SOMETHING ABOUT THE AUTHOR®

Something about
the Author *was named
an* **"Outstanding
Reference Source,"**
*the highest honor given
by the American
Library Association
Reference and Adult
Services Division.*

ISSN 0276-816X

SOMETHING ABOUT THE AUTHOR®

**Facts and Pictures about Authors
and Illustrators of Books for Young People**

volume 119

GALE GROUP

*Detroit
New York
San Francisco
London
Boston
Woodbridge, CT*

iccrz

STAFF

Scot Peacock, *Managing Editor, Literature Product*
Mark Scott, *Publisher, Literature Product*

Katy Balcer, Sara L. Constantakis, Kristen A. Dorsch, Lisa Kumar, *Editors;* Shayla Hawkins, Motoko Fujishiro Huthwaite, Simone Sobel, Denay Wilding, Thomas Wiloch, *Associate Editors;* Joshua Kondek, *Technical Training Specialist*

Alan Hedblad, *Managing Editor*
Susan M. Trosky, *Literature Content Coordinator*

Victoria B. Cariappa, *Research Manager;* Tracie A. Richardson, *Project Coordinator;* Maureen Emeric, Barbara McNeil, Gary J. Oudersluys, Cheryl L. Warnock, *Research Specialists;* Tamara C. Nott, *Research Associate;* Nicodemus Ford, Tim Lehnerer, Ron Morelli, *Research Assistants*

Maria L. Franklin, *Permissions Manager;* Edna Hedblad, Shalice Shah-Caldwell, *Permissions Associates*

Mary Beth Trimper, *Composition Manager;* Dorothy Maki, *Manufacturing Manager;* Stacy Melson, *Buyer*

Michael Logusz, *Graphic Artist;* Randy Bassett, *Image Database Supervisor;* Robert Duncan, *Imaging Specialist;* Pamela A. Reed, *Imaging Coordinator;* Dean Dauphinais, Robyn V. Young, *Senior Image Editors;* Kelly A. Quin, *Image Editor*

Library of Congress Catalog Card Number 72-27107

ISBN 0-7876-4707-1
ISSN 0276-816X

Printed in the United States of America

10 9 8 7 6 5 4 3 2 1

Contents

Authors in Forthcoming Volumes viii
Introduction ix
Acknowledgments xi

Authors in Forthcoming Volumes

Below are some of the authors and illustrators that will be featured in upcoming volumes of *SATA*. These include new entries on the swiftly rising stars of the field, as well as completely revised and updated entries (indicated with *) on some of the most notable and best-loved creators of books for children.

*Janet Ahlberg: English artist Ahlberg was a respected writer and illustrator whose works, in collaboration with her husband, Allan, were praised for their humor and warmth. Ahlberg, who died in 1994, was known for the acclaimed "Brick Street Boys" and "Jolly Postman" series, as well as stand-alone titles such as *Each Peach Pear Plum*.

*Joanna Cole: Since becoming a full-time writer in 1980, Cole has penned more than one hundred books for children, including *Cockroaches*, *How You Were Born*, and the "Magic School Bus" series. A proficient author in several genres, Cole's writings have earned enormous popular and critical acclaim. Each of her science books has been named an Outstanding Science Trade Books for Children from the National Science Teachers Association/Children's Book Council.

Malachy Doyle: Born in Northern Ireland, Doyle is noted for his retelling of classic Irish folktales. One such story appears in his book *The Children of Nuala*. Doyle has also earned recognition for books like *Jody's Beans,* which cover more universal themes.

*Leonard Everett Fisher: Fisher is a prolific painter, illustrator, and author. In addition to writing more than eighty books, he has illustrated more than one hundred and sixty by authors as diverse as Washington Irving, Madeline L'Engle, and Eric Kimmel. Among Fisher's numerous honors are the Parents' Choice Award for *The Seven Days of Creation* and the Children's Book Guild/*Washington Post* Nonfiction Award for *The White House*.

Rolf Heimann: A German-born Australian, Heimann uses his experience as a former graphic designer to illustrate his young adult books. One of Heimann's most recent works, *Knocking on Heaven's Door,* recounts his experiences as a protestor against French nuclear testing in the South Pacific.

Sylvia Long: Long is an award-winning illustrator of children's books, and is both author and illustrator for several picture books for preschoolers. Her titles include *Fire Race: A Karuk Coyote Tale*, which is based on a Native American myth, and *Alejandro's Gift*, which garnered praise for its illustrations.

Louise Marley: A versatile and gifted artist, Marley is a science fiction writer who also has a career as an opera singer and college music professor. Marley's love for music is evident in many of her book titles, including *The Glass Harmonica, Sing the Night*, and *Sing the Warmth*.

Richard Platt: Platt is the author of a growing list of informative books for young readers, and he also creates innovative multimedia projects. Some of his most popular works have been collaborations with Stephen Biesty on the "Cross-Section" and "Incredible" series.

*Gary Soto: A widely acclaimed poet, Gary Soto is also a respected children's writer. His poetry and prose for young adults include the books *Neighborhood Odes* and *The Cat's Meow*. Soto has received many honors for his work, including the American Book Award for his memoir *Living Up the Street*.

Vivian Walsh: Walsh is an American writer whose picture book *Olive, the Other Reindeer* and "Mr. Lunch" series are both based on her two dogs. Walsh collaborates on her books with her husband, illustrator J. Otto Seibold. The pair cite as their inspiration another husband-and-wife author team: H. A. and Margaret Rey, the creators of the beloved "Curious George" series.

*Jane Breskin Zalben: Best known for her picture books about the Jewish holidays, Zalben is a writer and illustrator whose books inform young readers about subjects as varied as AIDS and the Holocaust. *Beni's First Chanuka*, one of Zalben's most popular books, won a *Parents* magazine award in 1993.

Introduction

Something about the Author (*SATA*) is an ongoing reference series that examines the lives and works of authors and illustrators of books for children. *SATA* includes not only well-known writers and artists but also less prominent individuals whose works are just coming to be recognized. This series is often the only readily available information source on emerging authors and illustrators. You'll find *SATA* informative and entertaining, whether you are a student, a librarian, an English teacher, a parent, or simply an adult who enjoys children's literature.

What's Inside SATA

SATA provides detailed information about authors and illustrators who span the full time range of children's literature, from early figures like John Newbery and L. Frank Baum to contemporary figures like Judy Blume and Richard Peck. Authors in the series represent primarily English-speaking countries, particularly the United States, Canada, and the United Kingdom. Also included, however, are authors from around the world whose works are available in English translation. The writings represented in *SATA* include those created intentionally for children and young adults as well as those written for a general audience and known to interest younger readers. These writings cover the entire spectrum of children's literature, including picture books, humor, folk and fairy tales, animal stories, mystery and adventure, science fiction and fantasy, historical fiction, poetry and nonsense verse, drama, biography, and nonfiction.

Obituaries are also included in *SATA* and are intended not only as death notices but also as concise overviews of people's lives and work. Additionally, each edition features newly revised and updated entries for a selection of *SATA* listees who remain of interest to today's readers and who have been active enough to require extensive revisions of their earlier biographies.

New Autobiography Feature

Beginning with Volume 103, *SATA* features three or more specially commissioned autobiographical essays in each volume. These unique essays, averaging about ten thousand words in length and illustrated with an abundance of personal photos, present an entertaining and informative first-person perspective on the lives and careers of prominent authors and illustrators profiled in *SATA*.

Two Convenient Indexes

In response to suggestions from librarians, *SATA* indexes no longer appear in every volume but are included in alternate (odd-numbered) volumes of the series, beginning with Volume 57.

SATA continues to include two indexes that cumulate with each alternate volume: the Illustrations Index, arranged by the name of the illustrator, gives the number of the volume and page where the illustrator's work appears in the current volume as well as all preceding volumes in the series; the Author Index gives the number of the volume in which a person's biographical sketch, autobiographical essay, or obituary appears in the current volume as well as all preceding volumes in the series.

These indexes also include references to authors and illustrators who appear in Gale's *Yesterday's Authors of Books for Children, Children's Literature Review,* and *Something about the Author Autobiography Series.*

Easy-to-Use Entry Format

Whether you're already familiar with the *SATA* series or just getting acquainted, you will want to be aware of the kind of information that an entry provides. In every *SATA* entry the editors attempt to give as complete a picture of the person's life and work as possible. A typical entry in *SATA* includes the following clearly labeled information sections:

- *PERSONAL:* date and place of birth and death, parents' names and occupations, name of spouse, date of marriage, names of children, educational institutions attended, degrees received, religious and political affiliations, hobbies and other interests.

- *ADDRESSES:* complete home, office, electronic mail, and agent addresses, whenever available.

- *CAREER:* name of employer, position, and dates for each career post; art exhibitions; military service; memberships and offices held in professional and civic organizations.

- *AWARDS, HONORS:* literary and professional awards received.

- *WRITINGS:* title-by-title chronological bibliography of books written and/or illustrated, listed by genre when known; lists of other notable publications, such as plays, screenplays, and periodical contributions.

- *ADAPTATIONS:* a list of films, television programs, plays, CD-ROMs, recordings, and other media presentations that have been adapted from the author's work.

- *WORK IN PROGRESS:* description of projects in progress.

- *SIDELIGHTS:* a biographical portrait of the author or illustrator's development, either directly from the biographee—and often written specifically for the *SATA* entry—or gathered from diaries, letters, interviews, or other published sources.

- *BIOGRAPHICAL AND CRITICAL SOURCES:* cites sources quoted in "Sidelights" along with references for further reading.

- *EXTENSIVE ILLUSTRATIONS:* photographs, movie stills, book illustrations, and other interesting visual materials supplement the text.

How a SATA Entry Is Compiled

A *SATA* entry progresses through a series of steps. If the biographee is living, the *SATA* editors try to secure information directly from him or her through a questionnaire. From the information that the biographee supplies, the editors prepare an entry, filling in any essential missing details with research and/or telephone interviews. If possible, the author or illustrator is sent a copy of the entry to check for accuracy and completeness.

If the biographee is deceased or cannot be reached by questionnaire, the *SATA* editors examine a wide variety of published sources to gather information for an entry. Biographical and bibliographic sources are consulted, as are book reviews, feature articles, published interviews, and material sometimes obtained from the biographee's family, publishers, agent, or other associates.

Entries that have not been verified by the biographees or their representatives are marked with an asterisk (*).

Contact the Editor

We encourage our readers to examine the entire *SATA* series. Please write and tell us if we can make *SATA* even more helpful to you. Give your comments and suggestions to the editor:

BY MAIL: Editor, *Something about the Author,* The Gale Group, 27500 Drake Rd., Farmington Hills, MI 48331-3535.

BY TELEPHONE: (800) 877-GALE

BY FAX: (248) 699-8054

Acknowledgments

Grateful acknowledgment is made to the following publishers, authors, and artists whose works appear in this volume.

ATA, TE. Reisberg, Mira, illustrator. From an illustration in *Baby Rattlesnake*, told by Te Ata, adapted by Lynn Moroney. Children's Book Press, 1989. Story © 1989 by Lynn Moroney. Illustrations © 1989 by Mira Reisberg. Reproduced by permission.

BARNES, LAURA T. Barnes, Laura T., feeding her donkey, photograph. Reproduced by permission.

BONSALL, JOSEPH S. From the cover of *Outside*, by Joseph S. Bonsall. Ideals Children's Books, 1998. Illustrations © 1998 by Hambleton-Hill Publishing, Inc. Reproduced by permission.

BOOK, RICK. Book, Rick. From the cover of *Necking With Louise* by Rick Book. Red Dear Press, 1999. Reproduced by permission.

BRAITHWAITE, ALTHEA. All photographs reproduced by permission of the author.

CARLING, AMELIA LAU. Carling, Amelia Lau, with her family, photograph. Reproduced by permission.

CHARLIP, REMY. Charlip, Remy, illustrator. From a jacket of *Arm in Arm*, by Remy Charlip. Tricycle Press, 1997. Jacket art © 1997 by Remy Charlip. Reproduced by permission./ Charlip, Remy. From an illustration in *Peanut Butter Party: Including the History, Uses, and Future of Peanut Butter* by Remy Charlip. Copyright © 1999 by Remy Charlip. Reproduced by permission./Charlip, Remy, performing "March Dance Umbrella" (hands cupped, knees bent, vest with rings), 1978, photograph. © Johan Elbers 1997. Reproduced by permission.

CHILD, LAUREN. Child, Lauren. From the cover of *Clarice Bean That's Me* by Lauren Child. Candlewick Press, 1999. Reproduced by permission of Walker Books Ltd. Published in the U.S. by Candlewick Press, Inc., Cambridge, MA.

CLUTHA, JANET PATERSON FRAME. Frame, Janet, photograph by Jerry Bauer. Reproduced by permission.

CRESP, GAEL. Cresp, Gael, photograph. Reproduced by permission./ Cox, David, illustrator. From an illustration *The Tale of Gilbert Alexander Pig* by Gael Cresp. Barefoot Books, 1999. Illustrations copyright © 1999 by David Cox. Reproduced by permission.

DE SAULLES, TONY. De Saulles, Tony, illustrator. From the cover of *Suffering Scientists* by Nick Arnold. Scholastic, 2000. Reproduced by permission.

DUMAS, PHILLIPE. Dumas, Phillipe, illustrator. From an illustration in *A Farm: Reflections of Yesteryear*, by Phillipe Dumas, translated by Mary Logue. Creative Editions, 1999. © 1997 by l'Ecole des Loisirs. English text © 1999 by Creative Editions. Reproduced by permission./ Dumas, Phillipe, illustrator. From an illustration in *Odette: A Springtime in Paris*, by Kay Fender. Prentice Hall, 1978. © 1978 Kay Fender and Phillipe Dumas. Reproduced by permission./ Dumas, Phillipe, illustrator. From an illustration in *The Scarlet Ibis*, by James Hurst. Creative Education Inc., 1988. Illustrations © 1988 by Creative Education, Inc. Reproduced by permission.

EMBERLEY, MICHAEL. Emberley, Michael, illustrator. From an illustration in *Dinosaurs!*, by Michael Emberley. Little, Brown and Company, 1980. © 1980 by Michael Emberley. Reproduced by permission./ Emberley, Michael, illustrator. Cover of *It's Perfectly Normal*, by Robie H. Harris. Candlewick Press, 1996. Reproduced by permission of Walker Books Ltd. Published in the U.S. by Candlewick Press, Inc., Cambridge, MA.

FELTENSTEIN, DR. ARLENE (H.) Feltenstein, Arlene, photograph. Reproduced by permission./ Escriva, Vivi, illustrator. From an illustration in *Will the New Baby Be Bigger Than Me?*, by Dr. Joan Fallon and Dr. Arlene Feltenstein. Laredo Publishing Co., 1998. Reproduced by permission.

FOON, DENNIS. Foon, Dennis, photograph. Reproduced by permission./ Bridgman, Lorne, photographer. From the cover of *Doubling or Nothing*, by Dennis Foon. Annick Press Ltd., 2000. Reproduced by permission./ Foon, Dennis. From the cover of *Little Criminals*. Blizzard Publishing, 1996. Copyright © 1996 by Dennis Foon. Reproduced by permission./ Pasternak, Robert, illustrator. From the cover of *War*, by Dennis Foon. Blizzard Publishing, 1998. Copyright © 1995 by Dennis Foon. Reproduced by permission.

FRITZ, JEAN. Fritz, Jean, with a pigeon on shoulder, photograph. Reproduced by permission.

GANTOS, JOHN, JR. Borges, Jose Francisco, illustrator. From a jacket of *Desire Lines*, by Jack Gantos. Farrar, Straus and Giroux, 1997. Jacket woodcut (c) 1993 by Jose Francisco Borges. Jacket photograph (c) 1997 by Farrar, Straus and Giroux. Reproduced by permission./ Szpura, Beata, illustrator. From an illustration in *Jack's Black Book*, by Jack Gantos. Sunburst

Books, 1999. Cover art © 1997 by Beata Szpura. Reproduced by permission./ Rubel, Nicole, illustrator. From the cover of *Rotten Ralph*, by Jack Gantos. Houghton Mifflin Company, 1976. © John B. Gantos, Jr. and Leslie Rubel. Reproduced by permission.

GOLDBERG, WHOOPI. Goldberg, Whoopi (holding Golden Globe award in hand), photograph. AP/Wide World Photos, Inc. Reproduced by permission.

HAGER, TOM. Cover of *Linus Pauling and the Chemistry of Life*, by Tom Hager. Oxford University Press, 1998. Reproduced by permission.

HAWKES, NIGEL. Hawkes, Nigel. From the cover of *New Technology: Energy* by Nigel Hawkes. Twenty-First Century Books, 1994. (c) Aladdin Books Ltd. 1994. Reproduced by permission./ Hawkes, Nigel. From the cover of *The New Book of Mars* by Nigel Hawkes. Copper Beech Books, 1998. (c) Aladdin Books Ltd 1998. Reproduced by permission.

HOWARD, ELIZABETH FITZGERALD. Howard, Elizabeth Fitzgerald, photograph. Reproduced by permission./ Lewis, E. B., illustrator. From an illustration in *Virgie Goes to School with Us Boys*, by Elizabeth Fitzgerald Howard. Simon & Schuster Books for Young Readers, 2000. Illustrations (c) 2000 by E. B. Lewis. Reproduced by permission.

HUGHES, MONICA (INCE). Hughes, Monica, sitting with books in background, photograph. Reproduced by permission./ Clark, Brenda, illustrator. From *Little Fingerling* by Monica Hughes. Ideal's Children's Books, 1992. Illustration copyright (c) 1989 by Brenda Clark.

JOHNSON, SCOTT. Johnson, Scott, photograph. Reproduced by permission.

JONES, VEDA BOYD. Jones, Veda Boyd, photograph. AP/Wide World Photo. Reproduced by permission./ Moseley-Braun, Carol, Bill Clinton, and Al Gore, photograph. Bettmann/Corbis. Reproduced by permission.

KARR, PHYLLIS ANN. Org, Ed, illustrator. From the cover of *The Arthurian Companion*, by Phyllis Ann Karr. Chaosium, 1997. Reproduced by permission.

KEELY, JACK. Keely, Jack, illustrator. From the cover of *U Can Cartoon*, by Jack Keely. Walter Foster Publishing, 1997. (c) 1997 Walter Foster Publishing, Inc. Reproduced by permission.

KORMAN, GORDON (RICHARD). Korman, Gordon, photograph. Reproduced by permission of Gordon Korman./ Cover of *Losing Joe's Place*, by Gordon Korman. Scholastic Inc., 1990. (c) 1990 by Gordon Korman. Reproduced by permission./ Stutzman, Mark, illustrator. From *Nose Pickers From Outer Space* by Gordon Korman./ Swain, Ruth Freeman, photograph. Reproduced by permission./ Buehner, Mark, illustrator. From the cover of *The 6th Grade Nickname Game*, by Gordon Korman. Hyperion Paperbacks for Children, 2000. Cover illustration (c) 1998 by Mark Buehner. Reproduced by permission.

LALLY, SOINBHE. Lally, Soinbhe, photograph by Ann Cassidy. Reproduced by permission.

LAWRENCE, LOUISE. Kimball, Anton, illustrator. From a jacket of *Dream Weaver*, by Louise Lawrence. Clarion Books, 1996. Jacket illustration (c) 1996 by Anton Kimball. Reproduced by permission./ Hunt, Paul, illustrator. From a jacket of *Patchwork People*, by Louise Lawrence. Clarion Books, 1994. Jacket illustration (c) 1994 by Paul Hunt. Reproduced by permission.

LEVITIN, SONIA (WOLFF). Levitin, Sonia (seated outdoors with german shepard), photograph by Rose Eichenbaum. Reproduced by permission of Sonia Levitin.

LEWIN, TED. Lewin, Ted, photograph by Betsy Lewin. Reproduced by permission./ From an illustration in *Amazon Boy* by Ted Lewin. Macmillan, 1993. Reproduced by permission of Simon & Schuster Macmillan./ Lewin, Ted, illustrator. From an illustration in *Market!* by Ted Lewin. Lothrop, Lee & Shepard Books, 1996. (c) 1996 by Ted Lewin. Reproduced by permission.

LIPPINCOTT, GARY A. Lippincott, Gary A., illustrator. From an illustration in *Jeremy Thatcher, Dragon Hatcher*, by Bruce Coville. Harcourt Brace Jovanovich, 1991. Illustrations (c) 1991 by Gary A. Lippincott. Reproduced by permission./ *Storytime*, an original watercolor by Gary A. Lippincott. Reproduced by permission.

LYON, GEORGE ELLA. Lyon, George Ella, photograph. Reproduced by permission.

LYTLE, ROBERT A. Howell, Karen, illustrator. From a jacket of *Mackinac Passage: Summer Adventure* by Robert Lytle. AP/Wide World Photos. Reproduced by permission.

MAHY, MARGARET. Mahy, Margaret, photograph. Christchurch Press Company Ltd. Reproduced by permission./ Tseng, Jean, and Mou-sien Tseng, illustrators. From an illustration in *The Seven Chinese Brothers*, by Margaret Mahy. Scholastic Inc., 1990. Text copyright © 1990 by Margaret Mahy. Illustrations copyright © 1990 by Jean and Mou-sien Tseng. Reproduced by permission.

MARTIN, FRED. Martin, Fred, photograph. Reproduced by permission.

MATHERS, PETRA. Mathers, Petra, illustrator. From the cover of *Dodo Gets Married* by Petra Mathers. Atheneum, 2001. Reproduced by permission of the author.

MATHESON, RICHARD (CHRISTIAN). Matheson, Richard, photograph. Tor Books. Reproduced by permission./ Morris, Harry O., illustrator. From a jacket of *Dystopia: Collected Stories,* by Richard Matheson. Gauntlet Publications, 2000. Jacket art © 2000 by Harry O. Morris. Reproduced by permission.

MORRIS, JILL. Morris, Jill, photograph. Reproduced by permission.

MYERS, R(OBERT) E(UGENE). Eric Futran, photographer. From the cover of *Character Matters* by R. E. Myers. Good Year Books, 1999. Copyright © 1999 Good Year Books, an imprint of Addison-Wesley Educational Publishers, Inc. Reproduced by permission.

PEERS, JUDI(TH MAY WEST). Peers, Judi, photograph. Olan Mills Photography. Reproduced by permission.

PETERSON, KATHLEEN B. Peterson, Kathleen B., photograph. Reproduced by permission.

QUAY, EMMA. Quay, Emma, photograph. Reproduced by permission.

QUIN-HARKIN, JANET. Quin-Harkin, Janet, photograph. Reproduced by permission./ Cover of *One Crazy Christmas,* by Janet Quin-Harkin. Minstrel Books, 1996. (c) 1996 by Paramount Pictures. Reproduced by permission./ Daniel Weiss Associates, Inc., photographer. From the cover of *Who Do You Love?,* by Janet Quin-Harkin. Bantam Books, 1996. Cover art © 1996 by Daniel Weiss Associates, Inc. Reproduced by permission./ Ecco, Emily. From the cover of *Full House: Fireworks and Flamingoes* by Emily Ecco. Mistrel Books, 1997. Copyright © 1997 by Warner Bros. Reproduced by permission.

RANDLE, KRISTEN D. All photographs reproduced by permission of the author.

SCHRAM, PENINNAH. Schram, Peninnah, photograph. Reproduced by permission./ Allon, Jeffrey, illustrator. From a jacket of *Ten Classic Jewish Children's Stories*, by Peninnah Schram. Pitspopany, 1998. Illustration copyright (c) 1998 by Peninnah Schram. Reproduced by permission.

SCRIMGER, RICHARD. Johnson, Gillian, illustrator. From the cover of *The Nose From Jupiter* by Richard Scrimger. Tundra Books, 1998. Copyright (c) 1998 by Richard Scrimger. Reproduced by permission.

SEWALL, MARCIA. Sewall, Marcia, illustrator. From an illustration in *Nickommoh! A Thanksgiving Celebration,* by Jackie French Koller. Atheneum Books for Young Readers, 1999. Illustrations © 1999 by Marcia Sewall. Reproduced by permission./ Sewall, Marcia, illustrator. From an illustration in *People of the Breaking Day,* by Marcia Sewall. Atheneum Books for Young Readers, 1990. © 1990 by Marcia Sewall. Reproduced by permission./ Sewall, Marcia, illustrator. From an illustration in *The Green Mist,* adapted by Marcia Sewall. Houghton Mifflin Company, 1999. Copyright © 1999 by Marcia Sewall. Reproduced by permission./ Sewall, Marcia, illustrator. From an illustration in *The Pilgrims of Plimoth,* by Marcia Sewall. Atheneum, 1986. Copyright © 1986 by Marcia Sewall. Reproduced by permission.

STEDING, LAURIE. Steding, Laurie, photograph. Reproduced by permission.

STORAD, CONRAD J. Storad, Conrad J., photograph by John C. Phillips. Reproduced by permission./ Neely, Beth, and Don Rantz, illustrators. From an illustration in *Lizards for Lunch: A Roadrunner's Tale,* by Conrad J. Storad. Resort Gifts Unlimited, Inc., 1999. Text © 1999 by Resort Gifts Unlimited, Inc. Illustrations © 1999 by Beth Neely and Don Rantz. Reproduced by permission.

SWAIN, RUTH (FREEMAN). Swain, Ruth Freeman, photograph. Reproduced by permission.

THOMAS, MEREDITH. Thomas, Meredith, holding a sea creature, photograph. Reproduced by permission.

THOMPSON, SHARON (ELAINE). Thompson, Sharon, photograph. Reproduced by permission.

WALTON, DARWIN MCBETH. Walton, Darwin McBeth, photograph. Reproduced by permission.

WERLIN, NANCY. Werlin, Nancy, photograph by Harry Werlin. Reproduced by permission./ Wisnewski, Robert, illustrator. From the cover of *Are You Alone on Purpose?* by Nancy Werlin. Houghton Mifflin Company, 1994. Jacket copyright © 1994 by Robert Wisnewski. Reproduced by permission./ O'Rourke, Ericka, illustrator. From the cover of *Locked Inside,* by Nancy Werlin. Delacorte Press, 2000. Copyright © 2000 by Nancy Werlin. Reproduced by permission from Delacorte Press an imprint of Random House Children's Books, a division of Random House, Inc./ White, Craig, illustrator. From the cover of *The Killer's Cousin,* by Nancy Werlin. Delacorte Press, 1998. Jacket illustration copyright © 1998 by Craig White. Reproduced by permission.

WESTON, MARTHA. Weston, Martha, illustrator. From an illustration in *Bad Baby Brother,* by Martha Weston. Clarion Books, 1997. Text and illustrations © 1997 by Martha Weston. Reproduced by permission./ Weston, Martha, illustrator. From an illustration in *Cats Are Like That,* by Martha Weston. Holiday House, 1999. © 1999 by Martha Weston. Reproduced by permission./ Weston, Martha, illustrator. From an illustration in *How Will the Easter Bunny Know?* by Kay Winters.

something ABOUT THE AUThOR

AARDEMA, Verna 1911-2000
(Verna Aardema Vugteveen)

OBITUARY NOTICE—See index for *SATA* sketch: Born June 6, 1911, in New Era, MI; died May 11, 2000. Grade school teacher, journalist, and writer. Aardema received her B.A. degree from Michigan State College of Agriculture and Applied Science (now Michigan State University) in 1934; she began teaching elementary school that same year. Upon marrying her first husband, Albert Aardema, in 1936, Aardema stopped working, a depression-era custom for many women with income-earning spouses. After raising two children, she returned to teaching full-time in 1951, and taught for more than two decades before retiring in 1973. During this time, Aardema also became one of the most highly regarded adapters of African folktales for children. She was noted for creating authentic interpretations which skillfully incorporated the outstanding features of the oral tradition with wit, charm, and vitality. Best known for the cumulative pourquoi tale *Why Mosquitoes Buzz in People's Ears: A West African Tale* (1975) and for *Who's in Rabbit's House? A Masai Tale* (1977), the story of an outwitted caterpillar, she was also popular for her first collection of African folklore, *Tales from the Story Hat* (1960), in which listeners choose an object dangling from the storyteller's hat to represent their requests. Aardema retold tales from all directions of the compass in Africa, including tales from the Masai, the Ashanti, the Mpongwe, the Nkundo of Zaire, the Tonga, and the Swahili. Her stories deal with puzzles, tricksters, and heroes, and are all adapted from original tales held in the African and Mexican oral tradition. Known for her clear use of language as well as linguistic devices such as ideophones and repetitive sounds, Aardema enjoyed a writing career that spanned some four decades. Her most recent efforts included *Borreguita and the Coyote* (illustrated by Petra Mathers, 1991), *Anansi Finds a Fool* (illustrated by Bryna Waldman, 1992), *Misoso: Once Upon a Time Tales from Africa* (illustrated by Reynold Ruffins, 1994), *How the Ostrich Got Its Long Neck: A Tale from the Akamba of Kenya* (illustrated by Marcia Brown, 1995), *The Lonely Lioness and the Ostrich Chicks: A Masai Tale* (illustrated by Yumi Heo, 1996), *This for That: A Tonga Tale* (illustrated by Victoria Chess, 1997), and *Koi and the Kola Nuts: A Tale from Liberia* (illustrated by Joel Cepeda, 1999). Aardema won several awards for her books, many of which received Children's and Parents' Choice recognition along with notable book citations from the American Library Association. *Why Mosquitoes Buzz in People's Ears,* illustrated by Leo and Diane Dillon, was awarded the Caldecott Medal in 1976. *Who's in Rabbit's House* received the Lewis Carroll Shelf Award in 1978. After the death of her first husband, Aardema married Joel Vugteveen in 1975.

OBITUARIES AND OTHER SOURCES:

BOOKS

Something about the Author Autobiography Series, Volume 8, Gale, 1989, pp. 1-16.
St. James Guide to Children's Writers, 5th edition, St. James Press, 1999.

PERIODICALS

Publishers Weekly, May 29, 2000, p. 43.

ATA, Te 1895-1995

Personal

Born in 1895, in Tishomingo, OK; died in 1995; *Education:* Attended Oklahoma College for Women (now University of Science and Arts of Oklahoma), Carnegie Institute of Technology (now Carnegie-Mellon University), and Columbia University.

Career

Professional storyteller; performed professionally in New York City, Europe, and at the White House, Washington, DC.

Awards, Honors

Lake Te Ata in the state of New York was named in her honor.

Writings

(Compiler) *Indian Tales,* illustrated by Erika Weihs, L. W. Singer (New York City), 1968.
Baby Rattlesnake (for children), adapted by Lynn Moroney, illustrated by Mira Reisberg, Children's Book Press (San Francisco, CA), 1989.

Sidelights

The daughter of a Chickasaw tribal council member, Te Ata was a Native American storyteller of note who counted such famous people as Eleanor Roosevelt among her many fans. Before her death in 1995, she compiled some of her favorite stories in *Indian Tales,* and her cautionary story about a snake who pushes all the other animals around until it meets the boot of an Indian chief's daughter was adapted for children as *Baby Rattlesnake.*

Biographical and Critical Sources

PERIODICALS

Bloomsbury Review, April, 1991, review of *Baby Rattlesnake,* p. 8.
Bookbird, March, 1993, review of *Baby Rattlesnake,* p. 9.
Booklist, March 1, 1990, review of *Baby Rattlesnake,* p. 1351.
Bookwatch, February, 1990, review of *Baby Rattlesnake,* p. 7.
Bulletin of the Center for Children's Books, March, 1990, Kathryn Pierson, review of *Baby Rattlesnake,* p. 176.
Five Owls, January, 1993, review of *Baby Rattlesnake,* p. 52.
Horn Book Guide, January, 1990, review of *Baby Rattlesnake,* p. 275.
Kirkus Reviews, January 1, 1990, review of *Baby Rattlesnake,* p. 44.
Publishers Weekly, December 22, 1989, Diane Roback, review of *Baby Rattlesnake,* p. 56.
Reading Teacher, October, 1990, review of *Baby Rattlesnake,* p. 149.
School Library Journal, April, 1990, Carolyn Polese, review of *Baby Rattlesnake,* p. 86.*

Baby Rattlesnake begs and cries to get his rattle, but learns a lesson when he gets it too early and misuses it. (From Baby Rattlesnake, *by Te Ata, adapted by Lynn Moroney, and illustrated by Mira Reisberg.)*

B

BARNES, Laura T. 1958-

Personal

Born November 25, 1958, in Philadelphia, PA; daughter of John H. (an automotive dealer group executive) and Loraine (an artist; maiden name Lovell) Thompson; married Jefferson T. Barnes (an attorney), September 22, 1990. *Education:* University of Delaware, graduated, 1980.

Addresses

Home—444 Rosemont Ringoes Rd., Stockton, NJ 08559. *Office*—Barnesyard Books, Inc., P.O. Box 254, Sergeantsville, NJ 08557. *E-mail*—info@barnesyard-books.com and www.barnesyardbooks.com.

Career

Cross Keys Advertising and Marketing, Inc., Doylestown, PA, president and creative director, 1981-2000; Barnesyard Books, Inc., Sergeantsville, NJ, president and publisher, 1999—. Thompson Organization, Doylestown, vice president marketing; Bringhurst Funeral Home, member of board of directors; member of Heritage Conservancy, James A. Michener Art Museum, and Central Bucks Chamber of Commerce. *Member:* Society of Children's Book Writers and Illustrators, Publishers Marketing Association, Hunterdon County Historical Society, Delaware River Mill Society.

Writings

Twist and Ernest, illustrated by Carol A. Camburn, Barnesyard Books (Sergeantsville, NJ), 1999.
Teeny Tiny Ernest, illustrated by Camburn, Barnesyard Books, 2000.

Work in Progress

Ernest and the Christmas Wish, publication expected in 2002.

Sidelights

Laura T. Barnes told *SATA:* "After running and acting as the creative director at my own advertising and marketing firm for over twenty years, I realized that I was no longer finding the opportunity to be truly creative. My days were spent running the agency, managing projects, delegating duties, and dealing with decisions like health care benefits, lines of credit, et cetera.

Laura T. Barnes feeding her pony, Ernest.

"One day, while living in my converted barn and farm, Barnesyard, I simply started writing stories about my beloved animals. All of my ideas stem from day-to-day life watching and loving my adopted animals at the farm. Animals have so much to say and teach us, if we only take the time to stop, observe, and listen. I often say, 'I only write my books. The animals create the story.' It has been a rewarding experience to publish my first two books."

*   *   *

BONSALL, Joseph S. 1948-

Personal

Born May 18, 1948, in Philadelphia, PA; son of Joseph and Lillie Bonsall; married wife, Mary Ann, September 23, 1982; children: Sabrina Carver, Jen Stevens. *Politics:* Republican. *Religion:* Christian. *Hobbies and other interests:* Fishing, boating, tennis, working on his farm.

Addresses

Home—100 Surrey Hill Point, Hendersonville, TN 37075. *Office*—Mollythecat.com, 235 East Main St., PMB 256, Hendersonville, TN 37075. *E-mail*—Lilliesboy@aol.com.

Career

Musician. Member of Oak Ridge Boys (country vocal group), beginning 1973. Has also worked as a television host on the Nashville Network and as a motivational speaker.

Writings

FOR CHILDREN

Molly, illustrated by Erin Marie Mauterer, Ideals (Nashville), 1997.
The Home, Ideals, 1997.
Outside, Ideals, 1998.
Brewster, Ideals, 1999.

Also author of online book *Visit* at http://www.mollythecat.com.

Work in Progress

An autobiographical, inspirational book; a Civil War romance; two other novels.

Sidelights

Although his primary road to fame has been as lead singer in the popular and long-lived country western group the Oak Ridge Boys, Joseph S. Bonsall has won a host of new fans as the author of a series of children's books. His "Molly" stories, featuring engaging feline—and sometimes canine—characters, were inspired by Bonsall's own five cats: Molly, Old Pumpkin, Omaha, Gypsy, and Sally Ann.

The first book in the series, *Molly*, tells the story of how a young calico kitten was able to find a new home after the rest of her litter was taken to the animal shelter. She eventually finds a loving owner in Mother Mary, a woman who takes Molly in. The youngest of the four cats living at The Home, Molly longs to venture outside, and she learns the ways of the world by asking questions of the older, more experienced cats who share her space. While *School Library Journal* contributor Sally R. Dow contended that *Molly*, with its "vaguely religious overtones," contains a moral tone that is perhaps too strong, Bonsall intentionally injects such inspirational elements into his writing. As he noted in a *WritersClub* online interview, he feels a sense of responsibility toward his audience, "considering [my books] are influencing children . . . . [While] some bad things happen to Molly, . . . she's always looked after and she always ends up OK. Not always true in everyday life. But it will always be true as long as I'm writing Molly." In the Molly books, each of the animals places its faith in a "God of all Creatures."

Subsequent books in the Molly series include *The Home,* where readers learn more about Molly and her dream of going outside. *Outside* finds the young kitten's wishes granted, as she finds trouble on her tail. However, outside cats Spooker and the Dude teach Molly to be streetwise and avoid the bad-tempered stray known as Red Cat. *Brewster,* which Bonsall published in 1999, features a lovable bulldog that becomes a good friend to Molly despite his strength and somewhat fearsome appearance.

Although Bonsall's touring and performing schedule with the Oak Ridge Boys keeps his free time to a minimum, he still finds time to write, one of his favorite pastimes. "It is amazing how much time on the road there is to use your time positively," he explained to Matthew Carpenter for *Oaksworld.com.* "Motels, airplanes, bus rides. I even write at home." Home for Bonsall is a four-hundred-acre farm located near the heart of country music: Nashville, Tennessee.

The Molly books got their start in a hotel room in Las Vegas, while Bonsall was touring with his band. "I was going to be away from The Home for several weeks, and I was homesick for my family and really missing our new kitty at that time, Molly," he explained in an interview with John Mir for *Mollythecat.com.* Armed with encouragement and advice from several friends, Bonsall approached a few publishers with his story, but was turned down because of *Molly*'s moral and religious undertones: what the author described as "Friendship. Love. Sacrifice. Belief in God." Fortunately, when Bonsall returned home to Nashville, he found a willing publisher—Ideals—right in his own back yard.

As a means of giving something back to his many fans, Bonsall and his wife, Mary Ann, have formed the Joseph

Little Molly tastes the dangerous life of an outside cat in Joseph S. Bonsall's third Molly book. (Cover illustration by Erin Marie Mauterer.)

S. and Mary Ann Bonsall Foundation, an organization that provides scholarship money to send young, aspiring veterinarians and teachers to college. In 1999 he was the keynote speaker at the Literacy Volunteers of America, and he continues to do motivational speaking engagements in addition to his many obligations as a musician, author, farmer, and family man. Bonsall's advice to young people—not only aspiring writers but all kids with dreams—is a reflection of his own path to success. As he told Mir, "First of all, celebrate life. It is God's greatest gift to us. Take nothing for granted and do not sweat the small stuff. Work hard, sacrifice, put a stone on the pile each day and eventually the Mountain that is you will begin to form. Then, just follow your heart."

Biographical and Critical Sources

PERIODICALS

Horn Book, spring, 1998, p. 23.
Scottsdale Tribune, November 3, 1999, Betty Webb, "Oak Ridge Boys Lead Singer Turns Author."
School Library Journal, December, 1997, Sally R. Dow, review of *Molly,* p. 81.

ON-LINE

Molly the Cat, www.mollythecat.com (March 2, 2000).
Oaksworld.com, www.oaksworld.com (March 2, 2000).
WritersClub.com, www.writersclub.com (October 27, 1999).*

BOOK, Rick 1949-

Personal

Born June 29, 1949; son of Don (a farmer) and Lorraine (a homemaker; maiden name, Vallevand) Book; children: Christopher, Alison. *Education:* University of Saskatchewan, B.A., 1970.

Addresses

Home and office—38 Nursewood Rd., Toronto, Ontario, Canada M4E 3R8. *E-mail*—smplanet@inforamp.net.

Career

Freelance television and radio journalist and copywriter. Also works as a voice actor. *Member:* Canadian Authors Association, Alliance of Canadian Cinema, Television, and Radio Artists, Writers Union of Canada, Canadian Society of Children's Authors, Illustrators, and Photographers, Friends of Attawapiskat.

Rick Book's seven witty stories portray a teen's life in 1965 Saskatchewan.

Writings

The Lonely Seagull, Penumbra Press, 1993.
(With John Brown) *The Day They Saved Her Majesty* (anthology), Prentice-Hall Ginn, 1998.
Grandpa's Wooden Diary (anthology), Prentice-Hall Ginn, 1999.
Necking with Louise (young adult stories), Red Deer Press (Red Deer, Alberta), 1999.

Contributor to periodicals.

Work in Progress

A young adult novel about robots; an adult novel about the "dirty thirties."

Sidelights

Rick Book told *SATA:* "I've always written for a living, as a television and radio news reporter, writer of documentaries, speeches, magazine articles, and advertising material. It wasn't until my children asked me to repeat a bedtime story I'd made up that I considered writing for children. I wrote the story down; months later I sent it off to a publisher and forgot about it. Four months after that, I got a letter saying the company wanted to publish the book. That was many years ago. I've taken 'writing for children' classes and been a member of writers' groups for five years. One is led by the noted children's writer Kathy Stinson. Another group, also full of incredible writers, is led by Peter Carver, who eventually edited my book *Necking with Louise.* Since that book was published, faint hopes have stirred that writing might be more than a hobby someday.

"What I hope to achieve is, first, to get the book written. After I'd written *Necking with Louise,* I realized what I had wanted to say; that is, to convey my sense of good fortune and gratitude at having grown up on a farm in a small, rural community in western Canada. I also discovered how much I love the people who live there and the geography—that big, beautiful land and sky. I hope readers will identify with these people and places.

"Having a 'work habit' would be a good thing, wouldn't it? It suggests an often repeated action. The hardest thing I do in my life is to put myself in the chair. When I'm writing, I like to get up at five-thirty in the morning, make a strong pot of coffee, and start. Because I'm undisciplined, I set deadlines for myself. Then I get up at four-thirty. I sometimes write past noon, never past two o'clock, which is another reason why so many people have never heard of me.

"I've never had any purpose in writing other than to wrestle a story onto the page. The stories ooze up slowly like bubbles in a tar pond and demand to be written. It is only later, in retrospect, that I see what's important to me in this story or that character. These are happy discoveries; it's another way to enjoy the writing process after the writing is done!

"I did write a novel once that was full of righteousness and high purpose, an environmental clarion call for juvenile readers. It's deeply flawed and remains unpublished. Maybe someday I'll figure out how to fix it.

"The people in my writers' group (which also contains illustrators) are the most encouraging, generous, brave people I know. First, they and Peter Carver, the editor who leads us, taught me how to listen, to ask the dreaded question, 'What is the story here?' Their bravery in tackling tough issues in their lives provokes me to write stories I would never have considered.

"Other writers who have influenced me include the American naturalist Barry Lopez, Jack London, John Steinbeck, and Winston Churchill. As for artists, I like the Group of Seven because they painted the Canadian wild, Van Gogh because he was crazy and thought 'outside the box,' Marc Chagall because of the joy in his work, and William Kurelek because he painted scenes from my childhood.

"The advice I would give to aspiring writers and illustrators is: just do it! Write journals, write letters to the editor, write letters to your grandmother, write down your dreams. Buy and read lots of great books by great writers. Join organizations or go to meetings where there are writers or artists. Get a mentor. Buy him or her coffee or beer. Read *The Artist's Way*. Read it again. Ask for suggestions about other books to read. Write the stories you don't want to write. Pray for divine inspiration and courage. Write through your fear. Write like a pirate."

Biographical and Critical Sources

PERIODICALS

Booklist, October 15, 1999, Michael Cart, review of *Necking with Louise,* p. 442.

CITY Parent, August, 1999, Barbara Greenwood, "Short Stories Are Just What Teens Should Be Longing For," p. 33.

Globe and Mail (Toronto), July 10, 1999, Susan Perren, "How Peter Rabbit Came to Life, and Other Fantastic Tales."

Kirkus Reviews, July 1, 1999, review of *Necking with Louise,* p. 1051.

Publishers Weekly, August 2, 1999, review of *Necking with Louise,* p. 86.

Quill and Quire, April, 1999, Sheila A. Egoff, "Necking with Louise Misleads," p. 36.

Toronto Star, July 11, 1999, Keith Nickson, "Sweet Birds of Lust," pp. D25-D26.

ON-LINE

Amazon.com, www.amazon.com (August 25, 1999).

* * *

BOWEN, Rhys
See QUIN-HARKIN, Janet

Autobiography Feature

Althea Braithwaite

1940-

Althea

I was running a printing company when I first started writing for children, and my first books were the result of a silly conversation. My husband was away for a couple of weeks, learning how to operate a new printing machine that we were buying. Talking on the phone one evening, I said I was feeling bored, so Mike suggested I write a book. When I asked what about, he said impulsively the first thing that came into his head, "A giraffe." When I asked where to begin, he answered, "In the middle, of course! Where else?" At the print works the next morning, I came across a box of offcuts, strips of yellow paper, which had been trimmed off after printing a handbill or something for a customer. It made me think that if I was to draw a giraffe in black on yellow paper, it wouldn't need to be coloured in. So I wrote a story about a giraffe called Bimbo and an ant called Cuthbert, an unlikely couple of friends! For the illustration, I began in the middle of the giraffe's neck. Like many people, when they first start writing stories, I had difficulty in thinking of a good ending. In desperation, most children have used the

Althea Braithwaite with Tigger, 1944.

endings, "Waking up after a dream," "Living happily ever after," or "Going home to tea." In my book they go home and have strawberry jam for tea. I was really enjoying myself, and next I found a box of strips of grey paper, so I wrote a story about an elephant called Benjamin. But my main character Desmond came about because I have a carving of a dinosaur that I had bought at an exhibition. He's carved out of oak and looks very miserable. I decided to write about him and why he looked so sad—if you were a dinosaur living many of millions of years after your proper time, so you didn't have any friends, you might well be miserable. Because he looks out of place, people stare and point at him when he walks down the street, but eventually he gets asked to a party and when people get to know him, they find out how nice he is, and life is much better from then on! What I didn't know at that time was that children love dinosaurs. When writing stories about Desmond, I have little difficulty in thinking myself into his character, large, clumsy, and a bit shy—just how I feel on my less confident days.

I showed the three books to Mike when he came home. He liked them, but then they got put away in a drawer. A year or so later we were trying to think of something we could do on our printing machines instead of always doing work for other people, and Mike suggested we try printing and publishing my books. I thought it was a crazy idea, but after a while he persuaded me. I went to the zoo and looked more carefully at giraffes and elephants to learn how to draw them, then I did the books again, taking more care over both the illustrations and the words. I made the printing plates, and we printed five hundred copies of each

of the three books, using the long strips of coloured paper, so the books were an unusual size, like a chequebook.

The next job was to sell the books. We hadn't shown them to anyone and we both felt nervous and wondered whether people would like them. I went round some of the department stores and large bookshops in London. At that time there were not many female representatives and being the author and illustrator of the books I was selling made me even more of an oddity. Perhaps that was a help, because I managed to sell quite a few books. We had a small launch party to show them to local booksellers, which was reported in the local press. At this stage, no one, including ourselves, thought that we were actually going to make a business out of publishing books.

We mostly sold books in towns that we liked, making the visits a weekend jaunt and giving the best delivery service of any publisher. We set off in our VW bus on a Friday evening with a stock of books, lots of wrapping paper, and a typewriter. We would visit a town on Saturday morning, calling on all the bookshops and gift shops to try and get orders, then go back to the bus to pack the books and type the invoices, then deliver the books in the afternoon—and when possible, collect the money, too! We were then free to enjoy the rest of the weekend.

I wrote two more storybooks, encouraged by the interest—and the criticism! One was about Jeremy Mouse, who was frightened of the rain, because I wanted to draw a page of raindrops, and another about a pig called Peter, because I love pigs. When I tried to sketch some pigs in a field, they were all so friendly that it was difficult to get far enough away from them. These books actually got a review in a national Sunday newspaper, and this was followed up by a television station who wanted to make a programme about our publishing company.

Our son Duncan was born in 1969, soon after these books were published, so he appeared on television when he was only three weeks old! The first story I wrote after Duncan arrived was called *George and the Baby* and is about a dog being jealous on the arrival of a new baby. I wrote it because our dog Suki was jealous of Duncan and always tried to get on my lap with him. We were still doing small chequebook-size books at this stage, so I had to draw a friend's dachshund, or sausage dog, instead of our rather taller dog! I drew it from the dog's viewpoint, so I only had to draw people's feet and legs. This was a great relief because at this stage I was hopeless at drawing people. These small-size books were not popular with bookshops, who found them difficult to display properly. Libraries found them impossible too, as there was no room for the library ticket inside the cover. It was a shame, because they were fun to design and the shape was very popular with children, but in the end we did have to change to books of a more usual shape.

While we were still producing these miniature books and printing five hundred at a time, we had a very exciting order from America. An important toy buyer was in London for an international toy fair and spotted our books in a gift shop in Hampstead. After meeting him in London to show him more ideas for books, we had a nail-biting three weeks before receiving an order for twenty thousand books! It was this order which changed our attitude and made us feel we really were publishers! Later on Mike and I went on a sales trip to New York and came back with an order for one hundred thousand books from another publisher.

I am often asked if I thought when I was a child that I would be a writer. In fact I didn't actually learn to read until I was nearly eight, but I always loved books and having them read to me. My first publication, which I produced soon after I could read, was a newspaper. Rather than writing it myself, I was the editor, and I wrote letters to my parents and sister asking for contributions. I think I only managed to produce one issue. Much later, when I was about twelve or thirteen, I wrote a long, and I thought very exciting, adventure story. My sister, who is five years older than me, typed it for me, and I sent it to a magazine, but it was rejected. When I left school, I actually hoped to study photography. I was already developing and printing my own photographs, and I had won a couple of prizes in amateur competitions.

In all memories of my childhood, I am very aware that I was a person in my own right, not a toddler or a child. Perhaps it is because of this, that when I research and write my books, I always take children seriously and treat them as equals with adults.

To start at the beginning, my father was the eldest of four children. My grandmother brought them up in Southwold as her husband had been killed in the 1914-18 war. While at Cambridge University, he joined their Air Squadron and went on to make the Royal Air Force his career. He met my mother in Southwold as her family had a holiday house there, and they were married in Southwold church. My sister Gillian was born in 1935, and I came along five years later. I was born in Pinner, Middlesex. This was during the Second World War, and my father was on active service, so for the first year of my life, we lived with an elderly cousin, Pen. My sister, Gillian, who was five at the time, has clear memories of this. We all sat under the dining room table during air raids and apparently my mother shocked Cousin Pen by breast-feeding me.

We moved very frequently during the first few years of my life, and I know the approximate dates, as I have a list of my father's postings. My very earliest memory was before I could really talk, being on a ferry coming into port in Northern Ireland early one morning and looking through a porthole and seeing a train going along the coast. I said something like "chuff chuff," and was laughed at by my mother and sister and told we were on a boat. I remember being very pleased when they looked through the porthole and saw there actually was a train! My next clear memory was after we moved to London and I was sitting in a pram in the gardens of the flats where we lived. There was another child in a pram beside me, and a slightly older mobile child fetched us sticks, so we could fight each other. I was rather enjoying myself, perhaps I was winning, when the fight was broken up by shocked adults.

I was three and a half when we moved to North Coates in the north of England, and a beautiful cat called Ginger came to live with us. He wouldn't let anyone pick him up except me. I was allowed to scoop him up and carry him about, my arms around his front paws and the rest of his body hanging. One night when my parents were out, I woke up in the dark and imagined I could see enormous shadowy beetles crawling up the wall in the corner of my room. I

started to get dressed, was comforted, and put back to bed by Scottie, my father's batman, who looked after us. On another evening when my parents were entertaining, I crept downstairs and heard them all talking and laughing in the drawing room. I went back to bed and cried loudly to get my mother to come and talk to me and comfort me.

By the time I was five, we were back in London again. I went each day to a very small nursery school. I don't remember it, but I have a school photograph of me with the other eight pupils. Gillian was away at boarding school and home during the holidays. My first boyfriend, Andrew I think his name was, lived in the flats. He had red hair and freckles, and I was very jealous of another girl who liked him too. But then his mother asked my mother if I could go to tea.

I have vague, rather jumbled memories of being scared by air raids in the middle of the night and hiding down under the bedclothes. Later when my mother was aware that I was awake, we would all sit in the hall by the grandfather clock. One night across the river in Putney High Street, the cinema and next-door shop were hit by bombs, and we saw the sky lit up by the enormous fire. To stop me waking my parents too early in the mornings, I was shown the time on the grandfather clock and told when I could go into their bedroom, but I got it wrong and woke them at five o'clock instead of seven o'clock, or it may

The author's parents, Francis Joseph and Rosemary Braithwaite, on their wedding day, 1933.

have been four o'clock instead of eight o'clock. Even so I was allowed to snuggle down in their bed and stay quiet until a more reasonable hour. My only memory of food shortages was how long it took to shop, as we had to queue for everything. My mother was furious when, after waiting ages, she had to lose her place in the fish queue because a great fight broke out between Gillian and me outside the shop.

I still have hard skin at the end of my finger where, as a child, I cut it very badly one afternoon. I had a dolls' house and had been making a farmyard outside it. I needed straw for the pig sty. It was hard work cutting up paper with my blunt children's scissors, so I decided to use the photo trimmer in the desk in the drawing room, something that was strictly forbidden. When I cut the top off my finger, I quietly hid the trimmer behind the sofa and then went screaming to my mother. We went to the outpatients at the hospital where it was bound up.

At the end of the war, my father, then an Air Commodore, was a member of the advisory team travelling with politicians on a world peace mission. I remember him arriving back from Canada, unpacking his suitcase to show us the treats he had brought back. The luggage compartment on the aeroplane was not pressurised, so instead of my first experience of a banana, there was a mess of broken eggs and squashy black bananas amongst his clothes! What a disappointment. My mother joined him in Paris, which

Althea and her mother, 1940.

meant they were away for my sixth birthday. The person looking after me took me to lunch with Granny. We had delicious pink chicken. I later learnt this was salmon. Granny gave me an umbrella as a present, and coming home on the bus, I kept hoping that it might rain. I also had my first gas-filled balloon, which was up on my ceiling when I went to bed that night, but to my great disappointment was flop on the floor the following morning.

During the winter of 1946, there was thick snow and everything froze. A friend and I crawled through the hedge into Hurlingham Gardens, a posh country park next door to the flats. Lots of people were skating on the lake there, and we joined them sliding about pushing a chair. We came out through the main entrance and were stopped by the porter who told us that we shouldn't have been in there and that we were in great trouble and they would be round to see our parents. I was so scared that when I got home I went to bed for the day feeling very ill. My grandmother was there for the day, and I could hear my mother and granny discussing what could be wrong with me. I don't remember telling them.

I was seven when we sailed to Malta in a crowded troopship. My father had flown on ahead. We lived in a hotel for a few months until we found a house. The only thing I remember about it was coming downstairs and seeing an escaped Christmas turkey being chased through the hall of the hotel on Christmas Eve. It didn't put me off eating it the next day.

I went to my first "proper" school in Malta. I remember the dark classrooms with rows of desks. I was unable to read and didn't really cotton on to what I was supposed to be doing for a while, so I would happily sound out "c-a-t" as instructed, and then say "dog," because the helpful little black-and-white illustration looked more like a dog to me. In the music lesson during my first week in school, I was allowed to play the drums as a treat because I was new. After that I was only ever allowed to play the triangle. At the time I thought this was a punishment because I couldn't read. Much later I realised it was more to do with my being totally unmusical, to the extent that still I often can't hear the beat in music. I took after my father, who was teased that he only recognised "God Save the Queen" when everyone stood up.

I was more successful at acting, and in a production of the *Princess and the Pea,* I played the Queen and the King was my boyfriend Paddy. He was Irish, with dark hair and freckles. I can still remember my first line, "Look at the rain, it simply pours. I'm glad that we are safe indoors."

I was quite an organising child and invited my parents and sister to my fancy-dress party one evening. My mother put on my father's RAF uniform, and he wore one of her dresses. During the evening the front door bell rang, and they had the embarrassment of explaining to some people they didn't know well, who had arrived to a dinner party on the wrong night, that they didn't normally dress like that!

I have recently found some letters written by me, which show that as soon as I could read, I was writing phonetically spelt letters to my granny in London, telling her that I had learnt "to dithe with out eny body holeding my legs, but I coodent befor." The swimming was wonderful, most of it being straight into deep water, so jumping or diving was the best way of getting in. My father's commanding officer had the special privilege of using the RAF launch and during the summer he organised picnic parties to sandy beaches, with children and adults enjoying themselves together. The commanding officer asked me one year what I was going to do for my birthday, and I said I was having a picnic on a launch. "Oh really!" he said. "Your daddy hasn't asked me yet." But it was all right, I had my birthday boating party. Although Malta is very dry during the summer, it's beautifully green in spring, and I can remember the very lush botanical gardens and various expeditions into the countryside, including one with Edith, who looked after my sister and me, when we cooked sausages and found wild narcissi. It was in Malta that I became fascinated by nature, and I still have my first book on butterflies and moths that we had sent from England.

My father had a sailing boat, and he liked racing. Gillian was keen too. I used to go along sometimes and enjoyed it on days when there was not much wind, but I hated racing and, as I always seemed to be in the way, was usually used to balance the boat and had to stay crouching miserably in the wet, feeling seasick!

Swimming from rocks straight into deep water was very dangerous when it was rough, and I have the awful memory of standing with Edith in a crowd on the sea front watching two men drown. The force of the swell was too great for them to get out; it kept bringing them up near the land, then sucking them back down again. People were trying to throw them ropes. The sea made them seem alive long after they had drowned. I had nightmares for a long time afterwards. My other nightmare was falling from a great height. We didn't have a garden, but played on the roof. It had walls all round, but somehow in my dreams it seemed very unsafe. There was a balcony outside our bedroom, and I had flower pots in which I grew geraniums—I had made friends with someone who gave me lots of cuttings.

Gillian and I had pet tortoises, and they lived in our small yard outside the dining room. There was a raised flowerbed, and they both fell on their backs once, trying to get down from it. From then onwards they used the special ramp we had made for them. We also made them a garage shelter, a large square biscuit tin stood on its side with the lid providing an overhang. When it rained they would park themselves side by side in the tin. When they heard someone in the dining room, they would walk up and down in front of the door, necks stretched upwards, waiting to be fed on lettuce. Very sadly, they died of DDT poisoning after one winter when they had moved out of the box we had given them and hibernated by hiding behind the front door instead. We found them just before Easter. My parents had bought me a chocolate tortoise and thought it would be tactless to give it to me then, and so they had to rush out and buy a chocolate rabbit instead. I had already found the chocolate tortoise and overheard their plans. I was given the chocolate tortoise later in the year. We didn't have any other pets, but I was allowed to take Pixie, a neighbour's small dog, out for walks.

Friends of my parents taught them to speak "ego" language, putting "eg" before a vowel. *"Sego yegou cegan tegalk wegithegout egotheger pegeopegel egundegerstegandeging yegou."* The idea was that they could talk together without my sister and I understanding, but we soon learnt to speak it rather more fluently than they did.

We flew back to England when I was nine and lived in London for a while. I went to a girls' day school in Hampstead, which I enjoyed. Although I was still behind in some subjects, I did have the advantage that I could swim well. We had a weekly visit to the swimming pool, and in the annual sports I won various races and diving competitions. I had a great many friends, and in summer we would sit in the garden at lunchtime, discussing the mysteries of life ahead, and the fascinating things adults seemed to be keeping secret from us.

At home I kept busy. I was very keen on nature and made things such as a map of where birds migrated. I also made a pinbox camera which actually worked. I always meant to start a book about the things I thought my parents shouldn't do to me, so that I wouldn't inflict the same things on my own children, but unfortunately I never got around to this!

My parents gave me a pair of stilts for my birthday, and I learnt by walking up and down the street, eventually managing to use the top steps, making me tower above my parents.

One awful occasion sticks in my mind. I accidentally swallowed a pencil lead container by sucking it in and out of my mouth. The school asked me where I lived, and I was so scared that I couldn't even remember. They gave me lots

With Ginger, the pet cat, 1943.

Althea in her Brownie uniform, Malta, 1948.

of soft bread to eat. Eventually my mother was summoned, and I was taken off to hospital for an X-ray. I survived.

I am not sure that I would have passed the common entrance exam and gone to boarding school if my sister had not already been there. She thoroughly enjoyed boarding school and felt happy and successful, but I was looking forward to it with some trepidation. On getting there I found I was miserably homesick. Our parents thought it best for us to be at boarding school to avoid having to change schools every time my father was posted to another part of the world. Since I was very aware that they were making financial sacrifices so that we could be there, I always tried to hide my unhappiness. My main reason for disliking boarding school was because I could never have time on my own to be myself and to think my own thoughts. We were not allowed off the school premises, and even our own dormitories were out of bounds during the day. We slept in rooms with up to about eight other girls, each bed separated by a small locker. I found it difficult to conform and to fit in with what was wanted.

I cried easily, so I was an easy target for bullying, though I didn't experience any until I got to boarding school. I only have vague memories of the actual incidents, though recently under hypnosis I re-enacted the real fear that I felt when I was twelve. The sort of bullying I experienced was group teasing that they thought was fun, but got taken too far. I have tried to show how this can happen in the books I am writing at the moment, *Being Shy, Making Friends,* and *Feeling Angry.* During the day we were kept occupied all the time, with compulsory games every afternoon. I can well remember the misery of freezing blue knees, which itched and hurt as they warmed up, after a winter afternoon on the hockey field. I was over-plump and thought of myself as very fat and clumsy, and I was hopeless at gymnastics and all sport, except swimming. As the only swimming at Felixstowe was in the cold North Sea for a few weeks each year, I was no longer able even to

star at that. I didn't feel very successful in any subject other than art, which was not thought to be a serious subject. It came as a great surprise to me, and I think to all my family, when I very successfully passed all my school leaving exams.

Although I was miserable at school, we had some wonderful times during the holidays which were spent partly in Southwold, an ideal seaside town. It was marvellous to get away from London and to be free to go out by ourselves. We had bikes and were always allowed to go for walks and to cycle around Southwold on our own. Both lots of our grandparents were there and various aunts and uncles and cousins would come on holiday too. On one holiday, a friend and I had a secret camp in the gorse on the common, with a biscuit tin buried in it, containing our collection of important things. On another holiday my cousin and I played monopoly for days on end.

Later my parents bought our own cottage in Southwold. Being in the air force meant that we were always moving from one rented place to another, so this cottage was our first real home. I enjoyed going for long walks with my parents. My mother knew the names of all the wild flowers, and my father was interested in birds, so they encouraged me in my interest. On one walk with my father, he fell into a ditch. I was collapsed with laughter as he lay there, carefully taking off his watch and handing it to me before climbing out, wet and muddy all over.

We also spent part of our holidays at Brook House in Long Melford with Great Aunt Mary, a maiden aunt of my father's. Brook House seemed enormous and very old-fashioned to me. I had a tiny bedroom leading out of my parents' room. My bed was up against the window, and in summer I could watch the house martins nesting above my window which made going to bed in daylight good fun. The bath, with its claw feet, was in the middle of a large room, which was always cold even in summer. To have a bath in winter needed a lot of courage. The lavatory was at the other end of the house, down a long passage. It had a mahogany bench seat, which was the width of the room, with a hole for the actual toilet bowl. Aunt Mary never closed the door, so as I approached I would hear her call out, "I'm in here," and would have to retreat and come back later.

There were lots of rooms downstairs including the kitchen and walk-in larder, full of mouldy jam which had been made many years before—we were never allowed to eat the fresh new jam. Aunt Mary presided over meals in the dining room. It was not considered polite to ask what we were having for pudding, and we were always told to "wait and see." She had a large bosom and once lost a slice of cucumber down the front of her dress, which she pursued with a fork. Gillian was giggling uncontrollably at the other end of the table, and Mummy sent her to fetch a glass of water to get her out of the room.

Brook House had a huge garden divided by various walls and hedges, giving me all sorts of secret places to hide and have imaginary games. We also used to play tennis—and croquet, which I liked a lot. There were chickens to feed, outside cats, and toads which lived under the back doorstep. Daddy taught me to race earwigs by tickling them with grass, but if you tickled them too much they would turn around and run the other way. I grew my first lettuces and radishes with my father's help, too.

Aunt Mary was very kind, and the worst thing for me was that she would give children's parties for us each summer. All the children invited lived locally so they knew each other well. I felt very shy of them. If there is any threat of having to play games at a party, I'll still avoid it if at all possible. Aunt Mary died when I was thirteen and Brook House was sold, but I shall always have good memories of it.

My father was posted to Singapore during my last year at boarding school. It was a wonderful excuse to leave school as soon as I was sixteen. He and my mother and sister flew out there, and I stayed with Gran, my father's mother, for the holidays before I could join them. She was tiny and I always found her a very wise person to whom I could talk about anything. The ceiling of her sitting room was dark yellow; I assumed it had been decorated like that, but it was actually the result of her smoking. A parcel of two hundred cigarettes would arrive each week from Harrods. Before doing anything else in the mornings, she sat smoking while she completed the *Times* crossword. She once sent me a huge box of three dozen large Jaffa oranges at school, because she knew I loved oranges.

At the end of the summer term, after taking my exams, I felt very elated to be able to leave school, and I flew out to join my family in Singapore. It was tremendously exciting.

We were expecting to be there for a couple of years, so the first idea was for me to go to the RAF school and study for A levels. But I left after a week because there was no sixth form and no one had time to teach me. I agreed that instead I would let my sister teach me shorthand and typing. I did work quite hard, practising most mornings, and we didn't fight much!

Our time in Singapore was cut short when my father died in a flying accident just before Christmas that year. It makes me feel very emotional to try and write about it. I had been sailing with him the previous day, and I can still remember his eyes that day. Unlike my sister, I was still not all that keen on sailing, but on that day I had taken the helm and the jib, sailing the boat entirely on my own, and it had given him enormous pleasure that shone out through his blue eyes. It made me feel much loved and very close to him.

On the day he died, I knew that something was wrong before we were told. My mother and sister were Christmas shopping in Singapore, and I had gone up to the corner to post some letters as both Daddy and they seemed late coming back. An RAF car with two people in it was silently waiting at the corner of the road, and for some reason that gave me a very uneasy premonition. Normally I might have rung his office to ask if he would be home soon. Cookie had been waiting to serve lunch, and I decided to start without them, as I knew I wouldn't want it

"Brook House, Great Aunt Mary's house in Long Melford."

Suki, the author's beloved dog.

later. It was fried liver, and I couldn't really eat much. As soon as my mother and sister got back, my father's chief arrived to break the news to us that there had been a bad storm over the Pacific and that the Meteor aircraft my father was flying was missing. After the immediate shock of learning my father was dead, I didn't know what to do. The funeral was the next day. I could feel friends and their parents watching me, expecting me to cry, so I did a bit. But I really felt too numb and too much on public view to be able to react much. It was not until a couple of weeks later, on the ship coming home from Singapore, that I really let go and wept.

The voyage home gave us a few weeks to try and get used to my father being dead, but when we got back to England, we had to start having to face the realities of our new life without him. Mummy had been ill for most of the voyage home and was very run down. We spent the first couple of weeks living in London, while she tried to sort out what we should do. I remember it as being very cold, and it seemed to rain continuously.

My mother learnt that we were going to be very short of money, her widow's pension only being about one sixth of what my father had been earning. We decided to live at Southwold until we could find a flat we could afford. It was good to get back to our cottage there and to see Gran again. Gran was amazingly resilient and cheerful, having now outlived three of her four children. I spent the few months in Southwold taking photos, painting and reading, changing

my books whenever the library was open. When I was miserable I found painting particularly comforting, something I could lose myself in and feel better afterwards. I also went on long walks accompanied by Thabo, a lovely labrador belonging to a neighbour, and long cycle rides around the countryside. Once when the primroses were out, I hired a bike for the afternoon for my mother. It was supposed to be a treat for her! Also, according to my diary, I did a lot of the cooking and housekeeping.

I was hoping to go to the the London Polytechnic to study photography, and I was very disappointed to learn that I couldn't get a grant to do this because we had been living overseas. We couldn't afford to pay, so I reluctantly agreed to do a secretarial course instead. The course started in June, and we managed to find and move into a flat in London in time for this.

Once installed in our new flat in Kensington, we all got on with our lives. Gillian had already gone back to the job she had before we went to Singapore, as secretary at the Royal Philatelic Society. I did the secretarial course, then got a job working for King Edward's Hospital Fund as secretary to their training college, and my mother worked part-time in a dress shop. My sister got engaged to a Suffolk farmer and was married four months later. Money was very tight, and we had to sell the cottage in Southwold. I had started a five-year diary in Singapore, and it also covers the period when we were in London. It shows that I had a much more social life than I remember. I was always having friends to supper. I went to the cinema or theatre at least once a week and to dances at London University. I played squash, and in the summer we swam and played tennis. I was a member of a photographic club, and I made a lot of my own clothes. I was often away at weekends and went on several cycling holidays and stayed with friends in Holland and Germany. The cycling holidays were with two very good friends, Jackie and Nicky. On one holiday we explored the Isle of Wight, then cycled down to Brixham in Devon. We were not as sporty as most of the other people staying in youth hostels, and we usually started off and arrived long after everyone else. We managed over eighty miles on our longest day, rewarding ourselves with chocolate digestive biscuits after pushing our bikes to the top of steep hills.

Although my mother had quite a good social life going too, she was still finding it very difficult to live without my father, and after my sister got married, we were both very conscious of caring about each other, which sometimes stopped us from accepting invitations to go out or away for weekends. In 1960, after discussion and with her full approval, I decided to change jobs and move to Cambridge. I started off in a bed-sitting-room, then shared flats with various friends. Although sometimes lonely, I enjoyed the new freedom and independence. And about eighteen months after I moved to Cambridge, my mother was married to a widower, also a high ranking officer in the RAF.

My first couple of jobs were not very satisfying, and I only stayed in each for a few months. Then I found one that really suited me with Cambridge Consultants. It was a new company started by Tim Eiloart, a research student, his idea being to hire out the brainy people of the university to industry on a consultancy basis. When I started I was their only paid employee and ran their tiny one-roomed office. It only had room for a desk and three chairs. At the interview I said "yes," when asked if I could manage a typing pool, and I was made to write my own reference. I loved the job, working with a group of young and very enthusiastic graduates. To make some money we also set up a translation agency, and I had to find people who combined being fluent in another language with a scientific skill to cope with specialist translation work.

Our Cambridge office was in a crumbling building which was due for demolition. No one had done anything about finding a new office, and within days of it being knocked down, I found new offices around the corner in Jesus Lane. Now that we had more room, people working on projects or with ideas to discuss were dropping in daily, so I started providing lunch—pork pies, cold meats, and a large saucepan of soup cooked over a single ring. The soup would get more and more interesting towards the end of the week as I added a mixture of packets. I washed the saucepan on Fridays and started a new batch at the beginning of the week.

Through a friend of mine, I introduced Tim Eiloart to Clive Sinclair as we thought they would get on. They did, and Clive moved to Cambridge. As the work grew, the company took over workshop space in Histon Road and started employing instrument makers to make experimental machines. Work became, and has always continued to be, part of my life, rather than something I did just to earn money, and I would often work late with the others, finishing by going out for a meal or to the cinema with them.

In spite of my involvement with people at work, I had lots of other friends and a busy social life. During the five years I worked for CCL, I moved flats several times, bought a car, and acquired a puppy, Suki. Her mother, Pooch, belonged to Tim, so Suki was allowed to come to the office, and went everywhere with me. Pooch was a remarkable dog. She knew her way all-round Cambridge, and, if Tim was away, she would turn up at my flat, or at his girl friend's, or come to the office in search of him. Suki's father was, I was told, "a brown dog with a smile." Suki was not as bright as Pooch, but she was a very good chaperone when I wanted one, as she would sit and howl if anyone tried to put an arm round me or kiss me.

My first car was a very old Ford. It was difficult to get into gear and inclined to stall in traffic. I bought it soon after passing my driving test and drove to Southwold to show it off to Gran, who bravely came out for a drive with me. The windscreen wipers slowed and the lights dimmed if I went at any speed, so journeys in rain or at night took forever, and the combination of rain and dark was frightening. However I had some good times in it, and my friend Nicky and I even drove up to Scotland on holiday in it. I kept it for three years and in the end sold it at a profit as the male chauvinist who bought it was convinced that the awful noises were due simply to my bad driving and not the worn gears! My next car was a much newer turquoise blue Mini. I had to get an overdraft from the bank to buy it and had a letter from the bank manager wishing me "Many years of happy motoring."

After four years I decided I needed a change, as there was nothing more I could do for Cambridge Consul-

Braithwaite with son, Duncan, and husband, Mike Graham-Cameron, 1970.

tants. I was bored with running a translation agency, and it was frustrating not to be able to understand the technical side of the prototype and consultancy work.

Being surrounded by graduates made me wonder whether I needed more qualifications, and I applied to go to Sussex University and was offered a place. At the same time, various upheavals were going on at Cambridge Consultants, and they took over a building with a printing works in it. The owner, Rodney Dale, was also working for them, and the printing company was in financial difficulties. Rather than closing it, I was asked if I would like to run it and get it on its feet again. I think just being offered a place at university gave me the confidence I needed in my own ability, and I decided the printing company would be more of a challenge. It was. If I had known what was involved, I might have backed out. Tim was always good at recognising other people's abilities and pushing them into doing more than they realised they were capable of. Over the years I also learnt how to give people who worked for me the confidence to acquire new skills. For instance, one not very good secretary became an excellent printer, and she also had good skills as a manager.

When I agreed to take over the printing company, I didn't even know the difference between letterpress and litho printing. Tim's father was a printer in London, and I went and worked for him for a couple of weeks to learn something about printing methods and, more importantly, about costing and estimating. When I took over Polyhedron, we had no credit with suppliers, so every time we got

小さないのち── 2

ちょう

構成・絵＝アルセア　文＝小田英智

*A **Japanese** translation of **Butterflies,** written and illustrated by Braithwaite.*

a printing job, I had to go, cash in hand, to buy the paper to print it on. To begin with, I was resented by the four people already working there. They knew much more about printing than I did and didn't like a woman coming in and organising them. It was a struggle, but amazingly I did get

it running and on its feet again. I was soon learning a great deal about the mechanics of printing and found I had quite a good eye for design.

During this time, I met and got involved with Mike Graham-Cameron. He was married, but living a separate life from his wife, who was an actress. He was looking for a new job, and Tim, who was concerned that he might lose me if Mike had to move to a different part of the country, suggested I employ him. So I did, as sales manager. Selling was something I hated and something he was very good at. Due to his selling skills, the printing company began to expand, and we started to run out of space.

When his divorce eventually came through, we got married and moved to a village on the outskirts of Cambridge. We had chosen the house because it had large outbuildings and we were able to get planning permission to have a printing works in them. We moved the works out there, keeping the offices in Cambridge. Eventually we bought the printing company from Cambridge Consultants and moved everything to our home. I was pregnant, and we started to publish my picture books. Living at our work place made it easier for both of us. We decided to call the publishing company Dinosaur Publications after the main character I'd invented—Desmond the Dinosaur.

It was good to be able to work from home and both share in looking after Duncan. He was born at home. Our doctor had been round the corner at his pharmacist's twenty-first birthday party, so delivered Duncan at three o'clock in the morning wearing his dinner jacket! However worrying the daily problems of printing and publishing were, it was difficult to be anything but happy with our small son around. Each day was new to him, and when we brought him into our bed in the mornings while we opened the post and drank our coffee, he was always cheerful and excited.

I was surprised at how early babies start seeing pictures. Duncan was pointing at and recognizing objects in pictures long before he could talk. I made a poster for him by the side of his cot, with pictures of all the things he knew. I later designed and published an alphabet frieze full of different objects so other babies could have the same enjoyment

We moved again at the time of Duncan's third birthday. Both the printing and publishing companies were growing, and since we had only been given temporary planning permission, we had to find new and larger premises in which to live and work. We eventually found the house in which I still live, a large Edwardian villa, surrounded by trees and with stables behind it, which we converted into the print workshop. The house was big enough to use some of the ground floor as offices. After our move Duncan announced that we had moved house "because of his radiator." We learnt that he had had a frighteningly noisy radiator in his room at the previous house and obviously we had arranged the house move to get away from it! We felt awful. He had never complained about it, but assumed we knew—and therefore had done something about it.

We had taken Duncan everywhere with us during his first couple of years, but as he got older he had his own friends and needed the stimulus of going to playgroup. We needed to find someone to be around when we were out and to help look after him. When selling books at Hamley's toy shop we met Nita Sowter, who was working there. She wanted to get away from London and to illustrate books. She came to stay for a weekend and convinced us that she should live with us and look after Duncan. It worked extremely well for all of us, including Duncan, who found

her great fun and was very impressed by the green milk she magically produced from the larder at teatime.

Duncan was becoming a very useful critic, and I quite often changed words in stories as a result of his comments, for instance in *Desmond and the Carnival* the phrase "'the lions have escaped,' they cried" brought the comment, "Why did they cry?" So I changed it to "they shouted." I started writing books with Duncan directly in mind. At that time there was a shortage of factual books for young children. The ring road around Cambridge was being built, and Duncan was always asking me what the various machines did. I didn't know, so I researched and learnt all about the building of new roads so I could write *Making a Road*. Tim Hunkin did the pictures for us. He had just completed his degree in engineering at Cambridge University. He has a lovely quirky style of illustration and can draw machines that actually work. Tim illustrated a number of other books for us over the years, and when working on a book, he would turn up on his bicycle to stay with us, often inviting his friends to drop by too!

I also wrote the books *Going to the Doctor* and *Visiting the Dentist*. I had found that if I told Duncan about what was going to happen before an event, like going to have an injection, he might not like the idea, but he would be brave and cope with it. Pictures always make it easier to explain things and Nita illustrated these two books. As a result of doing them, I was asked to produce others, about hospitals and eye and ear tests, and also books on what it's

"Enyaki, our Greek cat, up a tree in Hungary," 1993.

"With my dog Tom, the hero in **Tom Takes Tea**," *1991.*

like to have asthma or diabetes. When doing these books I always seek children's advice when writing them, finding out what they found difficult or scary and how they have learnt to cope.

When I go into schools to talk about my work, I am often asked which I like best, writing or illustrating. Both give me enormous pleasure. Illustrating partly because I can lose myself in it and because I am always trying out new ways of achieving the illustration I have in my mind. The writing because I enjoy the research, meeting new people, and finding out about new things always becomes fascinating. After I have collected all the information together, it's always a struggle actually to write the book. It's a bit like doing a jigsaw puzzle, it slowly comes together, and I can see a pattern and a way of fitting all the information into the set number of pages.

As a result of the coverage in newspapers and magazines we received for our first books, I was asked to think up ideas for other publishers. Souvenir Press asked me to produce books for them, and I wrote some simple non-fiction books, including *Round and Round.* This was inspired by Duncan, who made up a song about clothes going round and round in the washing machine and cement going round and round in a cement mixer truck. It included skipping ropes, and dogs turning round and round before they lie down.

The National Trust, who look after historic houses and nature reserves, approached us to ask if we could think up ideas for special children's books. I have always loved natural history, so as a trial I wrote a book about British

wild animals, my idea being to give lots of interesting facts to encourage children to want to learn more. It was so successful that the first twenty thousand copies sold out in three months, and they asked for another book before the end of their season. Mike, Duncan, and I went up to Northumberland in the north of England, and we took a boat out to the Farne Islands, where I studied all the birds including puffins, which looked like clockwork toys as they waddled around the island. I learnt that they often nest in old rabbit holes. I made sketches, took lots of photographs, and wrote copious notes. Then after more research in libraries, we came back and I wrote the book, completed the illustrations, and got them checked by a professor of zoology at Cambridge University. He was very complimentary, saying that after spending so long among stuffed animals, the book made wild creatures come alive for him again. The book *All about Creatures on Islands and Things* was printed and the copies were in the shops six weeks after it had been commissioned.

During this time we also had the excitement of seeing the stories of *Desmond the Dinosaur* and some of my other characters including *Cuthbert and Bimbo,* the ant and giraffe, on children's television. I prepared storyboards for some and others were taken straight from the books.

When Nita Sowter left us to get married to the production manager in our printing company, we advertised for someone to take her place and were very lucky to find another all-rounder, Celia Henderson, who took on and enjoyed a wide range of duties from running the house and looking after Duncan to helping me with colour separation for the illustrations.

It was a very busy and exciting few years, but perhaps a bit too frenetic, and we didn't take enough time off to relax together. Sadly this had a detrimental effect on our marriage. Mike fell in love with a teacher at Duncan's school. He left me to live with her and her children, but continued to work with me. I shall always be grateful to Celia for the stability she gave Duncan during this emotionally difficult time.

After a year I decided I couldn't cope with Mike turning up daily and going "home" in the evenings, so he stopped working full-time, though he continued to do some freelance work for us. Christopher Wingate, who had been managing director of a large printing and publishing company that we worked with, came to Dinosaur as managing director. We worked well together, and he was also a wonderfully supportive friend. He, the people I worked with, and other friends all helped me to get over the emotional upset of splitting up with Mike. Initially Duncan was very angry with his father saying, "He should be here, looking after me, not going and looking after other children." He saw a lot of Mike, and gradually we got our lives together again. Work was still demanding and gave me great pleasure. I began to enjoy the freedom of not being married, doing things that Mike did not enjoy, like going for long and muddy walks across the marshes in Norfolk. I bought a cottage up there, and we had marvellous weekends and holidays, being taken boating by friends.

There is an annual international children's book fair in Italy. Publishers from all over the world plus some authors and illustrators descend on Bologna each April to show their books and to sell them from one country to another. The first year that Dinosaur had a stand there, Celia, Duncan, and I and a great friend Ann went by car to Italy, taking our books with us. On the way out we put the car on a train in Paris and travelled overnight to Nice, then drove round the coast into Italy. Duncan wore a T-shirt on which I had painted Desmond the Dinosaur and our stand number in case he should get lost in the enormous halls full of children's books. On our way back we were asked to stay with publishing friends in France. We shared the driving, which was reasonably grief free, except when Celia went round a roundabout the wrong way. I kept very quiet thinking it best not to panic her, and the other traffic obviously felt the same, because we were not even hooted at. Duncan had his seventh birthday cake on the ferry coming back to England.

A Japanese publisher at Bologna was very keen on my work and asked me to do a series of life-cycle books on *Flowers, Butterflies, Birds, and Frogs.* I wrote all four and illustrated the flower and butterfly books myself. I wanted to base the butterfly book on the swallowtail. I managed to find a centre where they were being bred. They let me have five caterpillars as long as I returned the pupa at the end. It was a bit disastrous as one caterpillar drowned and I lost another when it was changing into a pupa—though the following summer I had the great excitement of finding a swallowtail butterfly emerging from its pupa in a cupboard.

It's great fun when I can research, write, and illustrate from life, and I think it makes a more friendly and accessible book. For instance in *Growing Plants at Home,* a book about indoor gardening, not all my plants were perfect, and some of my illustrations show leaves with brown edges. Last summer I grew, sketched, and photographed lots of vegetables in pots in preparation for a book about gardening. Some of my story books grow out of real life too. I wrote two stories about my dog Tom, a large and very beautiful lurcher. It is written from his point of view. He used to steal food if it was left within reach and then give himself away by looking extremely guilty. *Tom Takes Tea* is about him stealing a chocolate cake.

Christopher was only with Dinosaur for three-and-a-bit years. He had two heart attacks, one after the first year from which he made a very good recovery. Mike came back to work full-time at Dinosaur after Christopher's heart attack, and I found I could work with him again. Christopher died of the second heart attack which he had on a train when he and I were travelling to Bologna. It was a very traumatic and sad time, made even more so by my mother dying three weeks later. She had had a serious operation some time before, from which she never fully recovered. It was a bad time, but again friends, family, and work helped me to come to terms with my emotions.

I have since written books on divorce, *I Have Two Homes,* and death, *When Uncle Bob Died,* as I know from my own and Duncan's experience that it helps to talk about one's feelings. These books are meant to be shared between a child and adult as a way to start talking. From doing radio phone-in programmes and talking to groups of people, I know that lots of people have found the books helpful.

After five years on my own, I married again. Edward also joined me in the business enterprises. My mother had left me some money, and we decided to use part of it to start a children's mobile bookshop. There are large areas in East Anglia which were not well served by bookshops, and we bought a secondhand caravan and a Land Rover so that Edward could convert the caravan into a travelling bookshop. It was stocked with children's paperbacks from all the main publishers, and he drove it to many schools and book fairs around the country. Although everyone was very keen on the idea, they didn't buy enough books to make it financially successful, so when it skidded off an icy winter road two years later, we could not afford to replace it.

Dinosaur Publications was growing to a size where we either had to find extra outside money to allow it to grow even more or sell up. We were wondering which to do when we had an offer from Collins Publishers, who wanted to buy the company. It was a difficult decision, but I was more interested in writing and illustrating books than in running a publishing company, so we decided to sell. For the next four years I was a consultant doing editorial work for them as well as writing for them and other publishers. However Collins published fewer and fewer new books and with the recession other publishers were also cutting back on their children's lists. I was finding it frustrating not to be able to do the books that I wanted to do.

After Duncan left school he worked in Cambridge. Then he and his girlfriend, Dawn, decided to go to Australia for a year. They worked for a while in Melbourne and bought an estate car and tent and travelled round the whole of Australia before coming back to England via Thailand. During the recession Edward was finding it difficult to get work too, so we decided to copy Duncan and Dawn and take off and travel just for the fun of it. We had always intended to take a couple of years off "one day" to explore the Mediterranean, and we had found a one-room apartment in Greece with this in mind. We bought a large Mercedes van which Edward converted into a camper van. We let our house to an American family and set off in April 1992. We travelled through France and Italy and arrived in Greece in June. We saw so many wonderful orchids and other wild flowers on the journey that by the time we arrived in Greece, I knew I wanted to work on books of Mediterranean flora and fauna for travellers. I took lots of photographs on the journey.

We lived in our apartment on the Peloponnesus opposite Delphi, going off in the camper every couple of months to explore a new part of mainland Greece. The following spring we had two fantastic months on Crete, living in the van and parking in beautiful spots. I was illustrating flowers each day and had never felt happier. It was wonderful to wake up each morning and step outside the van to be surrounded by the natural world, so much more beautiful than any man-made garden could ever be. We called in on official campsites once a week to have hot showers and to wash our clothes. The rest of the time we loved being in the wilds.

After another summer in Greece, when Duncan and Dawn and various friends visited us, we left, taking the long way back through Bulgaria, Romania, Hungary, Slovakia, and the Czech Republic. Calor gas was not available in Bulgaria and Romania, so we had the fun of collecting wood and cooking all our meals over open fires. I kept a diary, and I mean to write a book about our travels. This time there were three of us in the van. A small Greek cat had decided to accompany us. Her mother had lived with us all the time we had been in Greece and had dumped her daughter on us as a kitten. When we were packing the van, getting it ready to leave, the kitten kept jumping in and lying on the bed purring. We decided it would be cruel to leave her behind. She thoroughly enjoyed travelling, and when we stopped in the evenings she would go off and explore her new territory, always returning to the van, which had very definitely become her home. When it was too cold for us to leave the van door open for her, she would climb onto the back step and knock on the door to be let in. She soon learned to duck when we opened the door for her, as otherwise it knocked her to the ground.

After spending the winter in the south of France, we decided in the spring of 1994 to go to Spain. I wanted to see if the plants were very different from the east to the west of the Mediterranean region. The landscape in inland Spain is huge and dramatic. Again we were travelling in the camper and would drive up rough tracks to find wonderful places in which to live for a night or two. Many of the plants in Spain were the same as elsewhere, but I found some different ones, and we saw many more kinds of birds in southern Spain.

Animals have to go into quarantine for six months when they arrive in Britain, so we arranged for the cat to fly home in advance from Spain, on her own. It was a horrid thing for her to have to do, but she now thoroughly enjoys life in Cambridgeshire. She had kittens last year and her three daughters, each living with people whom we know, all had kittens this year, so there are now lots of half-Greek cats living in the fens. We have also heard her mother is well and still having kittens in Greece. I have still to write a cat's tale.

As I am no longer a publisher, I've discovered it takes several years for other publishers to come round to thinking that the books I want to write are a good idea. After two-and-a-half years away, I have only now been commissioned to write some of the books I had proposed before going away. In between, I'm still working on my Mediterranean books, using thousands of photographs I took in many countries.

As a child I didn't dream of becoming a writer and illustrator any more than I planned to run a printers or start a publishing company. These things happened because when the chances arose, I was able to grasp them. I'm a great believer in learning from experience and in teaching myself all the things I want to do. For many years now I have not had the security of a paid job, but I make a living from what I enjoy doing. Writing is just one of the ways of fulfilling myself. Learning new skills, painting, and travelling are equally important. The most difficult thing is trying to find the time to fit in all the wonderful and exciting possibilities.

Writings

FOR CHILDREN; FICTION; AUTHOR AND ILLUSTRATOR

Cuthbert and Bimbo, Dinosaur, 1967, Merrimack Book Service, 1978.

Benjamin, Dinosaur, 1967.
Desmond the Dinosaur, Dinosaur, 1967.
Jeremy Mouse, Polyprint, 1968, Merrimack Book Service, 1978.
Peter Pig, Polyprint, 1968, Merrimack Book Service, 1978.
Desmond Goes to Scotland, Dinosaur, 1968, Rourke, 1981.
George and the Baby, Dinosaur, 1968, Merrimack Book Service, 1978.
Desmond and the Fire, Dinosaur, 1969.
Desmond the Dusty Dinosaur, Dinosaur, 1969, Rourke, 1981.
Desmond Meets a Stranger, Dinosaur, 1971.
The Gingerbread Band, Dinosaur, 1970.
Smith the Lonely Hedgehog, Dinosaur, 1970, published in the U.S. as *Smith the Lonely Porcupine,* 1981.
Smith and Matilda, Dinosaur, 1971.
Desmond at the Carnival, Dinosaur, 1971, Rourke, 1981.
Tugby Is Given an Umbrella, Dinosaur, 1971.
Round and Round, Souvenir Press, 1971.
Up and Down, Souvenir Press, 1972.
The First National Trust Painting Book, Dinosaur, 1973.
The Second National Trust Painting Book, Dinosaur, 1973.
High in the Sky, Souvenir Press, 1973.
(Illustrated with others) *Althea's First Picture Book,* Dinosaur, 1974.
The First Country Book, Dinosaur, 1974.
Desmond Goes to New York, Dinosaur, 1975, Rourke, 1981.
The Third National Trust Painting Book, Dinosaur, 1975.
The Fourth National Trust Painting Book, Dinosaur, 1975.
The National Trust Second Country Book, Dinosaur, 1975.
Desmond and the Monsters, Dinosaur, 1975, Rourke, 1981.
The Second Country Book, Dinosaur, 1975.
Desmond and the Stranger, Dinosaur, 1976.
Desmond Goes Boating, Dinosaur, 1977, Rourke, 1981.
Colours and Cars, Souvenir Press, 1977.
Desmond and the Fancy Dress Party, Dinosaur, 1979, Rourke, 1981.
Desmond the Dinosaur Story Book, Dinosaur, 1979.
The Big Desmond Story Book, Dinosaur, 1980.
Jeremy Mouse and Cat, Dinosaur, 1980, Rourke, 1981.
Jeremy Mouse Was Hungry, Dinosaur, 1981, Rourke, 1981.
The Adventures of Desmond the Dinosaur, Dinosaur, 1981.
Desmond at the Zoo, Dinosaur, 1981, Rourke, 1981.
Desmond Starts School, Dinosaur, 1982.
(Illustrated with others) *Althea's Second Picture Book,* Dinosaur, 1983.
Desmond's Birthday Surprise, Dinosaur, 1984.
Desmond Goes to the Vet, Dinosaur, 1989.
Desmond's Christmas, Dinosaur, 1989.
Desmond's Postbag, Dinosaur, 1989.

NONFICTION; AUTHOR AND ILLUSTRATOR

The Flower, Souvenir Press, 1971.
All About Creatures on Islands and Things, Dinosaur, 1971.
All About Pines and Oakes and Things, Dinosaur, 1972.
All About Snails and Ladybirds and Things, Dinosaur, 1972.
All About Cuckoos and Robins and Things, Dinosaur, 1973.
All About Voles and Sticklebacks and Things, Dinosaur, 1973.

(Illustrated with Maureen Galvani) *A Visit to Canterbury Cathedral*, Dinosaur, 1975.

Day by Day Diary, Dinosaur, 1977.

A Flower, Longman, 1980, Longman USA, 1988 (originally published in Japanese by Kaisai-Sha, 1977).

(Illustrated with Maureen Galvani) *The Butterfly*, Longman, Green, 1980 (originally published in Japanese by Kaisai-Sha, 1977).

Animals at Your Feet, Dinosaur, 1980.

Address Book, Dinosaur, 1980.

How Was It Made?, Souvenir Press, 1980.

Desert Homes, Cambridge University Press, 1984.

Growing Plants at Home, Dinosaur, 1985, republished as *Green Finger Fun*, Dinosaur, 1988.

Under Sea Homes, Cambridge University Press, 1985.

Shapes of Things, Dinosaur, 1986.

Sizes of Things, Dinosaur, 1987.

OTHER FICTION

Victoria and the Flowerbed Children, illustrated by Barbara Sampson, Dinosaur, 1970.

Victoria and the Balloon Keeper, illustrated by Barbara Sampson, Dinosaur, 1971.

All About Squirrels and Moles and Things, illustrated by Christine Woodley, Dinosaur, 1971.

All About Guns and Armour and Things, illustrated by Sue Grahame, Dinosaur, 1972.

Going to the Doctor, illustrated by Nita Sowter, Dinosaur, 1973, Merrimack Book Service, 1978.

The New Baby, illustrated by Nita Sowter, Souvenir Press, 1973.

Going into Hospital, illustrated by Maureen Galvani, Dinosaur, 1973, reprinted with illustrations by Joanna Stubbs, Dinosaur, 1986.

Visiting the Dentist, illustrated by Maureen Galvani, Dinosaur, 1974, Merrimack Book Service, 1978, reprinted, illustrated by Ian Newsham, Dinosaur, 1986.

Going on a Train, illustrated by David L. Moore, Dinosaur, 1975.

Starting School, illustrated by Maureen Galvani, Dinosaur, 1975.

The Gingerbread Men, Maureen Galvani, Dinosaur, 1975.

A Baby in the Family, illustrated by Ljiljana Rylands, Dinosaur, 1975, Merrimack Book Service, 1978.

David and His Sister Carol, illustrated by Ljiljana Rylands, Dinosaur, 1976, Merrimack Book Service, 1978.

I Go to Playschool, illustrated by Nita Sowter, Souvenir Press, 1976.

Having an Eye Test, illustrated by Maureen Galvani, Dinosaur, 1978.

I Go to Hospital, illustrated by Ljiljana Rylands, Souvenir Press, 1977.

The Alphabet Book, illustrated by Ljiljana Rylands, Dinosaur, 1978.

My Babysitter, illustrated by Helen Herbert, Dinosaur, 1978.

Buildings Colouring Book, illustrated by Kate Fitzsimons, Dinosaur, 1979.

My Childminder, illustrated by Cynthia Pickard, Dinosaur, 1979.

I Go to a Party, Souvenir Press, 1979.

I Go Shopping, Souvenir Press, 1979.

About Bees and Honey, illustrated by Paula Youens, Dinosaur, 1979.

Moth and the Butterfly Collection, Dinosaur, 1979.

Costumes Colouring Book, illustrated by Kate Fitzsimons, Dinosaur, 1979.

Althea's Big Country Book, Dinosaur, 1979.

Visiting a Museum, illustrated by Maureen Galvani, Dinosaur, 1980.

Caterpillars to Butterflies, illustrated by Maureen Galvani, Dinosaur, 1980.

I Have Two Homes, illustrated by Isabel Pearce, Dinosaur, 1980.

Jane Is Adopted, illustrated by Isabel Pearce, Souvenir Press, 1980.

Wearing Many Hats, illustrated by Helen Herbert, Dinosaur, 1980.

Can You Moo?, illustrated by Ljiljana Rylands, Dinosaur, 1981.

My Sister, illustrated by Susan Morgan, Souvenir Press, 1981.

Having a Hearing Test, illustrated by Maureen Galvani, Dinosaur, 1981.

Know the Time, 1981.

Listen to Your Feet, illustrated by Ann Rees, Souvenir Press, 1981.

Riding on a Roundabout, illustrated by Helen Herbert, Dinosaur, 1981.

The School Fair, illustrated by Susan Morgan, Dinosaur, 1982.

Dinosaur's Book of Dinosaurs, illustrated by Ljiljana Rylands, Dinosaur, 1982.

My Night Away, illustrated by Susan Morgan, Souvenir Press, 1982.

The Year Around Us, Dinosaur, 1982.

When Uncle Bob Died, illustrated by Isabel Pearce, Dinosaur, 1982, reprinted with illustrations by Lisa Kopper, 1988.

I Can't Talk Like You, illustrated by Isabel Pearce, Dinosaur, 1982.

I Have Asthma, illustrated by Jean Howatt, Dinosaur, 1982.

Colours of Things, illustrated by Suzanna Gretz, Dinosaur, 1982.

I Have Diabetes, illustrated by Maureen Galvani, Dinosaur, 1983, reprinted with illustrations by Angela Owen, Dinosaur, 1991.

I Use a Wheelchair, illustrated by Maureen Galvani, Dinosaur, 1983, reprinted with illustrations by John Davey, 1991.

Friends, illustrated by Susan Morgan, Dinosaur, 1983.

I Want to Be an Engineer, Dinosaur, 1984.

More Dinosaurs from Dinosaur, illustrated by Barbara McGirr, Dinosaur, 1984.

My New Family, illustrated by Sue McMaster, Dinosaur, 1984.

The Pantomime, illustrated by Hilary Evans, Dinosaur, 1984.

Know the Time, illustrated by Susan Morgan, Dinosaur, 1985.

Starting School, illustrated by Joanna Stubbs, Dinosaur, 1985.

I Can't Hear Like You, illustrated by Jean Anderson, Dinosaur, 1986.

The Cakemaker, illustrated by Nita Sowter, Dinosaur, 1986.

Fruit Salad, illustrated by Jacqueline Wood, Dinosaur, 1987.

I Have Epilepsy, illustrated by Ann Baum, Dinosaur, 1987, reprinted with illustrations by Nicola Spoor, Dinosaur, 1991.

I Have a Mental Handicap, illustrated by Paul Dowling, Dinosaur, 1987.

Hippos at Home, illustrated by Bettina Paterson, Orchard, 1987.

Hippos Go Out, illustrated by Bettina Paterson, Orchard, 1988.

Lunchboxes, illustrated by Tim Archbold, Dinosaur, 1988.

Be Careful!, illustrated by Ian Newsham, Dinosaur, 1988.

If You Were a Gerbil, illustrated by John Rogan, Dinosaur, 1988.

Will It Rain Today?, illustrated by Colin Robinson, Dinosaur, 1988.

Crossing Roads, illustrated by Ian Newsham, Dinosaur, 1988.

I Have Eczema, illustrated by Sarah Altham, Dinosaur, 1988.

Opposites of Things, illustrated by Frances Cony, Dinosaur, 1988.

Speed of Things, illustrated by Susie Pritchatt, Dinosaur, 1988.

Colours of Things, illustrated by Susanna Gretz, Dinosaur, 1988.

How My Body Works, illustrated by Frances Cony, Dinosaur, 1989.

I Have Cancer, illustrated by Nicola Spoor, Dinosaur, 1989.

Flippers: Tom Takes Tea and Tom the Hero, illustrated by Rob McCaig, Pan Macmillan, 1993.

Cards to Paint and Window Pictures, National Gallery (London), 1996.

The Bullies, illustrated by Karin Littlewood, Black, 1996.

The Birthday Party, illustrated by Karin Littlewood, Black, 1996.

Alone at Home, illustrated by Karin Littlewood, Black, 1996.

Gila Gets Lost, illustrated by Karin Littlewood, Black, 1996.

My Two Families, photographs by Richard Clemence, Black, 1996.

Being a Friend, photographs by Charlie Best, Black, 1997.

Feeling Shy, photographs by Charlie Best, Black, 1997.

Telling the Truth, photographs by Charlie Best, Black, 1997.

Feeling Angry, photographs by Charlie Best, Black, 1997.

Feeling Jealous, photographs by Charlie Best, Black, 1998.

Feeling Scared, photographs by Charlie Best, Blac, 1998.

OTHER NONFICTION

Night, illustrated by Nita Sowter, Souvenir Press, 1972.

Water, illustrated by Nita Sowter, Souvenir Press, 1972.

Going on Wheels, illustrated by Nita Sowter, Souvenir Press, 1972.

Man in the Sky: The Early Years, illustrated by Timothy Hunkin, Colourmaster, 1972, Merrimack Book Service, 1978.

All About Poppies and Bluebells and Things, illustrated by Hilary Abrahams, 1973.

Making a Road, illustrated by Timothy Hunkin, Dinosaur, 1973, Merrimack Book Service, 1978.

Whirling Windmills, illustrated by Nita Sowter, Colourmaster International, 1973, Merrimack Book Service, 1978.

Bridges, illustrated by Hilary Abrahams, Colourmaster International, 1973.

Life in a Castle, illustrated by Hilary Abrahams, Colourmaster International, 1973, Merrimack Book Service, 1978.

Signposts of the Sea, illustrated by Timothy Hunkin, Colourmaster International, 1973, Merrimack Book Service, 1978.

Making a Car, illustrated by Timothy Hunkin, Dinosaur, 1974.

Building a House, illustrated by Colin King, Dinosaur, 1974.

How Life Began, illustrated by Mike Vince, Dinosaur, 1974, Merrimack Book Service, 1978.

Man Flies On, illustrated by Paul Wrigley, Colourmaster International, 1974, Merrimack Book Service, 1978.

Iron Roads, illustrated by Michael Vince, Colourmaster International, 1974.

Inland Waterways, illustrated by Denis Wrigley, Colourmaster International, 1974.

Fighting Fires, illustrated by Timothy Hunkin, Dinosaur, 1975.

Hospitals, illustrated by Maureen Galvani, Dinosaur, 1974, Merrimack Book Service, 1978.

Zoos, Dinosaur, 1975, Merrimack Book Service, 1978.

Cars, Dinosaur, 1975.

Farms, Dinosaur, 1975, Merrimack Book Service, 1978.

Life in the Garden, illustrated by Ann Biggs, Dinosaur, 1975.

Life in Ponds and Streams, illustrated by Ann Biggs, Dinosaur, 1975.

Life in Hedges and Verges, illustrated by Ann Biggs, Dinosaur, 1975.

Life on the Seashore, illustrated by Ann Biggs, Dinosaur, 1975.

Exploring Breckland, illustrated by Veronica Barge, East Anglica Tourist Board, 1975.

Exploring the Broads, illustrated by Veronica Barge, East Anglica Tourist Board, 1975.

Where Does Food Come From?, illustrated by Maureen Galvani, Dinosaur, 1976, Merrimack Book Service, 1978.

Moving House, illustrated by Maureen Galvani, Souvenir Press, 1976.

Frogs, illustrated by Maureen Galvani, Longman, 1980, Longman USA, 1988 (originally published in Japanese by Kaisai-Sha, 1977).

Birds, illustrated by Veronica Barge, Longman, 1980, Longman, 1988 (originally published in Japanese by Kaisai-Sha, 1977).

Castle Life, illustrated by Maureen Galvani, Dinosaur, 1976.

Flying in an Aeroplane, illustrated by Roger Phillippo, Dinosaur, 1977.

Thomas Telford: Man of Iron, illustrated by Timothy Hunkin, Dinosaur, 1977.

Bath from Roman Times, illustrated by Maureen Galvani, Dinosaur, 1977.

The Great Family Barnardo's, illustrated by Helen Herbert, Dinosaur, 1977.

Household Machines, illustrated by John Lobban and R. A. Sherrington, Puffin, 1977.

Spring, illustrated by Maureen Galvani, Souvenir Press, 1978.

Summer, illustrated by Maureen Galvani, Souvenir Press, 1978.

Autumn, illustrated by Maureen Galvani, Souvenir Press, 1978.

Winter, illustrated by Maureen Galvani, Souvenir Press, 1978.

A Visit to the Factory, illustrated by Jean Vaughan, Dinosaur, 1979.

Machines on a Farm, illustrated by Timothy Hunkin, Dinosaur, 1979.

Making a Book, illustrated by Tim Hunkin, Dinosaur, 1980, Rourke, 1981.

A First Big Picture Book, Dinosaur, 1980.

Animals at Home, illustrated by Maureen Galvani, Dinosaur, 1981.

What Is a Union?, illustrated by Chris Evans, Rourke, 1981, Dinosaur, 1981.

Making Plastics, illustrated by Timothy Hunkin, Dinosaur, 1981.

Leaves from Trees, illustrated by Barbara McGirr, Dinosaur, 1981.

The Stock Exchange, illustrated by Chris Evans, Dinosaur, 1982.

My Cat, illustrated by Gilian Hulse, Souvenir Press, 1982.

Ducks and Drakes, illustrated by Joe Blossom, Dinosaur, 1982.

Tree, illustrated by Barbara McGirr, Longman, 1982, Longman USA, 1988.

Foxes, illustrated by Helen Herbert, Longman, 1982, Longman USA, 1988.

Fish, illustrated by Paul Wrigley, Longman, 1983, Longman USA, 1988.

Snails, illustrated by Helen Herbert, Longman, 1983, Longman USA, 1988.

Caterpillars to Moths, illustrated by Maureen Galvani, Dinosaur, 1983.

Money in the Bank, illustrated by Susan Evans, Dinosaur, 1983.

Polar Homes, illustrated by Barbara McGirr, Cambridge University Press, 1983.

How a Zoo Works, illustrated by Ljiljana Rylands, Dinosaur, 1984.

Life in Ponds, illustrated by Barbara McGirr, Dinosaur, 1984.

Under the Magnifying Glass, illustrated by Alastair Burn, 1984.

Beside the Sea, illustrated by Maureen Galvani, Dinosaur, 1984.

Island Homes, illustrated by Barbara McGirr, Cambridge University Press, 1983.

Rain Forest Homes, illustrated by John Boyd Brent, Cambridge University Press, 1985.

Mountain Homes, illustrated by Barbara McGirr, Cambridge University Press, 1985.

Wool from Sheep, illustrated by Jane Dunn, Dinosaur, 1985.

Hedgehogs, illustrated by Joe B. Blossom, Longman, 1985.

Ladybirds, illustrated by Barbara McGirr, Longman, 1985, republished in the U.S. as *Ladybugs,* Longman USA, 1988.

Swans, illustrated by Joe B. Blossom, Longman, 1985, Longman USA, 1988.

Bats, illustrated by Barbara McGirr, Longman, 1985, Longman USA, 1988.

Living in Roman Times, illustrated by Chris and Hilary Evans, Dinosaur, 1986.

Special Care Babies, illustrated by Nicola Spoor, Dinosaur, 1986.

Farm Animals, illustrated by Barbara McGirr, Dinosaur, 1986.

Whale, illustrated by Barbara McGirr, Longman, 1987, republished as *Whales,* Longman USA, 1988.

Gorilla, illustrated by Barbara McGirr, Longman, 1987, republished as *Gorillas,* Longman USA, 1988.

Parrot, illustrated by Peter Gil, Longman, 1987, republished as *Parrots,* Longman USA, 1988.

Leopard, illustrated by Barbara McGirr, Longman, 1987.

Animals at Night, pictures by Gary Rees, Dinosaur, 1987.

Five Senses, illustrated by Emma Hughes, Dinosaur, 1987.

Farm Crops, illustrated by Jacqueline Wood, Dinosaur, 1988.

Insects, illustrated by Alan Male, Troll, 1990, published in England as *Insects and other Animals,* Eagle, 1990.

Trees and Leaves, illustrated by David More, Troll, Eagle, 1990.

What Makes Things Move?, illustrated by Robina Green, Troll, Eagle, 1991.

How Do Things Grow?, illustrated by Julie Douglas, Troll, Eagle, 1991.

NONFICTION; WRITTEN WITH HUSBAND, EDWARD PARKER

Jumbo Jets, illustrated by Peter Bailey, Black, 1992.
Cargo Ships, illustrated by Peter Kent, Black, 1992.
Railways, illustrated by Peter Kent, Black, 1992.
Windmills, Black, 1992.

ILLUSTRATOR; ALL WRITTEN BY TONY CROWLEY

Choosing a Job, Hobsons Press, 1974.
Finding a Job, Hobsons Press, 1974.
Starting a Job, Hobsons Press, 1975.
Keeping a Job, Hobsons Press, 1975.

OTHER

Some of Althea's books have been translated into several languages, including French, German, and Japanese.

C

CANNON, Eileen E(mily) 1948-
(Taffy Cannon)

Personal

Born December 1, 1948, in Chicago, IL; daughter of Joseph Phillip (a surgeon) and Mildred Eileen (a nurse; maiden name, Toll) Cannon; married William Christian Kamenjarin (an attorney), July 15, 1973; children: Melissa. *Education:* Duke University, A.B. (with distinction in political science), 1970, M.A.T., 1971.

Addresses

Home—P.O. Box 2520, Carlsbad, CA 92018. *Agent*—Jane Chelius Literary Agency, 548 2nd St., Brooklyn, NY 11215.

Career

Writer.

Awards, Honors

Academy Award nomination for live action short subject, 1975, for *Doubletalk.*

Writings

SCREENPLAYS

Doubletalk, 1975.

NOVELS; AS TAFFY CANNON

Convictions: A Novel of the Sixties, Morrow (New York City), 1985.
Mississippi Treasure Hunt (young adult novel), Juniper, 1996.
Guns and Roses, Perseverance, 2000.

"NAN ROBINSON" MYSTERY NOVEL SERIES; AS TAFFY CANNON

A Pocketful of Karma, Carroll & Graf (New York City), 1993.

Tangled Roots, Carroll & Graf (New York City), 1995.
Class Reunions Are Murder, Crest (New York City), 1996.

Sidelights

In 1985 Eileen E. Cannon, writing under the pseudonym Taffy Cannon, published her debut book, *Convictions: A Novel of the Sixties.* Since then she has written several mysteries, including *Mississippi Treasure Hunt,* a novel for young adult readers. In addition to fiction, Cannon is also the author of an Academy Award-nominated screenplay for the short film *Doubletalk.*

Cannon's young-adult novel, *Mississippi Treasure Hunt,* finds thirteen-year-old Vangie and her brother leaving their home in Malibu to visit their father and stepmother in Minnesota. While his children are visiting, Vangie's dad finds out that he has inherited an estate in Mississippi, so a summer in Minnesota quickly becomes a trip to the South. In a desk in the house her father inherits, Vangie discovers an old letter that alludes to the whereabouts of a mysterious treasure. She, her brother, and their grandfather solve the mystery with persistence and much help from the local library. *Kliatt* contributor Gerrie Human called Cannon's *Mississippi Treasure Hunt* "an ingeniously plotted mystery with realistic YAs portrayed."

Convictions, the author's first book, is the tale of two young, finishing-school friends who room together at Duke University during the 1960s and become drawn into the turbulence of the era. The narrator, Laurel Hollingsworth, looks back from the perspective of the late 1970s at her friend, Prentiss Granger, a beautiful and intelligent textile heiress forced underground by her accidental involvement in a murder. Cannon's portrait of the mood and feel of the era includes the 1968 Democratic convention in Chicago, the gap between traditional parents and rebellious, spoiled children, bomb plots, the FBI, and the acceptance of "free love" that triggers Prentiss's ultimate need for an abortion. It also offers "a compelling sense of place," according to *Los Angeles Times Book Review* contributor Marina Hirsch.

A reviewer for *Publishers Weekly* commented that Cannon's success in capturing the atmosphere of the 1960s was due in part to a narrator who is "so well-developed as a flesh-and-blood, humorous and self-deprecating commentator."

In 1993 Cannon published *A Pocketful of Karma,* her first mystery novel and the first in a series featuring attorney Nan Robinson, an investigator for the California State Bar. In *A Pocketful of Karma,* Robinson's former secretary, Debra LaRoche, seems to be missing, and the litigator-turned-investigator finds the search for her leading into the wilds of California popular culture: rock star groupies, Hollywood muscle boys, and past-life hypnotists. Robinson has doubts about hypnotic regressions and suspects several employees of the Past Lives Institute of murder, but nevertheless she finds herself attracted to Jonathan, the institute's director. Debra's body is eventually discovered in the trunk of the secretary's own car, her estranged husband also turns up dead, and Robinson herself becomes a target of Debra's mysterious assassin. *Wilson Library Bulletin* reviewer Gail Pool said Cannon "plays up her southern California setting well, distinguishing its identity and particular brands of looniness" from those in the rest of the country. A *Publishers Weekly* reviewer commented, "Cannon's skeptical heroine and her elusive villain stake out the wilds of L.A. in an auspiciously flavorsome foray."

In 1995's *Tangled Roots,* Cannon shifts the scene a bit further south to San Diego, where a flower nursery owner has been murdered and Robinson's brother-in-law, another flower grower, is the leading suspect. Attorney Robinson thinks her brother-in-law an unlikely perpetrator, but his gun and a wrapper from the unusual brand of gum he favors are found at the crime scene. Matters become more complex when it is learned that the man's pregnant wife once had an affair with the murder victim. Robinson's investigations lead her into a tangle of family relations, greenhouse employees, an amusement park conglomerate, and Anglo-Hispanic relations. Near the end, Cannon's sleuth, whom *Wilson Library Bulletin* reviewer Gail Pool described as "sharp" and "extremely appealing," almost becomes the fifth victim.

The third book in the "Nan Robinson" series, *Class Reunions Are Murder,* has attorney Robinson returning to Illinois for her twenty-year high school reunion where former class tramp Brenda Blaine surprises her by showing up, and then by turning up murdered.

Cannon has commented: "I always loved to write, but as a child it never occurred to me that I could *be* a writer. I thought writers were somehow anointed at birth, and since I hadn't been, I would have to find a real job. I kept looking for careers that would integrate writing until I discovered, in my mid-twenties, that writers were simply people who decided to write and then did so. Thus began an odyssey of challenge, adventure, creativity, and penury.

"Over the past quarter-century, I've tried just about every type of writing but advertising, which always seemed to be an immoral application of any gifts I might have (see penury, above). Along the way I supported myself as everything from a carnival barker to a professional feminist, accumulating material and moving through worlds I might never have otherwise encountered.

"I've never 'studied' writing, and I don't think it's something that can really be taught. Still, there are certain skills that can be acquired by writing and writing and then writing some more. It *is* an evolutionary process, and everything I do is built on what I've done before.

"From journalism I learned the importance of solid research, the significance of the single telling detail, that writer's block is a non-issue on deadline and that once you have your lead, a story or scene will write itself.. From screenwriting, I learned structure, pacing, visualization and that every word of dialogue should accomplish something.

"These different skills have come together in writing fiction, which provides all of the excitement of journalism without the constraint of having to tell the truth.

"Storytelling is magical to me, and the process of writing a wondrous exploration. To create people and worlds and events (and even commit the occasional murder) is a marvelous luxury, and one I cherish. Writing fiction allows me to explore issues and places and situations that I find interesting and to call it 'work' with a straight face. It never gets easier, but it's always exciting, and each new project presents unexpected joys and challenges. In the end, however, it all comes down to a simple truth: I write because I can't *not* write."

Biographical and Critical Sources

BOOKS

Detecting Women Two, Purple Moon (Dearborn, MI), 1996.

PERIODICALS

Booklist, February 15, 1993, p. 1038; February 1, 1995, pp. 992, 996.
Kirkus Reviews, April 15, 1985, p. 335; January 1, 1993, p. 24; January 1, 1995, p. 27.
Kliatt, September 1996, p. 6.
Library Journal, June 1, 1985, p. 142; February 1, 1993, p. 115; January, 1995, p. 142; February 1, 2000, p. 120.
Los Angeles Times Book Review, August 25, 1985, p. B1; August 15, 1993, p. 9.
Publishers Weekly, May 10, 1984, p. 221; January 11, 1993, p. 53; January 30, 1995, p. 88; February 12, 1996, p. 78.
Wilson Library Bulletin, May, 1993, p. 99; February, 1995, p. 73.*

CANNON, Taffy
See CANNON, Eileen E(mily)

*   *   *

CARLING, Amelia Lau 1949-

Personal

Born February 6, 1949, in Guatemala City, Guatemala; immigrated to the United States, 1966; daughter of Rodolfo (a store owner) and Graciela (a store owner; maiden name, Chang) de Lau; married Robert Carling; children: Laura Sulin, Ana Meili. *Education:* Occidental College, Los Angeles, B.A. (fine arts).

Addresses

Home—47 Lewis Parkway, Yonkers, NY 10705. *E-mail*—cmyk47@aol.com.

Career

Graphic designer, writer, and illustrator. Dial Books for Young Readers, New York City, assistant art director, 1987-97; Golden Books, New York City, art director—trade, 1997—. Has given readings from her work at schools, at the American Museum of Natural History, and at the Museum of Chinese in the Americas. *Exhibitions:* Museum of Chinese in the Americas, New York City, 1998-99.

Awards, Honors

Americas Award, Consortium of Latin American Studies, and Notable Book in the Field of Social Studies designation, National Council of Social Studies/Children's Book Council, both 1998, and Pura Belpre Honor

Amelia Lau Carling and family

Book for illustration, American Library Association, 2000, all for *Mama and Papa Have a Store.*

Writings

(And illustrator) *Mama and Papa Have a Store,* Dial (New York City), 1998.

Contributor of short story "El Cumpleanos de Sulin" in *Lectura* (reader), Scott Foresman, 1999. *Mama and Papa Have a Store* has been translated into Spanish.

Sidelights

A talented illustrator, Amelia Lau Carling has captured her childhood as the daughter of Chinese immigrants making a new home in Central America in *Mama and Papa Have a Store.* The winner of several picture book awards, including being named a Pura Belpre Honor Book in acknowledgment of Carling's colorful illustrations, *Mama and Papa Have a Store* shows readers a view of early twentieth-century, urban Maya culture through the eyes of its young narrator.

In the late 1930s, as World War II was just beginning in Europe, Carling's parents left their native village in the face of the Japanese invasion of China. The young couple settled in Guatemala, a Spanish-speaking country whose native people are of the Maya race. In their new home, the Laus raised their family, learned to adapt to Guatemalan society and language, and supported themselves by becoming shopkeepers. In her book honoring her parents' efforts, Carling describes a typical day in a Guatemalan shop: from opening for business, through interactions with customers, the midday meal with family, to the close of day. The young narrator, too young to go to school with her five siblings, takes in all the activity of the marketplace, from the street vendors, to the Mayan customers that come by bus from their Indian village to get supplies, to the family's Chinese neighbors who come by for a visit.

Calling *Mama and Papa Have a Store* a "pleasant family story" that has a "timeless" quality, *School Library Journal* contributor Pam Gosner added that "the engaging account ... introduc[es] an interesting melange of cultural elements as seen from the preschooler's point of view." Noting that Carling's "nicely rendered" watercolor illustrations provide the "authentic details" needed to make the story come alive for young readers, *Booklist* critic Lauren Peterson added that Carling's debut picture book would serve as an excellent "introduction to the concept of immigration." Praising Carling's ability to render the landscape of her past so vividly, a *Kirkus Reviews* writer applauded the work as "a remarkable and affectionate story of one family's resilience, ... of how a life can flourish under trying circumstances."

"In my first book I drew from my own rather unusual childhood in Guatemala," Carling explained to *SATA.* "First I gathered striking images that I sketched from memory. Then I put words on paper. There were many futile attempts at bringing the words and pictures together, many discouraging periods when I just put the whole thing away and gave up. But the images wouldn't leave me alone. Somehow, after a month-long hiatus, they would spring up again in my brain as if on their own, and compel me to sketch, write, and research. The process was unhurried but sporadic and tortuous. Fortunately, I kept going, and it finally pulled itself together after I learned to be disciplined and tackled the manuscript daily, even if for a few minutes, no matter what.

"Creating something is messy; there is no guarantee that when you start at A you'll get to B and end up with C, but it's worthwhile. And bringing it out to the world opens surprising doors. One woman came to a reading with two children in tow and explained that she had adopted one in Guatemala and one in China, and my book brought their stories together for her. I've met Latin American men and women who are Chinese now living in America and who find my story familiar, while most people find the notion of Chinese as Latinos very odd. Most of all, I derive pleasure from seeing how children read my story, think about their own family stories, and in turn write and draw pictures about them."

Biographical and Critical Sources

PERIODICALS

Booklist, July, 1998, Lauren Peterson, review of *Mama and Papa Have a Store,* p. 1885.
Kirkus Reviews, June 1, 1998, p. 810, review of *Mama and Papa Have a Store.*
School Library Journal, August, 1998, Pam Gosner, review of *Mama and Papa Have a Store,* p. 133.
Tiempos del Mundo (New York City), February 18, 1999, p. 1.

*   *   *

CHARLIP, Remy 1929-

Personal

Surname is pronounced Shar-lip; born January 10, 1929, in Brooklyn, NY; son of Max (a house painter) and Sarah (a poet; maiden name, Fogel) Charlip. *Education:* Cooper Union, B.F.A., 1949; further study at Black Mountain College, Reed College, Juilliard School of Music, Merce Cunningham Studio, Connecticut College, and Art Students' League of New York.

Addresses

Home—521 Precita Ave., San Francisco, CA 94110. *E-mail*—remy@remycharlip.com.

Career

Actor, dancer, choreographer, producer, stage director and designer, and filmmaker; author and illustrator of children's books; songwriter, conductor of drama workshops. Choreographer and actor with original Living Theatre Company; choreographer with London Contemporary Dance Theatre, 1972—, Scottish Theatre Ballet, 1973, Welsh Dance Theatre, 1974, and Remy Charlip Dance Company; costume designer and member of Merce Cunningham Dance Company for eleven years. Director, designer, actor, and dancer at Joyce Theater, Theatre Artand, Cafe La Mama, Brooklyn Academy of Music Opera House, and as first artist in residence at Museum of Contemporary Art, Los Angeles, CA, 1988; founding member of children's theatre group, the Paper Bag Players; toured with his own company, the International All Star Dance Company, with sponsorship from the first National Endowment for the Arts Choreography grant and the Pepsi-Cola Pavilion at the World's Fair, Osaka, Japan; director of opening piece presented by National Theatre of the Deaf on tour, 1971-72. Director, with Shirley Kaplan, of children's theatre at Sarah Lawrence College, 1967-71, and co-conductor of classes; lecturer, workshop director, or consultant at Harvard Summer School, Radcliffe College, University of California Santa Barbara, 1989, Hofstra University, 1991, and other schools. Co-designer and developer of a Black and Puerto Rican heritage museum in the Bronx, member of advisory panels, Connecticut Commission on the Arts, Brooklyn Children's Museum, Bay Area Dance Series, and Judson Poets' Theatre and Dance Theatre.

Awards, Honors

Ingram Merrill Award, 1961 and 1963; Obie Awards for direction, *Village Voice,* 1965, as producer and director of the Paper Bag Players, and 1966, for *A Beautiful Day;* Boys' Clubs of America Gold Medal (with Burton

Remy Charlip performing **March Dance Umbrella,** *1978.*

Supree), 1967, for *Mother, Mother, I Feel Sick, Send for the Doctor, Quick, Quick, Quick;* Yale University-Joseph E. Levine grant, 1968-69; *New York Times* Best Illustrated Books citation, 1969, first prize, Bologna Book Fair, 1971, both for *Arm in Arm;* two Gulbenkian Awards, 1972, for Scottish Theatre Ballet and London Contemporary Dance Theatre; Irma Simonton Black Award, Bank Street College of Education, 1973, for *Harlequin and the Gift of Many Colors;* Children's Science Book Award young honor, New York Academy of Sciences, 1975, for *Handtalk: New York Times* Best Illustrated Books citation, 1975, and *Boston Globe-Horn Book* Award, 1976, both for *Thirteen; New York Times* Best Illustrated Books citation, 1987, for *Handtalk Birthday;* Award for Professional Achievement, Cooper Union School of Fine Arts, NY, 1988. A library has been named in Charlip's honor in Greenville, DE, and he has been made a "laureate" by the San Francisco Public Library.

Writings

(With George Ancona and Mary Beth Miller) *Handtalk: An ABC of Finger Spelling and Sign Language,* photographs by Ancona, Parents' Magazine Press, 1974.
(With Lilian Moore) *Hooray for Me!,* illustrated by Vera B. Williams, Parents' Magazine Press, 1975.
What Good Luck! What Bad Luck!, Scholastic Book Services, 1977.
First Remy Charlip Reader, edited by Nancy S. Smith and Lisa Nelson, Contact Editions, 1986.
(With Mary Beth Miller) *Handtalk Birthday: A Number and Story Book in Sign Language,* photographs by George Ancona, Four Winds Press, 1987.
Amaterasu (performance piece), produced in Los Angeles, CA, 1988.
Young Omelet (play), produced at Hofstra University, Hampstead, NY, 1991.
(With San Francisco Arts Education Project) *Ideas for Teaching Arts to Children,* San Francisco Arts Education Project, 1995.
Why I Will Never Ever Ever Ever Have Enough Time to Read This Book, Tricycle Press (Berkeley, CA), 2000.

SELF-ILLUSTRATED

Dress Up and Let's Have a Party, W. R. Scott, 1956.
Where Is Everybody?, W. R. Scott, 1957.
(Author with Judith Martin) *The Tree Angel* (story and play), Knopf, 1961.
It Looks Like Snow, W. R. Scott, 1962.
(Author with Judith Martin) *Jumping Beans,* 1963.
Fortunately, Parents' Magazine Press, 1964.
(Author with Burton Supree) *Mother, Mother, I Feel Sick, Send for the Doctor, Quick, Quick, Quick,* Parents' Magazine Press, 1966.
I Love You, McGraw, 1967.
Arm in Arm: A Collection of Connections, Endless Tales, Reiterations, and Other Echolalia, Parents' Magazine Press, 1969.
(Author with Burton Supree) *Harlequin and the Gift of Many Colors,* Parents' Magazine Press, 1973.
(With Jerry Joyner) *Thirteen,* Parents' Magazine Press, 1975.

Sleepytime Rhyme, HarperCollins, 1999.
Peanut Butter Party: Including the History, Uses, and Future of Peanut Butter, Tricycle Press, 1999.

ILLUSTRATOR

Margaret Wise Brown, *David's Little Indian,* W. R. Scott, 1956.
Bernadine Cook, *The Curious Little Kitten,* W. R. Scott, 1956.
Margaret Wise Brown, *The Dead Bird,* W. R. Scott, 1958.
Betty Miles, *What Is the World?,* Knopf, 1958.
Ruth Krauss, *A Moon or a Button,* Harper, 1959.
Betty Miles, *A Day of Summer,* Knopf, 1960.
Betty Miles, *A Day of Winter,* Knopf, 1961.
Margaret Wise Brown, *Four Fur Feet,* W. R. Scott, 1961.
Sandol Stoddard Warburg, *My Very Own Special Particular Private and Personal Cat,* Houghton, 1963.
Ruth Krauss, *What a Fine Day for . . . ,* Parents' Magazine Press, 1967.
(With Demetra Maraslil) Jane Yolen, *The Seeing Stick,* Crowell, 1977.

Work in Progress

A movie script based on his book, *Harlequin and the Gift of Many Colors.*

Sidelights

Remy Charlip is the author and illustrator of a variety of acclaimed children's books that range from simple reading exercises to elaborate word games to visually innovative narratives. Charlip's diverse artistic background has contributed to his success as a children's writer; a choreographer, dancer, and stage director, he creates books that are noted for their animated pictures as well as stories that encourage children to imagine and improvise for themselves. "He elicits humor, fun, and gaiety from readers through magnificent manipulation of [his] art," Shelly G. McNamara writes in *Social Education.* An author who "tries to be both child and artist when he creates a story book," McNamara adds, Charlip "reaches all viewers with his common life experiences."

Charlip demonstrated a talent for art from a young age. In *Third Book of Junior Authors* Charlip recalled that "my first taste of glory in relation to art was in kindergarten when I filled up the blackboards with a drawing in colored chalks of an ocean liner with hundreds of portholes, and it was left up for Open School Week." He later attended Cooper Union, a fine arts college, but "being a painter seemed hopeless to me," he continued. Charlip turned to dance to learn how to express himself more fully. He spent eleven years with the Merce Cunningham Dance Theatre and helped found a theatre company for children. But he also used his artistic skills to help support himself by drawing and designing for books as well as the stage. He began illustrating his own stories with *Dress Up and Let's Have a Party,* which he wrote while waiting for an appointment with editor May Garelick one day. His next book, *Where Is Everybody?,* brought him critical attention for its simple, imaginative approach to introducing reading. As a new picture is added on each page a new word appears to match the picture, and the book becomes a game of appearance and disappearance until it asks the question of the title. "Not quite like any other easy-to-read book, this one is an original invitation to learning and to look," Ellen Lewis Buell remarked in the *New York Times Book Review*. A *New York Herald Tribune* writer also praised the book, for it "will please the children, give them amusing easy-reading, and perhaps inspire them to make similar booklets for themselves."

Charlip's *Fortunately* also contains a type of game within its story. The book follows a boy on his way to a birthday party; he is rescued from one mishap after another only to meet more trouble each time. With this story, Charlip "achieves a sense of wonder and spontaneity as the reader, teetering the whole time between fortunate and unfortunate adventures, is compelled to turn the pages," McNamara reported. The result is "an engagingly zany nonsense story, attractively illustrated," Zena Sutherland commented in *Bulletin of the Center for Children's Books,* and "the humor is the sort enjoyed by almost all small children."

Mother, Mother, I Feel Sick, Send for the Doctor, Quick, Quick, Quick, has the same kind of contagious humor encapsulated in its catchy rhymes, and its silhouette illustrations can be the inspiration for a shadow play. In the book, a doctor cures a little boy's illness by removing first one strange object, then another, from the boy's stomach. The result is "really good slapstick," Alice Dalgliesh of *Saturday Review* observed. Rachael R. Finne, writing in the *New York Times Book Review,* contended that the "wildly absurd plot ... is the result of the author's appreciation of nonsense."

Charlip again indulges his sense of word play in *Arm in Arm,* which avoids telling a specific story in favor of "creating a concentrated, imaginative awareness of language," according to Ingeborg Boudreau in the *New York Times Book Review.* The book contains illustrated puns, poems, dialogues, and riddles; the words move all over the page, and are even shaped to look like their

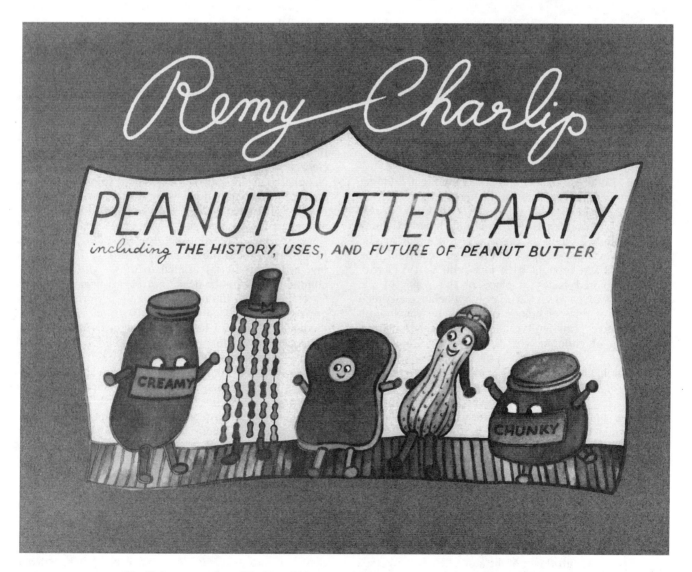

Charlip's watercolors illustrate his unusual history, recipe, joke, and activity book.

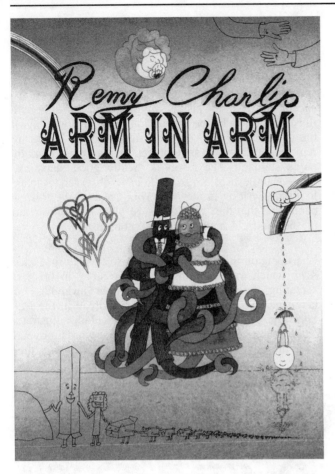

Witty plays on words and images fill Charlip's award-winning Arm in Arm.

subjects. Boudreau dubbed the book "a delight," adding that *Arm in Arm* is "one of the most kinetic picture books to appear in a long time." A *Publishers Weekly* critic likewise called *Arm in Arm* "unadulterated fun," and concluded: "Fun is *great* when it's the bright, rollicking, walking-in-space fun of Remy Charlip." The 1969 book was brought back into print in 1997, with brightly colored pages in place of the white of the original. *Booklist* reviewer Carolyn Phelan welcomed the return of this celebration of wordplay, concluding: "this creative book will challenge and charm a new generation of children."

To research his next book, *Harlequin and the Gift of Many Colors,* Charlip and coauthor Burton Supree traveled to Bergamo, Italy, where the Commedia Dell'Arte story of the acrobat originated. According to the legend, Harlequin's bright patchwork outfit was created because he had no costume of his own for the town carnival. The book took Charlip and his partner over two years to do, for both the writing and illustrating proved more difficult than they had expected. Charlip's elaborate effort with the illustrations pays off, according to many critics. While the tale of how Harlequin's friends donate parts of their costumes to make him an outfit is appealing, "one must return to the illustrations . . . to taste the full flavor of the story," Barbara Wersba commented in the *New York Times Book Review.* "An

enormous amount of thought and feeling has gone into these paintings," the critic continued, making for "a stunning book." Although *Junior Bookshelf* reviewer Marcus Crouch described the drawings as "elegant," he observed that the book seems "to turn in upon [itself] rather than to look out upon the world." But McNamara of *Social Education* finds *Harlequin* a moving story; it "shows, so effectively, the importance of love, sharing, and sacrificing for another," the critic commented. In addition, Charlip's "drawings capture the authenticity of detail, yet they appear simple, direct and fanciful."

Thirteen is a more complex, unpredictable book. Created with fellow author-illustrator Jerry Joyner, the book follows thirteen separate stories on each two-page spread, sometimes with little or no text. "The unusual format will inspire all ages," Barbara Elleman commented in *Booklist,* and the book's "graphic variety allows unlimited possibilities for the simple stories to be expanded." Anita Silvey similarly wrote in *Horn Book:* "*Thirteen* is not only original in its use of imagery, but it also suggests an entirely different approach to picture books . . . . The pictures do not illustrate a story, nor are they simply drawn as works of art; the images respond to each other—not to any verbal concept." But while *Thirteen* is a complex work, *New York Times Book Review* contributor Milton Glaser observed, its "absolute visual magic" is "executed with such decorative grace that it can be understood and experienced without discomfort." As a *Publishers Weekly* critic concluded, this "happy collaboration" contains "a wealth of surprises in a welcome contribution to children's books."

In 1974 Charlip employed the talents of photographer George Ancona and actress Mary Beth Miller of the National Theatre of the Deaf to explore nonverbal concepts of communication in *Handtalk: An ABC of Finger Spelling and Sign Language.* Miller and other characters act out and sign various concepts, including finger spelling of the alphabet. But *Handtalk* "is far from just another photo-illustrated handbook of finger spelling, nor is its appeal limited to those with a need to communicate with the deaf," a *Kirkus Reviews* contributor claimed. The authors' "energizing performance," the critic explained, is enough to make *Handtalk* a "mixed media hit." "Remy Charlip has designed *Handtalk* with the same clarity, humor and refreshing good sense found in his other books," contended *New York Times Book Review* critic Cynthia Feldman. As a result, *Handtalk* "comes as close as any inanimate medium can to capturing the liveliness and sparkle of a beautiful, expressive and often humorous method of communication," a *Science Books* reviewer concluded.

Charlip rejoined collaborators Ancona and Miller for the 1987 book *Handtalk Birthday.* The book tells of a surprise party for Mary Beth, and "the reader-viewer is challenged to use all sorts of visual cues to read the story in clips of hands, faces, and fingers in blurred motion," a *Kirkus Reviews* critic remarked. Like the original *Handtalk,* this book "is most successful in conveying the sense of sign as a vital, expressive and often personal language." A reviewer for *Booklist* found *Handtalk*

Birthday even more successful than the original: "Here the authors have presented words for all the signs; moreover, sentences are prompted by the birthday party atmosphere.... Mary Beth and company seem almost larger than life, and their enthusiasm is catching." "Exuberance, energy, and drama create high interest," Susan Nemeth McCarthy concluded in *School Library Journal,* and "this creative original story is an exciting way to share the joy of signing with children."

In the 1990s, several of Charlip's early books were brought back into print, often the artwork augmented by the new technologies that have revolutionized the world of children's books since Charlip began publishing in the 1950s. Among the works used to introduce a new generation of children to Charlip's brand of humor are *Arm in Arm* and *Hooray for Me!* The latter title first appeared in 1975, and offers a brightly colored, self-esteem boosting narrative. The 1996 edition "gives an old favorite a new look," Carolyn Phelan remarked in *Booklist.* The 1990s also saw two new titles from Charlip. The first, *Sleepytime Rhyme,* recalls the attractive simplicity and universality of Margaret Wise Brown's best work, according to *Booklist* reviewer Marta Segal. A rhythmic text, celebrating all the parts and ways of the child the mother loves, accompanies illustrations that are "crisp, simple, and bright," Segal commented. The result is a "sweet, gentle, bedtime book," this critic concluded.

Sleepytime Rhyme was quickly followed by *Peanut Butter Party,* a fanciful celebration of the world's best-loved food for kids. For lovers of peanut butter, Charlip offers suggestions about making art out of it, a recipe for edible play dough, the text for a peanut butter play in which smooth and chunky face off, as well as songs, rhymes, and jokes. The book concludes with a suggestion for a solo peanut butter party that requires meditating on a jar of the stuff. "There's a touch of *Hole Is to Dig* spontaneity here, ... that sandwiches pleasingly with the creative approach to playing with your food," remarked Deborah Stevenson in *Bulletin for the Center of Children's Books.* "Charlip's watercolor illustrations glorify the sticky stuff on every page," noted Lisa Gangemi Krapp in *School Library Journal,* concluding: "Like its subject, this unique book should have universal appeal."

Biographical and Critical Sources

BOOKS

Children and Books, by Zena Sutherland, Dianne L. Monson, and May Hill Arbuthnot, sixth edition, Scott, Foresman and Company, 1981, pp. 560-61.
Children's Literature Review, Volume 8, Gale (Detroit, MI), 1985, pp. 25-33.
Third Book of Junior Authors, edited by Doris De Montreville and Donna Hill, Wilson, 1972, Charlip, Remy, pp. 62-64.

PERIODICALS

Advocate, October 12, 1999, p. 75.

Booklist, October 1, 1975, Barbara Elleman, review of *Thirteen,* p. 231; March 15, 1987, Review of *Handtalk Birthday,* p. 1125; September 1, 1997, Carolyn Phelan, review of *Arm in Arm,* p. 128; November 15, 1999, Marta Segal, review of *Sleepytime Rhyme,* p. 633.
Bulletin of the Center for Children's Books, December, 1962, p. 62; February, 1965, Zena Sutherland, review of *Fortunately,* pp. 83-84; September, 1966, pp. 5-6; July-August, 1973, p. 167; July-August, 1999, Deborah Stevenson, review of *Peanut Butter Party,* p. 383.
Children's Book Review, Spring, 1975, p. 11.
Children's Book Review Service, April, 1975, p. 65.
Christian Science Monitor, May 7, 1975, p. B3.
Dance Magazine, February, 1995, p. 102.
Horn Book, June, 1957, p. 212; April, 1976, Anita Silvey, review of *Thirteen,* p. 148.
Interracial Books for Children Bulletin, vol. 11, nos. 1, 2, 1980, p. 24.
Junior Bookshelf, December, 1974, Marcus Crouch, review of *Harlequin and the Gift of Many Colors,* p. 334.
Kirkus Reviews, August 15, 1964, p. 808; March 15, 1966, pp. 299-300; May 15, 1969, p. 555; March 15, 1974, Review of *Handtalk,* p. 304; September 15, 1975, pp. 1060-61; February 15, 1987, Review of *Handtalk Birthday,* pp. 306-7.
Language Arts, May, 1976.
Los Angeles Times, February 18, 1988, Douglas Sadownick, "Charlip Trying to Cast Light on Sun Goddess"; February 20, 1988.
New York Herald Tribune, May 12, 1957, "Fun, Beauty, Fancy for First Readers," p. 24.
New York Times, December 8, 1969; December 5, 1975.
New York Times Book Review, June 23, 1957, Ellen Lewis Buell, "Looking and Learning," p. 22; August 21, 1966, Rachael R. Finne, review of *Mother, Mother, I Feel Sick, Send for the Doctor, Quick, Quick, Quick,* p. 20; July 20, 1969, Ingeborg Boudreau, review of *Arm in Arm,* p. 22; November 9, 1969, p. 62; March 11, 1973, Barbara Wersba, "He Rose to Find His Costume Had Become the Sky," p. 8; May 5, 1974, Cynthia Feldman, "Speaking of Other Ways," p. 41; October 5, 1975, Milton Glaser, review of *Thirteen,* p. 8; November 16, 1975; February 13, 1983, p. 30; October 25, 1987, p. 50.
Publishers Weekly, April 14, 1969, review of *Arm in Arm,* p. 97; April 23, 1973, Paul Doebler, "Story behind the Book: 'Harlequin,'" p. 62; March 11, 1974, p. 49; March 24, 1975, p. 48; August 11, 1975, review of *Thirteen,* p. 117; May 17, 1999, p. 81.
Saturday Review, April 16, 1966, Alice Dalgliesh, review of *Mother, Mother, I Feel Sick, Send for the Doctor, Quick, Quick, Quick,* p. 49.
School Library Journal, May, 1966, p. 138; May, 1975; December, 1975, p. 41; September, 1977; May, 1987, Susan Nemeth McCarthy, review of *Handtalk Birthday,* p. 83; October, 1989, p. 47; June, 1999, Lisa Gangemi Krapp, review of *Peanut Butter Party,* p. 112.
Science Books, September, 1974, review of *Handtalk,* p. 160.
Social Education, October, 1979, Shelley G. McNamara, "Naive Mural Art as a Vehicle for Teaching Elementary Social Studies," pp. 473-76.

Times Literary Supplement, December 6, 1974.
Washington Post Book World, July 8, 1973, p. 13.

ON-LINE

Remy Charlip's World, www.remycharlip.com (April 4, 2000).*

*   *   *

CHILD, Lauren 1965-

Personal

Born November 29, 1965, in Berkshire, England; father, an artist and art teacher; mother, an infant and primary teacher. *Education:* Attended Manchester Polytechnic, 1985-86; studied decorative arts with City and Guilds London, 1987-88.

Addresses

Home—London, England.

Career

Writer and illustrator. Founder of Chandeliers for the People (lampshade designers); also works for the creative agency Big Fish; designer of window displays and china dinnerware. Formerly worked as a waitress and painter.

Awards, Honors

Bronze Award, Smarties Book Prize, 1999, for *Clarice Bean, That's Me!*

Writings

FOR CHILDREN; AUTHOR AND ILLUSTRATOR

Clarice Bean, That's Me!, Candlewick Press (Cambridge, MA), 1999.
I Want a Pet!, Tricycle Press (Berkeley, CA), 1999.
I Will Never Not Ever Eat a Tomato, Candlewick Press, 2000 (published in England as *I Will Not Ever Never Eat a Tomato*, Orchard Books, 2000).
My Uncle Is a Hunkle, Orchard Books (London), 2000.

FOR CHILDREN; ILLUSTRATOR

Margaret Joy, *Addy the Baddy*, Viking (London), 1993.
The Complete Poetical Works of Phoebe Flood, introduction by John Whitworth, Hodder & Stoughton (London), 1997.

Work in Progress

Writing and illustrating *Beware of the Storybook Wolves*, publication by Arthur A. Levine Books (New York City) expected in 2001; and *Clarice Bean, Guess Who's Babysitting?*, Candlewick Press, 2001.

Sidelights

Lauren Child told *SATA:* "After growing up in the small market town of Marlborough, Wiltshire, as the middle child of three sisters and the daughter of two teachers, I have always been interested in the many aspects of childhood, from gazing into toy shop windows to watching American children's television shows and movies from the 1960s and 1970s. I still spend a lot of time looking in toy shops and have a large collection of children's books.

"After attending two art schools, where I admit that I did not learn much, I traveled for six months, still unsure about which career to embark upon. I have lived in many parts of London. I enjoy moving; it freshens me up. I am longing to go and live abroad for a while, but I'm not sure where.

"During the following years I did various things. I love designing and making things, and I find it incredibly exciting to see my drawings turned into objects. I didn't expect to be much good at writing and really started by accident. It was only when I came to write and illustrate *Clarice Bean* that I decided to devote my time to writing and illustrating books for children. It combines my fascination for childhood and my talent for designing and creating.

"*Clarice Bean* is a funky story about a girl called Clarice who has real girl power! It is based partly on growing up with my sisters and partly on things I saw when I was doing a lot of mindless staring out the window. The next book, *I Will Not Ever Never Eat a Tomato*, features two

Clarice shows real girl power in dealing with a chaotic family life in Lauren Child's colorful and unconventional self-illustrated work.

new characters, Charlie and Lola, and is a picture book about the magical world of food. The second Clarice Bean title is *My Uncle Is a Hunkle.*

"I am currently working on an animation project aimed at fairly young children. I am also busy designing various products and toys for children, as well as writing and illustrating. I like working on lots of different things at the same time, as it keeps me keen."

Biographical and Critical Sources

PERIODICALS

Booklist, April 15, 1999, review of *I Want a Pet!,* p. 1534.
Children's Book Review Service, April, 1999, review of *I Want a Pet!,* p. 98.
Horn Book, May, 1999, review of *I Want a Pet!,* p. 312.
Publishers Weekly, February 15, 1999, review of *I Want a Pet!,* p. 106; August 30, 1999, review of *Clarice Bean, That's Me!,* p. 83.
School Library Journal, May, 1999, Lisa Dennis, review of *I Want a Pet!,* p. 88; December, 1999, Maryann H. Owen, review of *Clarice Bean, That's Me!,* p. 88.*

*   *   *

CHRISTENSEN, Laurie
See STEDING, Laurie

*   *   *

CLUTHA, Janet Paterson Frame
1924-
(Janet Frame)

Personal

Born Janet Paterson Frame, August 28, 1924, in Dunedin, New Zealand; surname legally changed; daughter of George Samuel (a railway engineer) and Lottie Clarice (Godfrey) Frame. *Education:* Attended Dunedin Teachers Training College and Otago University.

Addresses

Office—P.O. Box 1118, Palmerston North, New Zealand.

Career

Writer.

Awards, Honors

Hubert Church Prose Awards for *The Lagoon: Stories, Scented Gardens for the Blind, A State of Siege,* and *Intensive Care;* New Zealand Literary Fund Award, 1960, for *Owls Do Cry;* New Zealand Scholarship in Letters, 1964, and Award for Achievement, 1969; Robert Burns fellowship, 1965, and H.D.L., 1978, both

from Otago University; Menton fellowship, 1974; Commander, Order of the British Empire, 1983; Wattie Book of the Year, Book Publishers Association of New Zealand, 1984, for *To the Is-Land: An Autobiography,* and 1986, for *The Envoy from Mirror City;* Commonwealth Writers Prize, 1989, for *The Carpathians.*

Writings

NOVELS; AS JANET FRAME

Owls Do Cry, Pegasus Press, 1957, Braziller, 1960.
Faces in the Water, Braziller, 1961.
The Edge of the Alphabet, Braziller, 1962.
Scented Gardens for the Blind, Pegasus Press, 1963, Braziller, 1964.
The Adaptable Man, Braziller, 1965.
A State of Siege, Braziller, 1966.
The Rainbirds, W. H. Allen, 1968, published as *Yellow Flowers in the Antipodean Room,* Braziller, 1969.
Intensive Care, Braziller, 1970.
Daughter Buffalo, Braziller, 1972.
Living in the Maniototo, Braziller, 1979, second edition, 1980.
The Carpathians, Braziller, 1988.

SHORT STORIES; AS JANET FRAME

The Lagoon: Stories, Pegasus Press, 1951, revised edition published as *The Lagoon and Other Stories,* 1961.
The Reservoir: Stories and Sketches, Braziller, 1963.
Snowman, Snowman: Fables and Fantasies, Braziller, 1963.
The Reservoir and Other Stories, Pegasus Press, 1966.
You Are Now Entering the Human Heart, Victoria University Press, 1983.

FOR CHILDREN; AS JANET FRAME

Mona Minim and the Smell of the Sun, illustrations by Robin Jacques, Braziller, 1969.

OTHER; AS JANET FRAME

The Pocket Mirror (poems), Braziller, 1967.
To the Is-Land: An Autobiography (also see below), Braziller, 1983.
An Angel at My Table: An Autobiography (also see below), Braziller, 1984.
The Envoy from Mirror City: An Autobiography (also see below), Braziller, 1985.
An Autobiography, Women's Press, Volume 1: *To the Is-Land,* Volume 2: *An Angel at My Table,* Volume 3: *The Envoy from Mirror City,* 1987.
The Janet Frame Reader, edited by Carole Ferrier, Women's Press, 1995.

Contributor of short stories to *Harper's Bazaar* and *New Yorker.*

Adaptations

A State of Siege was adapted as a film of the same title, directed by Costa-Gavras, released by Cinema 5, 1973. *An Angel at My Table* was filmed by Jane Campion in 1989, starring Kerry Fox. The film won over twenty national and international film awards.

Janet Frame

Sidelights

Considered one of New Zealand's most important writers, Janet Frame has authored several collections of stories, three volumes of autobiography, plus a book of poetry, but it is as a novelist that she is most admired. Calling her "a most distinguished and disturbing writer," Elizabeth Ward explains in the *Washington Post Book World* that "all her novels combine or juxtapose satirical social observation with a visionary dimension bordering perhaps on the morbid in its fascination with death and mental illness." In Carole Cooke's estimation, Frame "writes novels like spiders make lace—almost instinctively, without looking back," and, continues Cooke in the *Saturday Review,* "her books are so unlike what we expect a novel to be that they almost evanesce into their own mysticism." In *Contemporary Novelists,* W. H. New observes that "she has an uncanny ability to arouse the diverse sensibilities of shifting moods and to entangle in language the wordless truths of her inner eye."

Born in Dunedin, Frame grew up on the coast of South Island in the small town of Oamaru, characterized by Susan Wood in the *Washington Post Book World* as "physically, emotionally and culturally deprived." Her father worked for the railroad and her mother, who once served as a maid in the home of writer Katherine Mansfield, wrote poems that she sold door to door. Poor and painfully shy, Frame escaped the austerity of her childhood by reading and nurtured dreams of becoming a poet. As a young woman, however, she lacked self-esteem as well as a sense of her own identity. Eventually, she completed a teacher training course, but, rather than face evaluation by her superiors, she fled from the classroom and never returned. This perceived failure resulted in her attempted suicide; and after confiding the incident to a psychology professor, she found herself confined to a hospital's psychiatric ward. Mistakenly diagnosed as a schizophrenic, Frame endured years of hospitalizations and hundreds of shock treatments. She continued to write, though, and published her first book of stories, *The Lagoon,* while she was still a patient. When a hospital official happened to read about a literary award that the stories had won—an award about which even Frame was unaware—he released her from the hospital, and she thereby escaped the frontal lobotomy she was scheduled to undergo.

"Things began to change dramatically for Janet Frame after that," writes Wood. "She was befriended by one of her heroes, the New Zealand writer Frank Sargeson, who gave her a place to live and helped arrange a small stipend so that she could work on her first novel, *Owls Do Cry.*" The novel probes the memory of its mentally disturbed protagonist and reveals the deterioration of a financially and intellectually impoverished New Zealand family. It summoned much critical praise and, according to Robert Pick in the *New York Times Book Review,* it "was hailed as the first important novel to come out of New Zealand." One *New Yorker* critic calls Frame "a very sharp judge of character and a writer with a real narrative gift"; and in the *New York Herald Tribune Book Review* F. H. Bullock proposes that because of her "compassion" as a narrator, "and her poet's temperament," the author created a novel that "glows with the inner light of her human awareness." In a *Times Literary Supplement* review, Kevin Brown refers to the novel as a "tale of metamorphosis" and a "kind of personal archaeology, painstaking and intensely felt." In light of Frame's own years in psychiatric wards and the attendant "shock treatments that left her past in ashes," says Brown, "it is moving to watch her torchlit wandering in the labyrinth of memory."

Drawing again from personal experience, Frame's second novel, *Faces in the Water,* records one woman's years in a New Zealand asylum; or, in the words of Frances Hope in *Spectator,* it presents the reader with "a view into the madwoman's view out." A *Time* contributor finds Frame's writing "sensitive, and her evocation of madness unforgettable." And although Patrick Cruttwell wishes the novel had delved into why the character suffers, he acknowledges in the *Guardian* that it "is a piece of writing whose honesty and power are never in doubt." Considering it Frame's best book, Joyce Carol Oates explains in the *New York Times Book Review* that Frame deals with "the fluid boundary between sanity and madness, the watery depths of madness in which the normal 'see' their own faces." Oates thinks that "her novels exist for the purpose of illuminating certain mysteries for us—Miss Frame is obsessed with the mysteries of madness and death—the illumination is attempted through language, not through dramatic tension of one kind or another."

Frame's surrealistic next novel, *The Edge of the Alphabet,* presents a protagonist who, "in an effort to achieve her own identity ... narrowly observes the lives of half a dozen persons and finds them perpetually baffled, dogged by loneliness and a sense of ineffectuality, and all variously aware that communication between the living is impossible," according to a contributor to the *New York Herald Tribune Book Review.* William Peden in the *Saturday Review* notes that all the characters are "adrift in a limbo between illusion and reality which [the protagonist] calls 'the edge of the alphabet,' where 'words crumble' and communication is useless." Although Neal Ascherson suggests in *New Statesman* that "Frame launches at intervals into formidable harangues addressed over the reader's head," a *Times Literary Supplement* reviewer regards the narrative as "beautifully economical and told in a mixture of realism and fantasy, through interior monologue, snatches of dialogue, and flights of brilliant description."

Scented Gardens for the Blind presents, through interior monologue, three characters—a New Zealand genealogist working in England, his wife, and his daughter, who becomes mute upon leaving school. Calling it "the most remarkable novel that I have read in many years," Stanley Edgar Hyman proposes in his *Standards: A Chronicle of Books for Our Time:* "If it is not a work of genius ... it is surely a brilliant and overwhelming tour de force." The novel proved less successful to other critics. In the *New York Times Book Review,* for example, Peter Buitenhuis suggests that if "Frame intended this novel as a study in isolation and madness she has failed ... for there are clearly passages that have so strong a flavor of autobiography that she seems to have discharged the contents of her notebooks straight on to her pages." However, a contributor to the *Times Literary Supplement* believes that "any failure in communication on the part of the book as a whole, however, is redeemed by the beauty of the lyric style," adding that "there is no mistaking the power of Miss Frame's imagination and the anguish of her concern for suffering and beauty."

In *A State of Siege* the unmarried protagonist tries to start a new life by leaving her native New Zealand for an isolated island after years of teaching art and nursing her ailing mother, but while on the island she endures a night of terror and dies. In the *New York Times Book Review* Millicent Bell calls the novel "a study of the isolated and stagnant spirit struggling unsuccessfully for definition and expression," and relates it to Frame's "earlier explorations of lives cut off from outer relationship." Although Bell thinks that "Frame sets herself no easy task in seeking out interest in the drab stuff of a spinster's dreams and gropings," she adds that "Frame's gifts are unquestionably poetic—the description of personal mood and of nature. These, and a verbal wit are at her command." Finding it "an extraordinary novel," H. T. Anderson comments in *Best Sellers* that it "is worth the experience just for the richness and color of the prose alone." The New Zealand Film Commission assisted in adapting the book into a successful Golden Globe Award-winning film.

In *Yellow Flowers in the Antipodean Room,* published as *The Rainbirds* in England, Frame writes about an English immigrant to New Zealand who dies in an automobile accident only to return to life. "Life, however, rejects his resurrection," writes a *Time* reviewer. "He is fired from his job ... branded an anathema by society ... resented by his family for the inconvenience of his miracle." According to J. A. May in the *Christian Science Monitor,* the novel "has all the inevitability and awfulness of a Greek tragedy." For some critics, such as Oates, though, the novel did not quite achieve its potential. "One simply does not believe," says Oates in her *New York Times Book Review* piece, remarking that "this is a pity, for much of the novel is finely written, in a peculiar limpid style that seems a cross between Virginia Woolf and Samuel Beckett."

Intensive Care is the chronicle of two families living in Waipori, New Zealand, and includes several tragic elements and a futuristic era in which social problems are met by a computer that marks people for death. A critic for *Time* writes that *Intensive Care* continues Frame's preoccupation with history as "a hereditary malignancy that engulfs the present and dooms the future to madness, loneliness and death." While L. J. Davis compares the novel in a *Book World* review to "spending an evening in the company of a compulsively talkative, brilliant, neurotic woman obsessed with blood, disease, death, and the suffering of lonely people whose lives have gone all wrong," Arthur Edelstein finds it "a tangle of prose, verse, ballad, imaginary letters, and an enormous leap in the end to something like lyric allegory." Continuing in the *Southern Review,* Edelstein describes it as "bewildering yet powerful, an experience in which it cannot be determined how many layers of dream one has descended into, in which the characters dreaming seem themselves to be dreamed, as though all were the fevered conjurings of a patient in one of the novel's 'Recovery Units.'"

With the bizarrely plotted *Daughter Buffalo,* Frame concentrates again on death and insanity. According to J. A. Avant in *Library Journal,* the novel is "a strange, visionary work, as much a poem as a novel, with images of insanity, mutation, and death, and perceptions of how language changes reality." The book alternately tells the stories of its two protagonists; and, in the words of Barbara Harte in *Best Sellers,* Frame's technique "is virtually a novel within a novel, or a dual novel, and within this perilous framework, anathema to the insensitive amateur." Josephine Hendin, who labels it "a poem to the union of the living dead," continues in the *New York Times Book Review,* "Pathetic and ugly, sad and destructive, it has the grim power of life drawn up as a suicide pact.... But she writes with a beauty that confers a morbid grandeur, that makes poetry of the particular, the private, the enclosed."

"Language, in everyday use and in fiction, and its relation to experience—of self and others, nature and the denaturing effects of modern life—is the theme of *The Carpathians,*" writes Jayne Pilling in the *Times Literary Supplement.* The novel is described by Nancy Wartik in the *New York Times Book Review* as a "small masterpiece of literary craftsmanship, the work of an original thinker with a poet's ear for the sound and cadence of language." The story centers on a rich American whose author wife, in an attempt to end a long writing block, travels to exotic places "in search of contact with other people's experience," remarks Pilling. During a stay in New Zealand, a new galaxy is discovered that is simultaneously close and far away. Observing a frequent and "curious, combustible mix of modes at work" in Frame's novels, Pilling thinks that in *The Carpathians* the "possibilities are so rich that Frame needs several different narratives, Chinese box-style, to contain them." Moreover, Frame's autobiographical works illumine her fictional ones, says Pilling: "Frame has already given us the opportunity to see how a creative imagination works with felt and observed experience, since her autobiographical works can be read alongside her fiction, and it is richly rewarding to do so."

Fleur Adcock, writing in the *Times Literary Supplement*, maintains: "[Frame's] fictional and autobiographical writings are so closely interrelated that to read one work creates an appetite for the others; her various treatments of any subject enhance, rather than diminish, each other. Everything she presents is illuminated and thrown into sharp focus by the limpid clarity of a highly individual vision; she can be detached and passionate at the same time." Frame's *To the Is-Land* recalls her early childhood and is described by Helen Bevington in the *New York Times Book Review* as "a wistful tale, honestly and believably told, of the puzzling encounters of childhood, the recognitions, the gain and the loss." The book's title originated from what Ward says was Frame's "mispronunciation of the word 'island,' but eventually elevated into a kind of ideal state, neither the 'Was-Land' nor the Future, but the everlasting literal-minded here and now of the young." Ward indicates that while *Owls Do Cry* contains the same information as *To the Is-Land,* the latter is "much simpler and more lighthearted." Bevington suggests that "if one is to know Janet Frame better, hear the rest of it, one must consent to follow her on her journey to as many Is-Lands as there are."

An Angel at My Table continues Frame's personal story through her travels abroad, made possible by a government grant. According to Bevington in the *New York Times Book Review,* it "gives further evidence she has an arresting story to tell." Describing it as "fascinating, moving, and sometimes blackly humorous," Susan Wood writes in the *Washington Post Book World* that the book details Frame's misdiagnosis as schizophrenic and her long ordeal in and out of mental hospitals. "Simply living on her own, proving to herself that she was capable of existing in the world, seems to have been just what Frame and her writing needed.... What she has done," observes Wood, "is quite amazing and that she has done it with a sense of humor and without self-pity is more amazing still."

The Envoy from Mirror City, which continues the autobiographical trilogy, is regarded as "a memoir of travel and imagination" by Carol Sternhell in the *New York Times Book Review*. It begins with Frame's arrival in London at the age of thirty-two and ends eight years later with her journey home to New Zealand. Ward suggests in the *Washington Post Book World* that while "some readers will value the book for ... literary insights; others will appreciate more easily Janet Frame's comic spirit, her courage and honesty. For all these things, the entire trilogy is a work to treasure." While Sternhell suggests that the book is "less compelling than the earlier volumes," she concludes that "it's impossible not to be moved by this extraordinary portrait of a woman for whom art is life, a life well worth living."

Biographical and Critical Sources

BOOKS

Alley, Elizabeth, editor, *The Inward Sun: Celebrating the Life and Work of Janet Frame,* Daphne Brasell Associates Press (Wellington, NZ), 1994.
Baisnaee, Valaerie, *The Autobiographies of Simone de Beauvoir, Maya Angelou, Janet Frame, and Marguerite Duras,* Rodopi, 1997.
Contemporary Literary Criticism, Volume 96, Gale, 1997, pp. 164-221.
Contemporary Novelists, Sixth Edition, St. James Press, 1996.
Dalziel, Margaret, *Janet Frame,* Oxford University Press, 1981.
Evans, Patrick, *An Inward Sun: The Novels of Janet Frame,* New Zealand University Press, 1971; *Janet Frame,* Twayne, 1977.
Hyman, Stanley Edgar, *Standards: A Chronicle of Books for Our Time,* Horizon Press, 1966.
Irvine, Lorna, *Critical Spaces: Margaret Laurence and Janet Frame,* Camden House (Columbia, SC), 1995.
Mercer, Gina, *Janet Frame: Subversive Fictions,* University of Queensland Press (St. Lucia, Queensland), 1994.
Panny, Judith Dell, *I Have What I Gave: The Fiction of Janet Frame,* Braziller (New York City), 1993.
The Ring of Fire: Essays on Janet Frame, Dangaroo Press (Sydney), 1992.

PERIODICALS

Atlantic Monthly, October, 1961.
Best Sellers, July 15, 1966; June 15, 1970; October 1, 1972.
Books Abroad, spring, 1967; summer, 1967.
Books and Bookmen, June, 1967; July, 1973.
Book Week, August 16, 1964.
Book World, May 3, 1970, L.J. Davis, review of *Intensive Care.*
Christian Science Monitor, September 2, 1965; February 8, 1969.
Commonweal, October 19, 1962.
Guardian, January 19, 1962, Patrick Cruttwell, review of *Owls Do Cry.*
Harvard Advocate, winter, 1973.
Journal of Commonwealth Literature, August, 1977.
Library Journal, August, 1972; July, 1992, p. 132.
Ms., January-February, 1991, p. 67.
New Leader, August 13, 1960; August 14, 1967.
New Republic, September 11, 1965; May 31, 1975.

New Statesman, November 23, 1962, Neal Ascherson, review of *The Edge of the Alphabet.*

New Yorker, August 13, 1960; May 17, 1969; September 30, 1972.

New York Herald Tribune Book Review, August 14, 1960; September 23, 1962.

New York Review, February 27, 1969.

New York Times, February 3, 1969; December 13, 1989.

New York Times Book Review, July 31, 1960; October 8, 1961; August 18, 1963; August 16, 1964; July 18, 1966; September 11, 1966; November 11, 1966; February 9, 1969; May 3, 1970; August 27, 1972; September 16, 1979; November 21, 1982; October 7, 1984; October 6, 1985; January 22, 1989.

Observer Review, October 13, 1968.

Punch, February 7, 1968.

Saturday Review, September 9, 1961; September 29, 1962; April 19, 1969; October 27, 1979.

Southern Review, Summer, 1973, Arthur Edelstein, review of *Intensive Care.*

Spectator, January 19, 1962.

Time, September 22, 1961; August 6, 1965; March 21, 1969; May 18, 1970; August 6, 1979.

Times Literary Supplement, January 26, 1962; November 23, 1962; August 2, 1963; October 21, 1965; April 27, 1967; February 15, 1968; January 26, 1973; November 9, 1984; November 15, 1985; December 2, 1988.

Washington Post Book World, August 26, 1979; January 2, 1983; September 16, 1984; October 27, 1985.

World Literature Written in English, April, 1975; November, 1978.*

*   *   *

CRESP, Gael 1954-

Personal

Born April 2, 1954, in Benalla, Australia; daughter of Edward Thomas (a "fitter and turner") and Roma Carmel (a homemaker; maiden name, Hoskin) Cresp; married Stephen John Wilbourne (a computer consultant), May 10, 1975; children: Emily Jane, Elizabeth Alice, Rebecca Elana. *Education:* RMIT University, B.S. (librarianship), 1975; Chisholm Institute, graduate diploma in children's literature, 1982; Frankston TAFE, certificate in foundations of professional writing, 1990; Holmesglen TAFE, certificate in workplace training, 1999.

Addresses

Home—18 Boston Ave., Malvern East, Victoria 3145, Australia. *E-mail*—lantana@ozemail.com.au.

Career

Swinburne University of Technology, Hawthorn, Australia, librarian, 1994—. Professional storyteller, 1984—; presenter of storytelling workshops in Australia and elsewhere. *Member:* Storytelling Guild of Australia (president of Victoria branch, 1998-2000).

Writings

The Biography of Gilbert Alexander Pig, illustrated by David Cox, Benchmark/Cygnet (Melbourne, Australia), 1999, published as *The Tale of Gilbert Alexander Pig,* Barefoot Books, 2000.

Work in Progress

A picture book, *Fish for Breakfast,* publication expected in 2001; two manuscripts, *Exercise* and *Callie;* research on metaphors in traditional and fairy stories and their relevance to modern audiences.

Sidelights

Gael Cresp told *SATA:* "I have been a professional storyteller since 1984, although my father says I have been telling stories all my life. I have three children and, at last count, twenty-four nieces and nephews. I grew up in Seaford, a bay-side suburb forty kilometers south of Melbourne in Victoria. I am the second eldest of ten children, and that is why I have so many nieces and nephews!

"I use my own stories and poems in performance and undertake considerable research prior to adapting traditional stories for telling. I do not always know why I tell a particular story or adapt it in a particular way, although

Gael Cresp

some years down the track I can usually come up with a good explanation (that is, story!) about what it means.

"I work four days a week at a university library in Hawthorn, near Melbourne. I go around the library reminding people that they promised to carry out certain jobs before the next meeting. When they say that someone else has to do something first, I go to that person and find out what is stopping him or her from completing the task. I am often referred to a third person, and occasionally a fourth. Sometimes I feel like the old woman in the story of the pig who would not jump over the stile!

"Regarding *The Biography of Gilbert Alexander Pig,* I was prompted to tell the traditional story of the three little pigs from a contemporary perspective by the need to make the story relevant to people today. Once I began to use a black trumpet-playing pig, a modern setting followed logically.

"Traditional stories have information in them that will assist us in making decisions about our lives. When we are confronted with the need to make our own way in the world, we have some choices to make. The message I took from the traditional version of the story as a child was that there was no place for fun and games. I must work hard, build on strong foundations, and lock myself in (to a secure job and a proper house) if I were to be happy and successful. The story of Gilbert Alexander Pig began as a joke to poke fun at this idea and to suggest that there are, indeed, alternatives.

"I hope that every child or adult that comes to this story has heard the traditional tale of the three little pigs and notices and comments on the differences between the two tales. Any awareness or consideration of the alternatives that Gilbert Alexander Pig presents means my job has been well done. I would like people to admire Gilbert's courage, his tenacity, his athletic prowess, and his ability to negotiate. I would like them to admire the wolf because he finally listens and so actually gains friendship and a wonderful skill. I would like readers and listeners to be encouraged and empowered to make similar changes to the patterns of their lives. Most of all, I would like people to enjoy the story, to laugh at the dialogue and the illustrations, and to find the images and the story dancing in their minds long after the book is closed.

"The character of Gilbert Alexander Pig was inspired by the life of my friend, jazz trumpeter Gil Askey. To be a professional musician, even today, requires one to live differently than the majority of people. To play jazz on a trumpet is also to work on the edge of the music world (where string instruments and classical music are seen as

It was not long, however, before the Wolf heard the sound of the trumpet, smelled the smoke and the fish, and crept up on Gilbert Alexander Pig.

Cresp adds the power of music, as inspired by Motown jazz trumpeter Gil Askey, to the tale of the three little pigs in her **The Tale of Gilbert Alexander Pig.** *(Illustrated by David Cox.)*

the peak area). For Gil to do both of these things through the sixties and seventies was incredibly brave.

"The most remarkable thing about Gil is his lack of resentment and bitterness about the appalling treatment he and other black people received over the years. He has used his enormous talent to reach out to all kinds of people, to offer them a path into his joy in music and music-making. Gil has done a remarkable job of encouraging children—especially teenage boys—to undertake the difficult task of learning an instrument. The discipline to practice and the need to be cooperative in a band or orchestra are enormously valuable lessons to learn.

"I felt that Gil recognized that a lot of the resentment and violence offered to those who are different (black, 'arty') comes from fear and jealousy. His philosophy seems to be: Offer to share and to teach people, and they will become your friends."

D

De SAULLES, Tony 1958-

Personal

Born December 1, 1958, in Essex, England; son of Denys (an editor and writer) and Kate (a swimming teacher; maiden name, McDaniel) De Saulles; married Janet Lavelle (a hospital receptionist), January 14, 1984; children: Joe, Alice. *Education:* Attended West Surrey College of Art and Design, 1977-78; London College of Printing, B.A. (with honors), 1981. *Politics:* Conservative. *Religion:* Roman Catholic.

Addresses

Home—49 Shaw Green Lane, Prestbury, Cheltenham, Gloucestershire GL52 3BS, England. *E-mail*—tony@tonydes.demon.co.uk.

Career

Sudler & Hennessey, London, England, junior art director, 1981-82; Thames Head Book Packagers, Gloucestershire, England, designer, 1982-87; freelance illustrator, 1987—. Cheltenham and Gloucester College of Higher Education, part-time lecturer in graphic design and typography. *Member:* Association of Illustrators.

Awards, Honors

Rhone-Poulenc Best Children's Science Book Award (with Nick Arnold), 1997.

Writings

(Self-illustrated) *Ridiculous Rhymes,* Sherston Software, 1996.

ILLUSTRATOR

Nigel Nelson, *Body Talk,* Thomson Learning, 1993.
Nigel Nelson, *Signs and Symbols,* Thomson Learning, 1993.

Illustrator Tony De Saulles depicts the strange, painful, and sickening side of science with comic drawings.

Nigel Nelson, *Writing and Numbers,* Thomson Learning, 1994.
Nigel Nelson, *Codes,* Thomson Learning, 1994.

Nick Arnold, *Ugly Bugs,* Hippo Paperbacks (Leamington Spa, England), 1997.

Nick Arnold, *Blood, Bones, and Body Bits* (also see below), Hippo Paperbacks, 1997.

Nick Arnold, *Chemical Chaos* (also see below), Hippo Paperbacks, 1997.

Nick Arnold, *Nasty Nature,* Hippo Paperbacks, 1997.

Richard Wood, *Kitchens through the Ages,* Wayland (Hove, England), 1997.

Richard Wood, *Loos through the Ages,* Wayland, 1997.

Nick Arnold, *Fatal Forces,* Hippo Paperbacks, 1998.

Nick Arnold, *Disgusting Digestion,* Hippo Paperbacks, 1998.

Nick Arnold, *Sounds Dreadful,* Hippo Paperbacks, 1998.

Nick Arnold, *Blood, Bones, and Body Bits and Chemical Chaos: Two Horrible Books in One,* Scholastic (Leamington Spa), 1998.

Nick Arnold, *Vicious Veg,* Hippo Paperbacks, 1998.

Phil Gates, *Evolve or Die,* Hippo Paperbacks, 1999.

Nick Arnold, *Bulging Brains,* Hippo Paperbacks, 1999.

Nick Arnold, *Frightening Light,* Hippo Paperbacks, 1999.

Nick Arnold, *Ugly Bugs and Nasty Nature,* Scholastic, 1999.

Richard Wood, *Bathrooms,* Wayland, 1999, published as *Bathrooms through the Ages,* 2000.

Richard Wood, *Bedrooms through the Ages,* Wayland, 1999.

Nick Arnold, *Suffering Scientists,* Scholastic, 2000.

Nick Arnold, *Shocking Electricity,* Hippo Paperbacks, 2000.

Nick Arnold, *Deadly Diseases,* Hippo Paperbacks, 2000.

Nick Arnold, *Awfully Big Horrible Science Quiz Book,* Scholastic, 2000.

Nick Arnold, *Bulging Brains and Disgusting Digestion,* Scholastic, 2000.

Nick Arnold, *Micro Monsters,* Hippo Paperbacks, 2000.

Sidelights

Tony De Saulles told *SATA:* "Having escaped from a London advertising agency eighteen years ago, I now work from home in Gloucestershire, England. A home that I share with my wife, two children, a neurotic whippet, and an idle ginger cat. After many years of designing books, I've now progressed to illustrating them. My time is shared between the drawing board and the computer.

"The subject matter can vary enormously, but humor is one element that will always be found in my work. Ideas for illustrations come quickly as I read a manuscript: it's the drawing that takes the time. Nothing gives me more pleasure than producing something that will put a smile on someone's face—be it an adult or a child.

"I enjoy promoting my work at schools and book festivals. Children love jokes, poems, and drawings about things that are either smelly, slimy, rude, or ridiculous! I used to be 'told off' for producing all of the above ... now I'm paid for it!"

DUMAS, Philippe 1940-

Personal

Born September 26, 1940, in Cannes, Frances; son of Robert (a saddler and an amateur artist) and Jacqueline (Hermes) Dumas; married Kay Fender (a singer and writer), January 5, 1969; children: Alice, Emile, Jean, Robert, Louis. *Education:* Attended Ecole des Metiers d'Art, 1958-61, and Ecole Nationale Superieure des Beaux Arts, 1961-66. *Religion:* Protestant.

Addresses

Home—84 rue Chaptal, 92300 Levallois-Perret, France. *Office*—c/o L'Ecole des Loisirs, 11 Rue de Sevres, 75006 Paris, France.

Philippe Dumas illustrates the successes of a physically handicapped boy whose embarrassed older brother pushes him to learn to walk in The Scarlet Ibis. *(Written by James Hurst.)*

Day after day, the old man and the little bird played beautiful music in the Metro.

An old man and a little bird have a happy time in Paris before the bird moves on to a warmer climate in **Odette: A Springtime in Paris,** *a* **New York Times** *Best Illustrated Children's Book of the Year in 1988. (Written by Kay Fender and illustrated by Dumas.)*

Career

Painter and writer. *Military service:* Served with the French Cavalry, 1961-63. *Member:* Club de Saint Aubrin sur mer.

Awards, Honors

Prix Graphique, and one of *New York Times* Outstanding Books of the Year, both 1977, and *Boston Globe-Horn Book* Award honor book for illustration, 1978, all for *The Story of Edward; New York Times* cited *Odette: A Bird in Paris* as one of the Best Illustrated Children's Books of the Year, 1978; prix de la Fondation de France, 1981, for *Ce Changement-la* and 1985, for *Il Pleut, Il Pleut Bergere;* prix Beaugency (Funniest Book of the Year), 1987, for *Victor Hugo s'est egare.*

Writings

SELF-ILLUSTRATED; FOR CHILDREN

Laura, le terre-neuve d'Alice, L'Ecole des Loisirs, 1976, translation by wife, Kay Fender, published as *Laura, Alice's New Puppy,* David and Charles, 1979.

Histoire d'Edouard, Flammarion, 1976, translation by Gwen Marsh, published as *The Story of Edward*

(Junior Literary Guild selection), Parents Magazine Press, 1977.

Les Avatars de Benoit (title means "Ups and Downs of Benjamin"), L'Ecole des Loisirs, 1976, Dent, 1980.

La petite geante, L'Ecole des Loisirs, 1977, translation by Kay Fender published as *The Little Giant,* Dent, 1978.

Lucie, la fille d'Edouard, Flammarion, 1977, translation by Gwen Marsh published as *Lucy, Edward's Daughter,* Dent, 1977, translation by Michael Rosenbaum published as *Lucie: A Tale of a Donkey,* Prentice-Hall, 1980.

Ondine au fond de l'eau (title means "Ondine beneath the Waves"), L'Ecole des Loisirs, 1977.

Le Professeur Ecrouton-Creton (title means "Professor Ecrouton-Creton"), L'Ecole des Loisirs, 1977.

Menteries et verites (title means "Lies and Truths"), L'Ecole des Loisirs, 1978.

Cesar, le coq du village, Flammarion, 1978, translation by Deirdre Engel published as *Caesar, Cock of the Village,* Prentice-Hall, 1979 (published in England as *Caesar, the Village Cockerel,* Dent, 1979).

Laura et les bandits, L'Ecole des Loisirs, 1978, translation by Deirdre Engel published as *Laura and the Bandits,* David and Charles, 1980.

Le Maison, L'Ecole des Loisirs, 1979, translation by Elsie Fender published as *The House,* Dent, 1980.

Laura sur la route, 1979, translation by Deirdre Engel published as *Laura on the Road,* David and Charles, 1979.

L'Equitation et l'ecole espagnole de Vienne, Flammarion, 1980, translation by Mariana Fitzpatrick, published as *The Lippizaners and the Spanish Riding School of Vienna,* Prentice-Hall, 1981.

Laura perd la tete, 1981, translation published as *Laura Loses Her Head,* David and Charles, 1981.

Comptines francaises, comptines coquines, jeux de mots (title means "French Nursery Rhymes and Naughty Rhymes"), Flammarion, 1981.

Ce changement-la (title means "This Change"), L'Ecole des Loisirs, 1981.

Laura fete Noel (title means "Laura Celebrates Christmas"), L'Ecole des Loisirs, 1982.

Il Pleut, Il Pleut, Bergere, L'Ecole des Loisirs, 1985.

Peche a Pied (title means "Fishing in the Rock Pools"), L'Ecole des Loisirs, 1986.

Victor Hugo s'est egare, L'Ecole des Loisirs, 1987.

A Farm: Reflections of Yesteryear, Creative Editions (Mankato, MN), 2000.

OTHER SELF-ILLUSTRATED

Les Rats (title means "Rats"), Editions de Saint-Aubin, 1971.

(With Ionic Parlier) *Robidu,* Hachette, 1972.

Les brigands calabrais (title means "The Brigands of Calabria"), L'Ecole des Loisirs, 1977.

(With Boris Moissard) *Les contes a l'envers* (title means "Topsy-turvy Fairy Tales"), L'Ecole des Loisirs, 1977.

(With Boris Moissard) *Les Aventures du Vantard* (title means "Adventures of a Braggart"), L'Ecole des Loisirs, 1978.

Monsieur Menee (title means "Mr. Menee"), Editions Arthur Hubschmid, 1979.

Coffret de chansons (title means "Casket of Songs"), Flammarion, 1982.

Coffret d'histoires (title means "Casket of Stories"), Flammarion, 1983.

ILLUSTRATOR

Kay Fender, *Odette: A Bird in Paris*, Prentice-Hall, 1978 (published in England as *Odette: A Springtime in Paris*, Gollancz, 1978).

Theophile Gautier, *Le Roman de la Momie* (title means "The Story of the Mummy"), L'Ecole des Loisirs, 1979.

Charles Dickens, *Captain Boldheart* (juvenile), Dent, 1980.

Jan Dutourd, *Oeuvres romanesques* (title means "Selected Works"), Flammarion, 1980.

Marcel Ayme, *Les Contes du chat perche* (juvenile; title means "Tales of a Perched Cat"), Gallimard, 1980.

De nouvelles de Maupassant, 3 volumes (title means "Short Stories of Maupassant"), L'Ecole des Loisirs, 1981-82.

Roger Rudigoz, *Les Contes de la souris chauve* (juvenile; title means "Tales of a Baldheaded Mouse"), L'Ecole des Loisirs, 1982.

Andre Roux, adapter, *Bible en images: Ancien Testament* (title means "The Bible in Images: Old Testament"), L'Ecole des Loisirs, 1982.

Jakob Grimm and Wilhelm Grimm, *The Queen Bee*, Creative Education, 1984.

Anton Chekhov, *Histoires pour rire et sourire* (title means "Stories to Make You Laugh and Smile"), L'Ecole des Loisirs, 1984.

Haute de Gamme: l'art de vivre a la francaise, Flammarion, 1985.

James Hurst, *The Scarlet Ibis*, Creative Education, 1988.

Anne Trotereau, *Portraits devinettes d'auteurs illustres: pastiches et anagrammes,* L'Ecole des Loisirs, 1994.

Also illustrator of D. Merimee's *Chroniques du regne de Charles IX* (title means "Chronicles of the Reign of Charles IX"), and Guy de Maupassant's *Histoires fantastiques* (title means "Fantastic Stories"), both from L'Ecole des Loisirs.

Sidelights

Philippe Dumas once told *SATA:* "Some of my earliest memories center on World War II. I knew early on that my father was taken prisoner and then escaped to unoccupied southern France. My pregnant mother fled to Cannes, where I was born shortly after her arrival in 1940.

"After the German army invaded the unoccupied territory in November 1942, my parents no longer had any reason to hide in Cannes. So we returned to Paris. I was about three years old at the time. Paris was still in a state of great turmoil. There were frequent bomb alerts at night, and I recall many a night waiting in our bathrobes in the basement for the 'all clear' signal.... As a child I was deeply impressed by the violence which was going on all around me.

"I have four brothers and one sister. It was very important for me to grow up in a large family: it meant many books around the house, many games being played and many stories being told by the elders. I still dream of a big family, although we now have a girl and four boys, and my wife, Kay, is less enthusiastic about further expanding our numbers....

"I have always drawn. My father was an amateur painter and on Sundays when the weather was fine, I would go with him to draw outdoors. Then we would go to Julien's studio and draw a nude female. I was twelve years old and dreamed of becoming Van Gogh. Later, I studied painting at the Metiers d'Art and then attended the Ecole des Beaux Arts. It was a period during which theory was exceedingly important, and big words were used to express simple thoughts. I, on the other hand,

Dumas draws a family farm of yesteryear in his self-illustrated **A Farm.**

prefer people who say important things with simple words. Also, all of my teachers belonged to the abstract art movement. What I've always enjoyed in painting is the anecdotal and a narrative approach. I like art that, while not necessarily naive, is simple.

"Along with my paintings, I have always created half-drawn, half-written little stories. When I was in school, I wrote stories about my life as a pupil. Later I wrote stories about my fortunes or misfortunes in love. And I kept writing and drawing stories about my own life until I had children, at which point I began writing and illustrating stories for them. I've always done painting and illustration side-by-side. Although they are very different, they complement each other and, I'm interested in both mediums.

"I never wanted to be an illustrator. I cannot stand the traditional connotation of illustration: drawings that merely reiterate the text. Unless the illustrator is a genius, he is necessarily going to steal images from the reader's imagination. A good drawing can suggest many things, and I've always tried to accentuate something that is in the text without *specifically* being in it. That's what I call a 'picture-novel.' That's to say a novel where text and drawings are put together to serve a story without redundancies. It's more about annotating than illustrating. The books of the nineteenth century Swiss illustrator Rodolphe Topffer, who mixes drawings and text is really the model for my work....

"I like to do books that can be read by adults as well as by children, because it's often adults who read to kids. Children read differently from adults and look for different things in a book. The trick is to write books which can be read on several levels, thus surmounting the obstacle of categories. This is often baffling to editors because they tend to want clear identifications and labels. They are used to books made for particular age groups. This is something I don't understand—it's those rules. Take a tree in nature, for example: a child of two, an adolescent, and an old man will all perceive it differently. And that's the way it should be with books. To obtain this appeal when making a book is very difficult. One must achieve simplicity. We tend to start out in a complicated and convoluted way. The point is to take out everything that seems unnecessary, until the story is as direct and simple as possible without being puerile or falsely naive. That's the kind of work I am trying to do."

Philippe Dumas defines himself as something of a perpetual outsider, a stance with historical precedent in his family, which is Protestant in the predominantly Roman Catholic country of France. Dumas's books for children also cast him in the role of the outsider for they are often unusual in size and subject matter, and, for children in the United States, must be translated from the original French in which they were written. Though Dumas has written and illustrated numerous books for children and adults, and illustrated a number of books written by others, few have found their way to American publishers and reviewers. Among those that have is *Laura Loses Her Head,* in which two children and their large dog go to Paris to visit their grandfather. One day, while grandfather is away, the children decide to take a bath and the tub overflows, taking them for a wild ride down to the river, where they meet up with their none-too-happy grandfather. Dumas has also illustrated an edition of *The Queen Bee,* an adaptation of a little-known Brothers Grimm tale about a young man who teaches his brothers to be kind to animals. The animals then show their appreciation by helping all three brothers marry princesses.

Dumas moved away from fairy tales and fiction with *The Lippizaners and the Spanish Riding School of Vienna,* an historical account of the French horse riding tradition as it has been carried on at the Spanish School in Austria since the French Revolution. A reviewer in *Publishers Weekly* praised the energy of Dumas's meticulous illustrations and minimalist text, both of which display his admiration for his subject. This critic called *The Lippizaners* "one of the outstanding books of the year."

Dumas's admiration for his subject is evident again in his book *A Farm: Reflections of Yesteryear,* according to reviewers for *Publishers Weekly* and *Booklist.* In an oversize format that emphasizes the vast landscapes in which the nineteenth-century English farm is nestled, *A Farm* relies less upon an explanatory narrative and more upon Dumas's watercolor paintings, which the *Publishers Weekly* critic stated display "a reverent devotion to detail," yet "create a sense of bustle and activity." Each page focuses on one of the farm animals. The farm itself, with its many human inhabitants, is examined through views of fields, barns, the rooms where butter and cheese are made and stored, and various outbuildings. Though the book's large format and obscure subject matter might make it a questionable purchase for some libraries, "the book's beauty and charm can't be denied," Ilene Cooper proclaimed in *Booklist.*

Biographical and Critical Sources

PERIODICALS

Booklist, December 1, 1999, Ilene Cooper, review of *A Farm,* p. 698.
Publishers Weekly, November 20, 1981, review of *The Lippizaners,* p. 54; December 20, 1999, review of *A Farm,* p. 80.
School Library Journal, December, 1982, p. 48; November, 1984, p. 124.*

E

ELLIOTT, Janice 1931-1995

Personal

Born October 14, 1931, in Derby, England; died July 26, 1995; daughter of Douglas John (an advertising executive) and Dorothy (Wilson) Elliott; married Robert Cooper (a public affairs adviser for an oil company), April 11, 1959; children: Alexander. *Education:* Oxford University, B.A. (with honors), 1953. *Hobbies and other interests:* Sailing.

Addresses

Agent—Vivien Green, Richard Scott Simon Ltd., 43 Doughty Street, London WC1N 2LF, England.

Career

Journalist in London, England, 1954-62; novelist, freelance journalist, and critic, 1962—.

Awards, Honors

Secret Places was awarded the Southern Arts Award for Literature, 1981; fellow, Royal Society of Literature, 1989.

Writings

NOVELS FOR YOUNG PEOPLE

The Birthday Unicorn, Gollancz, 1970.
Alexander in the Land of Mog, Brockhampton Press, 1973.
The Incompetent Dragon, Blackie & Son, 1982.
The King Awakes, Walker Books, 1987.
The Empty Throne, Walker Books, 1988.

OTHER NOVELS

Cave with Echoes, Secker & Warburg, 1962.
The Somnambulists, Secker & Warburg, 1964.
The Godmother, Secker & Warburg, 1966, Holt, 1967.
The Buttercup Chain, Secker & Warburg, 1967.
The Singing Head, Secker & Warburg, 1968.

Angels Falling, Knopf, 1969.
The Kindling, Knopf, 1970.
A State of Peace (first novel in trilogy), Knopf, 1971.
Private Life (second novel in trilogy), Hodder & Stoughton, 1972.
Heaven on Earth (third novel in trilogy), Hodder & Stoughton, 1975.
A Loving Eye, Hodder & Stoughton, 1977.
The Honey Tree, Hodder & Stoughton, 1978.
Summer People, Hodder & Stoughton, 1980.
Secret Places, Hodder & Stoughton, 1981.
The Country of Her Dreams, Hodder & Stoughton, 1982.
Magic, Hodder & Stoughton, 1983.
The Italian Lesson, Hodder & Stoughton, 1985.
Dr. Gruber's Daughter, Hodder & Stoughton, 1986.
The Sadness of Witches, Hodder & Stoughton, 1987.
Life on the Nile, Hodder & Stoughton, 1989.
Necessary Rites, Hodder & Stoughton, 1990.
City of Gates, Hodder & Stoughton, 1992.
Figures in the Sand, Sceptre, 1994.

OTHER

The Noise from the Zoo and Other Stories, Sceptre (London, England), 1992.

Contributor to anthologies, including *Winter's Tales,* edited by A. D. Maclean, Macmillan, 1966; *Good Talk,* edited by Derwent May, Gollancz, 1968; *Penguin Modern Stories 10,* edited by Judith Burnley, Penguin, 1972; *Techniques of Novel Writing,* edited by A. S. Burack, Writer, Inc., 1973; *The Midnight Ghost Book,* edited by James Hale, Barrie & Jenkins, 1978; *Winter's Tales 25,* edited by Caroline Hobhouse, Macmillan, 1979; *The After Midnight Ghost Book,* edited by James Hale, Hutchinson, 1980; *The Twilight Book,* edited by James Hale, Gollancz, 1981; *The Best of the Fiction Magazines,* edited by Judy Cooke and Elizabeth Bunster, Dent, 1986.

Regular book reviewer for *Sunday Telegraph,* 1969—. Contributor of short stories to *Harper's Bazaar, Transatlantic Review, Nova,* and *Queen;* contributor of articles to newspapers and magazines, including *Sunday Times* and *Twentieth Century;* contributor of book reviews to *Sunday Times,* London *Times, New York Times,* and *New Statesman.* Former member of editorial staff, *House and Garden, House Beautiful, Harper's Bazaar,* and *Sunday Times.*

Adaptations

The Buttercup Chain, based on Elliott's novel of the same title, was produced by Columbia Pictures in 1969. *Secret Places,* an award-winning film based on the novel of the same title, was produced by Skreba in 1984 and released by Twentieth Century-Fox/TLC Films in 1985.

Sidelights

Janice Elliott's novels have been praised by many reviewers for their authentic evocation of atmosphere and mood. Reviewing *A State of Peace,* Elliott's first novel in a trilogy that explores the aftermath of World War II, a *Times Literary Supplement* contributor asserted that the author is "now firmly establishing herself as a novelist with notable talent for recreating times past . . . . [Her books] capture a remarkably authentic, solid and evocative background." David Haworth, reviewing the same book for *New Statesman,* commented on the difficulties of writing about recent history and added that "Elliott is not in the least daunted . . . . She evokes the immediate postwar world with accuracy and panache." Piers Brendon, writing in *Books and Bookmen,* described the novel as "an imaginative and deeply felt account of the vicissitudes of an upper middle class family in the London of the immediate post-war years. The atmosphere of demob drabness, poverty and points, bomb-sites and black marketeers is well conveyed . . . . I found this an involving and moving book—one which transmits life instead of trying to explain it."

In the *Dictionary of Literary Biography,* Virginia Briggs described *Summer People* as a novel of "social criticism." And while William Boyd commended Elliott for her "sure, deft touch," he was puzzled by the novel's futuristic setting, maintaining in the *Times Literary Supplement:* "The book's post-1984 world consists of a few layabout hippies on the beach, wandering stray dogs, hints that essential services are not all they could be, and dark talk of violence in the cities. The apocalyptic doom-laden atmosphere that's so patently striven for just doesn't emerge." John Mellors, however, is more impressed with Elliott's scenario, noting in the *Listener* that she creates "a sultry, threatening atmosphere, like the lull before a cosmic storm." Similarly, London *Times* critic Peter Tinniswood called the book "perfection," and added: "Gradually a complex and beautifully modulated picture is built up of a society crumbling in on itself . . . . It is a brilliantly imaginative work. Everything about it shimmers with quality of the highest order."

Several critics have commented on Elliott's economical use of language and images in conveying theme. "She builds meaning from snatches of conversation, exact portrayals of scene and mood," Mary Borg declared in the *New Statesman.* In a review of *The Kindling,* Borg wrote: "One is deeply impressed with the reverberations of the story. The effect is of gradual osmosis." And in an appraisal of *Secret Places* for the *Listener,* John Naughton asserted that "Elliott has succeeded in etching her characters, and their story, with a gossamer touch. Her book is full of eloquent understatement."

In the *Times Literary Supplement,* Lindsay Duguid describes Elliott's *Magic* as an impressionistic novel in which "parallel streams-of-consciousness" and "bits and pieces of information are slyly smuggled in" to establish a complex plot and "to encompass a generous notion of magic." Duguid continues: "By means of tight control and a contrastingly lavish use of irony, Elliott gives us a picture of human powers which is highly wrought but harmonious; the unequivocally fictional becomes the really real." And of *The Italian Lesson,* a novel set in Tuscany, Julia O'Faolain notes in the *Times Literary Supplement* that Elliott "plays variations on themes from E. M. Forster's Italian novels." O'Faolain speaks of the "economy" in the novel typical of Elliott, and believes that she "unfolds her story with wit and irony, keeping to the present tense and using short, affirmative sentences which build up tension."

Elliott's novel *Dr. Gruber's Daughter,* described by a *Kirkus Reviews* contributor as an "eccentric, quicksilvery and rather surprising Hitler-alive seriocomic novel," has been praised by many commentators for its fine characterizations and its sparkling wit. Mansel Stimpson suggested in the *Times Literary Supplement* that the success of *Dr. Gruber's Daughter* "lies in its strikingly individual and daring combination of comedy and drama." Stimpson added, however, that "the book's comedy is not a denial of its seriousness." Calling the book a "splendid" novel, Stimpson concluded: "Remembering the Nazi past, the book confidently asserts that people will be caught by history in the same way in the future: there will be other monsters, other victims, other passengers." Anita Brookner, who called the novel's plot "voluminous," remarked in the *Spectator,* "I finished the book with considerable admiration for [Elliott's] insight." And John Nicholson observed in the London *Times* that "Elliott is one of the most accomplished literary stylists at work in this country, with an imagination second to none and an extraordinarily consistent output." "Elliott writes like an angel," asserted Nicholson. "Her imagination is diabolical."

Reviewing Elliott's body of work in *Contemporary Novelists,* Hana Sambrook observed: "Most of Janice Elliott's carefully crafted novels share the same background (the affluent English middle class), the same period of time, the same preoccupation with the menopausal crises of well-established marriages, and, to a surprising extent, the same characters under different names . . . . The stress is on women's strength and ability to survive while men crack up and break." Sambrook mentions *Summer People, The Italian Lesson, Magic,* and two newer novels, *The Sadness of Witches* and *Necessary Rites,* as examples.

Elliott also wrote a number of books for younger readers, among them *The King Awakes,* a futuristic fantasy set in a post-nuclear world. The novel's twelve-year-old hero, Red, is accompanied on a thrilling journey of survival and discovery by his mother, his sister, and a wounded soldier named Artorius, who is actually the legendary King Arthur awakened from the sleep of a thousand years. *Junior Bookshelf* reviewer D. A. Young maintained that *The King Awakes* "will please readers with a taste for the fantastic and the perseverance to grasp the many threads which go to the making of this strange and beautiful complex piece of story telling."

Biographical and Critical Sources

BOOKS

Contemporary Literary Criticism, Volume 47, Gale, 1988.
Contemporary Novelists, sixth edition, St. James Press, 1996.
Dictionary of Literary Biography, Volume 14: *British Novelists since 1960,* Gale, 1983.

PERIODICALS

Books and Bookmen, September, 1971.
Books for Keeps, September, 1987, Pat Triggs, "Editor's Page," p. 3.
Chicago Tribune, October 23, 1985.
Junior Bookshelf, December, 1987, D. A. Young, review of *The King Awakes,* p. 281.
Kirkus Reviews, July 15, 1969, review of *Angels Falling,* p. 735; December 1, 1986, review of *The Italian Lesson,* p. 1744; December 1, 1987, review of *Dr. Gruber's Daughter,* p. 1638; May 1, 1995.
Listener, April 10, 1980; March 5, 1981.
Nation, September 11, 1967.
New Statesman, June 12, 1970; July 16, 1971.
New Yorker, March 23, 1987.
New York Times Book Review, January 17, 1988, review of *Dr. Gruber's Daughter,* p. 12.
Publishers Weekly, November 21, 1986; December 4, 1987; September 9, 1988; September 7, 1992, review of *The Noise from the Zoo;* August 9, 1993, review of *City of Gates;* May 22, 1995, review of *Figures in the Sand.*
Saturday Review, April 8, 1967.
School Librarian, review of *The King Awakes,* August, 1988, p. 107.
Spectator, March 15, 1975; March 28, 1981; September 17, 1983; September 6, 1986.
Times (London), April 30, 1980; March 18, 1982; September 15, 1983; April 18, 1985; September 4, 1986.
Times Literary Supplement, July 21, 1966; July 11, 1970; July 23, 1971; October 13, 1978; April 18, 1980; March 13, 1981; March 19, 1982; September 9, 1983; April 19, 1985; September 19, 1986; September 18, 1987; January 1, 1988; March 31, 1989; October 19, 1990; October 9, 1992.
Washington Post Book World, November 8, 1970.

EMBERLEY, Michael 1960-

Personal

Born June 2, 1960, in Boston, MA; son of Edward R. (an artist and writer) and Barbara (a writer and craftsperson; maiden name, Collins) Emberley. *Education:* Attended Rhode Island School of Design, 1979-80, and California College of Arts and Crafts, 1981-82. *Hobbies and other interests:* Bicycle racing.

Addresses

Home—1036 Winsor Ave., Oakland, CA 94610.

Career

Writer and illustrator, 1980—.

Writings

SELF-ILLUSTRATED

Dinosaurs! A Drawing Book, Little, Brown (Boston), 1980.
The Sports Equipment Book, Little, Brown, 1982.
More Dinosaurs! And Other Prehistoric Beasts: A Drawing Book, Little, Brown, 1983.
Ruby, Little, Brown, 1990.
The Present, Little, Brown, 1991.
Welcome Back, Sun, Little, Brown, 1993.

ILLUSTRATOR

Zachary Judd, *Roller Coaster Ride,* Silver Burdett & Ginn (Morristown, NJ), 1992.
Robert L. May, *Rudolph's Second Christmas,* Applewood Books, 1992.
Robert L. May, *Rudolph the Red-Nosed Reindeer,* Applewood Books, 1994.
Robie H. Harris, *It's Perfectly Normal: Changing Bodies, Sex, and Sexual Health,* Candlewick Press, 1994.
Robie H. Harris, *Happy Birth Day!,* Candlewick (Cambridge, MA), 1996.
Robie H. Harris, *It's So Amazing! A Book about Eggs, Sperm, Birth, Babies, and Families,* Candlewick, 1999.
Robie H. Harris, *Hi, New Baby!,* Candlewick, 2000.

Sidelights

Michael Emberley retains strong memories from his childhood of rowing to the ocean with friends and riding his bicycle along the narrow winding road of his hometown in Massachusetts. After graduating from high school, he began working with his father, an established children's book author and illustrator. With his father's encouragement, Emberley eventually branched off into his own style of illustrating and began to work on ideas for his own children's books. Since then, he has produced books that teach young children how to draw dinosaurs, and written and illustrated several picture books, often drawing upon classic children's literature. He has also teamed up with a number of authors to illustrate their stories, and with Robie H. Harris, who has

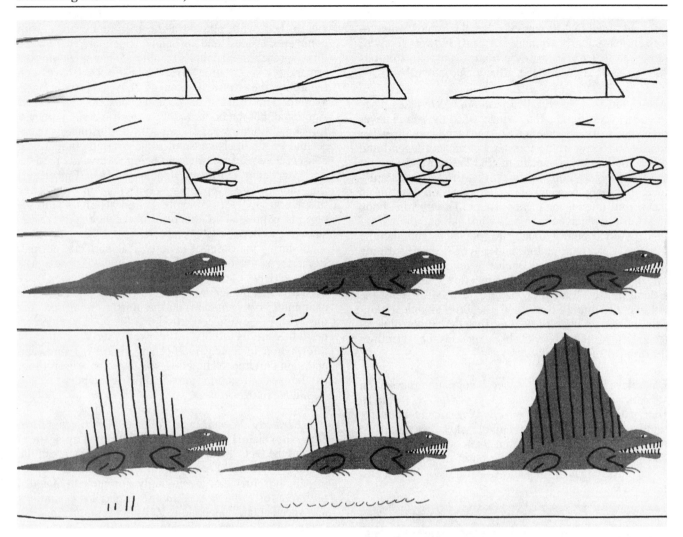

Michael Emberley shows how to draw ten dinosaurs in his **Dinosaurs.**

written several books intended to inform and reassure children about their bodies and sexuality.

For his first effort, *Dinosaurs!: A Drawing Book,* Emberley chose ten well-known dinosaurs and presented children with simple instructions on how they can be drawn. A *Publishers Weekly* reviewer called *Dinosaurs!* "An amusing and instructive book." Though a *Kirkus Reviews* contributor compared Emberley's step-by-step art lessons for children unfavorably to his father's works on drawing, *School Library Journal* critic Lynn S. Hunter called the son's drawings "more complex" than his father's, but concluded that fans of the elder Emberley's books "are sure to enjoy this one." Similarly, *More Dinosaurs! And Other Prehistoric Beasts: A Drawing Book,* was generally well received by reviewers; W.A. Handley, who critiqued the book for *School Library Journal,* predicted that "budding artists will love this one."

Emberley turned to storytelling with his next effort, *Ruby,* a version of the Little Red Riding Hood folktale. In Emberley's rendition, a mouse is asked by her mother to take a bag of triple-cheese pies to her sick grandmoth-er. To get there, Ruby must travel through a dangerous city, and along the way she encounters a con artist reptile and a very friendly cat, both of whom she manages to outwit. A *New York Times Book Review* critic praised Emberley's text and illustrations as "very clever." Although a *Publishers Weekly* critic feared only "readers on the older end of the intended age spectrum" will understand Emberley's "somewhat sophisticated humor," Martha Topol wrote in *School Library Journal* that "this Red Riding Hood variation has enough plot twists and innovation to keep readers involved and interested."

In Emberley's next work, *The Present,* set in Denmark, Uncle Arne buys a pocket knife as a gift for his nephew's birthday, but decides he likes it so much he will keep it himself. He then buys an old bicycle and fixes it up to give to his nephew, but realizes he must learn how to ride it in order to deliver it. Many reviewers praised Emberley's cinematic technique, which comical-ly shows Uncle Arne learning to ride a bicycle; others noted that the author gives an adult figure concerns a child can understand. Although a *Publishers Weekly* writer found the book "droll but somewhat wordy," the critic admitted that Emberley's "gentle, homey watercolors are particularly winning." Ann A. Flowers likewise remarked in *Horn Book:* "the homey, busy illustrations ... are just right for the affectionate story."

Also set in Scandinavia, *Welcome Back, Sun* takes place in Norway, during the long winter when the sun is never seen. The story centers on a little girl who convinces her family to follow in the footsteps of ancient legend and climb the highest mountain to find the sun and show it the way home. Along the way, the girl and her family meet their neighbors, who, too, are intent on ushering in the spring after a long gray winter. This picture book was warmly received by critics who, like one *Publishers Weekly* contributor, found it "both an enlightening glimpse of another culture and a lyrical, heartwarming story." Others, like Lisa Dennis, a reviewer for *School Library Journal*, singled out Emberley's drawings for special praise: "Emberley captures the feel of both the cold, gray 'murky time' and the brilliant, clear sunshine," Dennis attested, adding that the author/illustrator's "captivating artwork" ably expresses the warmth of the family relationships.

Emberley has illustrated several nonfiction books on sexuality and physical development, written by Robie H. Harris. In the first, *It's Perfectly Normal,* intended for middle-grade readers, the author takes her audience through the facts of life—from intercourse, conception, and birth, to topics such as the onset of puberty, birth control, AIDS, and sexual abuse—with the help of a bird

Emberley illustrates the facts of life in Robie H. Harris's nonfiction book for middle-graders.

and a bee who play straight man/funny man with comments, asides, and questions. For many reviewers, this approach to teaching sexuality to young people was remarkably successful. "It is the best book I have seen regarding the physical changes that puberty brings," averred Tim Moses in *Boston Book Review.* Some suggested that the book may be a controversial purchase for some libraries, and Emberley's illustrations were seen to be the likely cause of some consternation among conservative readers. "Besides being warm and unaffected," Stephanie Zvirin attested in *Booklist,* Emberley's illustrations "are eyepoppers—especially in a book for this age group." Part of Emberley and Harris's philosophy, as expressed in the title of the book, is that as strange and occasionally embarrassing as sexuality may seem during the onset of puberty, it is perfectly normal. Emberley's illustrations, depicting human nudes in a wide variety of shapes, sizes, and colors, a boy masturbating, intercourse between two people, and a girl examining her genitalia in the mirror, reinforce that message. Reviewers concurred that the book's effectiveness lies in its ability to convey lots of important information in a way intended to relax, reassure, and entertain children. "The book will serve as a useful tool in the sex education curriculum," contended Nancy Vasilakis in *Horn Book.*

It's Perfectly Normal was followed by *Happy Birth Day!,* in which Harris and Emberley teamed up again to present the facts about birth couched in a story about the first day of life for a newborn infant. "All the milestones of a baby's first day are lovingly chronicled," noted a reviewer for *Publishers Weekly.* "Emberley's paintings are spectacular," Stephanie Zvirin wrote in *Booklist,* continuing: "Large, realistic, and softly colored, they literally glow as they catch the tender moments." With their next joint effort, *It's So Amazing!: A Book about Eggs, Sperm, Birth, Babies, and Families,* Emberley and Harris provide a look at human sexuality similar in format to their *It's Perfectly Normal,* but for a younger audience. The result is "an equally outstanding book," contended Amy Brandt in *Booklist.* As in the earlier book, Emberley's illustrations run the gamut from humorous cartoons to straightforward graphic illustrations of the human body and reproductive systems, and the bird and the bee are back to provide comic relief, ask questions, and reinforce and define important concepts. And, as in the earlier book, according to *Publishers Weekly,* the authors successfully convey a wealth of important information "with candor and humor, neatly distilling various aspects of sex, reproduction and love."

Author and illustrator Michael Emberley, the son of author and illustrator Ed Emberley, is also the brother of author and illustrator Rebecca Emberley. The trio put their heads together to produce *Three: An Emberley Family Sketch Book,* in which each contributes stories, poems, drawings, and other tidbits, all playing on the theme of three-ness. Michael Emberley's contribution showcases his several styles of illustration, including pen-and-ink, watercolor, and crayon artwork, offering stories and poems to go with each. "Children will be intrigued by this big book of fun, which celebrates togetherness and individuality all in one family," pre-dicted Kathleen Squires in *Booklist.*

Biographical and Critical Sources

PERIODICALS

Booklist, March 15, 1980, Barbara Elleman, review of *Dinosaurs!,* p. 1055; September 15, 1994, review of *It's Perfectly Normal,* p. 133; May 1, 1996, Stephanie Zvirin, review of *Happy Birth Day!,* p. 1502; August, 1998, Kathleen Squires, review of *Three: An Emberley Family Sketch Book,* p. 1993; January 1, 2000, Amy Brandt, review of *It's So Amazing!,* p. 912.

Boston Book Review, 1995, Tim Moses, review of *It's Perfectly Normal.*

Bulletin of the Center for Children's Books, May, 1991, p. 216; October, 1993, Roger Sutton, review of *Welcome Back, Sun,* pp. 42-43.

Five Owls, January, 1995, p. 55.

Horn Book, September-October, 1991, Ann A. Flowers, review of *The Present,* p. 582; March-April, 1995, Nancy Vasilakis, review of *It's Perfectly Normal,* p. 214.

Kirkus Reviews, May 1, 1980, review of *Dinosaurs!,* p. 576.

New York Times Book Review, March 10, 1991, review of *Ruby,* p. 29.

People Weekly, May 15, 1995, p. 40.

Publishers Weekly, January 25, 1980, review of *Dinosaurs!,* p. 341; November 11, 1983, p. 48; October 12, 1990, review of *Ruby,* pp. 62-63; May 31, 1991, review of *The Present,* p. 75; September 13, 1993, review of *Welcome Back, Sun,* p. 130; July 18, 1994, p. 248; June 17, 1996, review of *Happy Birth Day!,* p. 63; June 29, 1998, p. 58; December 20, 1999, review of *It's So Amazing!,* p. 80.

Quill & Quire, October, 1993, p. 44.

School Library Journal, May, 1980, Lynn S. Hunter, review of *Dinosaurs!,* p. 54; February, 1984, W.A. Handley, review of *More Dinosaurs!,* pp. 68-69; October, 1990, Martha Topol, review of *Ruby,* p. 90; September, 1991, p. 232; January, 1994, Lisa Dennis, review of *Welcome Back, Sun,* p. 88.

Washington Post Book World, February 12, 1984, p. 11.

Wilson Library Bulletin, September, 1991, p. 108.*

* * *

ESEKI, Bruno
See MPHAHLELE, Ezekiel

F

FELTENSTEIN, Dr. Arlene (H.) 1934-
(Dr. Arlene Maletta)

Personal

Born April 14, 1934, in Yonkers, NY; daughter of Louis (in business) and Viola (a homemaker; maiden name, Klein) Pollack; married Jerome P. Feltenstein, February 26, 1956 (divorced, October, 1994); married Joseph Ramon Maletta (a realtor), October 17, 1999; children: (first marriage) George, Richard. *Education:* Hunter College of the City University of New York, B.A. (cum laude), 1956, M.S. (education), 1962; Wellness Institute, Seattle, WA, certificate in clinical hypnotherapy, 1993; American Holistic College of Nutrition, M.S./B.S., Ph.D. (with honors), 1995; also attended Mamaroneck Teachers Institute, Foundation for Mind Research, Lincoln Center Institute for Aesthetic Education, and Fordham University, between 1968 and 1993. *Politics:* Republican. *Religion:* Jewish. *Hobbies and other interests:* Playing the piano, musical composition.

Addresses

Home and office—5231 East Muriel Dr., Scottsdale, AZ 85254. *E-mail*—DocA5@aol.com.

Career

Health and wellness counselor and curriculum specialist at public school in Larchmont, NY, 1968-94; Winners Outpatient Obesity Treatment Center, Yonkers, NY, nutritional director, 1994-96; private practice of nutritional counseling. Teacher at New York Chiropractic College; Samaritan Village, designer of nutritional education program for AIDS patients and staff, 1995-96.

Writings

(With Joan Fallon) *Will the New Baby Be Bigger Than Me?*, illustrated by Vivi Escriva, Laredo Publishing (Beverly Hills, CA), 1999.
Am I Still Special?, Laredo Publishing, 2000.

Also author of *The Nutritional Approach to Health: Living with AIDS,* 1996.

Work in Progress

Spencer's Steinway; A Novel Novel.

Arlene Feltenstein

50

Dr. Feltenstein pairs up with Dr. Joan Fallon for Will the New Baby Be Bigger Than Me? *(Illustrated by Vivi Escriva.)*

Sidelights

Dr. Arlene Feltenstein told *SATA:* "In 2000 I became a Bat Mitzvah at Temple Solel in Scottsdale, Arizona. The preparation took two years. Married to a Christian, I join him in celebrating his holidays as well as my own. I love music, play the piano, compose a bit, and write or adapt stories for children's plays. I create the scripts, music, and lyrics. I work on my own autobiography daily. Will it be published? I'm not sure."*

*　　　*　　　*

FOON, Dennis 1951-

Personal

Born November 18, 1951, in Detroit, MI; son of Alvin Nathan (in business) and Shirley (a teacher; maiden name, Weiss) Foon; married Jane Howard Baker, May 2, 1975 (divorced June, 1982); children: Rebecca Howard, Aliayta Foon-Dancoes. *Education:* University of Michigan, B.A. (with honors), 1973; University of British Columbia, M.F.A., 1975.

Addresses

Home—647 East 12th Ave., Vancouver, British Columbia, Canada V5T 2H7. *Agent*—(for television and film) Harrison Arts Management, #303A-489 College St., Toronto, Canada M6G 1A5; (for plays for young people) Peter Zednik, Green Thumb Theatre, 1885 Venables, Vancouver, British Columbia, Canada V5L 2H6.

Career

University of British Columbia, Centre for Continuing Education, Vancouver, instructor in playwriting, 1974-79; Green Thumb Theatre for Young People, Vancouver, co-founder and artistic director, 1975-88. Play-

wright-in-residence at Young People's Theatre, Toronto, 1983-84; lecturer and workshop director; consultant to Canada Council, Provincial Educational Media Centre, and National Film Board of Canada; consultant to *Sesame Street Canada,* 1988-92. *Member:* International Association of Children's Theatre (vice president, 1979-82), Professional Association of Canadian Theatres (member of board, 1978-79), Composers, Authors, and Publishers Association of Canada, Writers Guild of Canada, Playwrights Union of Canada, Canadian Actors Equity Association.

Awards, Honors

Avery Hopwood Award, University of Michigan, 1972, for story "The Quivering Scarecrow Flinch"; *Writer's Digest* Award, 1973, for story "Putting It to Linda on a Sunday Afternoon"; CBC Literary Award, 1985, for *The Short Tree and the Bird That Could Not Sing;* British Theatre Award for best production for young adults, 1986, for *Invisible Kids;* Chalmers Award, 1987, for *Skin,* and 1995, for *The Short Tree and the Bird That Could Not Sing;* International Arts for Young Audiences Award, 1989, for outstanding contribution to theater for young audiences; Scott Newman Award, 1990; British Columbia Film Award "Leo" for best screenplay, 1996, Top Ten Award, Writers Guild of Canada, 1997, and Gemini Award, 1997, all for *Little Criminals;* Jesse Richardson Career Achievement Award, 1998; Robert

Dennis Foon

Wagner Award for best screenplay, Columbus TV Festival, 1998, for *White Lies.*

Writings

PUBLISHED PLAYS

The Last Days of Paul Bunyan (one-act), Playwrights Canada, 1977.

The Windigo (one-act; first produced in Vancouver, British Columbia, at Green Thumb Theatre, May, 1977), Talonbooks, 1978.

Raft Baby (one-act; first produced at Green Thumb Theatre, March 25, 1978), Talonbooks, 1978.

Heracles (one-act; first produced on tour in British Columbia and Alberta by Axis Mime Theatre and Green Thumb Theatre, May 22, 1978), Talonbooks, 1978.

New Canadian Kid (one-act; first produced on tour in British Columbia by Green Thumb Theatre, October, 1981; also see below), Pulp Press, 1982.

The Hunchback of Notre Dame (adapted from the novel by Victor Hugo; two-act; first produced at Vancouver Playhouse Mainstage, November, 1981), Playwrights Canada, 1983.

Trummi Kaput (adapted from the German play by Volker Ludwig; two-act; produced on tour in Canada by Grips Theatre, Berlin, and Green Thumb Theatre, May, 1982), published in *Canadian Theatre Review,* May, 1983.

Skin [and] *Liars* (*Skin* first produced at Project One, Vancouver, 1984; *Liars* first produced by Green Thumb Theatre, 1986), Playwrights Canada, 1988.

New Canadian Kid [and] *Invisible Kids* (*Invisible Kids* first produced at Unicorn Theatre, London, England, 1985), Pulp Press, 1989.

Words We Call Home (monologue; first produced as *Children's Eyes* in Vancouver at New Play Centre, 1983), UBC Press, 1990.

Mirror Game, (first produced at La Quinzaine International Theatre Festival, Quebec City, by Green Thumb Theatre, 1988), Blizzard Pub. (Winnipeg, Canada), 1992.

Seesaw (first produced in Vancouver, 1994), Blizzard, 1993.

Chasing the Money: A Play (Manitoba Theatre for Young People, 1999), Blizzard, 2000.

UNPUBLISHED PLAYS

Peach (one-act), first produced at Vancouver East Cultural Centre, April 28, 1976.

(Co-creator) *Hotsy Totsy,* first produced at Arts Club Theatre, 1978.

La Malice, Voyageur (one-act), first produced at Green Thumb Theatre, May, 1979.

Dr. Smyrichinsky's Brother (two-act), first produced in Montreal, Quebec, at Montreal Playwright's Workshop, May, 1982.

Afternoon Tea, first produced at New Play Centre, 1986.

Bedtimes and Bullies (adaptation of Ludwig's play), first produced by Young People's Theatre, 1987.

ZAYDOK: A Comedy for Adults, first produced at New Play Centre by Touchstone Theatre, October, 1987.

Sunspots, first produced in Vancouver, 1995.

Kip's high-stakes gambling nearly ruins his life. *(Cover photo by Lorne Bridgman.)*

OTHER

(Contributor) Cathy Ford, editor, *The Canadian Short Fiction Anthology,* Intermedia Press, 1976.

(With Judith Mastai, Brian Thorpe, Fran Gebhard, and Wendy Van Reisen) *Feeling Yes, Feeling No: A Child Sexual Abuse Prevention Program,* produced by Green Thumb Theatre, 1982.

(With Brenda Wright) *Am I the Only One? A Child's Book on Sexual Abuse,* Douglas & McIntyre, 1985.

Differences, National Film Board of Canada, 1986.

The Short Tree and the Bird That Could Not Sing (Book-of-the-Month Club selection), illustrated by John Bianchi, Groundwood, 1986.

Wheels (television drama), Canadian Broadcasting Corp. (CBC-TV), 1987.

Boogeymen (television drama), CBC-TV, 1987.

War, Blizzard Pub., 1995.

Little Criminals (television drama by CBC-TV, 1996), Blizzard, 1996.

White Lies (television drama), CBC-TV, 1998.

Double or Nothing: A Novel, Annick Press, 2000.

Also author of *Loss,* a television drama commissioned by KCTS, of *Baby,* a television drama for CBC-TV, and of *Jenny & the Queen of Light,* North Play Productions.

Contributor of articles, fiction, and poems to periodicals, including *GRAIN, Afterthoughts,* and *ANON.*

Adaptations

Feeling Yes, Feeling No has been produced on film by the National Film Board of Canada. *Skin* was filmed by Intercom Films in 1988; *New Canadian Kid* was produced as a videoplay by Hy Perspectives Media Production in 1982, and *Invisible Kids* was produced in the same format by Winnipeg Videon in 1987; *La Malice, Voyageur* was produced for radio by the Provincial Educational Media Centre, Vancouver, British Columbia, in March, 1979, and *Children's Eyes* was broadcast on CBC Radio's "Vanishing Point" series in December, 1985.

Sidelights

Dennis Foon once commented: "Over the last eight years I have been deeply involved in child advocacy theatre, writing and/or directing plays for the young that help give them some tools to better cope with a complex

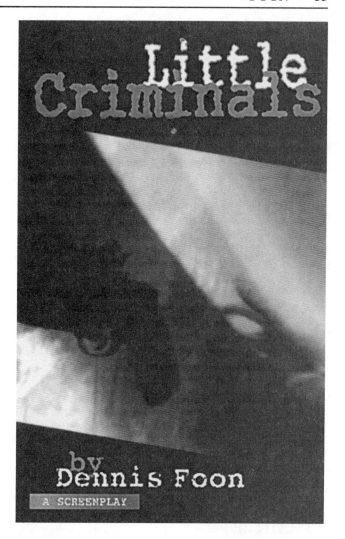

Eleven-year-old boys are the criminals in Foon's dramatic portrayal of life on the streets.

Based on actual interviews, Foon's War *captures the lives of four young teenagers growing up in violent times. (Cover art by Robert Pasternak.)*

and confusing world. This work with Green Thumb Theatre has taken me across North America and Europe and has led to a number of international collaborations."

Though predominantly a playwright, Foon is also the author of a number of books and television specials that address the disturbing topics of sexual abuse and troubled children. His television production, *Little Criminals,* investigates the plight of child and teen gang members. "Are they criminals or victims?," Foon is quoted as saying in a *Maclean's* article by Marci McDonald. McDonald wrote that the author interviewed well over one hundred young "toughs" in order to accurately create Des, the eleven-year-old leader of a gang in *Little Criminals.* Foon has a passion for increasing awareness of the problems that many children face today as well as a "rage at injustice to small spirits—especially the growing number of young people like Des, the casualties of a society that has abandoned him," McDonald remarked.

Foon is the author of many plays, published and unpublished. David H. Jenkinson, writing in *Twentieth-Century Children's Writers,* noted that Foon's plays "generally contain few characters and require little elaborate staging, are available to small companies and can reach wide audiences." McDonald commented on the "gritty, kitchen-sink style realism" of Foon's plays. McDonald added: "In Foon's plays, kids grappled with racial slurs and school bullies, the tug-of-war of divorce and the humiliation of alcoholic parents. His plotlines were spun with such compelling credibility and innovative charm that his dramas were produced in schools across the country and around the world from Dublin to New Zealand."

Biographical and Critical Sources

BOOKS

Jenkinson, David H., "Dennis Foon," *Twentieth-Century Children's Writers,* 4th edition, St. James Press, 1995.

PERIODICALS

Books in Canada, December, 1986; March, 1989; November, 1992.
Canadian Children's Literature, number 46, 1987; number 57, 1990; summer, 1996.
Canadian Theatre Review, spring, 1983.
Chimo!, September, 1982.
Globe and Mail, May 20, 2000.
Maclean's, January 22, 1996, Marci McDonald, "Pint-sized Perpetrators," p. 58.
Montreal Sunday Express, July 11, 1982.
Vancouver Sun, November 29, 1983; November 23, 1998; April 22, 2000.

*   *   *

FRAME, Janet
See CLUTHA, Janet Paterson Frame

*   *   *

FRITZ, Jean (Guttery) 1915-

Personal

Born November 16, 1915, in Hankow, China; daughter of Arthur Minton (a minister and YMCA missionary) and Myrtle (Chaney) Guttery; married Michael Fritz, November 1, 1941; children: David, Andrea. *Education:* Wheaton College, A.B., 1937; study at Columbia University. *Hobbies and other interests:* Reading, traveling.

Addresses

Home—50 Bellewood Ave., Dobbs Ferry, NY 10522. *Agent*—Gina MacCoby Literary Agency, 1123 Broadway, Suite 1010, New York, NY 10010. *E-mail*—jfritz60@aol.com.

Career

Author of historical biographies and novels for young people. Silver Burdett Co., New York City, research assistant, 1937-41; Dobbs Ferry Library, Dobbs Ferry, NY, children's librarian, 1955-57; Jean Fritz Writers' Workshops, Katonah, NY, founder and instructor, 1962-70; Board of Co-operative Educational Service, Westchester County, NY, teacher, 1971-73; Appalachian State University, Boone, NC, faculty member, summer, 1980-82. Lecturer.

Awards, Honors

New York Times outstanding book of the year citations, 1973, for *And Then What Happened, Paul Revere?,* 1974, for *Why Don't You Get a Horse, Sam Adams?,* 1975, for *Where Was Patrick Henry on the 29th of May?,* 1976, for *What's the Big Idea, Ben Franklin?,* 1981, for *Traitor: The Case of Benedict Arnold,* and 1982, for *Homesick: My Own Story; Boston Globe-Horn Book* honor book citations, 1974, for *And Then What Happened, Paul Revere?,* 1976, for *Will You Sign Here, John Hancock?,* and 1980, for *Stonewall;* named outstanding Pennsylvania author, Pennsylvania School Library Association, 1978; Honor Award for Nonfiction, Children's Book Guild, 1978 and 1979, for the "body of her creative writing"; American Book Award nomination, 1980, for *Where Do You Think You're Going, Christopher Columbus?,* and 1981, for *Traitor: The Case of Benedict Arnold;* LL.D., Washington and Jefferson College, 1982, Wheaton College, 1987; Child Study Award and Christopher Award, both 1982; Newbery Honor Book Award, American Book Award, and *Boston Globe-Horn Book* honor book, all 1983, all for *Homesick: My Own Story; Boston Globe-Horn Book* Nonfiction Award, 1984, for *The Double Life of Pocahontas,* and 1990, for *The Great Little Madison;* Regina Award, 1985; Laura Ingalls Wilder Award, 1986; Orbis Pictus Award, National Council of English Teachers, 1989, for *The Great Little Madison;* Knickerbocker Award for Juvenile literature, 1992; many of Fritz's books have been named notable books by the American Library Association.

Writings

FOR CHILDREN

Bunny Hopwell's First Spring, illustrated by Rachel Dixon, Wonder, 1954.
Help Mr. Willy Nilly, illustrated by Jean Tamburine, Treasure, 1954.
Fish Head, illustrated by Marc Simont, Coward, 1954.
Hurrah for Jonathan!, illustrated by Violet La Mont, A. Whitman, 1955.
121 Pudding Street, illustrated by Sofia, Coward, 1955.
Growing Up, illustrated by Elizabeth Webbe, Rand McNally, 1956.
The Late Spring, illustrated by Erik Blegvad, Coward, 1957.
The Cabin Faced West, illustrated by Feodor Rojankovsky, Coward, 1958.
(With Tom Clute) *Champion Dog, Prince Tom,* illustrated by Ernest Hart, Coward, 1958.
The Animals of Doctor Schweitzer, illustrated by Douglas Howland, Coward, 1958.

Jean Fritz

How to Read a Rabbit, illustrated by Leonard Shortall, Coward, 1959.

Brady, illustrated by Lynd Ward, Coward, 1960.

Tap, Tap Lion, 1, 2, 3, illustrated by Shortall, Coward, 1962.

San Francisco, illustrated by Emil Weiss, Rand McNally, 1962.

I, Adam, illustrated by Peter Burchard, Coward, 1963.

Magic to Burn, illustrated by Beth Krush and Joe Krush, Coward, 1964.

Surprise Party (reader), illustrated by George Wiggins, Initial Teaching Alphabet Publications, 1965.

The Train (reader), illustrated by Jean Simpson, Grosset, 1965.

Early Thunder, illustrated by Ward, Coward, 1967.

George Washington's Breakfast, illustrated by Paul Galdone, Coward, 1969.

And Then What Happened, Paul Revere?, illustrated by Margot Tomes, Coward, 1973.

Why Don't You Get a Horse, Sam Adams?, illustrated by Trina Schart Hyman, Coward, 1974.

Where Was Patrick Henry on the 29th of May?, illustrated by Margot Tomes, Coward, 1975.

Who's That Stopping on Plymouth Rock?, illustrated by J. B. Handelsman, Coward, 1975.

Will You Sign Here, John Hancock?, illustrated by Trina Schart Hyman, Coward, 1976.

What's the Big Idea, Ben Franklin?, illustrated by Margot Tomes, Coward, 1976.

The Secret Diary of Jeb and Abigail: Growing Up in America, 1776-1783, illustrated by Kenneth Bald and Neil Boyle, Reader's Digest Association, 1976.

Can't You Make Them Behave, King George?, illustrated by Tomie de Paola, Coward, 1977.

Brendan the Navigator, illustrated by Enrico Arno, Coward, 1979.

Stonewall, illustrated by Stephen Gammell, Putnam, 1979.

Where Do You Think You're Going, Christopher Columbus?, illustrated by Margot Tomes, Putnam, 1980.

The Man Who Loved Books, illustrated by Trina Schart Hyman, Putnam, 1981.

Traitor: The Case of Benedict Arnold, illustrated with engravings and prints, Putnam, 1981.

Back to Early Cape Cod, Acorn, 1981.

The Good Giants and the Bad Pukwudgies (folktale), illustrated by Tomie de Paola, Putnam, 1982.

Homesick: My Own Story, illustrated by Margot Tomes, Putnam, 1982.

The Double Life of Pocahontas, illustrated by Ed Young, Putnam, 1983.

China Homecoming, illustrated with photographs by Mike Fritz, Putnam, 1985.

Make Way for Sam Houston!, illustrated by Elise Primavera, Putnam, 1986.

Shh! We're Writing the Constitution, illustrated by Tomie de Paola, Putnam, 1987.

China's Long March: 6000 Miles of Danger, illustrated by Yang Zhr Cheng, Putnam, 1988.

The Great Little Madison, illustrated with engravings and prints, Putnam, 1989.

Bully for You, Teddy Roosevelt!, illustrated by Mike Wimmer, Putnam, 1991.

George Washington's Mother, illustrated by DyAnne DiSalvo-Ryan, Putnam, 1992.

(With Katherine Paterson, Fredrick and Patricia McKissack, Margaret Mahy, and Jamake Highwater) *The World in 1492,* illustrated by Stefano Vitale, Holt, 1992.

Surprising Myself, photographs by Andrea Fritz Pfleger, Owen (Katonah, NY), 1992.

The Great Adventure of Christopher Columbus: A Pop-up Book, illustrated by Tomie de Paola, Putnam & Grosset, 1992.

Just a Few Words, Mr. Lincoln: The Story of the Gettysburg Address, illustrated by Charles Robinson, Grosset & Dunlap, 1993.

Around the World in a Hundred Years: From Henry the Navigator to Magellan, illustrated by Anthony Bacon Venti, Putnam, 1994.

Harriet Beecher Stowe and the Beecher Preachers, illustrated with engravings and prints, Putnam, 1994.

You Want Women to Vote, Lizzie Stanton?, illustrated by DyAnne DiSalvo-Ryan, Putnam, 1995.

Why Not, Lafayette?, illustrated by Ronald Himler, Putnam, 1999.

OTHER

Cast for a Revolution: Some American Friends and Enemies, 1728-1814 (adult biography), Houghton-Mifflin, 1972.

(Contributor) William Zinsser, editor, *Worlds of Childhood: The Art and Craft of Writing for Children,* Houghton-Mifflin, 1990.

Book reviewer, *San Francisco Chronicle,* 1941-43, and *New York Times,* 1970—. Contributor of short stories to periodicals, including *Seventeen, Redbook,* and *New Yorker.*

Fritz's papers are housed in a permanent collection in the Children's Literature Collection at the University of Oregon, Eugene, and included in the Kerlan Collection at the University of Minnesota, and in a collection at the University of Southern Mississippi.

Adaptations

Fritz's writings have been recorded on audio cassette.

Work in Progress

Leonardo's Horse.

Sidelights

Jean Fritz is a highly regarded author of historical biographies for young people. *Horn Book* magazine contributor Mary M. Burns has stated: "No one is better than Jean Fritz at making history interesting as well as comprehensible. She has the ability to define a theme, support it with facts, and transform a collection of data into a synthesis that reads like an adventure story." Fritz has written biographies of many heroes of the American Revolution, including George Washington, Paul Revere, Samuel Adams, and John Hancock, as well as other significant figures in history before and after this much-studied era, including Christopher Columbus, Pocahontas, Elizabeth Cady Stanton, and Harriet Beecher Stowe. Fritz has won numerous awards for this work, and critics highlight her ability to bring alive complex events and people from the past through the use of humor and the inclusion of personal details that are usually left out of historical accounts.

As a child growing up in China, the daughter of missionaries, Fritz turned to writing as a "private place, where no one could come," as she recalled in a *Publishers Weekly* interview. She began keeping a journal, into which she copied passages from books and poems written by others; later, "it became a place for her to articulate her feelings about people and life. Years later she drew upon it in her writings for children," according to O. Mell Busbin in *Dictionary of Literary Biography.* Living in China as an American focused much of Fritz's fantasy life on the land of her parents' birth, which they spoke of frequently and with much feeling. "I think it is because I was so far away that I developed a homesickness that made me want to embrace not just a given part of America at a given time but the whole of it," Fritz wrote in an article for *Horn Book.* "No one is more patriotic than the one separated from his country; no one is as eager to find roots as the person who has been uprooted."

Fritz is credited with producing biographies that are consistently well-crafted, realistic, thoroughly researched, and often witty accounts of the characters who have shaped and influenced history. For example, in her *Language Arts* review of *Traitor: The Case of Benedict Arnold,* Ruth M. Stein noted that Fritz's "books exemplify criteria for good biographies—accuracy, interest, relevance to our times, and insight into the person, the period and contemporaries. . . . However cozy the style and informal the writing, the scholarship is solid, yet unobtrusive. Primary and secondary material are woven so neatly into the narrative, you scarcely notice the internal documentation . . . . She manages to clarify her protagonist and the positions he took, even though she cannot be accused of remaining unbiased." And Georgess McHargue remarked in the *New York Times Book Review* that "Jean Fritz has what amounts to perfect pitch when writing history or biography for young people."

Fritz's talent for bringing historical figures to life is a major source of her popularity with readers and critics alike. As Busbin states in *Dictionary of Literary Biography:* "In her biographies Fritz attempts to get at the truth of the individual through his likes, dislikes, worries, joys, successes, failures. In each case she reveals the humanity of individuals, presenting their lives as revealed in diaries, letters, and other original sources. Through her humorous style she paints a full, believable picture of each individual, using specific, exact language and precise detail. She refuses to create fictional dialogue for the characters in her biographies; the only conversation found in these books is that which she has discovered in letters, diaries, journals, and other original sources, which she draws upon plentifully." "I like being a detective, a treasure hunter, an eavesdropper," Fritz revealed to Richard Ammon in a profile for *Language Arts.* "I look for personalities whose lives make good stories. I like complicated people, persons who possessed contradictions or who have interesting quirks."

Fritz once shared her thoughts on the perennial popularity of biographies: "I think young people of almost any age or ability read biographies for the same reason that adults do—or would if they could find what they want. We all seek insight into the human condition, and it is helpful to find familiar threads running through the lives of others, however famous. We need to know more people in all circumstances and times so we can pursue our private, never-to-be-fulfilled quest to find out what life is all about. In actual experience we are able to see so few lives in the round and to follow them closely from beginning to end. I, for one, need to possess a certain number of relatively whole lives in the long span of history."

Fritz has summed up her feelings on writing about the past in this manner: "My interest in writing about American history stemmed originally, I think, from a subconscious desire to find roots. I lived in China until I was thirteen, hearing constant talk about 'home' (meaning America), but since I had never been 'home,' I felt like a girl without a country. I have put down roots quite firmly by now, but in the process I have discovered the joys of research and am probably hooked. I eavesdrop on the past to satisfy my own curiosity, but if I can surprise children into believing history, I will be happy, especially if they find, as I do, that truth is stranger (and often funnier) than fiction."

Fritz began her career as a writer in the 1950s by publishing children's picture books such as *Bunny Hopwell's First Spring* and *Help Mr. Willy Nilly*. She soon branched out into historical narratives and gained a reputation as a stellar biographer of American heroes with titles published in the 1960s and 1970s, such as *Why Don't You Get a Horse, Sam Adams?*, *Who's That Stopping on Plymouth Rock?*, and *Can't You Make Them Behave, King George?* In the 1980s, Fritz continued to publish biographies on pivotal figures in American history, but moved beyond the core group around George Washington and the signers of the American Constitution with titles such as *Where Do You Think You're Going, Christopher Columbus?*, *The Double Life of Pocahontas*, and *Make Way for Sam Houston!* Like her earlier biographies, these later works take on subjects often written about before by others. However, reviewers compare Fritz's accounts favorably to those written by others, for she is unfailingly clear, interesting, and accessible.

The 1990s often found Fritz venturing beyond the shores of the United States in her quest for biographical material. In 1992, Fritz contributed to *The World in 1492,* a compendium of six essays that offers a worldwide glimpse of human history five hundred years ago from the perspective of six different geographic locations. Though the depth of information offered is necessarily limited, reviewers noted, the scarcity of books offering world history to students in middle school makes the contribution invaluable. "The cumulative effect presents a global pattern of currents and undercurrents making up the swirling ocean of human existence 500 years ago," Patricia Manning commented in *School Library Journal*. Fritz's own *Around the World in a Hundred Years: From Henry the Navigator to Magellan* also focuses on the fifteenth century. Here the author presents a series of European explorers whose conquest of the world beyond the shores of Europe helped make more accurate maps available for the first time, and also reaped untold profits for the Spanish and Portuguese monarchies through the enslavement of native peoples. Critics noted that Fritz does not shy away from telling unflattering truths about characters often hailed as heroes in the annals of history, and that her characteristic wit is also ever-present. "Those [students] seeking a broader picture will find this an intriguing view of the age of exploration," predicted Carolyn Phelan in *Booklist*.

Fritz returned to the time of the American Revolution with the publication of *George Washington's Mother,* a humorous biography of the mother of the first president of the United States, that "depicts Mary Ball Washington as a manipulative and stubborn worrywart," according to Gale W. Sherman in *School Library Journal*. Geared for a younger audience than most of Fritz's historical narratives, *George Washington's Mother* was perceived by reviewers as intended to teach younger children something about early American history through anecdotes that emphasize how even important people are sometimes embarrassed by the behavior of their mothers.

Also intended for early-grade readers is Fritz's *Just a Few Words, Mr. Lincoln: The Story of the Gettysburg Address*. In this short history, Fritz concisely explains the causes of the American Civil War and relates the story of the battle of Gettysburg, where 23,000 Union soldiers died. The author refutes the legend that has Lincoln writing his famous speech on the train ride to Gettysburg, and includes the text of the speech at the end of the book. Though carefully designed and written with a younger audience in mind, *Just a Few Words, Mr. Lincoln,* like Fritz's books for older children, "informally yet ably conveys the significance of Lincoln's eloquent speech," according to a reviewer for *Publishers Weekly*.

In *Harriet Beecher Stowe and the Beecher Preachers,* Fritz returned to the Civil War era by focusing on the woman whom Lincoln credited with starting the war to end slavery through the publication of her protest novel, *Uncle Tom's Cabin*. Fritz describes Stowe's childhood as one of nine children born to a fire-and-brimstone preacher who was disappointed she was born a girl. "With her usual respect for young readers, Fritz explores not only a life, but also a family, an era, and vitally important social movements," remarked Sally Margolis in *School Library Journal*. Fritz notes that while Harriet Beecher Stowe was punished as a child for seeking creative expression in writing, as an adult it was the profits from Stowe's writing that supported her husband and six children. "How she managed to write at all, given the circumstances under which she struggled, is the central conflict in a biography which reads like a novel," according to Mary M. Burns in *Horn Book*. *Harriet Beecher Stowe and the Beecher Preachers* is often compared to two other biographies of the author of *Uncle Tom's Cabin* published near-contemporaneously. *Bulletin of the Center for Children Books* reviewer Deborah Stevenson favored Fritz's version for several reasons: "the portrayals here are livelier, . . . and the style is informative but conversational and unintimidating, qualities that make it more suitable for preteens than [the other books]."

In *You Want Women to Vote, Lizzie Stanton?*, Fritz celebrates another female hero of the nineteenth century. Like Beecher Stowe, Stanton was born to a father who wished she had been born a boy and spent much of her life chasing her father's approval. And, like Beecher Stowe, Stanton was able to balance the acute demands of motherhood and housekeeping with the demands of her political conscience, finding the time to help organize and lead the American suffrage movement, and in the process, becoming the "Grand Old Woman of America," as Mary M. Burns noted in her review in *Horn Book*. Some reviewers claimed that Fritz manages to tell the story of Stanton's life in such an entertaining manner that students may want to read it for the story rather than for the history. Indeed, Stanton "comes alive for middle graders in a narrative with almost novelistic pacing, a dose of humor, and an affectionate point of view," proclaimed a critic for *Kirkus Reviews*.

Fritz offers a different perspective on the American Revolution in *Why Not, Lafayette?*, a portrait of the French nobleman who was inspired by the colonists' bid for freedom to fight alongside Washington and other Republican heroes of the war against Britain. The author portrays her protagonist as stifled by the boredom of his life in Paris, electrified by news of the colonists' struggle, on fire with admiration for General Washington, and a lifelong idealist in pursuit of republicanism. Fritz follows Lafayette from the years that made him a hero in the eyes of a new country, to the tricky years of the French Revolution, and his triumphal tour of the United States in his later life. As usual, Fritz relies on the effective inclusion of personal details to draw the reader into the reality of the life being studied: "readers will be stirred even at this distance by Lafayette's accomplishments," predicted a contributor to *Kirkus Reviews*. Though reviewers disagreed about the degree to which Fritz is successful in portraying the important players in both the French and American revolutionary scenes, a reviewer for *Publishers Weekly* came down on the affirmative side of the question and concluded that *Why Not, Lafayette?* is "lively, vigorous and just plain fun to read."

Biographical and Critical Sources

BOOKS

Children's Literature Review, Gale (Detroit, MI), Volume 2, 1976, Volume 14, 1988.
Dictionary of Literary Biography, Volume 52: *American Writers for Children since 1960: Fiction*, Gale, 1986.
Hostetler, Elizabeth Ann Rumer, *Jean Fritz: A Critical Biography*, University of Toledo, 1981.
Norton, Donna E., *Through the Eyes of a Child: An Introduction to Children's Literature*, 2nd edition, Merrill, 1987.
Something about the Author Autobiography Series, Volume 2, Gale, 1986.

PERIODICALS

Booklist, November 1, 1992, Carolyn Phelan, review of *The World in 1492*, p. 506; October 1, 1993, Kay Weisman, review of *Just a Few Words, Mr. Lincoln*, p. 347; May 15, 1994, Carolyn Phelan, review of *Around the World in a Hundred Years*, p. 1676; September 15, 1999, Randy Meyer, review of *Why Not, Lafayette?*, p. 253.
Bulletin of the Center for Children's Books, March, 1961; March, 1974; November, 1975, Zena Sutherland, review of *Where Was Patrick Henry on the 29th of May?*, p. 44; July-August, 1982; June, 1994, Betsy Hearne, review of *Around the World in a Hundred Years*, p. 319; October, 1994, Deborah Stevenson, review of *Harriet Beecher Stowe and the Beecher Preachers*, p. 45; October, 1995, Elizabeth Bush, review of *You Want Women to Vote, Lizzie Stanton?*,

pp. 53-54; December, 1999, Elizabeth Bush, review of *Why Not, Lafayette?*, p. 128.
Catholic Library World, July-August, 1985.
Early Years, February, 1982.
Five Owls, May-June, 1987; May-June, 1994, Mary Bahr Fritts, review of *Around the World in a Hundred Years*, p. 108.
Horn Book, October, 1967; January-February, 1985; July-August, 1986; March-April, 1993, Anita Silvey, review of *The World in 1492*, p. 226; July-August, 1994, Mary M. Burns, review of *Around the World in a Hundred Years*, p. 471; September-October, 1994, Mary M. Burns, review of *Harriet Beecher Stowe and the Beecher Preachers*, pp. 606-07; January-February, 1996, Mary M. Burns, review of *You Want Women to Vote, Lizzie Stanton?*, pp. 89-90; November, 1999, Margaret A. Bush, review of *Why Not, Lafayette?*, p. 756.
Kirkus Reviews, August 1, 1995, review of *You Want Women to Vote, Lizzie Stanton?*, p. 1109; October 1, 1999, review of *Why Not, Lafayette?*, p. 1579.
Language Arts, February, 1977; April, 1980; September, 1982, Ruth M. Stein, review of *Traitor: The Case of Benedict Arnold*, p. 605; March, 1983, Richard Ammon, "Profile: Jean Fritz," pp. 365-69; September, 1994, Miriam Martinez and Marcia F. Nash, review of *George Washington's Mother*, pp. 371-72.
Los Angeles Times Book Review, July 25, 1982, Barbara Karlin, review of *And Then What Happened, Paul Revere?*, *What's the Big Idea, Ben Franklin?*, and *Where Was Patrick Henry on the 29th of May?*, p. 9.
New Yorker, December 6, 1982, Faith McNulty, review of *Homesick: My Own Story*.
New York Times Book Review, November 9, 1980, Georgess McHargue, "Early Explorers," pp. 60-61; November 14, 1982, James A. Michener, "China Childhood," pp. 41, 57.
Publishers Weekly, July 24, 1981; October 26, 1992, review of *The World in 1492*, p. 73; September 20, 1993, review of *Just a Few Words, Mr. Lincoln*, p. 72; September 20, 1999, review of *Why Not, Lafayette?*, p. 89.
San Francisco Chronicle, April 3, 1985.
School Library Journal, November, 1967; October, 1992, Gale W. Sherman, review of *George Washington's Mother*, p. 103; November, 1992, Patricia Manning, review of *The World in 1492*, p. 115; October, 1993, Leda Schubert, review of *Just a Few Words, Mr. Lincoln*, p. 118; September, 1994, Sally Margolis, review of *Harriet Beecher Stowe and the Beecher Preachers*, p. 227; September, 1995, Rebecca O'Connell, review of *You Want Women to Vote, Lizzie Stanton?*, p. 208.
Top of the News, June, 1976.
Voice of Youth Advocates, August, 1994, Joanne Johnson, review of *Harriet Beecher Stowe and the Beecher Preachers*, p. 166.

G

GANTOS, Jack
See GANTOS, John (Bryan), Jr.

* * *

GANTOS, John (Bryan), Jr. 1951-
(Jack Gantos)

Personal

Born July 2, 1951, in Mount Pleasant, PA; son of John (a construction superintendent) and Elizabeth (Weaver) Gantos (a banker); married Anne A. Lower (an art dealer), November 11, 1989; children: Mabel Grace. *Education:* Emerson College, B.F.A., 1976, M.A., 1984. *Politics:* Liberal Democrat. *Religion:* Roman Catholic.

Addresses

Home—24 Holyoke St., Boston, MA 02116. *Office*—Emerson College, Division of Writing, Literature and Publishing, 1001 Beacon St., Boston, MA 02116. *Agent*—Fran Leibowitz, Writers House, 21 West 26th St., New York, NY 10010.

Career

Author and educator. Emerson College, Boston, MA, part-time writing instructor, 1978-80, adjunct instructor, 1980-86, assistant professor, 1986-92, associate professor of creative writing and literature, 1992-95, professor of creative writing and literature, 1995—. Visiting professor at Brown University, 1986, University of New Mexico, 1993, and Vermont College, 1996. Frequent speaker at schools, libraries, and educational conferences, and facilitator of writing workshops. *Member:* American Association of University Professors, National Council of Teachers of English, Society of Children's Book Writers and Illustrators, Writer's Guild.

Awards, Honors

Best Books for Young Readers citation, American Library Association, 1976-93, for the "Rotten Ralph" series; Children's Book Showcase Award, 1977, for *Rotten Ralph;* Emerson Alumni Award, Emerson College, 1979, for Outstanding Achievement in Creative Writing; Massachusetts Council for the Arts Awards finalist, 1983, 1988; Gold Key Honor Society Award, 1985, for Creative Excellence; National Endowment for the Arts grant, 1987; Quarterly West Novella Award, 1989, for *X-Rays;* Children's Choice citation, International Reading Association, 1990, for *Rotten Ralph's Show and Tell;* Batavia Educational Foundation grant, 1991; West Springfield Arts Council (WESPAC) grant, 1991; Parents' Choice citation, 1994, for *Not So Rotten Ralph;* New York Public Library Books for the Teenage, 1997, for *Jack's Black Book;* Silver Award, 1999, for *Jack on the Tracks;* Great Stone Face Award, Children's Librarians of New Hampshire, National Book Award finalist for Young People's Literature, ALA Notable Children's Book, NCSS and CBC Notable Children's Trade Book in the Field of Social Studies, *School Library Journal* Best Book of the Year, *Riverbank Review* Children's Book of Distinction, New York Public Library "One Hundred Titles for Reading and Sharing," all 1999, Iowa Teen Award, Iowa Educational Media Association, Flicker Tale Children's Book Award nomination, North Dakota Library Association, Sasquatch Award nomination, all 2000, all for *Joey Pigza Swallowed the Key;* National Endowment for the Arts Fellowship for Creative Writing, fiction; Gantos has also received other regional and child-selected awards.

Writings

"ROTTEN RALPH" PICTURE BOOK SERIES; ILLUSTRATED BY NICOLE RUBEL

Rotten Ralph, Houghton Mifflin (Boston), 1976.
Worse than Rotten, Ralph, Houghton Mifflin, 1978.
Rotten Ralph's Rotten Christmas, Houghton Mifflin, 1984.
Rotten Ralph's Trick or Treat!, Houghton Mifflin, 1986.
Rotten Ralph's Show and Tell, Houghton Mifflin, 1989.

Rotten Ralph, a very bad cat who nevertheless is loved unconditionally by his young owner, debuted in 1976 in the first of the series created by Jack Gantos and Nicole Rubel.

Happy Birthday Rotten Ralph, Houghton Mifflin, 1990.
Not So Rotten Ralph, Houghton Mifflin, 1994.
Rotten Ralph's Rotten Romance, Houghton Mifflin, 1997.
The Christmas Spirit Attacks Rotten Ralph, HarperCollins (New York), 1998.
Rotten Ralph's Halloween Howl, HarperCollins, 1998
Back to School for Rotten Ralph, HarperCollins, 1998.
Wedding Bells for Rotten Ralph, HarperCollins, 1999.

The "Rotten Ralph" books have been translated into other languages, including Hebrew and Japanese.

PICTURE BOOKS; ILLUSTRATED BY NICOLE RUBEL

Sleepy Ronald, Houghton Mifflin, 1976.
Fair-Weather Friends, Houghton Mifflin, 1977.

Aunt Bernice, Houghton Mifflin, 1978.
The Perfect Pal, Houghton Mifflin, 1979.
(With Nicole Rubel) *Greedy Greeny,* Doubleday (New York), 1979.
Swampy Alligator, Simon & Schuster (New York), 1980.
The Werewolf Family, Houghton Mifflin, 1980.
Willy's Raiders, Parents Magazine Press (New York), 1981.
Red's Fib, Jim Henson Associates, 1985.

"JACK HENRY" SERIES; AUTOBIOGRAPHICAL FICTION FOR MIDDLE-GRADE READERS; PUBLISHED BY FARRAR, STRAUS (NEW YORK)

Heads or Tails: Stories from the Sixth Grade, 1994.
Jack's New Power: Stories from a Caribbean Year, 1995.

Jack's Black Book, 1997.
Jack on the Tracks: Four Seasons of Fifth Grade, 1999.

OTHER

Zip Six: A Novel (adult novel), Bridge Works (Bridgehampton, NY), 1996.
Desire Lines (young adult novel), Farrar, Straus, 1997.
Joey Pigza Swallowed the Key (fiction for middle-graders), Farrar, Straus, 1998.

Also author of novella *X-Rays.* Contributor of short story "Cradle Hold" to *No Easy Answers: Short Stories about Teenagers Making Tough Choices,* edited by Donald R. Gallo, Delacorte, 1997, and short story "The Penny Tree" for *Storyworks* magazine, October, 1999.

Adaptations

Joey Pigza Swallowed the Key, read by the author, was released on audio cassette by Listening Library in 1999; *Heads or Tails: Stories from the Sixth Grade* has also been released on audio cassette. The "Rotten Ralph" books have been adapted for television. Two Rotten Ralph animated specials were produced and broadcast on the Disney Channel; in addition, the BBC is producing individual programs based on the character for broadcast in the European and Asian markets; Fox Family Channel is planning on broadcasting the programs in the United States.

Work in Progress

Rotten Ralph Feels Rotten, for Houghton Mifflin; *The Duck Pond,* for Farrar, Straus; *Living in the Library,* a young adult novel; *Brasilia,* an adult novel.

Sidelights

A popular and prolific author of books for readers ranging from the early primary grades through high school, as well as for adults, John Gantos, Jr. (better known as Jack Gantos), is considered by many critics and readers to be both a gifted humorist and an insightful observer of childhood feelings and behavior. Gantos has written witty cautionary tales, middle-grade fiction that presents bittersweet reflections on the pains and pleasures of growing up, and young adult fiction that deals frankly with serious themes. However, he is perhaps best known as the creator of Rotten Ralph, a large, anthropomorphic, red cat whose devilish, mostly unrepentant behavior is always forgiven by his owner, Sarah, a patient and loving little girl. Gantos has collaborated on the multi-volume series of picture books that feature the rascally feline with illustrator Nicole Rubel, an artist whose bright colors and bold designs are generally thought to complement the author's brisk, droll prose style well and to add to the huge popularity of the character.

Gantos is also well known for creating the "Jack Henry" books, autobiographical fiction that describes the experiences of the author's alter ego as a fifth-, sixth-, and seventh-grader. Other popular books by Gantos include *Joey Pigza Swallowed the Key,* a story about a boy with Attention Deficit Disorder (ADD), and *Desire Lines,* a young adult novel about how a teenage boy outs two lesbian classmates in order to save his own reputation. Throughout his works, Gantos has addressed issues that are meaningful to young people, such as the nature of friendship, dealing with jealousy and loneliness, being forgiven and accepted, the importance of playing fair and doing the right thing, and learning how to fit into the often baffling world of adults. Although some of the author's works are considered exaggerated, irreverent, and unsubtle and include elements that are considered gross or unsettling, many critics have noted the positive values in his books, as well as their outrageous humor and underlying poignancy. Gantos is generally regarded as a talented, imaginative writer who understands children and what appeals to them.

Born in Mount Pleasant, Pennsylvania, Gantos is the eldest son of John Gantos, Sr., a construction superintendent and salesman of Lebanese Catholic descent, and Elizabeth Weaver Gantos, a bank employee and Lutheran who came from Mount Pleasant. Gantos comes from a family of four children; he has an older sister, Betsy, and two younger brothers, Pete and Eric. As a first grader, Gantos was in the Bluebird reading group, which he later discovered was for slow readers. He began expressing his creativity at an early age. Gantos has noted that his favorite game as a small boy was to pretend that his clothes were on fire and then to roll down a hill to save himself. When he was in the second grade, Gantos received his first diary. He once told *SATA,* "I had an older sister who was very smart. She was in fifth grade and I liked to do everything that she did.... One day my mother came home from work and gave her a diary.... When I saw that diary, I wanted one, too. My mother said I was too young to have a diary but I didn't think so. I pitched a fit. I howled and sobbed. 'I want a diary,' I cried. 'I want a diary.' She finally gave me one. 'But you better write in it every day,' she said." Gantos did as his mother requested. He recalled, "I wrote the date, the weather, and what I ate for breakfast, lunch, and dinner. Food was the most important thing in the world to me and so I wrote about it all the time." Gantos also collected what he now calls "a lot of junk"—shells, rocks, stamps, pennies, bottle caps, baseball cards, butterflies, and what he has termed "lots more good stuff."

As a second grader, Gantos moved with his family from Pennsylvania to Barbados, where his father felt he could find more work. Young Jack was able to move all of his collections by putting them into his diaries—gluing, pasting, and even drilling holes in the books. The move to Barbados prompted a change in Jack's journal entries. He said, "I began to write about all the stuff that was in my diary. I wrote about where I caught my bugs. I wrote about the stamps I collected. I wrote stories about the photographs I had saved. And I became a lot more excited about keeping a diary because so much of what I wrote about had personal meaning to me. To this day I still put lots of junk in my notebooks and write about it. The junk and stuff has become the details in much of my

Tragedy results from sixteen-year-old Walker's participation in a witch-hunt against two lesbian classmates in Gantos's novel for young adults. (Woodcut by Jose Francisco Borges.)

writing." While in Barbados, Gantos attended British schools that emphasized the importance of reading and writing; he claims that by fifth grade he had managed to learn ninety percent of what he knows now. When the family moved from Barbados to south Florida, Gantos found that his new classmates were less interested in their studies and that his teachers generally acted more as disciplinarians than as instructors. Consequently, he retreated to an abandoned bookmobile and read. Gantos began collecting anecdotes—many of which he over-heard standing outside of the teacher's lounge—in the sixth grade. In addition, he began writing down his own thoughts and feelings. Gantos told *SATA,* "Most of the stories were from real life. I saw a plane crash and wrote about it. My father rescued a drowning husband and wife in the ocean. He was heroic, and I wrote about it. Once my sister accidentally started a grease fire in the kitchen. The whole house almost burned down but my mom was only thankful that we were safe. She wasn't even angry, and I wrote about how she loved us. I wrote many more stories from my life." Many of these stories were later to provide the inspiration for the author's "Jack Henry" series.

In junior high, Gantos went to a school that had once been a state prison. Once again, he spent most of his time reading outside of the classroom. Gantos decided to become a professional writer when he was in high school. He told an interviewer from Amazon.com, "[M]y diary and journal writing background gave me a lot of confidence that writing was something I had loved all my life." After graduating from high school, Gantos left Florida to attend Emerson College in Boston. While at Emerson, Gantos met art student Nicole Rubel; the pair became friends and decided to work together on picture books for children. Gantos wrote in *Fifth Book of Junior Authors and Illustrators,* "She had illustrated a book without words and when I saw it I asked for permission to write the story. We started that way." The author told *SATA,* "I made a lot of mistakes. I thought children's books had to be sweet, warm, and gen-tle . . . . " After Gantos received his first rejection letters, he was frustrated. "Then," he recalled, "I remembered what one of my teachers had told me. She said, 'Write about what you know.' I was sitting at my desk and I looked down at the floor and saw my lousy, grumpy, hissing creep of a cat that loved to scratch my ankles, throw fur around the house, and shred the clothes in my closet." His cat became Rotten Ralph, and a new antihero was born. Gantos's first book, *Rotten Ralph,* was published in 1976, the year that he received his B.F.A. in creative writing from Emerson College and decided to become a freelance writer. Gantos told *SATA,* "It was a great day when I saw that first published book. All the hard work had paid off."

In *Rotten Ralph* the title character indulges in bad behavior at home, such as crashing his bike into the dining room table; sawing the tree limb that supports the swing of his owner, Sarah; and wearing Father's slippers. Sarah's family takes him to the circus, but Ralph misbehaves so badly that he is left there as punishment. While in the circus, Ralph becomes unhappy as a performer, and he runs away. He is found, ill and underfed, by Sarah, who welcomes him back home. It appears that Ralph has learned his lesson and will become less rotten, but Gantos gives indications that Ralph will continue to be his impish self. Writing in *Language Arts,* Ruth M. Stein called *Rotten Ralph* a "successful first book by both author and illustrator." Although Zena Sutherland of *Bulletin of the Center for Children's Books* noted, "There's some humor in the situation, but it seems overworked," *Washington Post Book World* critic Brigitte Weeks called *Rotten Ralph* "a moral tale" that children will "highly appreciate" for seeing a cat in trouble instead of a child.

In subsequent volumes of the series, Ralph continues to be naughty and to get away with it. He ruins Christmas, Thanksgiving, Halloween, Valentine's Day, Show and Tell, birthday parties, and even a wedding. In addition, Ralph engages in such activities as teasing his cousin Percy, a sweet, well-mannered cat of whom he is jealous; rubbing garbage and dog food on himself so as not to have to kiss Petunia, the host of a Valentine's Day party that he does not want to attend; leading a trio of neighborhood alley cats on a day-long spree in order to show them that he is not a softy because he is a house cat; trying to prevent Sarah from making new friends at school; clawing his way into Santa Claus's sack on Christmas Eve; and stealing Aunt Martha's wedding bouquet, which he presents to Sarah as a peace offering. In *Not So Rotten, Ralph,* Sarah—who, at her most exasperated, simply chastises Ralph mildly—takes him to Mr. Fred's Feline Finishing School, where he is hypnotized into good behavior; however, Sarah misses the old, mischievous Ralph, and successfully lures him back into his natural state. In all of the books in the series, Sarah always gives Ralph her unconditional love, no matter how many stunts he pulls.

Critics have noted that Ralph, with his tricks, ploys, and demands for attention, is very much like a child, and that children are attracted to his gleeful overindulgence. In addition, reviewers have acknowledged that Ralph is popular with children because he ultimately gets away with his crimes and is still accepted by Sarah, who is described as having "the patience of a saint" by one *Publishers Weekly* contributor in a review of *Rotten Ralph's Trick or Treat.* In their review of *Rotten Ralph's Rotten Christmas,* Donnarae MacCann and Olga Richard stated, "Rotten Ralph may be satirizing the arrested development of the spoiled child, but the character of Sarah serves as a wry comment upon overindulgent parents." Ann A. Flowers of *Horn Book* added, "It is a pleasure to see big, red, devilish Ralph up to his old tricks and acting like a jealous child; he is convincing and might even bring some understanding to children with the same problem." Writing in the *Horn Book* about *Rotten Ralph's Rotten Romance,* Elizabeth S. Watson said, "It's no wonder kids love Ralph—what a perfect vicarious way to get back at all those well-meaning adults who make you go to parties where everyone else seems to be having a great time." Assessing the same title in *Booklist,* Stephanie Zvirin commented that this work, like all of the books in the series, "allows children the vicarious thrill of being unabashedly naughty. But at the same time it provides assurance that even in the face of bad behavior they'll still be loved—something worth talking about."

Not all observers, though, are fond of Rotten Ralph. For example, a reviewer in *Children's Book Review Service* called *Worse than Rotten, Ralph* a "do-it-yourself guide to mayhem which can be summed up in a few phrases—ridiculous, garish, and makes no sense," while *School Library Journal* critic Mary B. Nickerson added, "The unrelieved, gratuitous mayhem is, depending on one's age, either boring or threatening." John Peters, writing about *Rotten Ralph's Trick or Treat* in *School Library Journal,* noted that "the humor has worn too thin, and Ralph has no redeeming qualities." However, most reviewers find Ralph's adventures both amusing and appealing and extol Gantos's slyly written texts and Rubel's psychedelic line drawings. In his review of *Back to School for Rotten Ralph* in *Booklist,* Michael Cart called Ralph "a cat so rambunctiously rotten that you've just gotta love him," while a reviewer for *Horn Book* added, "Gantos's skillful examination of the child's world is once again evident as the author probes a common negative emotion and suggests, but never preaches, a positive outcome." Ilene Cooper, writing in *Booklist* about *Wedding Bells for Rotten Ralph,* puts it succinctly: "Wow, is this cat rotten!"

In addition to their works about Rotten Ralph, Gantos and Rubel have collaborated on several other picture books. They began with *Sleepy Ronald,* a book about a little rabbit whose constant sleepiness—on roller skates, on the diving board, in the bathroom, and in rehearsals for a Wagnerian opera—brings him trouble until his friend Priscilla realizes that Ronald's ears droop over his eyes and fool him into thinking that it is nighttime. A critic in *Kirkus Reviews* concluded, "A limp ending if ever we heard one, especially since Rubel's ... palette is bright enough to wake the dead." However, *School Library Journal* reviewer Allene Stuart Phy called Ronald "the funniest rabbit to appear in some time," and Betsy Hearne of *Booklist* called the book "pretty farfetched, but ... pretty funny, too." In *Aunt Bernice,* young Ida's parents are going away for the summer, so her Aunt Bernice and her dog, Rex, come to babysit. Aunt Bernice's behavior—such as laughing at a mushy movie, which gets her and Ida kicked out of the theater, and dressing up as a gorilla to scare Ida's friends at a slumber party—embarrasses her niece, and Rex drools and gets his fleas all over everything. Finally, Ida realizes that she is growing fond of Bernice and Rex despite their shortcomings. A reviewer for *Publishers Weekly* commented, "The spiffy nonsense of Gantos is perfectly complemented, once more, by Rubel's nutty, brashly colored cartoons. Like *Rotten Ralph* and their other books, their new one is a comic masterpiece." A critic in *Kirkus Reviews* similarly stated that "for the first time since *Rotten Ralph,* Gantos's story provides a suitable outlet for Rubel's manic energy."

Besides children and anthropomorphic animals, Gantos and Rubel also use supernatural figures as the main characters in their picture books. In *Greedy Greeny,* a little green monster has a nightmare after eating the watermelon that his mother was saving for dinner—as well as everything else in the refrigerator. Greeny dreams that he has become the watermelon and that he is going to be served to his family; his shouts awaken his mother, who calms and forgives him. Writing in *Booklist,* Denise M. Wilms stated, "Humorously didactic, this picture book has the kind of tight, well-placed plot and comic elements that make it a good, working story.... Appealing, even if the off-beat isn't your cup of tea," while a critic for *Kirkus Reviews* called *Greedy Greeny* a "holy terror of a guilt dream" and a "close-to-home fantasy" before concluding that the book is "[f]ar-out fun with a firm base." In *The Werewolf Family* two werewolf parents and their two werewolf children come to a party on the night of the full moon. The family is the picture of decorum before their transformations. However, after they become werewolves, the family dispenses spiders and snakes to babies and puts the other guests in medieval torture instruments such as racks and hanging manacles before returning home. A critic for *Kirkus Reviews* noted, "If you can accept a sort of Rocky Horror Show equivalent for the picture-book set, Gantos and Rubel are the pair to give it punch." A reviewer for *Children's Book Service* said, "Aside from being dull, this story ... is also distasteful and possibly offensive." However, Patricia Homer concluded in *School Library Journal* that *The Werewolf Family* "really does take advantage of the immense popularity of monsters and the macabre, but children are bound to be attracted."

While writing his picture books in collaboration with Rubel, Gantos began working part-time at Emerson College as a writing instructor. After receiving his master's degree in creative writing from Emerson, Gantos became an associate professor of creative writing and literature there. He married art dealer Anne A. Lower in 1989; the couple have a daughter, Mabel Grace. In 1993, Gantos became Graduate Coordinator for the M.A. degree in creative and professional writing at Emerson and also built the M.A./M.F.A. degree concentration in children's book writing and literature.

In 1994, Gantos produced the first of his "Jack Henry" books, *Heads or Tails: Stories from the Sixth Grade.* In this collection of autobiographical and semi-autobiographical vignettes, Jack, who has lived in nine houses and has gone to five schools because of his dad's desire to find a better job by moving from place to place, is living in southern Florida. The text, which is written in diary form, is accompanied by samples of Jack's handwriting and photocopied items such as a mouse skin and a squashed bug. Jack gets into situations with family, friends, and neighbors and at school. He fights with his know-it-all sister, attends the funeral of his maternal grandfather, sees his dog eaten by an alligator, and generally tries to do the right thing but lands in trouble. However, Jack bounces back, and in the process performs what Michael Cart called in *School Library Journal* "acts of unself-conscious kindness." Cart continued, "Jack's a survivor, an 'everyboy' whose world may be wacko but whose heart and spirit are eminently sane and generous." In his conclusion, Cart called *Heads or Tails* a "memorable book" and Gantos a "terrific writer with a wonderfully wry sensibility, a real talent for turning artful phrases, and a gift for creating memorable characters." A *Publishers Weekly* reviewer commented that the author "makes an auspicious foray into new ground" and concluded that a "bittersweet resonance filters the humor in these stories and lingers most welcomely."

In the second volume of the series, *Jack's New Power: Stories from a Caribbean Year,* Jack and his family have moved from Florida to Barbados. Among his other adventures, Jack makes new friends, thinks his parents are lost at sea, gets his heart broken, sees his dad rescue a drowning couple who turn out to be English royalty, loses his birthday money to a shady friend of his father's, and searches for a lost boy who turns up dead. He also thinks that he has gained the power to make things happen and, in the process of trying to be a man, conquers his fear of horses. As in the first volume, Gantos presents readers with both laughable moments and serious thoughts. Writing in *Booklist,* Susan Dove Lempke said that "the eight stories here convey with

sharp humor Jack's uncomfortable yet exhilarating early adolescence." The critic concluded that readers will "anxiously await the next installment of Jack's life." Elizabeth S. Watson added in *Horn Book* that, as in the first book in the collection, "the first-person narrative authentically reproduces the language and observations of twelve-year-olds. Quirky and funny with some good advice subtly inserted."

In *Jack's Black Book* Jack is back in Florida after the end of his seventh-grade year. Deciding that he wants to be a serious writer, Jack buys a black book in which to write a novel. His junior high, a former detention center, is a magnet school for training in shop; consequently, the pressure is on him to do well in this subject. Jack makes a dog coffin for his class project, and then has to dig out his dead dog in order to pass seventh grade. When he tries to make a summer business by writing postcards for hire, Jack loses out when a client, a prisoner out on furlough, doesn't like his work and tosses his typewriter into the ocean. Hanging out with his next-door neighbor, juvenile delinquent Gary Pagoda, Jack gets a tattoo of his dead dog on his big toe. He decides to give up his schemes to concentrate on just being himself. A critic for *Kirkus Reviews* noted that Gantos "trots out one disgusting and dangerous event after another to give his morose protagonist material for jokes." The critic added, "With a mean-spirited reliance on shock and cheap laughs, the book gets some tacked-on introspection at the end." Writing in *Horn Book,* a reviewer noted, "There's enough descriptive disaster, some good solid writing, and a bizarre plot that even reluctant adults can't help but appreciate."

Gantos is also the author of *Jack on the Tracks: Four Seasons of Fifth Grade,* a prequel to the other volumes in the "Jack Henry" series. In this book, Jack bonds with his father when he eats a fifty-pound steak, accidentally kills his cat, writes a gross story that appalls his teacher, is locked out of the house naked for putting a live roach in his sister's mouth, and hides from what he thinks are two escaped convicts (actually two of his friends) by lying in a shallow hole along the railroad tracks as a train passes overhead. Jack also wonders why he cries all the time, tries to exercise more self-control, and resolves to do the adult thing rather than the childish one. Writing in *Booklist,* Susan Dove Lempke stated, "[Gantos's] books about Jack Henry ... succeed precisely because they present a hilarious, exquisitely painful, and utterly on-target depiction of the life of an adolescent and preadolescent boy."

Gantos became a full professor at Emerson College in 1995. The next year he went to Vermont College, where he became a core faculty member, designed the M.F.A. program, and taught a class on writing for children before returning to Emerson. He has also been a visiting professor at other universities. Gantos produced *Zip Six,* an adult novel, in 1996. In this work, a drug dealer meets an Elvis impersonator in prison, becomes his manager on the prison circuit, and is betrayed by him on the outside. In 1997 Gantos published *Desire Lines,* a young adult novel about sixteen-year-old Walker, a loner who lives in Fort Lauderdale, Florida, and spends much of his time alone on a golf course. Walker has been spying on two classmates, Karen and Jennifer, who have been making love at a duck pond on the course. When an anonymous teenage preacher comes to the school trying to enlist students for the hate group headed by his father, a minister who builds a church in the town, the boy tries to entice Walker, who refuses to participate. The boy then tries to blackmail Walker by accusing him of being gay. In order to prove his masculinity, Walker forms an alliance with three tough classmates in a gang they call the Box. When the Box members desecrate the new church and Walker is caught, the boys in the Box turn on him and pressure him to identify gays at their school. Walker outs Karen and Jennifer to save himself. When Karen confronts him at school, she asks Walker if he was the person who identified her and her lover, but he refuses to admit the truth. At the duck pond, Walker watches while Karen shoots Jennifer, then herself, in a suicide pact. Jennifer dies, but Karen survives to come back to school, where she again confronts Walker. Walker learns that the Box ratted him out. However, he still refuses to acknowledge his act to Karen. At the end of the novel, Walker is left alone with his guilt. A critic noted in *Publishers Weekly,* "Gantos projects an unsettling image of cowardice and survival of the toughest.... The author reduces the players of this drama to near-stereotypes whose 'desire lines' (chosen paths) are not all that different; in doing so he transmits a one-sided (and pessimistic) view of humanity." A critic in *Kirkus Reviews* stated that Gantos "is explicit when demonstrating how a climate of fear and suspicion can be concocted in a community, and how insecure young people—gay, straight—can be tormented by it."

In 1998 Gantos published what has become one of his most critically acclaimed works: *Joey Pigza Swallowed the Key.* In this book, which is directed at middle graders, Joey, a boy in the early primary grades, has attention deficit disorder (ADD) and hyperactivity. He inadvertently does things like swallowing his house key, cutting off his fingernail in a pencil sharpener, and slicing off the tip of his classmate's nose while running with a pair of scissors. Sent to a special education center for six weeks, he is given regulated medication and learns how to manage his behavior. Joey feels strong and hopeful when his treatment is completed. At the end of the story, he returns to his old school, where he is allowed to sit and read in the Big Quiet Chair. Throughout the book, which is narrated by Joey with flashes of humor, readers learn that he has been emotionally abused by his grandmother, who, like Joey, is hyperactive. *Horn Book* critic Jennifer M. Brabandee noted that Joey's "own brand of goodness has an unaffected charm and an uncloying sweetness. Joey is always explaining to people that he's a good kid; readers of this compelling tragicomedy will know almost from the start that Joey's not just a good kid—he's a great kid." Susan Dove Lempke added in *Booklist,* "Most teachers and students know at least one child with attention deficit hyperactivity disorder (ADHD), and this book will surely help them become more understanding, even as they enjoy Gantos's fresh writing style and tart

sense of humor." Writing in *School Library Journal,* Shawn Brommer commented, "from the powerful opening lines and fast-moving plot to the thoughtful inner dialogue and satisfying conclusions, readers will cheer for Joey, and for the champion in each of us."

A frequent speaker at schools, libraries, conferences, and festivals, Gantos is also the facilitator of writing workshops on children's literature for students and teachers. Regarding his literary career, Gantos once said, "I write for children because they are sincere and authentic in their reactions. I write for adults because I am an adult and I need to write about subjects, dreams, and characters outside the limited scope of the children's genre. I enjoy my work as much as possible. I read good books and I want to write good books." Writing in *Fifth Book of Junior Authors and Illustrators,* Gantos said, "There are many myths as to what a children's book writer is: perhaps a socially retarded adult, a dreamer who lives in a pink bubble, a moral pervert. I don't care if writers are all of the above as long as they write great fiction for children." Gantos once told *SATA* that he was passing by the window of a book store where copies of *Rotten Ralph* were on display: "Several children were

Seventh-grader Jack buys a black book in which to write a novel about his hilarious misadventures. (Cover illustration by Beata Szpura.)

chanting 'Rotten Ralph ... Rotten Ralph ... Rotten Ralph ...' over and over. For a writer to receive such sincere attention is rare. They are a good audience and deserve good books."

Biographical and Critical Sources

BOOKS

Children's Literature Review, Volume 18, Gale, 1989, pp. 140-43.

Holtze, Sally Holmes, editor, *Fifth Book of Junior Authors and Illustrators,* H. W. Wilson Co. (New York City), 1983.

PERIODICALS

Booklist, October 1, 1976, Betsy Hearne, review of *Sleepy Ronald,* p. 251; October 15, 1979, Denise M. Wilms, review of *Greedy Greeny,* p. 351; December 1, 1995, Susan Dove Lempke, review of *Jack's New Power,* p. 616; November 15, 1996, Stephanie Zvirin, review of *Rotten Ralph's Rotten Romance,* p. 593; August, 1998, Michael Cart, review of *Back to School for Rotten Ralph,* p. 201; December 15, 1998, Susan Dove Lempke, review of *Joey Pigza Swallowed the Key,* p. 752; June 1, 1999, Ilene Cooper, review of *Wedding Bells for Rotten Ralph;* September 1, 1999, Susan Dove Lempke, review of *Jack on the Tracks,* p. 132.

Bulletin of the Center for Children's Books, July, 1976, Zena Sutherland, review of *Rotten Ralph,* p. 174.

Children's Book Review Service, November, 1978, review of *Worse than Rotten, Ralph,* p. 22; December, 1980, review of *The Werewolf Family,* p. 24.

Emergency Librarian, November 1, 1997.

Horn Book Magazine, November-December, 1984, Ann A. Flowers, review of *Rotten Ralph's Rotten Christmas,* p. 740; March-April, 1996, Elizabeth S. Watson, review of *Jack's New Power,* p. 231; November-December, 1996, Elizabeth S. Watson, review of *Rotten Ralph's Rotten Romance,* p. 723; January, 1998, review of *Jack's Black Book,* p. 70; September, 1998, review of *Back to School for Rotten Ralph,* p. 598; November-December, 1998, Jennifer M. Brabandee, review of *Joey Pigza Swallowed the Key,* pp. 729-30.

Kirkus Reviews, August 15, 1976, review of *Sleepy Ronald,* p. 903; February 15, 1978, review of *Aunt Bernice,* pp. 173-74; February 1, 1980, review of *Greedy Greeny,* pp. 120-21; October 1, 1980, review of *The Werewolf Family,* p. 1293; February 15, 1997, review of *Desire Lines;* August 1, 1997, review of *Jack's Black Book,* p. 1221.

Language Arts, May, 1977, Ruth M. Stein, review of *Rotten Ralph,* p. 582.

Publisher's Weekly, February 6, 1978, review of *Aunt Bernice,* p. 101; August 22, 1988, review of *Rotten Ralph's Trick or Treat,* p. 95; June 6, 1994, review of *Heads or Tails,* p. 66; February 24, 1997, review of *Desire Lines,* p. 92.

School Library Journal, October, 1976, Allene Stuart Phy, review of *Sleepy Ronald,* p. 97; October, 1978, Mary B. Nickerson, review of *Worse than Rotten, Ralph,* p. 132; October, 1980, Patricia Homer, review of *The Werewolf Family,* p. 134; October, 1986, John Peters, review of *Rotten Ralph's Trick or Treat,* p. 160; June,

1994, Michael Cart, review of *Heads or Tails,* p. 128; November, 1995, p. 119; December, 1998, Shawn Brommer, review of *Joey Pigza Swallowed the Key,* p. 124.

Teaching Pre-K-8, March, 1996.

Washington Post Book World, June 13, 1976, Brigitte Weeks, review of *Rotten Ralph,* p. 112.

Wilson Library Bulletin, February, 1985, Donnarae MacCann and Olga Richard, review of *Rotten Ralph's Rotten Christmas,* p. 404.

ON-LINE

Amazon.com, www.amazon.com (April 28, 2000).*

—*Sketch by Gerard J. Senick*

*   *   *

GOLDBERG, Whoopi 1955-
(Caryn E. Johnson)

Personal

Born Caryn E. Johnson, November 13, 1955 (some sources give dates ranging from 1949 to 1954), in New York, NY; daughter of Emma (a nurse and teacher) Johnson; married, 1962 (divorced 1974); married David Edward Claessen (a cinematographer), September, 1986 (divorced, 1988); married Lyle Trachtenberg (a labor organizer), c. 1994 (divorced c. 1995); children: (first marriage) Alexandrea Martin.

Addresses

Home—New York. *Agent*—William Morris Agency, 151 El Camino Dr., Beverly Hills, CA 90212.

Career

Actress. Worked variously as a bank teller, bricklayer, and mortuary cosmetologist, 1974 to late 1970s; comedienne, first with the Blake Street Hawkeyes Theater and later as one-woman show, late 1970s to 1985; film, television, and theater actress and comedienne, 1985—. Works with numerous charitable organizations, often in a fund-raising capacity, including the Comic Relief series, which raises money for AIDS research.

Actress in films, including *The Color Purple,* Warner Bros., 1985; *Jumpin' Jack Flash,* Twentieth Century-Fox/Lawrence Gordon/Silver Pictures, 1986; *Fatal Beauty,* Metro-Goldwyn-Mayer, 1987; *Burglar,* Warner Bros., 1987; *The Telephone,* 1988; *Clara's Heart,* Warner Bros., 1988; *Beverly Hills Brats,* 1989; *Homer & Eddie,* Kings Road, 1989; *The Long Walk Home,* New Visions, 1990; *Ghost,* Paramount, 1990; *Wisecracks,* 1991; *House Party 2,* 1991; *Soapdish,* Paramount, 1991; *Sarafina!,* Hollywood Pictures, 1992; *The Magical World of Chuck Jones,* 1992; *The Player,* Guild/Spelling Entertainment/Avenue, 1992; *Sister Act,* Touchstone, 1992; *Loaded Weapon 1* (also known as *National Lampoon's Loaded Weapon 1*), Three Arts Entertainment/New Line Cinema, 1993; *Made in America,*

Warner Bros., 1993; *Sister Act 2: Back in the Habit,* Touchstone, 1993; *The Lion King* (animated), Disney, 1994; *Liberation,* 1994; *Naked in New York,* 1994; *Corrina Corrina,* New Line Cinema, 1994; *Star Trek: Generations,* Paramount, 1994; *The Pagemaster* (animated), Twentieth Century-Fox, 1994; *The Little Rascals,* Universal/Amblin, 1994; *The Celluloid Closet,* Brillstein-Grey Entertainment/Sony/Telling, 1995; *Boys on the Side,* Warner Bros., 1995; *Moonlight and Valentino,* Gramercy/Working Title/Polygram, 1995; *Theodore Rex* (also know as *T. Rex*), J & M Entertainment/New Line Cinema/Shooting Star Entertainment, 1995; *Bogus,* Warner Bros., 1996; *The Associate,* Buena Vista/Hollywood Pictures/Interscope/Polygram, 1996; *Ghosts of Mississippi* (also known as *Ghosts from the Past*), Castle Rock/Columbia, 1996; *In & Out,* Paramount, 1997; *An Alan Smithee Film: Burn Hollywood Burn* (also known as *An Alan Smithee Film and Burn Hollywood Burn*), Cinergi/Hollywood Pictures, 1997; *State and Maine,* 1998; *How Stella Got Her Groove Back,* Twentieth Century-Fox, 1998; and *The Deep End of the Ocean,* Via Rosa/Columbia/Mandalay, 1998.

Actress in television series, including *Star Trek: The Next Generation,* syndicated, 1988-94; *Bagdad Café,* CBS, 1990; *Captain Planet and the Planeteers* (animated), syndicated, 1990; (host) *The Whoopi Goldberg Show,* 1992; and (host) *Hollywood Squares,* 1998. Guest on television series, movies, award shows, and specials, including *Rock the Vote,* MTV; *Moonlighting,* ABC, 1985; *A Different World,* NBC, 1987; *Dolly,* ABC, 1987; *Kiss Shot,* 1989; *Happy Birthday, Bugs!: Fifty Looney Years,* 1990; *The Sunshine Boys,* 1995; *Muppets Tonight,* 1996; (host) *The 1996 Academy Awards Show,* 1996; *Tales from the Crypt Presents: Bordello of Blood* (also known as *Bordello of Blood*), Universal, 1996; *Cinderella* (also known as *Rodgers & Hammerstein's Cinderella*), Walt Disney, 1997; and *In the Gloaming,* 1997. Appears in music videos, including *Aretha Franklin's Jumping Jack Flash; Bonnie Raitt's You Got It; Voices that Care;* and *Michael Jackson's Liberian Girl.* Appeared in commercials for MCI Friends & Family long distance, 1995.

Awards, Honors

Drama Desk Award for outstanding one-person show, 1984-85; Image Award, National Association for the Advancement of Colored People (NAACP), 1985; Grammy Award for best comedy recording, 1985, for *Whoopi Goldberg: Direct from Broadway;* Golden Globe Award for best actress in a dramatic role, and Academy Award nomination for best actress, both 1986, both for *The Color Purple;* Image Award, NAACP, 1990; British Academy of Film and Television Arts Award for best actress in a supporting role, 1990, Academy Award for best supporting actress, Golden Globe award for best performance by an actress in a supporting role in a motion picture, American Comedy Award for funniest supporting female—motion picture, all 1991, all for *Ghost;* Woman of the Year, Hasty Pudding Club, 1993; Golden Globe nomination for best performance by an actress in a motion picture—comedy/

Whoopi Goldberg

musical, 1993, for *Sister Act;* ShoWest Award, female star of the year, 1993; Image Award nominations, NAACP, 1996, for *Boys on the Side* and *Happily Ever After: Fairy Tales for Every Child;* Image Award nomination, NAACP, 1997, for *Ghosts of Mississippi;* Image Award nomination, NAACP, 1998, for *Cinderella;* also recipient of numerous other awards.

Writings

Alice (for children), illustrated by John Rocco, Bantam (New York City), 1992.
Book (autobiography), R. Weisbach (New York City), 1997.

Also author of scripts for one-woman comedy shows, including *Moms,* 1984.

SOUND RECORDINGS

Whoopi Goldberg, Geffen, 1985.
(With others) *The Best of Comic Relief,* Rhino, 1986.
Fontaine: Why Am I Straight?, MCA Records, 1988.
(With others) *The Best of Comic Relief 2,* Rhino, 1988.
(With others) *The Best of Comic Relief 3,* Rhino, 1989.
(With others) *The Best of Comic Relief '90,* Rhino, 1990.

Also performed as reader on Joel Chandler Harris's *Jump!: The Adventures of Brer Rabbit,* adapted by Van

Dyke Parks and Malcolm Jones, Harcourt (San Diego, CA), 1990.

Sidelights

In 1992 actress, comedienne, and activist Whoopi Goldberg added "writer" to her list of occupations with the publication of *Alice,* an adaptation of Lewis Carroll's *Alice in Wonderland.* Goldberg's Alice is a young, African-American girl living in New York City who dreams of becoming rich. She enters numerous lotteries, and finally one day she wins what she believes is a great sum of money. Together with her friend Robin (a variation on Carroll's Mad Hatter character) and an invisible rabbit named Sal, she boards a bus for Manhattan—the equivalent of the original Alice's slide into the rabbit hole—to claim her prize. Downtown she finds unscrupulous adults who try to cheat her out of her prize, but she manages to hold on to her winning ticket, only to find that it's worthless: the ticket only qualifies her to purchase a piece of swampland property in Florida. A fortune teller delivers the story's moral: "Dear, you are rich. Look at your wonderful friends who stick by you whether you win or lose. Think about the wild adventure you've had. No amount of money could buy these things." Suzanne Curley, writing in the *Los Angeles Times Book Review,* conceded that Carroll would "probably not" approve of Goldberg's adaptation, but also commended "Whoopi's breezy storytelling" and asked, "wouldn't you love to see Whoopi bring [Carroll's] 'Jabberwocky' into the 20th Century?"

In her career Goldberg has overcome a number of adverse situations—including critical reactions to a string of failed movies between the high points marked by *The Color Purple* in 1985 and her Academy Award-winning comeback with *Ghost* in 1990. Before her break into stardom in 1983 with a successful Broadway show, she had been a single mother on welfare, and before that she had struggled with drug addiction.

It must, however, be noted that aspects of Goldberg's life story are subject to debate. She was born Caryn E. Johnson in New York City in 1955, though some sources identify the year as between 1949 and 1954. By some accounts she was raised in poverty, though according to Nancy Jo Sales in *New York,* "As public housing goes, the Chelsea Projects" where Goldberg lived as a child "aren't actually that bad." As for tales that she was "a teenage junkie from the ghetto," Sales wrote, "In fact, Caryn Johnson was a nice Catholic-school girl." Sales quoted a former neighbor as saying, "I don't know why she goes around saying she was a drug addict and all that stuff. I knew her mother. Caryn was a nice girl." According to Sales, Goldberg herself told *Newsday* that the media had exaggerated the facts of her own involvement with drugs, which invited easy stereotypes: "[Drug abuse] coupled with the fact that I'm black! From the ghetto! On welfare! My mother was like, 'Excuse me? I don't think so.' She was, uh-huh, very agitated."

But perhaps the most important and indisputable fact about Goldberg's childhood is that she dreamed of becoming a star from the beginning. Life was certainly not easy in her home: she and her brother were raised by a single mother, Emma Johnson, after her father abandoned them, and with her offbeat personality, Goldberg was not popular in school. She found release in movies, often watching three or four a day. Her favorite was *It Happened One Night,* starring Clark Gable and Claudette Colbert. During the broadcast of the Academy Awards each year, she would stand up in the living room of the family's small apartment and regale her mother and brother with the acceptance speeches she would one day make. At the age of eight, her mother enrolled her in acting classes at the Helena Rubinstein Children's Theater, and she briefly attended New York's prestigious High School of the Performing Arts.

But Goldberg dropped out of high school, at which time the much-vaunted drug episodes began. Whatever the extent of her involvement with LSD or (as some accounts say) heroin, the situation was serious enough that she went into treatment. Goldberg ultimately married her drug counselor, with whom she had a daughter, but the two were soon divorced. In 1974 a friend gave her a one-way ticket to Los Angeles, and Goldberg, taking her daughter Alexandrea with her, headed west. She found her way to San Diego, where she became involved in the theater while working various jobs, including stints as a bank teller, a bricklayer, and a cosmetologist responsible for making up the faces of corpses in a mortuary. During this time she also began to adopt the stage name "Whoopi Cushion" (which she pronounced with a French accent, as "koo-SHAWN"), after a well-known novelty item that makes an flatulent sound when someone sits on it. Her mother said the name sounded absurd, so she changed the last name to Goldberg, thus playing on the equally bizarre idea of a black woman with a Jewish name.

In 1980 Goldberg and her partner in comedy shows, Don Victor, had an opportunity to perform in San Francisco, but Victor quit before they even had a chance to begin. She opted to move north anyway, and in Berkeley she began to develop a comic routine that involved numerous characters. Many of these combined humor with biting social commentary. The brainless "Surfer Chick," it turns out, has become that way because of a coat-hanger abortion she performed on herself; in another role, a black girl washes herself with bleach in a futile attempt to look white.

On the success of her show, Goldberg began to tour the United States, and in 1984 enjoyed a big break with a show on Broadway. More successes followed as renowned film director Mike Nichols offered to produce her show. Nor was Nichols the only influential figure impressed by her talents: director Steven Spielberg invited her to appear in his upcoming film adaptation of Alice Walker's novel *The Color Purple.* Through her starring role as Celie in Spielberg's 1985 film, Goldberg quickly became a superstar. A few years before, she had gone on welfare to support herself and her daughter; now she was nominated for an Academy Award.

But the Oscar she had dreamed of eluded her that year, and for many years that followed, as she appeared in a string of films that failed either with critics or fans or both. She continued to command enormous salaries for her pictures, including more than two million dollars in 1987 for *Fatal Beauty,* a film that earned only eleven million dollars. Meanwhile, critics had begun to speculate that Goldberg's career had already peaked; then, in 1990, success came in an unlikely package.

The supernatural love story *Ghost* had not seemed like a potential blockbuster: traditionally the fourth of July weekend is a significant release date for summer movies, and it came out after the holiday. In addition, it faced competition from such big-budget action thrillers as *Die Hard 2* and *Total Recall,* which starred Arnold Schwarzenegger. But *Ghost* became a surprise hit, the largest money-maker of 1990 with nearly 198 million dollars in domestic box-office receipts. For her role as the high-spirited con woman Oda Mae Brown, a psychic, Goldberg received an Oscar nomination—and this time she won. On March 25, 1991, Goldberg finally got to make the acceptance speech she had spent years composing. Goldberg was only the second black woman in film history, after Hattie McDaniel's award for *Gone with the Wind* in 1939, to win an Oscar for best supporting actress.

Some of Goldberg's subsequent films were successes, including *Sister Act* in 1992; others—including the 1993 sequel, for which she received eight million dollars— were not. In the latter year, her career hit a low point from a public relations standpoint: "I will be surprised," she told Sales in 1997, "if your editor doesn't say, 'Remind them about the Friars Club.'" At a celebrity roast at the prestigious Friar's Club, she and Danson, the former star of TV's *Cheers,* appeared in blackface, a form of makeup by which white vaudeville actors at the turn of the century made themselves appear to be black, which is now considered a symbol of racism and derogatory attitudes toward African Americans. Furthermore, the script of Danson and Goldberg's "comedy" routine—much of which she wrote—was filled with offensive racial, sexual, and scatological terminology.

Goldberg and Danson ceased to be romantically involved, but she weathered the sharp criticism that came in the wake of the Friar's Club incident. She also endured sometimes negative critiques of her films. By 1997 she was "tired of movies," she told Sales, and was rehearsing to appear in a Broadway production of the musical *A Funny Thing Happened on the Way to the Forum.* She was also involved with actor Frank Langella, whom she had met while making the movie *Eddie* (1996). Setting the stage for her interview, Sales described the unlikely-looking couple: "It's 10 a.m. and Whoopi's draped in a coarse beige tunic and roomy pants, athletic socks, floppy shoes" whereas Langella "has got on a pair of pants so soft you could polish diamonds with them; a shirt so white it seems to glow."

Other contrasts abound, not least of which is the fact that Goldberg is black and Langella (like Danson and most of her companions in the past) is white. Whereas Goldberg is flamboyant, Langella is soft-spoken and reserved. But as Sales went on to show, the pairing of opposites constituted a form of completion. Goldberg had dreamed of becoming Langella's friend, she said, since first seeing him in a movie when she was fourteen years old. Langella recalled that while he was going through a divorce during the filming of *Eddie,* Goldberg gave him a book by German poet Rainer Maria Rilke. "I randomly opened it," he told Sales, "to see what I would read and how it would relate to us. It said that the tragedy of people when they fall in love young is that half a person falls in love with half a person. Rilke says wait, wait, wait, until you are mature and a whole person falls in love with a whole person." Langella, Sales wrote, "regards Whoopi with this unbridled sort of loving amazement." Describing their sense of completion in one another, Langella told Sales, "Whoopi often says we're like two broken toys trying to mend each other."

Biographical and Critical Sources

BOOKS

Adams, Mary Agnes, *Whoopi Goldberg: From Street to Stardom,* Dillon Press (New York City), 1993.

African American Almanac, sixth edition, Gale (Detroit, MI), 1994.

Blue, Rose, and Corinne J. Naden, *Whoopi Goldberg: Entertainer,* Chelsea House (New York City), 1995.

Contemporary Black Biography, Volume 4, Gale (Detroit, MI), 1993.

Contemporary Theater, Film, and Television, Volume 13, Gale (Detroit, MI), 1995.

DeBoer, Judy, *Whoopi Goldberg,* Creative Education (Mankato, MN), 1997.

Dictionary of Twentieth-Century Culture, Volume 5: *African American Culture,* Gale (Detroit, MI), 1996.

Katz, Sandy, *Whoopi Goldberg,* Chelsea House (Philadelphia), 1996.

Parrish, James Robert, and Don Stanke, *Hollywood Baby Boomers,* Garland (New York City), 1992.

Parrish, James Robert, *Whoopi Goldberg: Her Journey from Poverty to Mega-Stardom,* Carol Publishing (Secaucus, NJ), 1997.

Smith, Jessie Carney, *Notable Black American Women,* Gale (Detroit, MI), 1992.

Thomas, Nicholas, editor, *The International Directory of Films and Filmmakers,* Volume 3: *Actors and Actresses,* St. James (Detroit, MI), 1992.

Unterbrink, Mary, *Funny Women,* McFarland & Company (Jefferson, NC), 1987.

Who's Who among African Americans, Gale (Detroit, MI), 1994.

PERIODICALS

Advocate, September 15, 1998, review of *Hollywood Squares,* p. 20.

Adweek Eastern Edition, October 25, 1999, Simon Butler, "Makin' Whoopi," p. 5.

Booklist, November 1, 1992, p. 520; March 15, 1993, p. 1345; November 1, 1997, Cynthia Alexa, "Koi and the Kola Nuts," p. 494; September 15, 1999, Sue-Ellen Beauregard, "America's Libraries Change Lives," p. 272.

Bulletin of the Center for Children's Books, February, 1993, p. 176.

Entertainment Weekly, October 24, 1997, Alexandra Jacobs, review of *Book,* p. 60; September 18, 1998, Joe Flint, "The X & O Files," p. 52; November 27, 1998, Lisa Schwarzbaum, review of *The Rugrats Movie,* p. 56; October 24, 1997, p. 60; February 19, 1999, Ken Tucker, "Twasn't Brillig," p. 116; March 19, 1999, Lisa Schwarzbaum, "The Lost Boy," p. 68; April 2, 1999, Ken Tucker, p. 36; May 28, 1999, p. 148; December 3, 1999, Tricia Johnson, "Gimme Shelter," p. 18.

Harper's Bazaar, October, 1992, Mark Matousek, review of *Alice,* p. 72.

Interview, April, 1999, Wyclef Jean, "Whoopi Meets Wyclef," p. 66; October, 1999, p. 126.

Jet, November 3, 1997, "Whitney Houston and Brandy Star in TV Movie 'Cinderella,'" p. 44; December, 1998, p. 64; February 1, 1999, p. 36; April 5, 1999, "Whoopi Goldberg Delights Worldwide Audience as Host of 71st Annual Academy Awards," p. 55; April 12, 1999, Sylvia P. Flanagan, "The Deep End of the Ocean," p. 46; February 21, 2000, "Whoopi Sells Her Farm in Connecticut for $915,000," p. 34.

Ladies Home Journal, March 2000, Margie Friedman, "Whoopi's World," p. 82.

Library Journal, February 1, 1998, Susan McCaffrey, "Audiobook," p. 131.

Library Quarterly, January, 2000, Clara M. Chu, "America's Libraries Change Lives," p. 172.

Los Angeles Times Book Review, September 27, 1992, Suzanne Curley, review of *Alice,* p. 12.

Magpies, November, 1993, p. 34.

New York, September 14, 1992, p. 110; Nancy Jo Sales, February 17, 1997, pp. 40-45.

New York Times Book Review, November 8, 1992, p. 56.

Parents Magazine, December, 1992, p. 88.

People, June 6, 1994, p. 35; November 17, 1997, Mitchell Fink, "Whoopi Goldberg Has Sold an Idea to CBS for a Prime-Time Dramatic Series She Calls 'Harlem,'" p. 53; December 1, 1997, Thomas Fields-Meyer, review of *Book,* p. 52; August 24, 1998, p. 33; December 21, 1998, Terry Kelleher, "Hollywood Squares," p. 27; March 8, 1999, Chuck Arnold, "Chatter," p. 166; November 8, 1999, Terry Kelleher, "Tube," p. 31; January 17, 2000, p. 35; March 13, 2000, Samantha Miller, "Siteseeing on the Net," p. 23.

Publishers Weekly, November 3, 1997, "Audiobook," p. 41; January 11, 1999, p. 26.

School Librarian, August, 1993, p. 76.

School Library Journal, January, 1993, p. 76.

Variety, November 2, 1998, Ray Richmond, review of *A Knight in Camelot,* p. 36; February 22, 1999, Ray Richmond, "Alice in Wonderland," p. 88; March 1, 1999, Emanuel Levy, "The Deep End of the Ocean," p. 77; March 13, 2000, Bill Higgins, "Ruby for Whoopi," p. 51.*

GRAYSON, Devin (Kalile) 1970-

Personal

Born July 19, 1970, in New Haven, CT. *Education:* Graduate of Bard College; attended post-grad classes at University of California-Berkeley.

Career

Writer. Formerly worked for a health maintenance organization (HMO).

Writings

(With Yvel Guichet) *Relative Heroes* (comic book), DC Comics, 2000.

Also author of *Batman: Gotham Knights,* DC Comics, and "Like Riding a Bike," in *The Batman Chronicles #7,* DC Comics. Has also contributed to a *Batman Plus* special issue, and the *Catwoman* and *Nightwing* annuals for 1997.

Sidelights

Devin Grayson is notable for being the first woman to pen a regular Batman series of comics. Born in Connecticut and raised in San Francisco, Grayson is the daughter of left-wing political activists. She spent her youth dreaming of becoming an actor, and in pursuit of that goal participated in numerous Bay Area amateur theatrical productions. At Bard College, in up-state New York, Grayson fell into writing fiction in a sociology class when, for an assignment on an individual who had greatly influenced her, she invented a character named Flynn, whose exploits in the jungles of Zaire were brought to a tragic end in a waterfall accident. Grayson recounted the episode in the third person on her webpage on www.2kcomics.com: "Flynn was fond, apparently, of singing old Doris Day songs, and so as the essay ended on a quivering rendition of 'Que Sera, Sera,' Grayson looked up nervously to see her classmates deeply touched by Flynn's plight. After laughing herself sick in the college courtyard, Grayson began to pursue a career in fiction in earnest."

A youthful attempt at writing a novel was abandoned, however, when Grayson met and fell in love with Batman comics at the age of twenty-two. In 1997, she was given her first chance to write for the series, resulting in a story called "Like Riding a Bike," for the *Batman Chronicles #7.* In an interview with Cathy Grossman for CNN.com's WomenCONNECT.com, Grayson described the experience of being a novice comics writer: "What I brought to the table was, first and foremost, a dedicated willingness to learn. I got it right away that this was a very unique medium and that it was really going to challenge me as a writer. My joke is that given the strict (22-page) counts and the leanness of the dialogue, it's a little like writing haiku—the format and demands of the finished product are that arbitrary and that inflexible. I was also strongly self-motivated, crazy in love with the characters, and, perhaps most significantly, not a long-term comic fan. It's all new to me. Sometimes that means that I make ridiculous mistakes ... But sometimes it means that I come up with a new take on one of the classic elements of the superhero genre, or get something so totally wrong as to make it new and right again."

Grayson's original contribution to the superhero comics genre is called *Relative Heroes,* and it exemplifies the author's conviction that the "evil forces" in comics of the twenty-first century reside within the characters themselves. As Grayson told Grossman: "Whether it be a matter of destroying the ecological well-being of our home, or sacrificing the sacred trust of our families in astounding acts of violence and neglect, or disregarding the spiritual needs of our selves and our communities, the demon we come up against again and again is our own mortal and existential crisis." In *Relative Heroes,* Grayson invents characters, who, like many of the superhero protagonists of the past, gain their super powers at the same time they experience a tragic loss. In this case, the characters are a family of teenagers who lose their parents in a car crash. "Being fans of the superhero genre, they automatically assume that this means they've 'had an origin' and should now be a superhero team," Grayson explained to Grossman. Though Jeff Jensen, writing in *Entertainment Weekly,* faulted Grayson and co-author Yvel Guichet, for short-changing the novelty of their premise by rushing the teenagers into the business of superhero rescuing, he concluded with the hope that in subsequent issues of *Relative Heroes,* "Grayson and Guichet can tell stories that don't trivialize their emotionally rich premise."

Biographical and Critical Sources

PERIODICALS

Entertainment Weekly, April 21, 2000, Jeff Jensen, review of *Relative Heroes,* p. 72.

ON-LINE

2K.com, www.2kcomics.com (February 17, 2000).
WomenCONNECT, www.WomenCONNECT.com (February 15, 2000).*

H

HAGER, Tom 1953-

Personal

Born April 18, 1953, in Portland, OR; married Lauren Kessler (a writer), July 7, 1984; children: three. *Education:* Portland State University, B.S., 1975; Oregon Health Sciences University, M.S. (with honors; medical microbiology and immunology), 1978; University of Oregon, M.S. (with honors; journalism), 1981.

Addresses

Home—84898 South Willamette St., Eugene, OR 97405. *Office*—Office of Communications, University of Oregon, Eugene, OR 97403. *E-mail*—relhager@oregon.uoregon.edu. *Agent*—Nat Sobel, Sobel Weber Associates, Inc., 146 East 19th St., New York, NY 10003.

Career

National Cancer Institute, Bethesda, MD, science writer in Office of Cancer Communications, 1981; Aster Publishing, Eugene, OR, editor, 1982-83; University of Oregon, Eugene, adjunct assistant professor of journalism, 1983—, director of Office of Communications, 1995—. *Member:* Council for the Advancement and Support of Education.

Awards, Honors

More than ten national and district awards, Council for the Advancement and Support of Education (CASE), between 1985 and 1993; National Gold Award for Periodicals Resources Management, CASE, 1989; national award for best feature writing, CASE, 1993; *Force of Nature* was selected as a "best sci-tech books of 1995" by *Library Journal.*

Writings

(With wife, Lauren Kessler) *Aging Well,* Facts on File, 1987.

Tom Hager portrays the life of two-time Nobel Prize winning chemist Linus Pauling.

Force of Nature: The Life of Linus Pauling, Simon & Schuster, 1995.
Linus Pauling and the Chemistry of Life (biography for young readers), Oxford University Press (New York City), 1998.
Linus Pauling: A Centenary Volume, Oregon State University Press (Corvallis, OR), in press.

Contributor to *The Pauling Symposium: A Discourse on the Art of Biography,* Oregon State University Press, 1996. Correspondent, *Journal of the American Medical Association,* 1981-83. Contributor of more than a hundred articles to magazines and newspapers, including *Engineering and Science, Self, Reader's Digest,* and *Medical Post.* Founding editor, *LC,* 1982-83; contributing editor, *Oregon,* 1982-84, and *American Health,* 1983-88; editor, *Oregon Quarterly,* 1985-95.

Biographical and Critical Sources

PERIODICALS

Booklist, May 15, 1998, Randy Meyer, review of *Linus Pauling and the Chemistry of Life,* p. 1614.
Curriculum Review, November, 1998, review of *Linus Pauling and the Chemistry of Life,* p. 13.
Horn Book Guide, fall, 1998, review of *Linus Pauling and the Chemistry of Life,* p. 414.
Kirkus Reviews, April 15, 1998, review of *Linus Pauling and the Chemistry of Life,* p. 579.
School Library Journal, August, 1998, Carolyn Angus, review of *Linus Pauling and the Chemistry of Life,* p. 174.
Science Activities, spring, 1999, Markham B. Schack, review of *Linus Pauling and the Chemistry of Life,* p. 38.
Science Books and Films, October, 1998, review of *Linus Pauling and the Chemistry of Life,* p. 207; December, 1998, review of *Linus Pauling and the Chemistry of Life,* p. 279.

*   *   *

HARRIS, Mary K(athleen) 1905-1966

Personal

Born September 22, 1905, in Harrow, Middlesex, England; daughter of Roland E. and Mary (Mackey) Harris. *Education:* Attended Harrow County School for Girls, 1916-22. *Religion:* Roman Catholic. *Hobbies and other interests:* History, painting, the Ecumenical Movement.

Career

Writer.

Writings

FOR CHILDREN

Gretel at St. Bride's, illustrated by Drake Brookshaw, Nelson (London), 1941.
The Niche over the Door, Sheed, 1948.
Fear at My Heart, Sheed, 1951.
Henrietta at St. Hilary's, Staples Press, 1953.
The Wolf, Sheed, 1955.
Thomas, Sheed, 1956.
I Am Julie (novel), Crowell, 1956, published in England as *My Darling from the Lion's Mouth,* Chatto & Windus, 1956.

A Safe Lodging, illustrated by Don Bolognese, Sheed, 1957.
Emily and the Headmistress, Faber, 1958.
Lucia Wilmot (novel), Chatto & Windus, 1959.
Seraphina, Faber, 1960.
Elizabeth, Sheed, 1962.
Helena, Sheed, 1964.
Penny's Way, Faber, 1964.
The Bus Girls, Faber, 1965.
Jessica on Her Own, Faber, 1968.

Sidelights

Mary K. Harris's books were inspired by her experiences as a schoolchild. As a young girl, she noticed how unkind children were to one another and concluded that they only behaved badly because they were in groups. She determined that, individually, each child must surely be as appalled as she was by their behavior. As an adult, she used this early fascination with relationships to create stories for children. In *Gretel at St. Bride's* Harris sharply depicts the themes of childhood isolation and children's inability to understand the lives of their classmates. The Gretel of the title is a refugee from Nazi Germany who is certain that all the other children ever worry about is candy and getting on the hockey team.

Harris's books are set in all sorts of schools, including boarding schools, grammar schools, and secondary schools. Ann Thwaite wrote in *Twentieth-Century Children's Writers* that Harris was an entertaining writer who "explored with amused understanding the different pressures on adolescent girls as they come to terms with life, with the conflicting demands of home and school, and the difficulties and rewards of friendship." While her books were not contrived to prove a point, she did approach her writing with a sense of purpose. Thwaite observed that Harris "aimed to make ordinary life interesting and meaningful. She felt it important to help children to understand themselves and each other, to make them realize, as she herself had not realized until much later, that children are also vulnerable."

Biographical and Critical Sources

BOOKS

St. James Guide to Children's Writers, fifth edition, St. James Press, 1999.

PERIODICALS

Booklist, September 15, 1956.
Center for Children's Books Bulletin, March, 1968, p. 110.
Kirkus Reviews, January 15, 1968, p. 57.
Library Journal, August, 1956.
New York Times, August 5, 1956.*

HAWKES, Nigel 1943-

Personal

Born September 1, 1943, in Fulmer, England; son of Ronald William (a company director) and Kathleen Mary (a homemaker) Hawkes; married Jo Beresford (a company director) May 23, 1971; children: Georgina, William, Alexander. *Education:* Attended Sedbergh School, Yorkshire, 1957-62; St. Catherine's College, Oxford, B.A., 1966, M.A., 1969. *Religion:* Church of England. *Hobbies and other interests:* Gardening, walking, opera.

Addresses

Home—Well House, Front Rd., Woodchurch, Kent, England. *Office*—The Times, 1 Penninghorst, London, E1 9XN England.

Career

Journalist for *Nature,* 1966-69, and *Science Journal,* 1969-71; *Observer,* London, England, journalist, 1972-

Nigel Hawkes discusses the newest technology being used to make current energy sources more efficient and to tap renewable sources such as wind, water, solar, and nuclear power to meet future energy needs. (Cover photos by David Hardy and Sandia; illustrations by Alex Pang and Peter Harper.)

90; *Times,* London, science editor, 1990—. Governor for the British Nutrition Foundation, 1999—. *Member:* Association of British Science Writers.

Awards, Honors

British Nutrition Foundation Prize, 1992; CBE, 1999.

Writings

The Computer Revolution, Dutton, 1971.
Early Scientific Instruments, Abbeville Press, 1981.
Nuclear, Franklin Watts, 1981.
Food and Farming, Franklin Watts, 1982.
Space Shuttle, Gloucester Press, 1982.
Computers: How They Work (picture book), illustrated by Paul Cooper, Elsa Godfrey, and Rob Shone, Franklin Watts, 1983.
Computers in Action (picture book), Franklin Watts, 1983.
Microprocessors, Scribner's, 1984.
Nuclear Power (picture book), Gloucester Press, 1984.
Computers in the Home (picture book), Franklin Watts, 1984.
Robots and Computers (picture book), Franklin Watts, 1984.
Farms (picture book), Silver Burdett (Morristown, NJ), 1985.
Oil (picture book), illustrated by Ron Hayward Associates, Gloucester Press, 1985.
Chernobyl: The End of the Nuclear Dream, Vintage, 1986.
Nuclear Safety (picture book), illustrated by Ron Hayward Associates, Gloucester Press, 1986.
The Heroin Trail (picture book), illustrated by Ron Hayward Associates, Gloucester Press, 1986.
Nuclear Arms Race (picture book), illustrated by Ron Hayward Associates, Gloucester Press, 1986.
AIDS (picture book), illustrated by Ron Hayward Associates, Gloucester Press, 1987.
Gun Control (picture book), illustrated by Ron Hayward Associates, Gloucester Press, 1988.
Toxic Waste and Recycling (picture book), Gloucester Press, 1988.
Space Shuttles: A New Era? (picture book), illustrated by Ron Hayward Associates, Gloucester Press, 1989.
Nuclear Power, Rourke (Vero Beach, FL), 1990.
Safety in the Sky (picture book), illustrated by Ron Hayward Associates, Gloucester Press, 1990.
(Editor) Julie Flint and others, *Tearing Down the Curtain: The People's Revolution in Eastern Europe,* Hodder & Stoughton (London), 1990.
Glasnost and Perestroika, Rourke, 1990.
Structures: The Way Things Are Built, Macmillan, 1990.
Vehicles, Macmillan, 1991.
Genetic Engineering (picture book), Gloucester Press, 1991.
Into Space (picture book), Gloucester Press, 1992.
Medicine and Health, Twenty-First Century Books, 1994.
Communications (picture book), Twenty-First Century Books, 1994.
Energy (picture book), Twenty-First Century Books, 1994.
Space and Aircraft (picture book), Twenty-First Century Books, 1994.

Transportation on Land and Sea (picture book), Twenty-First Century Books, 1994.

Structures and Buildings (picture book), Twenty-First Century Books, 1994.

Mysteries of the Universe, Copper Beech Books (Brookfield, CT), 1995.

The Fantastic Cutaway Book of Spacecraft, illustrated by Alex Pang, Copper Beech Books, 1995.

Amazing Achievements: A Celebration of Human Ingenuity, Thunder Bay Press (San Diego), 1996.

The New Book of Mars (picture book), Copper Beech Books, 1998.

Planes and Other Aircraft (picture book), Copper Beech Books, 1999.

(With Steve Parker and Barbara Tay) *Science,* Aladdin, 1999.

Ships and Other Seacraft (picture book), Copper Beech Books, 1999.

Climate Crisis, Copper Beech Books, 2000.

Genetically Modified Foods, Copper Beech Books, 2000.

Sidelights

Science writer Nigel Hawkes is the prolific author of children's nonfiction books on such wide-ranging topics as food, health issues, computers, vehicles, energy, and outer space. Many of his highly illustrated books concisely introduce young readers to complicated topics.

Among his handful of books on vehicles, Hawkes has penned two on space shuttles. In his 1983 book *Space Shuttle,* he traces the history of reusable spacecraft and gives readers a glimpse inside a working shuttle. According to a *Junior Bookshelf* reviewer, the work will "feed the curiosity" of young readers. Six years later Hawkes returned to the topic, writing *Space Shuttles: A New Era?* In this update he discusses contemporary events—such as the first mission after the shuttle *Challenger* exploded—describes both American and Soviet shuttle programs, and remarks on future plans for the shuttles. Jonathan Betz-Zall, writing in *School Library Journal,* found Hawkes's views on the shuttle programs to be "especially insightful" and termed the work overall an "enlightening piece of journalism." Hawkes returned to the subject again with his 1994 title *Space and Aircraft.* Steven Engelfried, writing for *School Library Journal,* determined that this book, in which Hawkes discusses probes, supersonic jets, and space shuttles, "works well as a basic introduction."

Hawkes has also penned books on health issues, such as food, farming, illegal drugs, and medical techniques and research, and gun control. *The Heroin Trail,* an overview on the history, production, and effects of heroin use, includes large, full-color and black-and-white photographs that combine with the text to portray the ruin that heroin use causes. According to both Sue Diehl in *School Library Journal* and Ilene Cooper of *Booklist,* this account provides a "useful overview" of the heroin story. However, Betsy Hearne, writing in the *Bulletin of the Center for Children's Books,* wondered if the "sensationalized shock effect" would repel some readers, thus preventing them from reading this cautionary tale.

Hawkes describes the features of Mars and the discoveries of the Pathfinder missions. *(Cover illustration by Richard Rockwood.)*

In a similar, highly illustrated format, Hawkes's *AIDS* presents basic information on AIDS (Acquired Immune Deficiency Syndrome). Topics covered include the virus, spread of the disease, and AIDS prevention, information that a *Kirkus Reviews* critic determined "is presented clearly, simply, and often." Likewise, Ilene Cooper predicted in her *Booklist* review that students would consider *AIDS* a "satisfactory overview" of the topic. In *Medicine and Health,* Hawkes introduces young readers to such modern medical technology as diagnostic testing, drug development, and surgical techniques, while in *Genetic Engineering* he considers the advantages and disadvantages of changing the genetic makeup of plants, animals, and human beings. About *Genetic Engineering,* a *Kirkus Reviews* critic declared, "There's much here to learn and enjoy." Citing the use of full-color photographs, and "excellent diagrams," Denise L. Moll concluded in *School Library Journal* that it is "an appealing title for those students who find science intimidating."

In the environmental field, Hawkes has written about such topics as energy, toxic waste, and recycling. In *Energy* he explains the workings of wind-powered turbines and solar energy cells, giving "just enough information to lead curious readers to more detailed works," to quote Eunice Weech of *School Library Journal.* "An intriguing overview of its subject," seconded Carolyn Phelan in her *Booklist* review. In *Oil,* part of a series on fuels, Hawkes describes the source of fossil fuels, the methods of producing and delivering them, and the importance of oil as fuel. Because of their design, books in this series are "ideal for slow readers," judged Meryl Silverstein in *School Library Journal.* So too, in *Toxic Waste and Recycling,* Hawkes gives readers an overview of the dangers of improperly disposing of hazardous waste, which *Booklist* critic Denise M. Wilms judged to be "best suited to readers needing a quick international overview" of the topic.

Hawkes has written several titles on nuclear power. He presents the methods of generating atomic power and the controversy surrounding the use of this energy in *Nuclear Power.* According to Dennis Ford in *School Library Journal,* this "concise yet detailed" explanation includes an "excellent layout on the operation of fission reactors." With *Nuclear Safety* Hawkes presents opposing opinions on whether or not nuclear power is safe, discussing the nuclear accidents at Three Mile Island in 1979, Sellafield in 1956, and Chernobyl in 1986. For the author's "even-keeled approach and his coverage of Chernobyl," *School Library Journal* critic Jeffrey A. French recommended this title.

Politics and atomic energy combine in Hawkes's books *The Nuclear Arms Race* and *Glasnost and Perestroika.* In the former, the author traces the history of nuclear arms stockpiling, as well as nuclear testing and deterrence strategies. The material comes in a "compact presentation" that "will give readers pause," remarked Babara Elleman in *Booklist.* In *Glasnost and Perestroika,* Hawkes chronicles Russian history of the later decades of the twentieth century, discussing changes made after Mikhail Gorbachev rose to power.

Biographical and Critical Sources

PERIODICALS

Booklist, November 15, 1986, Barbara Elleman, review of *Nuclear Arms Race,* p. 507; January 1, 1987, Ilene Cooper, review of *The Heroin Trail,* p. 709; December 15, 1987, Ilene Cooper, review of *AIDS,* p. 708; August, 1988, Denise M. Wilms, review of *Toxic Waste and Recycling,* p. 1926; July, 1994, Carolyn Phelan, review of *Energy,* p. 1939.

Bulletin of the Center for Children's Books, March, 1987, Betsy Hearne, review of *The Heroin Trail,* p. 126.

Growing Point, July, 1987, p. 4840.

Horn Book Guide, spring, 1996, p. 103.

Junior Bookshelf, April, 1983, review of *Space Shuttle,* p. 75; December, 1990, p. 295.

Kirkus Reviews, October 1, 1987, review of *AIDS,* p. 1462; November 1, 1988, pp. 1604-05; March 15, 1991, review of *Genetic Engineering,* p. 393.

Los Angeles Times Book Review, October, 17, 1993, p. 10.

Magpies, November, 1991.

New York Times Book Review, November, 29, 1993, p. C18.

School Library Journal, August, 1983, p. 66; March, 1985, p. 166; April, 1985, Dennis Ford, review of *Nuclear Power,* p. 97; March, 1986, Meryl Silverstein, review of *Oil,* p. 158; May, 1987, Sue Diehl, review of *The Heroin Trail,* pp. 98-99; August, 1987, Jeffrey A. French, review of *Nuclear Safety,* p. 84; July, 1989, Jonathan Betz-Zall, review of *Space Shuttles: A New Era?,* p. 93; August, 1990, p. 170; December, 1991, Denise L. Moll, review of *Genetic Engineering,* pp. 122-23; August, 1994, Eunice Weech, review of *Energy,* p. 163; January, 1995, p. 118; February, 1995, Steven Engelfried, review of *Space and Aircraft,* p. 107; December, 1995, p. 117; August, 1990, p. 170.

*   *   *

HIGH, Philip E(mpson) 1914-

Personal

Born April 28, 1914, in Biggleswade, England; son of William (a bank clerk) and Muriel High; married Pamela Baker, August 17, 1950; children: Jacqueline, Beverly. *Education:* Attended high school in Canterbury, England. *Politics:* Tory. *Religion:* "Raised Church of England, now agnostic."

Addresses

Home—4 King St., Canterbury, Kent CT1 2AJ, England. *Agent*—E.J. Carnell Literary Agency, Roneybury Bungalow, near Old Harlow, Essex CM20 2EX, England.

Career

Worked as an insurance agent, realtor, shop assistant, psychic medium, and journalist, 1935-50; East Kent Road Car Co. Ltd., England, bus driver, 1950-79; writer, 1955—. *Military service:* Served in the Royal Navy during World War II.

Writings

SCIENCE FICTION NOVELS

No Truce with Terra, Ace Books, 1964.
The Prodigal Sun, Ace Books, 1964.
The Mad Metropolis, Ace Books, 1966, published in England as *Double Illusion,* Dobson, 1970.
Reality Forbidden, Ace Books, 1967.
These Savage Futurians, Ace Books, 1967.
Twin Planets, Paperback Library, 1967.
The Time Mercenaries, Ace Books, 1968.
Invader on My Back, R. Hale, 1968.
Butterfly Planet, R. Hale, 1968.
Come, Hunt an Earthman, R. Hale, 1973.
Sold—for a Spaceship, R. Hale, 1973.
Speaking of Dinosaurs, R. Hale, 1974.
Fugitive from Time, R. Hale, 1977.
Blindfold from the Stars, Dobson, 1979.

Contributor to magazines and newspapers, including *Authentic Science Fiction.*

Sidelights

Philip High once said, "I write because I have to write. Once an idea is formed, it prods and nags until I begin. Once started, I keep hours that no work union would tolerate. My wife keeps calling me for meals, my friends write and ask if I am dead because I don't answer letters. I am hooked on the damn thing and my Muse stands over me with a whip.

"I have never claimed to be a great literary figure. I am a storyteller and a square one to boot. I like all the loose ends tied up by the last page and I am psychologically incapable of writing anything but a happy ending. I suppose, deep down, I write as an off-beat do-gooder, hence the happy ending solution.

"My advice to young writers is to write the type of yarn you like reading the best. If you like reading Westerns more than anything else, don't try to write a detective story. Soak yourself in Westerns, then try your hand. I papered an entire wall with rejection slips until I tried the form of literature I like most, science fiction. My first short story in this field was accepted at first attempt. Note: I don't think this rule applies to poetry. I love verse, but have written only nine poems (never considered for publication) which I can read without shuddering."

High's novels are characterized by an emphasis on story lines, bizarre settings, and stylistic straightforwardness. In *Twin Planets* alien invaders wreak havoc on a future alternate Earth, and the humans there are compelled to try to help our Earth avoid the same fate. Aliens are the antagonists in *Invader on My Back,* as well. In this book, the aliens have separated people into groups by personality type, but they all have one thing in common—a fear of looking up as the result of their subservient status. In *Reality Forbidden* dream machines exist that are capable of lulling humans into conformity. Don D'Ammassa observed in *Twentieth-Century Science-Fiction Writers,* "Indeed, one of the many recurring themes in High's novels is a dread of conformity and the value of the individual."

Biographical and Critical Sources

BOOKS

Twentieth-Century Science-Fiction Writers, third edition, St. James (Detroit, MI), 1991.

PERIODICALS

Booklist, September 1, 1989, p. 15.
Books and Bookmen, April, 1970, p. 26.
Fantasy Review, July, 1985, p. 17; November, 1985, p. 26.
Library Journal, August, 1989, p. 152.
Times Literary Supplement, November 28, 1968, p. 1346.*

HOWARD, Elizabeth Fitzgerald 1927-

Personal

Born December 28, 1927, in Baltimore, MD; daughter of John MacFarland (a teacher and in real estate) and Bertha McKinley (a teacher and clerk; maiden name, James) Fitzgerald; married Lawrence Cabot Howard (a professor), February 14, 1953; children: Jane Elizabeth, Susan Carol, Laura Ligaya. *Education:* Radcliffe College, A.B., 1948; University of Pittsburgh, M.L.S., 1971, Ph.D., 1977. *Politics:* Democrat. *Religion:* Episcopalian. *Hobbies and other interests:* African folklore, French conversation, symphony concerts, grandchildren, family history.

Addresses

Home—919 College Ave., Pittsburgh, PA 15232. *Agent*—Kendra Marcus, Book Stop Literary Agency, 67 Meadow View Rd., Orinda, CA 94563.

Career

Boston Public Library, Boston, MA, cataloging assistant, 1948-51, children's librarian, 1951-56; Hofstra College (now Hofstra University), Hempstead, NY, research assistant in political science, 1956-57; Episcopal Diocese of Pittsburgh, Pittsburgh, PA, resource director, 1972-74; Pittsburgh Theological Seminary, Pittsburgh, reference librarian, 1974-77; University of Pittsburgh, Pittsburgh, visiting lecturer in library science, 1977-78; West Virginia University, Morgantown,

Elizabeth Fitzgerald Howard

assistant professor, 1978-81 and 1982-85, associate professor, 1985-91, professor of library science, 1991-93. Member of Radcliffe Alumnae Association Board of Management, 1969-72, Ellis School Board of Trustees, 1969-75, Magee-Women's Hospital Board of Directors, 1980-94, QED Communications Board of Directors, 1987-92, and Beginning with Books Board of Directors, 1987-93; member of vestry, Calvary Church, 1991-95. *Member:* American Library Association (member of Caldecott committee, 1984), Association for Library Services to Children (board member), International Board on Books for Young People, Society of Children's Book Writers and Illustrators, National Council of Teachers of English, Beta Phi Mu.

Awards, Honors

American Library Association notable book citation, 1990, Hedda Seisler Mason honor book, Enoch Pratt Library, 1991, and *Booklist* Picture Books of the '80s, all for *Chita's Christmas Tree;* Parents' Choice Award (picture book category), and Teacher's Choice Award, International Reading Association, both 1992, both for *Aunt Flossie's Hats (and Crab Cakes Later).*

Writings

America as Story: Historical Fiction for Secondary Schools, American Library Association, 1988, 2nd edition (with Rosemary Coffey), 1997.
The Train to Lulu's, illustrated by Robert Casilla, Bradbury, 1988.
Chita's Christmas Tree, illustrated by Floyd Cooper, Bradbury, 1989.
Aunt Flossie's Hats (and Crab Cakes Later), illustrated by James Ransome, Clarion, 1991, reprinted (10th anniversary edition), 2001.
Mac and Marie and the Train Toss Surprise, illustrated by Gail Gordon Carter, Four Winds, 1993.
Papa Tells Chita a Story, illustrated by Floyd Cooper, Four Winds, 1995.
What's in Aunt Mary's Room?, illustrated by Cedric Lucas, Clarion, 1996.
When Will Sarah Come?, illustrated by Nina Crews, Greenwillow, 1999.
Virgie Goes to School with Us Boys, illustrated by E. B. Lewis, Simon & Schuster, 2000.
Lulu's Birthday, illustrated by Pat Cummings, Greenwillow, in press.

Sidelights

Elizabeth Fitzgerald Howard once told *SATA* about the source for her stories for children: "It was inevitable that I would think back to my own childhood when I began to write stories for children. My sister Babs and I really did take *The Train to Lulu's.* This book was my first effort to try to capture for today's young readers some of the unique and yet universal experiences of children in one mid-century African-American family. *Chita's Christmas Tree* tells of old-time Christmas as celebrated in my father's family. Chita, my father's first cousin, now age eighty-four, was the daughter of one of

Baltimore's first African-American doctors. This is a glimpse of a little known facet of African-American life. *Aunt Flossie's Hats (and Crab Cakes Later)* celebrates my mother's sister, Aunt Flossie. A teacher in Baltimore schools, she lived to be almost 101, staying in the same house for sixty-five years and never throwing anything away. There are more stories about Aunt Flossie. And there are stories to be told about my father's father, and his five brothers, who came to Baltimore from Tennessee, and practiced law, medicine, pharmacy, and real estate. And great-grandfather John Henry Smith and his dry dock at Baltimore Harbor. And my mother's uncle Jimmy who owned a grocery store with—to quote Aunt Flossie—'fine terrapins and the best peaches anywhere.' I still hope to write about my sister and me growing up in Mrs. Ella Ford's rooming house, our quarters in the attic, and sharing the one bathroom with the several black graduate students on the second floor.

"This is a time of great richness in children's books by and about African Americans," Howard continued. "But there is so much still to be told . . . . There is still a need for more and more books so that children of all colors may discover more and more about growing up black in America—what is different and what is familiar, and how we are all connected."

Howard told *SATA,* "As I have continued writing stories based in people in my family—and reading similar stories by other authors—I have come to believe that the 'family story'—whether based on more recent memory or handed down over generations—might be considered a genre of children's literature similar to the folktale genre . . . . Doesn't the family story pass along memories and traditions, values and expectations, just as the folktale does? And the truth that stories connect us is attested to by audience members when I talk about my writing. When I conclude a presentation for adults, I often stress the real fact that all our families are rich with stories, and that our stories from different ethnic or racial or religious traditions have so much in common. But even if I haven't mentioned this, inevitably, members of the audience tell me excitedly that *Aunt Flossie's Hats (and Crab Cakes Later)* reminded them of their own loved aunts or grandmas who 'never threw anything away,' or *Mac and Marie and the Train Toss Surprise* evoked a wonderful surprise from their Uncle Abner or great-grandpa. And how many can remember a train (or bus or plane) trip to visit relatives? People feel that the incidents related in family stories are shared experiences. These stories show how we are connected. While I write to portray little known facets of African-American life and history, at the same time I am writing about our shared history, the history that connects us."

Howard's picture books have been welcomed for providing a glimpse into African-American life of the past in stories that celebrate the joy of simple pleasures and close family relationships. For example, in *Papa Tells Chita a Story,* a little girl sits on her father's lap after dinner and listens while he tells of his adventures during the Spanish American War. Papa's story effortlessly blends the factual and the fantastical as he battles alligators and other wild animals on a trek across Cuba to deliver a secret message and win a medal. *School Library Journal* critic Ruth Semrau noted that the story might inspire students to tell their own family stories.

Other family stories from Howard emphasize positive lessons for young children. In *Virgie Goes to School with Us Boys,* which is set in the Reconstruction South, little Virgie is determined to go to school just like her five older brothers, even though this means walking seven miles to the school on Monday morning and staying at the school all week. Reviewers proclaimed that Howard's rendition of Virgie's bravery as she faces the sometimes frightening trek in order to go to school is winning. "Virgie is a radiant heroine," attested a reviewer for *Publishers Weekly,* who added that "Howard proves herself adept at plucking a large-scale episode from history and adapting it to the scale of a picture book." In an author's note, Howard relates the social and familial history of the story, which is based on one told by her grandfather's brother. "Children will respond to the wonderful pictures and the implicit and moving message about the value of learning," predicted GraceAnne A. DeCandido in *Booklist.* Howard similarly pulls a homely moral from the simple story told in *When Will Sarah Come?,* which recounts how young Jonathan passes the time playing with his grandmother on the day his older sister Sarah attends school for the first time. "Younger siblings will love listening to this description of being left behind," remarked Marta Segal in *Booklist.*

The characters and incidents in *Aunt Flossie's Hats (and Crab Cakes Later)* are also based on Howard's family history. In this book, which celebrates "the ways in which shared memories can be a thread, invisible yet strong, that ties generations together," according to a critic in *Publishers Weekly,* sisters Sarah and Susan are regaled by stories when they visit their great-great-aunt Flossie, whose prodigious collection of hats each comes with its own bit of history. Susan and Sarah return to Aunt Flossie's in *What's in Aunt Mary's Room?,* where they are introduced to the family Bible that resides in the room in Flossie's house where Aunt Mary lived. This Bible was a gift in honor of Flossie's grandfather and contains a thumbnail sketch of the family history, which Susan is allowed to add to by carefully writing in her own and her sister's names and birth dates. Carolyn Phelan praised the book as "a warm family story that many children will enjoy," in her *Booklist* review.

In *Mac and Marie and the Train Toss Surprise,* Howard "succeeds once again in making a small incident come alive," claimed Linda Greengrass in *School Library Journal.* Here, a little boy who dreams of becoming a railroad engineer in turn-of-the-twentieth-century Baltimore waits in high anticipation for the night when his Uncle Clem, who works in the dining car of the Seaboard Florida Limited, will drop a package for them in their yard as the train speeds by. In her review in *Horn Book,* Mary M. Burns also compared *Mac and Marie and the Train Toss Surprise* favorably with Howard's other nostalgic family stories, remarking that this one not only effectively renders the excitement that

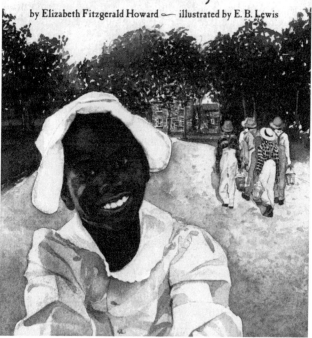

Virgie is determined to attend school with her five older brothers in the post-Civil War south. (Cover illustration by E. B. Lewis.)

children feel when their relatives make a special effort to please them, "but also celebrates the pride of ordinary folk made extraordinary by their sense of dignity and their indomitable spirit."

Biographical and Critical Sources

PERIODICALS

Booklist, February 15, 1996, Carolyn Phelan, review of *What's in Aunt Mary's Room?,* p. 1026; October 15, 1999, Marta Segal, review of *When Will Sarah Come?,* p. 454; November 1, 1999, GraceAnne A. DeCandido, review of *Virgie Goes to School with Us Boys,* p. 525.

Five Owls, September, 1993, p. 4; September, 1994, pp. 1-3.

Horn Book, May-June, 1993, Mary M. Burns, review of *Mac and Marie and the Train Toss Surprise,* p. 317; September-October, 1995, p. 626.

Publishers Weekly, February 15, 1991, review of *Aunt Flossie's Hats (and Crab Cakes Later),* p. 88; March 15, 1993, p. 85; December 20, 1999, review of *Virgie Goes to School with Us Boys,* p. 80.

School Library Journal, June, 1993, Linda Greengrass, review of *Mac and Marie and the Train Toss Surprise,* p. 76; June, 1995, Ruth Semrau, review of *Papa Tells Chita a Story,* p. 87.

HUGHES, Monica (Ince) 1925-

Personal

Born November 3, 1925, in Liverpool, England; naturalized Canadian citizen, 1957; daughter of Edward Lindsay (a mathematician) and Phyllis (Fry) Ince; married Glen Hughes, April 22, 1957; children: Elizabeth, Adrienne, Russell, Thomas. *Education:* Attended the Convent of the Holy Child Jesus, Harrowgate, Yorkshire, England; and Edinburgh University, 1942-43. *Religion:* Roman Catholic. *Hobbies and other interests:* Swimming, walking, traveling, beachcombing ("very difficult on the prairies"), gardening, sewing, puzzles, church activities.

Addresses

Home—13816 110-A Ave., Edmonton, Alberta, Canada T5M 2M9. *Agent*—The Pamela Paul Agency, 253 High Park Ave., Toronto, Ontario, Canada M6P2S5.

Career

Author and editor. Dress designer in London, England, 1948-49, and Bulawayo, Rhodesia (now Zimbabwe), 1950; bank clerk in Umtali, Rhodesia, 1951; National Research Council, Ottawa, Ontario, laboratory technician, 1952-57; full-time writer, 1975—. Writer-in-residence at several universities, including University of Alberta, 1984-85, and at Canadian public libraries.

Monica Hughes

Secretary, Writers Guild of Alberta, 1988-89. *Military service:* Women's Royal Naval Service, 1943-46. *Member:* Canada PEN, Writers Union of Canada, Canadian Society of Children's Authors, Illustrators, and Performers, International Board of Books for Young People (IBBY), SF Canada, Writers Guild of Alberta.

Awards, Honors

Vicky Metcalf Award, Canadian Authors Association, 1981, for body of work, and 1983, for the short story "Iron-Barred Door"; Alberta Culture Juvenile Novel Award and Bay's Beaver Trophy Award, both 1981, Canada Council Children's Literature Award, 1982, for *Guardian of Isis;* R. Ross Annett Award, Writers Guild of Alberta, Canada Council Children's Literature Award, Young Adult Canadian Book Award, and Best Book for Young Adults citation, American Library Association (ALA), all 1983, the Silver Feather Award, the Federal Association of Women Doctors of Germany, 1986, and the Booken Leeuw (Book Lion) Award for young adult fiction, the Netherlands, 1987, all for *Hunter in the Dark,* which was also designated a Deutscher Jugendbuchpreis honour book (Germany); International Board of Books for Young People (IBBY) Honour List, and ALA Best Books for Young Adults citation, both 1982, Phoenix Award, Children's Literature Association, 2000, for *The Keeper of the Isis Light;* Guardian Award runner-up, 1983, for *Ring-Rise, Ring-Set;* Hans Christian Andersen Award nomination, IBBY, 1984, for body of work; R. Ross Annett Award, 1984, for *Space Trap;* R. Ross Annett Award, 1986, for *Blaine's Way;* International Order of Daughters of the Empire (IODE) Book Award, 1989, for *Little Fingerling;* Alberta Achievement Award, 1986; City of Edmonton Cultural Creative Arts Award, 1988; Canadian Library Association Notable Book citation, 1991, for *Invitation to the Game;* Children's Book Centre Award, 1992, and R. Ross Arnett Award, 1993, for *Crystal Drop;* Red Cedar Young Reader's Choice Award nomination, British Columbia, 1997-98, for *Castle Tourmandyne;* Silver Birch Award nomination, Ontario Library Association, 2000, for *The Other Place;* Phoenix Award, Children's Literature Association (International), 2000, in special recognition of literary merit for the "Isis" trilogy.

Writings

FICTION; FOR CHILDREN AND YOUNG ADULTS

Gold-Fever Trail: A Klondike Adventure, illustrated by Patricia Peacock, LeBel (Edmonton, Alberta), 1974.

Crisis on Conshelf Ten, Copp Clark (Toronto), 1975, Atheneum (New York), 1977.

Earthdark (sequel to *Crisis on Conshelf Ten*), Hamish Hamilton (London), 1977, Methuen (Toronto), 1981.

The Ghost Dance Caper, Hamish Hamilton, 1978.

The Tomorrow City, Hamish Hamilton, 1978, Methuen (Toronto), 1982.

Beyond the Dark River, Atheneum, 1979, Thomas Nelson (Toronto), 1979.

Hunter in the Dark, Atheneum, 1982, Clarke, Irwin (Toronto), 1982.

Ring-Rise, Ring-Set, Watts (New York), 1982, Methuen, 1982.

Beckoning Lights, illustrated by Richard A. Conroy, LeBel, 1982.

The Treasure of the Long Sault, illustrated by Richard A. Conroy, LeBel, 1982.

My Name Is Paula Popowich! illustrated by Leoung O'Young, Lorimer (Toronto), 1983.

Space Trap, Watts, 1983, Groundwood (Vancouver), 1983.

Devil on My Back, MacRae, 1984, Atheneum, 1985.

Sandwriter, MacRae, 1984, Holt (New York), 1988.

Mike, Chasseur de Tenebre, Pierre Tisseyre (Montreal), 1985.

The Dream Catcher (sequel to *Devil on My Back*), Methuen, 1986, Atheneum, 1987.

Blaine's Way, Irwin, 1986.

Log Jam, Irwin, 1986, published in England as *Spirit River,* Methuen (London), 1988.

The Promise (sequel to *Sandwriter*), Methuen (London), 1989, Simon & Schuster, 1992.

The Refuge, Doubleday (Toronto), 1989.

Invitation to the Game, HarperCollins (Toronto),1990, Simon & Schuster, 1991.

The Crystal Drop, HarperCollins (Toronto), 1992, Simon & Schuster (New York), 1993.

The Golden Aquarians, HarperCollins (Toronto), 1994, Simon & Schuster, 1995.

Castle Tourmandyne, HarperCollins (Scarborough, Ontario), 1995.

Where Have You Been, Billy Boy? HarperCollins, 1995.

The Seven Magpies, HarperCollins, 1996.

The Faces of Fear, HarperCollins, 1997.

The Story Box, HarperCollins, 1998.

The Other Place, HarperCollins, 1999.

"ISIS" TRILOGY; YOUNG ADULT SCIENCE FICTION

The Keeper of the Isis Light, Atheneum, 1980, Hamish Hamilton, 1980.

The Guardian of Isis, Hamish Hamilton, 1981, Atheneum, 1982.

The Isis Pedlar, Atheneum, 1982, Hamish Hamilton, 1982.

PICTURE BOOKS AND EASY READERS

(Reteller) *Little Fingerling* (picture book), illustrated by Brenda Clark, Kids Can Press (Toronto), 1989, Ideals Children's Books (Nashville), 1992.

A Handful of Seeds (picture book), illustrated by Luis Garay, Lester (Toronto), 1993, Orchard Books (New York), 1996.

Jan's Big Bang (easy reader), illustrated by Carlos Freire, Formac (Halifax), 1997.

Jan and Patch (easy reader; sequel to *Jan's Big Bang*), illustrated by Carlos Freire, Formac, 1998.

Jan on the Trail (easy reader), illustrated by Carlos Freire, Formac, 2000.

OTHER

(Editor and contributor) *What If . . . ? Amazing Stories* (anthology), Tundra Books (Toronto and Plattsburgh, NY), 1998.

Contributor of essays and short stories to anthologies, including *Magook,* McClelland & Stewart, 1977; *Owl's*

Fun Book for Spring, Summer, and Fall, Grey de Pencier, 1982; *Out of Time,* Bodley Head, 1984; *Dragons and Dreams,* Harper, 1985; *The Windows of Dreams,* Methuen, 1986; *Canadian Children's Treasury,* Key Porter, 1988; *Canadian Children's Annual,* Grolier, 1988; *Take Your Knee Off My Heart,* Methuen, 1990; *Mother's Day,* Methuen, 1992; *Too Young to Fight: Memories from Our Youth During World War II,* Stoddart, 1999. Hughes's books have been translated into several languages, including Danish, Dutch, Finnish, French, German, Italian, Japanese, Norwegian, Polish, Swedish, and Swiss. Teacher's guides, lesson plans, and student activity packages for several of Hughes's works are available online. Hughes's papers are housed in permanent collections at the University of Calgary, Alberta, and at the de Grummond Collection, University of Southern Mississippi.

Work in Progress

Jan on the Trail (third story in the series), for Formac, 2000; *Storm Warning,* a young adult novel.

Sidelights

An English-born, Canadian author of fiction, short stories, and picture books, as well as a reteller and editor, Monica Hughes is considered one of Canada's best writers for children and young adults. Noted for writing successful works in several genres, including the picture book, the contemporary realistic novel, and the survival story, she is also well known as an advocate of science fiction. Hughes, who uses the settings of distant galaxies or future times in order to address the problems faced by young people in today's society, creates science fiction that is acknowledged for combining exciting stories with incisive exploration of social and moral issues. In addition, her works are recognized for their plausibility, authenticity, and integrity. Hughes is also praised for her careful research, attention to detail, and ability to create fully realized worlds and rounded characters. Called a serious anthropologist and philosopher, she is acclaimed as a particularly astute observer of human nature. One of Hughes's most popular works is the "Isis" trilogy, a trio of science fiction novels for young people that chronicle the evolution of a colony on a faraway planet over three generations while describing the coming-of-age of several teenage characters. She is also well known for writing *Hunter in the Dark,* a young adult novel about a sixteen-year-old boy who comes to terms with his impending death from leukemia while on a quest to shoot his first deer.

Hughes often uses her adopted country of Canada—in the past, present, and future—as the setting for her books, and she draws her themes from her experiences as a Canadian. She also features native Canadian peoples, such as Inuits and Cree and Blackfoot Indians, in several of her works. Noted for centering each of her novels on a major social, moral, or economic issue, she treats such topics as adaptation to alien environments, the erosion of natural resources, the preservation of heritage, the misuse of technology, and the loss of individuality. Among Hughes's most frequent themes are the importance of communication; the value of tolerance and kindness; the interrelationship of culture, environment, and humanity; and the meaning of being a person. In her works, Hughes presents young men and women, often orphans or outsiders, who face crises that could have potentially devastating consequences, both for themselves and for their societies. By accepting their challenges, these young people come closer to maturity. They often learn to live in simpler cultures that value the land while becoming more open to others. At the end of several books, the protagonists return home to try and work within their respective societies.

As a writer, Hughes favors a smooth, straightforward style that is noted for its evocative, graceful quality. She is recognized as an author who has brought genre fiction to a new level; her works, though considered relevant to Canadian readers, are regarded as universal in scope. Although Hughes is sometimes criticized for ethnic stereotyping as well as for the lack of continuity or explanation in some of her works, she is generally considered a talented, intelligent, and inventive writer who writes books that are both entertaining and thought-provoking. Writing in *Canadian Children's Literature,* Gerald Rubio called Hughes "one of the best Canadian—and perhaps world—authors of juvenile fiction at work today." Kit Pearson, who is herself considered a notable Canadian author, stated in the *Christian Science Monitor,* "Because of one writer—Monica Hughes—Canada shines in the field of science fiction." Pearson concluded by calling Hughes "[p]erhaps her country's most distinguished writer for children...." Writing in *In Review,* Irma McDonough predicted that Hughes "is writing books that will ... be considered classics by many new generations of young people."

Born in Liverpool, England, Hughes is the daughter of Edward Lindsay Ince, a prominent mathematician, and Phyllis Fry Ince; Hughes also had a sister, Liz, who is now deceased. At the time of her birth, both of Hughes's parents worked at the University of Liverpool. When she was a few months old, the family moved to Egypt, where her father became the head of the mathematics department at the University of Cairo. The family returned to England in 1931 when E. L. Ince obtained a position at the University of London. By the time she went to school, Hughes could already read; she was taught to read by her mother and grandmother, who often read aloud to her and her sister. The girls attended the Notting Hill and Ealing High School, a day school near their home in the London suburb of West Ealing. In her second year at the school, Hughes went to the British Museum to see the Rosetta Stone. Back in the classroom, she inscribed cuneiform characters on clay tablets and made hieroglyphics. Writing in her *Something about the Author Autobiography Series* (*SAAS*) entry, she recalled, "I began to make a connection between the words I was learning to put together in our English class and those ancient languages. It was all part of the same magic, a way of preserving words and story." The teachers also read aloud to the students, not from, as Hughes noted, "the kind of storybooks that we could

read for ourselves, but from more difficult material: the myths and beliefs of Early Man, for instance, and the Norse Sagas. I still remember the day when the teacher read to us the story of the death of Balder the Beautiful.... and how we sat at our desks with the tears streaming down our faces. This is when I discovered the idea of Hero, a concept that has been very important to my writing life." In an article in *Canadian Children's Literature,* Hughes wrote, "I think perhaps the most fortunate thing that ever happened to me happened [at the age of seven] ... I've always known, since that school, that magic lay between the covers of books, and that all that was necessary to do to partake of the treasures was to open the covers and plunge in."

Hughes decided that she wanted to be an archeologist, specializing in Ancient Egypt—that is, until she got scared by the film *The Mummy* starring Boris Karloff. At school, she won the class prize two years in a row and was given *Swallows and Amazons* and *Swallowdale,* two holiday romances by the English children's writer Arthur Ransome. In the class library, she discovered the fantasies and realistic fiction of another popular English author for the young, E. Nesbit. Hughes, who has called Edith Nesbit her favorite writer, recalled that she "brought me to the world of possible magic, which is quite different from the magic of myths and fairy tales." In 1936, the Ince family moved to Edinburgh, Scotland. Hughes recalled, "The city seemed to me dismally cold and grey, and our school was quite dreadfully boring.... The world seemed as dull and grey as the weather, and I longed for the colour and excitement of Egypt."

However, she soon discovered the Carnegie Library, in which, as she noted, "was all the colour and magic that my life lacked." She devoured works beloved by children such as *The Wind in the Willows* and *Black Beauty,* the novels of Charles Dickens and Robert Louis Stevenson, and historical adventure stories and romances by nineteenth-century writers such as Anthony Hope, Alexandre Dumas, H. Rider Haggard, and Baroness Orczy. When she discovered the speculative adventures of Jules Verne, which she read in both English and French, Hughes found that the "science fiction bug had bitten me." Her father, who was an amateur astronomer, gave Hughes a book by Sir James Jeans called *The Mysterious Universe,* which, as she wrote in *Sixth Book of Junior Authors and Illustrators,* "opened my eyes to the magic of the skies as E. Nesbit had opened them to the magic of amulets and psammeads." Writing in *Canadian Children's Literature,* she added that "E. Nesbit's world of fantasy and the astronomy of my father were beginning to come together, even though I didn't know it at the time." Hughes soon began to tell stories to her younger sister and to dream of becoming a writer.

During World War II, Hughes was sent to school in Argyllshire on the west coast of Scotland. The school was in a hunting lodge that was like, as Hughes recalled in *SAAS,* "the castle out of one of my nineteenth-century novels." The author was later to draw on her experience in *The Seven Magpies,* a mystery story set in a Scottish school during World War II. After a year, Hughes was sent to the Convent of the Holy Child Jesus in Harrowgate, Yorkshire. She noted that it "was an excellent school, and I loved my two years there." Encouraged to write fiction as well as the required essays and compositions, Hughes won a prize for the best story—a chocolate bar, which was considered a luxury during wartime. E. L. Ince passed away at the end of her second year at the school. Although Hughes had planned to attend Oxford University and study English literature, her father's death made this impossible. Hughes enrolled at Edinburgh University at sixteen and decided to take an honors mathematics degree.

At the end of her freshman year, she volunteered for service in the Royal Navy and became a member of the Women's Royal Naval Service. On her eighteenth birthday, she went to London, where she spent the next two years working on one of the most secret projects of the war, the breaking of the German code. London was bathed in darkness during the war; when peace was declared, the lights came on again. Hughes wrote in *SAAS,* "That was the most magical thing, I believe, after almost six years of darkness. And it was pleasant to go to sleep without fear of a raid. I had had three near misses, enough to make me understand how fragile and beautiful life was." Transferred into meteorology, Hughes was sent to a fleet arm air base in the northeast of Scotland—an area she called "[t]he end of the world"—in order to map the data coming into the RAF station. On her night watches, she would look up at the stars and imagine what life there was like.

In 1948, Hughes was released from the Navy and went to live with her mother and sister in London. After taking a course in dress designing, she worked as a freelancer in the garment trade and for a theatrical costumier. A friend suggested that Hughes might like to visit her home in Southern Rhodesia, so she got a work permit and set out for Cape Town. For the next two years, Hughes lived in Rhodesia, which is now called Zimbabwe. She worked at a local dress factory, did some modeling, and had a job in a bank in Umtali, a small city on the border between Zimbabwe and Mozambique. When her mother wrote to her that her sister, Liz, was ill, Hughes returned to England. She worked at dress design, but also began to write more seriously. Hughes noted in *SAAS* that, even though she was dissatisfied with her articles and short stories, writing "was something I *knew* I had to do." When she got the urge to travel again, Hughes decided to go to Australia. She intended to go to Canada and get various jobs as she worked her way across to the Pacific Ocean. Regarding Canada, she recalled, "I didn't intend to stay more than a single winter, if I could help it."

Hughes wrote in *Canadian Children's Literature,* "Canada was really a great shock and it became a catalyst that brought me face to face with myself." In 1952, she landed in Ottawa and found a job as a laboratory technician at the National Research Council, where she tested airplanes and new materials and discussed the possibility of flying saucers and life on Mars with her coworkers. Hughes generally found social life in Ottawa a bit lacking. "For lack of companionship," she wrote in *SAAS,* "I began to live inside my head, inventing characters who talked to each other while I listened in." Hughes rented a typewriter and began to write a novel. She moved to writing short stories in the science fiction genre. When the fledgling author joined a writing group, she met a friend who introduced her to Glen Hughes, a fellow writer who was also creating science fiction; the couple were married in 1957 and have four children, Elizabeth, Adrienne, Russell, and Thomas. While living in London, Ontario, where her husband worked with the federal government, Hughes began to write again. The family moved to Edmonton, Alberta, when Glen Hughes received a new government position in 1964. In Edmonton, Hughes painted in oils, wove tapestries on a loom, and wrote. "I never stopped writing," she noted, "even though I never sold a single short story, article, or novel."

After the death of her mother and sister, Hughes found it difficult for a time "to go on doing the creative things that had been bubbling up within me." However, in 1971, she picked up a book in the library, *Writing for the Juvenile and Teenage Market* by Jane Fitz-Randolph. Hughes decided to spend a year attempting to write professionally. First, she read books by such authors as Rosemary Sutcliff, Alan Garner, Penelope Lively, Peter Dickinson, and Jill Paton Walsh, as well as books on the art of writing for young people. As she wrote in *Canadian's Children's Literature,* "All the books I read said, 'Write about what you know.' ... I realized that really I had very few roots and it's hard to write without roots—particularly if you want to write with authority. I just had to go back to those very beginnings of being a human being who had known how to write and how to read, and draw on that authority of just being a human being on earth."

After a few false starts, Hughes wrote *Gold-Fever Trail: A Klondike Adventure,* a story for middle graders that was commissioned by publisher John LeBel to act as an adjunct to social studies courses in Alberta. In this work, which was published in 1974, thirteen-year-old Harry and his eleven-year-old sister, Sarah, face separation when their mother dies. Their father, prospecting for gold in the Yukon, has not been heard from, so the children embark on a journey to find him. After many exciting adventures, including finding gold for themselves, Harry and Sarah are reunited with their father. Writing in *In Review,* Marion Brown stated, "I think that *Gold-Fever Trail* shows great promise and that Monica Hughes should be encouraged," while Marion Pope, writing in *The World of Children's Books,* added that the story "has high appeal to children and adults alike and can stand on its own as a valuable addition to Klondike literature."

Shortly after completing *Gold-Fever Trail,* Hughes saw a film by the naturalist Jacques Cousteau in which he spoke about one of his designs, an underwater habitat called Conshelf One. Hughes wondered what would it be like to live under the sea and to be a child growing up there. These thoughts prompted her first work of science fiction, *Crisis on Conshelf Ten*. Addressed to young adults and set in the twenty-first century, the novel describes how Kepler Masterman, a teenage boy born and raised on the Moon, comes to Earth for the first time with his father, who has been sent to persuade the government to give the colony more money and influence. Kepler is sent to live with relatives in an underwater community, Conshelf Ten, where he discovers the Gillmen, a surgically altered race evolving in secret who are sabotaging essential oil and fishery plants. At the end of the novel, Kepler convinces the Gillmen to stop their violent actions. Gerald Rubio, writing in *Canadian Children's Literature*, called *Crisis on Conshelf Ten* "epic in scope, structure, and theme," while *Booklist* reviewer Barbara Elleman added that Hughes's "picture of twenty-first century undersea living ... is fascinating. Readers intrigued with the futuristic genre may well get caught up in the story." *Earthdark*, the sequel to *Crisis on Conshelf Ten*, addresses the exploitation of colonists and natural resources. In this work, Kepler returns to the Moon colony with news of governmental reform. The novel also includes a romance between Kepler and Ann, a girl from the colony. A reviewer for *Children's Book News* noted that, with *Earthdark*, Hughes "gives teenage readers science fiction at its best," while *Junior Bookshelf* critic A. R. Williams concluded, "it is about time someone at least hinted at resettlement problems and cultural mutation in an imagined but not impossible dream of colonisation of the spheres."

In 1980, Hughes produced the first volume of her "Isis" trilogy, *The Keeper of the Isis Light*. This work, which is set in the twenty-second century, introduces one of the author's most popular characters, Olwen Pendennis. As an infant, Olwen was brought to the planet Isis by her late parents, scientists who were researching the arid, radiation-filled environment. Before their deaths, Olwen's parents programmed a robot, the Guardian, to take care of her. The Guardian, seemingly emotionless but actually kind and loving, has taken care of Olwen, now sixteen, from the time that she was four. In order to facilitate her survival on Isis, the Guardian has given Olwen enlarged lungs, broad nostrils, and tough greenish skin. Olwen meets Mark London, a seventeen-year-old boy who is part of a group of settlers who come to Isis from Earth, and falls in love. However, Mark and the other settlers reject Olwen because of her appearance. Rejecting medical treatment to restore her to human form, Olwen, who experiences human emotion for the first time in years, decides that she wants to remain as she is. She chooses isolation over conformity, retreating to the upland area of Isis and leaving the more lush valley to the settlers. Writing in *Canadian Children's Literature*, Gerald Rubio said of *The Keeper of the Isis Light*, "In many respects it is the best work Monica Hughes has produced; it is, however, so unique that comparisons are not really valid." Irma McDonough stated in *In Review*, "William Faulkner talks about 'the old universal truths lacking which any story is ephemeral and doomed—love and honour, and pity and pride,

and compassion and sacrifice.' And when I thought of these truths the first book that came to mind was a science fiction, an unlikely candidate perhaps, but *The Keeper of the Isis Light* reverberates in the reader's mind long after she reads the last word because these truths enrich Olwen's story."

In the second volume of the series, *The Guardian of Isis*, the settlers who came from Earth to Isis are living at a subsistence level and are involved in a taboo-laden religion based on misconceptions of history. The settlers are led by a reactionary president, Mark London, Olwen's love interest from the previous novel. When Jody N'Kumo, a twelve-year-old boy whose ancestors came from East Africa, rebels against the society, he is banished by the President to the realm of the Ugly One—Olwen Pendennis. Jody finds Olwen and her Guardian. With their help, he saves his people from a flood. At the end of the novel, Guardian predicts that Jody is the future president who will abolish the old order and bring about positive change. Writing in the *Junior Bookshelf*, Marcus Crouch said, "It is a long time since I was so impressed by a book about the future.... Monica Hughes brings before us the strange world of Isis in all its beauty, and integrates setting and action and character in exemplary fashion. Her book is an excellent 'read,' a tract on society and a relevant commentary on the history of our own times." Calling Jody "a compelling character," *School Library Journal* contributor Jody Roacher concluded that *The Guardian of Isis* "is a well-written and finely descriptive narrative which contains several ideas worthy of contemplation by young minds."

The final volume of the series, *The Isis Pedlar*, introduces humor and romance to the trilogy. An Irish space trader, Mike Flynn, comes to the planet and exploits the settlers, duping them into mining for valuable firestones by using drugs and magic tricks. However, Mike's teenage daughter Moira realizes his plan and thwarts it with the help of Guardian and David N'Kumo, the nephew of Jody from the previous book. Moira and David fall in love, and Moira decides to stay on Isis and marry David. At the end of the novel, Jody N'Kumo becomes president of the colony, and Guardian decides to leave Isis to oversee Mike Flynn's future travels. Writing in the *Times Educational Supplement*, Jessica Yates noted, "Monica Hughes has a particular skill in depicting primitive, self-sufficient cultures, whether on our planet or an alien world. The resourceful heroes, Jody and David, are black, descended from Africans on Earth, and this is necessary for the plot because they can better endure the thin atmosphere of upper Isis." However, the critic notes, "the question at least needs to be asked, given that a con-man was necessary to the plot, how automatic was the decision that he should be Irish?" Calling the "Isis" trilogy "surely the most impressive achievement in young adult literature to appear in a very long time," in *Quill and Quire* Rubio dubbed *The Isis Pedlar* "a daring tour de force" that is "an aesthetically satisfying conclusion to the Isis epic."

With *Hunter in the Dark,* a young adult novel published in 1982, Hughes created what is one of her most acclaimed books. In this coming-of-age story, sixteen-year-old Mike discovers that he has leukemia. He goes through physical changes, medical treatments, and the reactions of family and friends. Trying to find a way to come to terms with his fate, he goes alone to the foothills of Alberta in order to kill a deer, his first. He find the deer, an impressive buck. As he tracks it, Mike goes on a spiritual journey. When he comes face to face with the deer, Mike refuses to kill it. He comes to an understanding of both life and death, and is thus able to return home with a peaceful spirit. Writing in *Twentieth-Century Children's Writers,* Rubio noted that *Hunter in the Dark* "remains Hughes's masterpiece." Irma McDonough commented in *In Review,* "Hughes has faced a difficult task with integrity.... There is a sadness attached that allows for no rejoicing in Mike's rage to live. It is a sobering book but an honest one. And young readers deserve honesty." *Quill and Quire* contributor Paul Kropp called *Hunter in the Dark* "perhaps the most important Canadian young-adult novel of the year," while *Maclean's* writer Cathleen Hoskins noted that Hughes "writes with a gutsy realism that bodes well for the future of intelligent juvenile fiction in this country."

Hughes has written several stories that are told in two volumes. Among the most well-received are *Devil on My Back* and *The Dream Catcher,* science fiction novels set in the twenty-first century. In *Devil on My Back,* fourteen-year-old Tomi, a boy whose father rules the computer-driven underground center Arc One, is caught in a slave revolt and escapes to the outside world. Tomi revels in his new lifestyle, which stresses healthy living and open affection. When a precious saw breaks, he risks his life to return to Arc One for more tools and seeds. Margery Fisher of *Growing Point* called *Devil on My Back* "one of the most moving and thoughtful of Monica Hughes's remarkable sequence of speculative tales," while *Horn Book* critic Anita Silvey concluded, "The implication of the denouement—that the young must seek to change their world rather than to escape from it—gives the story the kind of philosophical underpinning that characterizes the best of science fiction."

In *The Dream Catcher,* fourteen-year-old Ruth, who feels that she is a misfit, runs away from her community of Arc Three, one of several cities established after the world's oil supplies ran out. Ruth sets out to look for Arc One; when she is caught, she learns from the authorities that she is valuable because of her psychic powers. Ruth begins receiving messages in dreams. When she discovers that these messages are coming from Lord Tomi, the hero of *Devil on My Back,* Ruth joins forces with Tomi to defeat the regime that oppresses the citizens of Arc. Writing in *School Librarian,* Tony O'Sullivan stated, "This is a quietly absorbing and reflective novel which sees itself as part of a larger series in which problems of individual freedom and social good are explored with a degree of freshness." Zena Sutherland of *Bulletin of the Center for Children's Books* noted, "This meshes nicely with the first book but

Only a finger-length tall, Issun Boshi seeks his fortune and overcomes two monsters by resourcefulness and good manners in Hughes's retelling of a Japanese folktale. (Cover illustration by Brenda Clark.)

stands firmly on its own, a compelling narrative with strong characters and a plot that has good structure and momentum."

With the young adult novels *Sandwriter* and *The Promise,* Hughes moved into the realm of fantasy. *Sandwriter* describes how sixteen-year-old Antia, a princess of the twin continents Komilant and Kamalant, is sent to the desert country of Roshan as the prospective bride of its prince, Jodril. Willful, spoiled, and impressionable, Antia is under the romantic spell of her evil tutor, Eskoril, who wants to take over the two continents. Eskoril convinces Antia to spy on Jodril. She accidentally discovers the valuable secret of the desert—twin lakes under the sand, one containing water and the other crude oil. The lakes are guarded by the Sandwriter, an ancient priestess whose magic ensures the survival of Roshan. After Antia betrays the secret that she has found, she realizes that she has acted foolishly and joins with Sandwriter and Jodril to save the country; in the process, she learns wisdom, loyalty, and modesty and falls in love with Jodril. At the end of the novel, Antia and Jodril pledge their unborn child to be Sandwriter's successor. *Canadian Children's Literature* critic Gertrud Lehnert noted that after Antia rejects Eskoril as a traitor and fights him, she "remembers nonetheless the love she once felt for him and thus remains faithful to herself. This seems to me a remarkable switch in a book for young readers ... *Sandwriter* communicates some of the essential ambivalence of human lives and feelings instead of offering a simple ready-made solution." Writing in *Bulletin of the Center for Children's Books,* Roger Sutton added, "There's not much suspense here, and too much quasi-mythic musing instead of action, but feisty and headstrong Antia is a true heroine, and the book could serve as a stepping stone to the books of Robin McKinley and other stories about 'girls who do things.'"

The Promise introduces Ramia, the daughter of Antia and Jodril from the previous book, who is sent against her will to Sandwriter in order to fulfill the pledge made by her parents. Ramia is escorted to Sandwriter's cave by a young man, Atbin, who shows her kindness. Rebellious at first, Ramia learns to accept her new life. However, after four years, the spartan lifestyle and her need for companionship cause Ramia to have a breakdown. Sandwriter sends Ramia to live with an ordinary couple for a year; she is reunited with Atbin, and they fall in love. Ramia is faced with a dilemma: should she marry Atbin and have a normal life or accept her vocation as the heir to Sandwriter? At the end of the novel, Ramia returns to Sandwriter, sacrificing her own desires in order to serve her country. *Quill and Quire* contributor Frieda Wishinsky stated, "Sequels do not often achieve the power, fluency, and characterizations of the original. *The Promise* ... is an exception. An engrossing tale of love and commitment, it stands fully on its own." Writing in the *Times Educational Supplement,* Neil Philip commented, "What lifts *The Promise* above the common run of the fantasies it resembles, and above *Sandwriter,* is the way in which the author deals with the romantic possibilities inherent in this situation, and manifested in Ramia's relationship with Atbin.... This is a maturely drawn relationship, in which every turn has its possibilities of fulfillment and love." Assessing both books, Lehnert concluded that Hughes "succeeds in evoking the atmosphere of two realms within her imagined planet, particularly the beautiful and terrifying world of the desert, and in obliquely raising our consciousness of different ways of treating nature. One may read these books as dealing with ecological problems, or as describing a person's search for herself or for her duty toward society. But any pedagogical purpose is unobtrusively transmitted in a well-told story."

In addition to her books for older children and adolescents, Hughes is the creator of several books for younger readers. She is the author of two picture books, *Little Fingerling,* a retelling of a Japanese folktale, and *A Handful of Seeds,* a story that was published for UNICEF. In *Little Fingerling* Hughes describes how Issun Boshi, a tiny but courageous young man, goes to Kyoto, Japan, to seek his fortune. He becomes the favorite in the home of a merchant and falls in love with his daughter, Plum Blossom. When Issun Boshi overcomes two evil giants, he uses their magic and, with Plum Blossom's help, becomes a handsome samurai warrior. A critic in *Booklist* called *Little Fingerling* "[a]n elegant retelling," while *Books in Canada* critic Linda Granfield noted that Hughes's "detailed descriptions enhance rather than overload the story." Granfield concluded that Hughes and illustrator Brenda Clark "have striven to produce an authentic Japanese ambience and have been extremely successful. Their research has brought history alive in a picture book."

In *A Handful of Seeds,* young Concepcion, a Hispanic girl, is forced to move from a farm to a barrio after the death of her grandmother. All that she takes with her is a handful of seeds. In the city, Concepcion meets a gang of homeless orphan children who survive by stealing and picking through garbage. She teaches them to grow vegetables from the seeds that she brought from home. When the police chase and beat the children, the garden is destroyed. However, the children help Concepcion to replant it; later, they have a feast. Another gang of hungry orphans shows up, so Concepcion gives them some food and seeds as well as training in how to grow their own garden. *School Library Journal* reviewer Maria Redburn stated, "Hughes's well-written narrative does not hide the ugliness of life in the *barrio.* However, the easy resolution of Concepcion's problems makes the story seem like a fairy tale. Nonetheless, it is a good vehicle for introducing a difficult subject." Writing in *Quill and Quire,* Sarah Ellis commented, "[S]uch a book could be plodding and dull. It is not. Hughes writes with a clean, pared-down style that gives this story of social realism a fable-like feel." Ellis concluded that *A Handful of Seeds* "is not a solution to the complex problems of poverty and development. But it is not a bad place to start, for any age."

Hughes is also the creator of three stories for early primary graders about Jan, a little girl who wants to be in her school's science fair and to get a puppy of her own. In addition, Hughes is the editor of a collection of stories and poems for young adults in which Canadian authors such as Tim Wynne-Jones, Joan Clark, Alice Major, and the editor herself address the question "what if?" She has also contributed several short stories to anthologies edited by others.

Hughes commented in the *St. James Guide to Young Adult Writers,* "I write in response to my excitement at the wonder of our world, and sometimes in response to my dismay at what we are doing to it." Writing in *Canadian Children's Literature,* Hughes noted that, in addition to being entertaining, one of the functions of a good writer for children "is to help them explore the world and the future. And to find acceptable answers to the Big Questions: 'What's life about?' 'What is it to be human?' ... [T]hose are the questions that demand truthful answers, not pat ones. So I think my chief criterion for a story for children ... is that one should write as truthfully as possible, even if it isn't easy or painless. One faces oneself in the darkest inside places of one's memory and one's subconscious, and out of that comes both joy and sorrow. But always—and I think ... this is perhaps the second crucial thing for children—always there must come hope. And then one writes and one scribbles out and then one writes again, and then maybe after half a dozen drafts (as one of my favourite writers, Alan Garner, says) maybe—then—a book will emerge. And if it is good enough, it will probably be for children."

Biographical and Critical Sources

BOOKS

Children's Literature Review, Volume 9, Gale, 1985, pp. 61-79.

Gallo, Donald R., editor, *Speaking for Ourselves, Too,* National Council of Teachers of English, 1993.

Holtze, Sally Holmes, editor, *Sixth Book of Junior Authors and Illustrators,* Wilson, 1989, pp. 140-42.

McDonough, Irma, editor, *Profiles: Authors and Illustrators, Children's Literature in Canada,* Canadian Library Association, 1982, pp. 78-80.

Meet the Authors and Illustrators, Scholastic, 1991.

Pendergast, Tom and Sara Pendergast, editors, *St. James Guide to Young Adult Writers,* second edition, St. James, 1999, p. 400.

Presenting Children's Authors, Illustrators, and Performers, Pembroke, 1990.

Silvey, Anita, editor, *Children's Books and Their Creators,* Houghton, 1995.

Something about the Author Autobiography Series, Volume 11, Gale, 1991, pp. 149-62.

Twentieth-Century Children's Writers, third edition, St. James, 1989, pp. 473-74.

Van Belkon, Edo, editor, *Northern Dreamers: Interviews with Canadian Authors of Science Fiction, Fantasy, and Horror,* Quarry Press, 1998.

Writing Stories, Making Pictures, Canadian Children's Book Centre, 1994.

PERIODICALS

ALAN Review, spring, 1992, pp. 2-5.

Booklist, April 15, 1977, Barbara Elleman, review of *Crisis on Conshelf Ten,* p. 1266; June 15, 1990, review of *Little Fingerling,* p. 2000.

Books in Canada, December, 1989, Lisa Granfield, "A Boatload of Babies," p. 23; March, 1997, p. 36.

Bulletin of the Center for Children's Books, July-August, 1987, Zena Sutherland, review of *The Dream Catcher,* p. 211; March, 1988, Roger Sutton, review of *Sandwriter,* p. 138.

Canadian Children's Literature, Number 26, 1982, Monica Hughes, "The Writer's Quest," pp. 6-27; Number 17, 1989, Gerald Rubio, "Monica Hughes: An Overview," pp. 20-26; Number 61, 1991, Gertrud Lehnert, "Futurist Roles for Women," pp. 82-84.

Children's Book News, December, 1978, review of *Earthdark,* p. 2.

Christian Science Monitor, October 5, 1984, Kit Pearson, "A Harvest of Children's Books from Canada," pp. B8-B9.

Growing Point, September, 1984, Margery Fisher, review of *Devil on My Back,* p. 4309.

Horn Book Magazine, June 1, 1985, Anita Silvey, review of *Devil on My Back,* pp. 317-18.

In Review, Autumn, 1974, Marion Brown, review of *Gold-Fever Trail: A Klondike Adventure,* pp. 49-50; February, 1981, Irma McDonough, "Profile: Monica Hughes," pp. 11-13; April, 1982, Irma McDonough, "A Creative National Literature for Children," pp. 5-13.

Junior Bookshelf, June, 1977, A. R. Williams, review of *Earthdark,* p. 179; October, 1981, Marcus Crouch, review of *The Guardian of Isis,* p. 212.

Maclean's, June 28, 1982, Cathleen Hoskins, "Reading for Sleeping-Bag Adventures," pp. 56-57.

Quill and Quire, April, 1982, Paul Kropp, review of *Hunter in the Dark,* p. 32; March, 1983, Gerald Rubio, review of *The Isis Pedlar,* p. 67; January, 1990, Frieda Wishinsky, review of *The Promise,* p. 16; April, 1993, Sarah Ellis, "Into the *Barrio,*" p. 35; October, 1998, pp. 44-45; December, 1998, p. 38.

Reading Teacher, April, 1992, pp. 634-41.

School Librarian, February, 1987, Tony O'Sullivan, review of *The Dream Catcher,* p. 64.

School Library Journal, February, 1983, Jody Roacher, review of *The Guardian of Isis,* p. 77; March, 1996, Maria Redburn, review of *A Handful of Seeds,* p. 176.

Times Educational Supplement, November 19, 1982, Jessica Yates, "Space Invaders," p. 34; February 16, 1990, Neil Philip, "A Rebel's Choice," p. 68.

World of Children's Books, Spring, 1978, Marion Pope, "Yukon-Icons," pp. 25-27.

ON-LINE

Monica Hughes, www.ecn.ab.ca/mhughes (May 10, 2000).

—Sketch by Gerard J. Senick

J

JOHNS, Janetta
 See QUIN-HARKIN, Janet

*   *   *

JOHNSON, Caryn E.
 See GOLDBERG, Whoopi

*   *   *

JOHNSON, Scott 1952-

Personal

Born November 23, 1952, in Chicago, IL; son of Roy and Gladys (Hurt) Johnson; married Susan Newton, September 28, 1985; children: Ethan Lucas, Jordan Guthrie, Caleb Nathaniel. *Education:* Indiana University, B.A. (with honors), 1974; University of Massachusetts, M.F.A., 1978. *Hobbies and other interests:* Backpacking, hiking, bicycling, acoustic music (guitar and mandolin).

Addresses

Home—25 Wright Ave., Mahopac, NY 10541. *Office*—c/o Pleasantville High School, 60 Romer Ave., Pleasantville, NY 10570. *Agent*—Richard Parks Agency, 138 East 16th St., New York, NY 10003. *E-mail*—woodchip@computer.net.

Career

Pleasantville High School, Pleasantville, NY, teacher of English and creative writing, 1978—. Writer. *Member:* Sierra Club, Nature Conservancy.

Awards, Honors

Fulbright exchange teacher, 1983; National Endowment for the Humanities independent study fellowship, 1987;

"Best Books for Young Adults" selection, American Library Association (ALA), 1993, for *One of the Boys;* "Best Books of 1999," *School Library Journal,* "Best Books for Young Adults," ALA, 2000, and "Quick Picks for Reluctant Readers," ALA, 2000, all for *Safe at Second.*

Scott Johnson

Writings

YOUNG ADULT NOVELS

One of the Boys, Atheneum, 1992.
Overnight Sensation, Atheneum, 1994.
Safe at Second, Philomel, 1999.

Contributor of articles and short stories to *English Journal, TriQuarterly,* and *Ploughshares.*

Sidelights

Scott Johnson once told *SATA:* "There aren't too many second chances in life, and writing for young people, for me, is a way to get back and live through some of those choices and decisions I had to make—and often didn't make too wisely." Johnson's ability to empathize with adolescents comes from his continuing contact with them in his position as a high school teacher. He first discovered young adult novels as a teacher; his favorites, he recalls for *SATA,* provided him "with a direct line to my past, to those adolescent sensations that haunted and tortured all of us, and other times left us soaring with glee. That teenager from long ago is still inside, still seeing the world as unjust and overly complicated, still crying out for understanding, some guidance and maybe a little bit of attention. We need to listen to that teenager, and [young adult] books help to put us in touch."

When Johnson began to dream of becoming a writer, he took inspiration from the stories he had heard as a child: "There was something in fiction that reminded me of the tales told around the fire on my old Boy Scout camping trips. Tales swapped, with everyone hoping the next one would be even better—scarier, wilder, more real than life. And as we lay there, each snap of a twig or rustle of a leaf outside our tent was surely the telltale sign of some creature we had thrilled to around the fire, drawing near, long after the last story was spoken. That's how fiction works, I think. 'Good story,' we say, when the storyteller reaches the end, but that's not the half of it. The true measure of fiction is how much it grows inside you, how much the tale still burns after the campfire is only embers."

In his first novel, *One of the Boys,* Johnson sets up a classic dilemma for his young protagonist, Eric. Eric's desire to belong to the gang that has formed around newcomer Marty leads him to participate in some unsavory pranks. Eric persists in following the crowd until he realizes the cost in self-respect from doing what he knows is wrong. Randy Meyer remarked in *Booklist:* "The pain and promise of friendship come clear in a story that demonstrates that there are no easy choices." Unlike other stories about following a false leader down the wrong path, *One of the Boys* offers few insights into the character of ne'er-do-well Marty, noted a reviewer for *Publishers Weekly.* "Instead, Johnson deftly stresses Eric's development from mindless stooge to independent, ethical individual," according to the *Publishers Weekly* critic. Likewise, Gerry Larson commented in *School Library Journal* that young adult readers will recognize both Eric and Marty from their own experi-

ences, going on to observe that "believable characters, realistic dialogue, and smooth plot foreshadowing render a thought-provoking story."

Johnson's second book, *Overnight Sensation,* tells a similar story with a female protagonist. During the summer before her senior year, Kerry Dunbar goes to work on her aunt and uncle's farm, where the unaccustomed labor causes her to lose weight. With the help of a college-age cousin, she is further transformed from the social know-nothing of her earlier years in high school to the beauty who catches everyone's eye when she returns home in the fall. She quickly falls in with a heavy-drinking crowd, and one night the group breaks into a friend's garage, accidentally setting fire to it. The event marks the end of Kerry's days as one of the popular kids in school. "Using incidents familiar to young adults, the author creates an engrossing story of a young woman's moral deterioration and subsequent redemption," remarked Merri Monks in *Booklist.* Although a reviewer for *Publishers Weekly* did not think that adolescent readers would find Kerry a sympathetic character, the critic noted that Johnson's "first-person narrative is on key and the dialogue rarely falters." In *Voice of Youth Advocates,* Susan Dunn called *Overnight Sensation* "a good novel of adolescent angst that many teens will be able to relate to."

Johnson again focuses on the intense relationships between young people in his third effort, *Safe at Second,* in which star pitcher Todd and his sidekick Paulie must reevaluate their identities and their relationship to each other when Todd loses an eye to a line drive. Before the accident, Todd is already auditioning for the major leagues, and Paulie imagines his future only in terms of helping the person who has been his friend his entire life. After the accident, Paulie continues to identify himself in terms of his friend's needs, but begins to realize that Todd's loss of nerve on the pitching mound, and his plans for the future, are questions Todd must resolve for himself. Along the way, Paulie is forced to move beyond the safe boundaries of the identity he had carved out for himself and become more of an individual. "It is a measure of Johnson's craft that he can deprive these two worthy young men of the future they covet yet convince his readers that the unimagined life beyond the diamond may still hold some charm," pronounced Elizabeth Bush in *Bulletin of the Center for Children's Books.* Although a contributor to *Kirkus Reviews* found some flaws in Johnson's characterizations, the critic concluded that *Safe at Second* is an "unusually thoughtful, if slightly uneven, tale [that ends] on a high note."

Biographical and Critical Sources

PERIODICALS

Booklist, April 1, 1992, Randy Meyer, review of *One of the Boys,* p. 1438; April 1, 1994, Merri Monks, review of *Overnight Sensation,* p. 1436; June 1, 1999, p. 1829.
Bulletin of the Center for Children's Books, July, 1999, Elizabeth Bush, review of *Safe at Second,* p. 390.
Kirkus Reviews, June 1, 1999, review of *Safe at Second,* p. 884.

Publishers Weekly, April 6, 1992, review of *One of the Boys,* p. 66; March 7, 1994, review of *Overnight Sensation,* p. 73.

School Library Journal, May, 1992, Gerry Larson, review of *One of the Boys,* p. 133.

Voice of Youth Advocates, June, 1994, Susan Dunn, review of *Overnight Sensation,* p. 84.

*   *   *

JONES, Veda Boyd 1948-

Personal

November 30, 1948, in Sulphur Springs, AR; daughter of Raymond E. (chief clerk at the electric company) and Dorothy (an American Red Cross worker; maiden name, Brown) Boyd; married Jimmie L. Jones (an architect), November 15, 1975; children: Landon, Morgan, Marshall. *Education:* Crowder College (Neosho, MO), A.A. (in history), 1968; Pittsburg State University (Pittsburg, KS), B.A. (in history), 1970; University of Arkansas, M.A. (in history), 1974; Missouri Southern State College, teaching certificate, 1976. *Hobbies and other interests:* Sailing.

Addresses

Home—505 W. 34th St., Joplin, MO 64804-3613. *E-mail*—vjones@janics.com.

Career

Blue Cross, Blue Shield of Oklahoma, Tulsa, assistant manager of actuarial services, 1973-75; freelance writer, 1982—; Crowder College, instructor, 1993; Institute of Children's Literature, instructor, 1993—. Member of the Joplin Public Library Board, 1999—, secretary, 2000—. *Member:* Society of Children's Book Writers and Illustrators, Ozark Writers League, Missouri Writers' Guild, American Association of University Women-Joplin Branch (president, 1987-89).

Awards, Honors

Winner, 1993 *Writer's Digest* writing competition in the articles division, for "Naturalist Rachel Carson"; numerous awards from the Missouri Writers' Guild (including Best Children's Fiction, 1993; Best Magazine Article, 1996; Best Historical Article, 1997; Best Adult Fiction, 1993, 1997, 1998, 1999; and Best Romance Novel, 1997, 1998); best contemporary romance, readers' poll in Heartsong Presents, 1995, for *Callie's Mountain;* Crowder College Distinguished Alumnus Award, 1995.

Writings

JUVENILE

Bible Story Coloring Book, Barbour (Ulrichsville, OH), 1996.

Adventure in the Wilderness, illustrated by Adam Wallenta, Barbour, 1997.

Cincinnati Epidemic, Barbour, 1997.

The New Citizen, Barbour, 1998.

Tara Lipinski, Chelsea House (Philadelphia, PA), 1998.

Coming Home, illustrated by Adam Wallenta, Barbour, 1999.

Caves, illustrated by Ryan Durney, Seedling, 1999.

Government and Politics, Chelsea House, 1999.

Nicole Bobek, Chelsea House, 1999.

Selena ("They Died Too Young" series), Chelsea House, 2000.

Thomas Jefferson: Author of the Declaration of Independence, Chelsea House, 2000.

Alexander Hamilton: First Secretary of the Treasury, Chelsea House, 2000.

Ewan McGregor, Chelsea House, 2000.

The Senate, Chelsea House, 2000.

Native Americans of the Northwest Coast, Lucent (San Diego, CA), 2000.

Selena ("Latinos in the Limelight" series), Chelsea House, 2001.

Ernest Hemingway, Chelsea House, 2001.

Veda Boyd Jones

Carol Moseley-Braun receives support from Bill Clinton and Al Gore in her 1992 bid for U.S. senator. (From Government and Politics, *written by Jones.)*

OTHER

April's Autumn, Avalon, 1991.
Gentle Persuasion, Heartsong Presents, 1993.
Under a Texas Sky, Heartsong Presents, 1993.
The Governor's Daughter, Heartsong Presents, 1993.
A Sign of Love, Heartsong Presents, 1994.
Callie's Mountain, Heartsong Presents, 1995.
Callie's Challenge, Heartsong Presents, 1996.
A Question of Balance, Heartsong Presents, 1997.
A Sense of Place, Heartsong Presents, 1998.

Contributor of novellas collected in the following anthologies published by Barbour: *Christmas Treasures,* 1996, *Summer Dreams,* 1997, *Christmas Dreams: Four New Love Stories from Christmas Present,* 1997, *I Do: A Romantic Collection of Inspirational Novellas,* 1998, and *Gift of Love,* 2000. Contributor of stories and articles to magazines, including *Cricket, Highlights, Humpty Dumpty, Writer, Writer's Digest,* and *Woman's World.*

Work in Progress

A middle-grade novel with the working title of *The Corner of Bush and Moffet.*

Sidelights

Veda Boyd Jones told *SATA:* "I was born in Arkansas and spent the first nine years of my life in a town of 466 people, mostly relatives. Although my family moved to a metropolis (Neosho, a town of almost ten thousand) in Missouri when I was in the fourth grade, I returned to Arkansas for graduate school at the University of Arkansas, where my father had attended school. I can call those hogs with the best of them, and now it's actually fashionable to say 'y'all' and know what it means.

"I never consciously intended to be a writer, although I edited the school paper in high school and at the junior college I attended. It was a decade later when I decided to write and submit my work for publication. After I had read some romance novels and said, 'I can do better than that,' my life as a writer began.

"I learned that it wasn't as easy to write a romance as it looked. But I was determined, and I loved creating characters and manipulating them. I wrote five contemporary romance manuscripts before one sold. So, I'm a firm believer in the adage that 'writing is ten percent inspiration and ninety percent perspiration.

"While I was in the midst of writing about falling in love, my three sons, Landon, Morgan, and Marshall, asked me to write something for them. I took time to write a story not only for them, but starring them. It sold to *Cricket* magazine, and I was immediately bitten by the children's writing bug.

"Most of my fiction writing for children comes directly from my sons' experiences. Sometimes my own small-town upbringing sneaks into my writing—big porches, long summer days, lightning bugs, five-cent bottles of pop. I use my emotional experiences, too—the tears from falling off a bike twelve times before victoriously riding four feet, the joy of catching snowflakes on my tongue, and the fascination of watching a snake slither into the pond.

"When writing nonfiction, I use the research skills I was taught in college, and I've learned that the reference librarian is a writer's best friend. I don't settle for finding a fact in one source. I keep digging until I find other facts to substantiate it. When writing biographies, I like to immerse myself in the subject's world until I know his reasons for making the choices he made in his life.

"If we met in a crowded room you would remember me, simply because I'm short, almost four-foot nine. Standing out in a crowd isn't always a good thing, especially for an adolescent who's trying to blend into the group, but I've found its good points. I never had to worry that my dates would be shorter than I. And I've learned to talk easily with strangers so they will help me with items on the top shelves of grocery stores. Of course, my boys used me as a measuring stick until they all passed me, which was usually in their fourth-grade years.

"My husband, who's almost six feet, is an architect. We have always gotten along well except for the summer we built the new room onto our house. He thought I should anticipate his needs: he's holding a hammer, I should hand him nails; he's lifting one end of the board, I should pick up the other end. Of course, I didn't. His dream is to someday design and build us a house. I'm all for it (I want my dream library/study), but we have an agreement. All I will do is carry him a cold drink from time to time. He'll get someone else to be his assistant.

"I write on a computer in the new room, right next to the pool table and the fireplace and close to the kitchen refrigerator. My dream library/study would rival that of Professor Higgins' in *My Fair Lady*. For now, I'm settling for more bookcases in our new room. (We've been in the 'new room' now for fifteen years, but we still call it that.)

"I love writing. I can't imagine a more satisfying life."

K

KARR, Phyllis Ann 1944-

Personal

Born July 25, 1944, in Oakland, CA; daughter of Frank Joseph (an educator) and Helena (an educator; maiden name, Beckmann) Karr; married Clifton A. Hoyt, June 2, 1990. *Education:* Colorado State University, A.B., 1966; Indiana University at Bloomington, M.L.S., 1971. *Politics:* "Independent." *Religion:* Catholic.

Addresses

Home—Barnes, WI. *Agent*—Owlswick Literary Agency, 4426 Larchwood, Philadelphia, PA 19104.

Career

East Chicago Public Library, Roxana Branch, East Chicago, IN, branch librarian, 1967-70; Hamill & Barker Antiquarian Booksellers, Chicago, IL, shop assistant, 1971; University of Louisville Library, Louisville, KY, cataloguer, 1972-77; writer, 1977—. Volunteer reader and monitor for Recording for the Blind, Louisville; member of Communiversity Band, Rice Lake, WI, 1978-91. *Member:* International Wizard of Oz Club, Early English Text Society, Mystery Writers of America, Science Fiction Writers of America, Friends of the University of Michigan Gilbert and Sullivan Society, Phi Sigma Iota, Beta Phi Mu.

Writings

My Lady Quixote, Fawcett, 1980.
Frostflower and Thorn, Berkley, 1980.
Lady Susan (based on the unfinished novel by Jane Austen), Everest House, 1980.
Meadow Song, Fawcett, 1981.
Perola, Fawcett, 1982.
The Elopement, Fawcett, 1982.
The Idylls of the Queen, Ace Books, 1982.
Frostflower and Windbourne, Berkley, 1982.
Wildraith's Last Battle, Ace Books, 1982.

The King Arthur Companion, Reston, 1983.
At Amberleaf Fair, Ace, 1986.

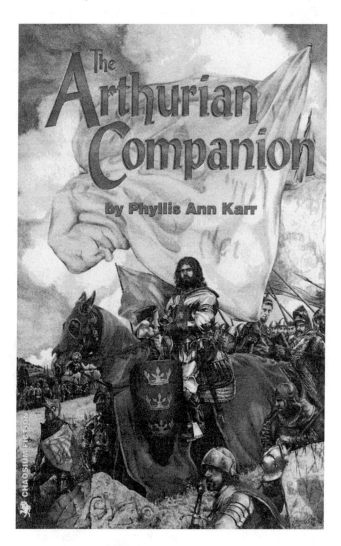

Containing one thousand entries, Phyllis Ann Karr's alphabetical guide references the people, weapons, artifacts, and geography of the Arthurian legend. (Cover illustration by Ed Org.)

The Gardener's Boy, Buckethead Enterprises (Albuquerque, NM), 1988.

Also contributor to magazines, including *Ellery Queen,* and to numerous anthologies. Author of column, "Thoughts from Oakapple Place," *GASBAG,* 1970—. Assistant editor for *Fantasy and Terror,* 1975-76. Karr's papers have been solicited for the University of Oregon Special Collections.

Sidelights

Phyllis Ann Karr has written fantasy fiction, a study on Arthurian literature, and historical mystery and romance. Her first major stories were short mysteries for *Ellery Queen's Mystery Magazine,* although she had previously published short fantasy stories in small-press magazines. These tales featured Torin and Toymaker, and were less about sword and sorcery than about rural people living in magical worlds. Although developed through short stories, Torin also appears in the fantasy-mystery novel *At Amberleaf Fair.*

Karr is best known for her stories about the sorceress Frostflower and the swordswoman Thorn. Her first fantasy novel, *Frostflower and Thorn,* describes a world in which men are farmer priests and women are warriors. When Thorn, a young warrior, becomes pregnant, she approaches Frostflower to hasten time so she can deliver the baby within a day. As a result, both women are banished, and the novel tells of their adventures together. The women are very different in their ways of thinking, and they tend to clash. Mike Ashley noted in the *St. James Guide to Fantasy Writers* that the interaction of the "ill-mixed characters" is what gives the series its strength. Karr used a similar dynamic in *Wildraith's Last Battle,* a non-series book about a cruel goddess-turned-human and a mercenary. In the next series book, *Frostflower and Windbourne,* Karr adds elements of mystery as the two women help another sorceress who is accused of murdering a man.

Karr's loves for mystery, fantasy, and Arthurian legend come together in *The Idylls of the Queen* in which Guinevere organizes a banquet and Sir Patrise is killed right in front of Arthur and the other knights. Ashley observed, "This gave Karr a chance to explore the motives and lives of the knights from a new angle, making it one of the most refreshing of recent Arthurian novels."

"The first goal of fiction is to entertain," Karr once said. "True entertainment is difficult unless there is also some philosophic or other thought-provoking content, but the first duty of the fiction crafter is to tell a story on a clear, coherent level, readily comprehensible to the reader. I think fiction took a wrong turn when the 'literary' authors like James Joyce became a separate breed from the 'popular' authors of fiction. Cervantes, Dickens, and others are great because they have both a popular and a critical appeal, even though the popular may have come first and have been followed only later by the critical. The best style is the invisible style, though there are

exceptions. I, personally, write because it is an inner need to maintain my balance. Fiction satisfies the need better than nonfiction and is also easier to write, as a rule.

"I can translate from non-technical French, Russian, and Middle English (from verse into verse in the latter) and hope someday to add Polish and maybe Latin. But translation seems an even harder field to break into than original composition. My biggest break to date in getting paid for my writing was the good fortune of obtaining an agent.

"From 1984 to 1989, I rented a cottage in Birchwood, Wisconsin, for a writing retreat. Through the bookmobile that serves both Birchwood and Barnes, my future husband made contact with me, seeking a fellow reader of science fiction and fantasy. A first marriage for both of us, it is turning out well worth the wait: more than ever, I rejoice that I never rushed into a relationship, but held out for the right partner."

Biographical and Critical Sources

BOOKS

St. James Guide to Fantasy Writers, St. James (Detroit, MI), 1996.

PERIODICALS

Booklist, September 15, 1982, review of *The Idylls of the Queen,* pp. 92, 94.
Book World, October 6, 1985, review of *Wildraith's Last Battle,* p. 11.
Fantasy Review, December, 1986, Michael M. Levy, review of *At Amberleaf Fair,* p. 35.
Library Journal, September 15, 1980, Kathy Piehl, review of *Lady Susan,* p. 1879; January 15, 1981, review of *Frostflower and Thorn,* p. 170; February 15, 1983, Barbara J. Dunlap, review of *The King Arthur Companion,* p. 384.
Ms., October, 1981, Valerie Eads, "A First: Woman Warrior Day," p. 19.
Publishers Weekly, July 25, 1980, review of *Lady Susan,* p. 147.
Reference Services Review, Volume 23, number 4, 1995, p. 64.
Voice of Youth Advocates, December, 1982, Kristie A. Hart, review of *Idylls of the Queen,* p. 38.
Washington Post Book World, October 6, 1985, p. 11.*

* * *

KEELY, Jack 1951-

Personal

Born August 9, 1951, in Binghamton, NY; son of Kenneth (a machinist) and Myrtle (a writer and English teacher) Keely. *Education:* Rhode Island School of Design, B.F.A., 1973; Cranbrook Academy of Art, M.F.A., 1976.

Jack Keely gets readers started cartooning—from how to draw characters with different emotions, personalities, and ages to drawing animals, action figures, and special effects.

Addresses

Home—2219 3/4 Echo Park Ave., Los Angeles, CA 90026. *E-mail*—jkeely@gte.net.

Career

Writer, illustrator, and cartoonist. Taught illustration and design at Ohio University, Athens, and North Carolina State University, Raleigh. Worked as a book and magazine illustrator in New York City and as an advertising art director; creator of images for greeting cards, advertisements, puzzles, games, and novelty gifts.

Writings

ILLUSTRATOR

Planet Dexter's Shake, Rattle, and Roll! Cool Things to Do with Dice (That Grown-ups Don't Even Know About), Addison-Wesley (Reading, MA), 1995.
Instant Creature! The Swimming Critters from Way Back Then!, Addison-Wesley, 1995.

Sylvia Branzei, *Planet Dexter's Grossology,* Addison-Wesley, 1995.
Michael A. DiSpezio, *Planet Dexter's Visual Foolery!,* Planet Dexter (Reading), 1995.
Bill Haduch and David Williams, editors, *Balls: The Book with Bounce!,* Addison-Wesley, 1996.
Beth Wolfensberger Singer, *The Hairy Book: The Uncut Truth about the Weirdness of Hair,* Addison Wesley Longman (Reading), 1996.
Sylvia Branzei, *Animal Grossology: The Science of Creatures Gross and Disgusting,* Addison Wesley Longman, 1996.
Liz Doyle, *Planet Ant,* Planet Dexter, 1996.
Liz Doyle, *The Toobers and Zots Travel Companion,* Planet Dexter, 1996.
Daniel Weizmann, *Take a Stand!,* Penguin Putnam (New York City), 1996.
Kristin Harpster, *Marco! Polo! Eleven Pool and Water Games,* Price Stern Sloan (Los Angeles, CA), 1997.
Beth Wolfensberger Singer, *Lefty: A Handbook for Left-Handed Kids,* Planet Dexter, 1997.
Sylvia Branzei, *Grossology Begins at Home,* Addison Wesley Longman, 1997.
Sylvia Branzei, *Virtual Grossology,* Addison Wesley Longman, 1997.
Barbara Saffer, *Science Questions and Answers: The Human Body; for Ages 6-8,* Lowell House (Los Angeles), 1998.
The Art of Cartooning, Walnut Grove Press, 1998.
Magical Lands, Penguin Putnam, 1998.
Animal Friends, Penguin Putnam, 1998.
Dressing Up, Penguin Putnam, 1998.
Tasty Treats, Penguin Putnam, 1998.
S. Price, *Crazy Ballet Game,* Penguin Putnam, 1998.
Sylvia Branzei, *Hands-on Grossology: The Science of Really Gross Experiments,* Planet Dexter, 1999.
It's Not Just Tissues, Penguin Putnam, 1999.
U Can Cartoon!, Walter Foster Publishing, 2000.

Also illustrator of *Calculator Mania, How High Is Pepperoni, Starting Out in Cartooning, The Toobers and Zots Home Companion,* and *Money Madness.*

OTHER

Self-illustrated books include *Step-by-Step Cartooning with Jack Keely,* Walter Foster Publishing.

Adaptations

Keely's cartoon characters have been translated into "animatronic" displays for a museum exhibition based on the "Grossology" series. His characters have served as models for dolls, puppets, and plastic figures.*

*   *   *

KORMAN, Gordon (Richard) 1963-

Personal

Born October 23, 1963, in Montreal, Quebec, Canada; son of Charles Isaac (an accountant) and Bernice (a journalist and author; maiden name, Silverman) Korman. *Education:* New York University, B.F.A., 1985. *Hobbies and other interests:* Music, travel, sports.

Addresses

Home—7905 Bayview Ave., #506, Thornhill, Ontario, Canada L3T 7N3. *Office*—c/o Scholastic Inc., 555 Broadway, New York, NY 10012. *Agent*—Curtis Brown Ltd., 10 Astor Pl., New York, NY 10003.

Career

Writer, 1975—. *Member:* Writers Union of Canada, Canadian Society of Children's Authors, Illustrators, and Performers (CANSCAIP), Society of Children's Book Writers and Illustrators.

Awards, Honors

Air Canada Award, Canadian Authors' Association, 1981, as "Most Promising Writer under Thirty-five"; Ontario Youth Award, International Year of the Youth Committee of the Ontario Government, 1985, for contributions to children's literature; Children's Choice Award, International Reading Association, 1986, for *I Want to Go Home!*, and 1987, for *Our Man Weston;* Markham Civic Award for the Arts, 1987; American Library Association (ALA) Editors' Choice and ALA Best Book citations, 1988, for *A Semester in the Life of a Garbage Bag;* ALA Best Book citation, 1991, for *Losing Joe's Place;* Manitoba Young Readers' Choice Award, 1992, for *The Zucchini Warriors;* Junior Library Guild selection, and "Our Choice" book citation, Canadian Children's Book Center, both 1992, both for *The Twinkie Squad.*

Writings

FOR CHILDREN AND YOUNG ADULTS

This Can't Be Happening at Macdonald Hall!, illustrated by Affie Mohammed, Scholastic, 1977.
Go Jump in the Pool!, illustrated by Lea Daniel, Scholastic, 1979.
Beware the Fish!, illustrated by Daniel, Scholastic, 1980.
Who Is Bugs Potter?, Scholastic, 1980.
I Want to Go Home!, Scholastic, 1981.
Our Man Weston, Scholastic, 1982.
The War with Mr. Wizzle, Scholastic, 1982.
Bugs Potter: Live at Nickaninny, Scholastic, 1983.
No Coins, Please, Scholastic, 1984.
Don't Care High, Scholastic, 1985.
Son of Interflux, Scholastic, 1986.
A Semester in the Life of a Garbage Bag, Scholastic, 1987.
The Zucchini Warriors, Scholastic, 1988.
Radio Fifth Grade, Scholastic, 1989.
Losing Joe's Place, Scholastic, 1990.
Macdonald Hall Goes Hollywood, Scholastic, 1991.
(With mother, Bernice Korman) *The D-minus Poems of Jeremy Bloom,* Scholastic, 1992.
The Twinkie Squad, Scholastic, 1992.
The Toilet Paper Tigers, Scholastic, 1993.
The Three Z's, Scholastic, 1994.

Gordon Korman

Why Did the Underwear Cross the Road?, Scholastic, 1994.
Something Fishy at Macdonald Hall, Scholastic, 1995.
The Chicken Doesn't Skate, Scholastic, 1996.
(With B. Korman) *The Last-Place Sports Poems of Jeremy Bloom: A Collection of Poems About Winning, Losing, and Being a Good Sport (Sometimes),* Scholastic, 1996.
Liar, Liar, Pants on Fire, illustrated by JoAnn Adinolft, Scholastic, 1997.
The Sixth Grade Nickname Game, Hyperion, 1998.
Nose Pickers from Outer Space, Hyperion, 1999.
Planet of the Nose Pickers, Hyperion, 2000.
Touchdown Stage Left, Hyperion, 2000.
Your Mummy Is a Nose Picker, Hyperion, in press.
No More Dead Dogs, Hyperion, in press.

"MONDAY NIGHT FOOTBALL CLUB" SERIES, PUBLISHED BY HYPERION

Quarterback Exchange: I Was John Elway, 1997.
Running Back Conversion: I Was Barry Sanders, 1997.
Super Bowl Switch: I Was Dan Marino, 1997.
Heavy Artillery: I Was Junior Seau, 1997.
Ultimate Scoring Machine: I Was Jerry Rice, 1998.
(With James Buckley, Jr., and Brian Peterson) *NFL Rules!: Bloopers, Pranks, Upsets, and Touchdowns,* 1998.

"SLAPSHOTS" SERIES, PUBLISHED BY SCHOLASTIC

The Stars from Mars, 1999.
All-Mars All-Stars, 1999.
The Face-Off Phony, 2000.

Cup Crazy, 2000.

OTHER

Korman's books have been translated into French, Swedish, Danish, Norwegian, and Chinese.

Adaptations

The "Monday Night Football Club" series has been adapted for the Disney Channel TV series, *The Jersey.*

Sidelights

Canadian author Gordon Korman once described himself to Leslie Bennetts in the *New York Times* as a "gutless troublemaker" at school, always demonstrating a healthy disrespect for authority, but never pushing such skepticism into outright anarchy. Such a description might fit some of Korman's cast of imaginary characters just as well. There are the roommates Boots and Bruno who keep coming back for more adventures

Sixteen-year-old Jason and two friends take over his brother's apartment for a summer of parties, girls, no parents ... and comic chaos.

at Macdonald Hall; Bugs Potter who nudges the bounds of authority to the limit, though not into chaos; the imaginative liar Zoe Bent in *Liar, Liar, Pants on Fire;* even a nose-picking alien in *Nose Pickers from Outer Space* and its sequels. Korman writes about and for kids from middle grades to high school; humor is the name of the game, with touches of teen insight here and there. The successful "tried-and-true" Korman formula is, according to Connie Tyrrell Burns writing in *School Library Journal:* "zany situations; a fast pace; likable, well-drawn characters; contemporary dialogue; and lots of humor."

Since publishing his first book when he was only fourteen years old, Korman has written a slew of best-selling novels for children and young adults. His slapstick humor, madcap adventures, and high-spirited, rebellious characters have helped make his books popular favorites with school-age readers across Canada and the United States. "Many of Mr. Korman's plots revolve around the frustrations of rambunctious boys forced to submit to stuffy academic authorities," noted Bennetts. From sports stories with a comic edge, to classroom tales bordering on the gross, Korman has made a major industry of humorous insurrection and adolescent empowerment.

Korman was born in Montreal, Quebec, where his father worked as an accountant and his mother wrote an "Erma Bombeck-type column" for a local newspaper, as he told Bennetts. In elementary and junior high school, Korman was always fond of writing—especially his own brand of zany stories and scenarios. "I wasn't a big reader for some reason," he remarked to Chris Ferns in *Canadian Children's Literature.* "But I always tried to put in creativity where I could: if we had a sentence with all the spelling words for that week, I would try to come up with the stupidest sentences, or the funniest sentences, or the craziest sentences I could think of."

A classroom assignment at the age of twelve developed into Korman's first published work, *This Can't Be Happening at Macdonald Hall!* The precocious Korman was only fourteen when this first novel was published. Set at a Canadian boarding school, the novel features Bruno Walton and "Boots" Melvin O'Neal. Roommates and best friends, the two get into their fair share of scrapes, usually led by the intrepid Bruno. So effective is the pair at their pranks, that the headmaster of the school, Mr. Sturgeon, known fondly to the students as "The Fish," decides to separate them. The ensuing plot of the book recounts the duo's attempts to get The Fish to reunite them. A surprising best-seller, this first novel set Korman on a course he has held to for over two decades and forty books. He continued writing while a student, finishing a book a year during summer vacations. Bruno and Boots have made a number of appearances over the years. In *Go Jump in the Pool!,* another roommate introduced in the first novel, a rich hypochondriac, uses his stock market wizardry to help raise money for a swimming pool at the school; in *Beware the Fish!,* a further roommate, science whiz

Drimsdale, comes to the rescue with Boots and Bruno to stop declining enrolment at their school.

The fourth novel in the series, *The War with Mr. Wizzle,* features the girls who reside across the road at Miss Scrimmage's Finishing School For Young Ladies. These same girls maintain a high profile in *The Zucchini Warriors,* in which the Macdonald Hall football team secretly recruits one of the female students to become the quarterback of their pitiful team. When a movie company uses the school for a setting, Bruno tries to become a star in *Macdonald Hall Goes Hollywood.* A reviewer for *Publishers Weekly* found that title to be a "rollicking tale," with "plentiful" laughs.

In his seventh outing at Macdonald Hall, the 1995 *Something Fishy at Macdonald Hall,* Korman presents Boots and Bruno upstaged by an anonymous prankster who delights in water balloons and blue dye in the swimming pool. But all fingers initially point to the prankish duo, and soon Bruno and Boots are on the trail of the person trying to frame them. "Fans of the series will delight in another tale of madcap humor, peopled with some of the funniest, most ridiculous adults in middle-grade fiction," Burns concluded in a *School Library Journal* review. Dave Jenkinson, writing in *Quill and Quire,* commented that middle-grade readers "will not only find the usual zany humour they have come to expect from Korman but a well-crafted mystery as well." Jenkinson further noted, "As always, everything comes together in a tumultuous but satisfying conclusion that will leave readers eagerly awaiting Korman's next Macdonald Hall escapade."

In the intervening years between his first Macdonald Hall novel and his seventh, Korman's fertile imagination has taken him in many directions. His other best-selling books feature characters that similarly test boundaries of authority. Bugs Potter, in the 1980 novel *Who Is Bugs Potter?* and the 1983 novel *Bugs Potter: Live at Nickaninny,* is a rock-and-roll drummer who lives for his music. Simon Irving in Korman's 1986 novel, *Son of Interflux,* organizes a high school campaign to save school land from being purchased by his father's corporation. Artie, appearing in the 1984 publication *No Coins, Please,* pulls off scams for money whenever his summer camp group visits the city, to the frustration of his counselors.

Korman's early books relied to a large extent on wildly improbable coincidence and "contrivance of events," as Korman explained to Ferns. *Our Man Weston,* for example, is a wild adventure in which teenager Sidney West foils a spy, saves a high-tech Air Force plane, and solves several other mysteries, including the location of two missing golden retrievers. In the second *Bugs Potter* book, the erstwhile rock drummer is stranded with his family on a wilderness holiday, where he stages a concert and discovers a missing tribe of Indians. Korman's complex and comic plots demonstrate that "few writers are as adept at creating fast-paced and hilarious plots," as Peter Carver noted in *Quill and Quire.*

Jeff and Wiley discover an unbelievable power in nicknames and nearly ruin their friendship as they compete to find a nickname for the new girl. (Cover illustration by Mark Buehner.)

As Korman moved into adolescence and adulthood, receiving a B.F.A. degree in dramatic and visual writing from New York University in 1985, so did his characters, and he began to more fully develop their personalities and relationships with each other. His slapstick humor, although remaining a significant part of the action in his stories, began to share the stage with some realistic depictions of adolescent life. In his 1985 *Don't Care High,* Paul wakes up the apathetic students at his new high school. And in his 1987 novel, *A Semester in the Life of a Garbage Bag,* Korman introduces Raymond Jardine, whose desire to win a school contest (and therefore spend the summer in Greece rather than at his uncle's New Jersey fish-gutting plant) stimulates a chain of events in the life of his English class partner, Sean Delancey. There is no shortage of absurdity in this novel. Among the characters who become involved in the plot are Sean's grandfather, a yo-yo prodigy, his younger sister (whom Sean calls "Genghis Khan in training"), and his rival in romance, the muscular but not-so-bright Steve "Cementhead" Semenski. Along with the caricatures and absurdity, however, there are real teenage emotions and interrelations. Ferns commented in his review of *A Semester in the Life of a Garbage Bag* in *Canadian Children's Literature* that Korman's "lunatic comic inventiveness ... is accompanied by a perceptive eye for the quirks of adolescent behaviour." The critic added that "the comedy and the observation almost seem to be pulling in different directions," and summarized that, although in this novel he is stretching into new, not yet mastered territory, "Gordon Korman's comic imagination is as fertile as ever."

Radio Fifth Grade, Korman's 1989 novel about a student-run radio show, contains Korman's customary zany elements—a stubborn parrot, a school bully who insists on radio air time to read his short stories about kittens, and an adviser who is too busy reading pulp science fiction to help the students with the show. The book was praised by Todd Morning in *School Library Journal* for its comic value. "This story works well on the level of sheer farce," Morning stated, going on to claim that "Korman is good at creating chaotic, if not always believable, situations." A *Publishers Weekly* critic, however, found value beyond the book's humor, stating that *Radio Fifth Grade* is "feelingly written, and earns a place with the best middle-grade fiction; more than a romp, it has genuine charm."

Korman's 1990 book, *Losing Joe's Place,* is the story of Jason Cardone and two friends who, at the age of sixteen, sublet Jason's brother's Toronto apartment while he is away in Europe. Everything that can go wrong does go wrong for the three boys while they strive to pay their rent each month. Again, the story is filled with the farcical characters and chaotic situations for which Korman is known, though the book offers more than its comic strain. Several critics noted the depth of characterization of Jason, who narrates the tale. Shirley Carmony remarked in *Voice of Youth Advocates* that Jason "is a lovable adolescent whose hopes and fears are rather typical ones for a 16 year old boy. His humorous viewpoint is a pleasure." Jack Forman concluded in his *School Library Journal* review of *Losing Joe's Place:* "Surprisingly, it's not the quick twists and turns of the farcical plot that keep this very funny story moving. It's Jason's spirited narrative, his self-effacing sense of humor, and his finely tuned ear for the ridiculous that make these unbelievable antics work and create characters from these caricatures."

In later books Korman has dealt with characters who, while still battling against authority, also outfox their more successful peers. The 1992 novel *The Twinkie Squad,* for instance, relates the goings on of a middle school "Special Discussion Group" for difficult students. Douglas Fairchild inspires his fellow Twinkies to consider their group "Grand Knights of the Exalted Karpoozi," and the students become embroiled in trouble and plots. "Again Korman has used humor to

explore and explain the problems of growing up," *Voice of Youth Advocates* contributor Patsy H. Adams remarked. Praising the characters as "well developed and very familiar," the critic added that the book could be "shared by parent, or grandparent and child." Similarly, *The Toilet Paper Tigers* recounts the transformation of a collection of misfits into a championship baseball team. "With their abundant quirks, the cartoonish characters are an engaging lot," wrote a *Publishers Weekly* critic.

More wacky plot elements and rambunctious characters are served up in novels such as *Why Did the Underwear Cross the Road?, The Chicken Doesn't Skate, Liar, Liar, Pants on Fire, The Sixth Grade Nickname Game,* and *Nose Pickers from Outer Space* and its sequels. Justin, Jessica, and Margaret are determined to win the Good Deed Contest in *Why Did the Underwear Cross the Road?,* besting their peer competitors by catching car thieves. Reviewing this title in *School Library Journal,* Suzanne Hawley concluded, "Korman's book has a galloping plot full of humor, and young readers are sure to enjoy it." Reviewing the same book in *Quill and Quire,* Phyllis Simon noted that the author "delivers his

Ten-year-old Devin discovers that the nerdy, nose-picking exchange student living with his family is an alien with a nose computer who may save the planet. (Cover illustration by Mark Stutzman.)

signature brand of fast-paced humour and frenetic plot-making."

In *The Chicken Doesn't Skate,* the action shifts south of the border to a Minnesota school. Milo's science project on food chains features Henrietta, a chicken who becomes the hockey team's mascot in their bid for a winning season. *Booklist*'s Bill Ott commented, "Korman tells the hilarious story of how a group of kids with little in common ... are thrown together in the hullabaloo over Henrietta's fate." Ott further noted, "This is a genuinely funny, refreshingly unpretentious novel." Zoe Bent is the biggest liar in the third grade in *Liar, Liar, Pants on Fire.* She lies to cover up former lies; lies even when the truth will suffice. But a friend soon convinces her that she has a special gift—a vivid imagination. "The message that everyone is special in their own way is a bit heavy-handed," observed Robin L. Gibson in a *School Library Journal* review of the novel, "but it is, nonetheless, a message that children cannot hear too often."

In the 1998 *The Sixth Grade Nickname Game,* again set south of the Canadian border, this time in Pennsylvania, Jeff and Wiley are inseparable friends, born only hours apart and now joined at the hip emotionally and psychically. They love making up nicknames for their schoolmates, but when the new girl, Cassandra, steals both their hearts, best friends suddenly become competitors. "Korman is at his amusing best here," wrote Janice M. Del Negro in the *Bulletin of the Center for Children's Books.* "This is a funny, fast-paced grade-school romp that is going to cross gender lines with ease," Del Negro concluded. Reviewing the novel in *Booklist,* Carolyn Phelan felt that the "story captures the ambience of sixth grade with humor and empathy," while Sheree Haughian noted in *Quill and Quire* that "Korman has not lost his gift for satire."

In *Nose Pickers from Outer Space,* ten-year-old Devin thinks the exchange student, Stan, is a real nerd and a nose picker to boot, until he discovers that he's actually an alien from the planet Pan on a mission to Earth. His incessant nose picking is actually the activation of a nose computer, as Stan tries to convince his planet that Earth and not Mercury should become the in-spot vacation destination for Pan's inhabitants and thus avoid relocation of the planet to the back of the galactic beyond. "This lightweight sf for middle readers will likely delight Korman fans who usually can't get enough of his slapstick humor, frenzied action, and comic characters," concluded *Booklist* reviewer Karen Hutt. A contributor to *Publishers Weekly* remarked, "Korman's tongue is in his cheek as often as Stan's finger is in his nose, creating a light and silly caper that will, as the series obviously intends, bring on ample laughs." Intergalactic hi-jinks are continued in *Planet of the Nose Pickers* and *Your Mummy Is a Nose Picker.*

Korman has also written two sports series for middle-grade readers, "Monday Night Football Club" and "Slapshots." In the first series, a mysterious old football jersey transforms one young boy into John Elway, and then other friends get into the game, becoming sports greats from Barry Sanders to Jerry Rice. In "Slapshots," the Martians are the newest hockey team in their league, hailing from the small town of Mars, and they battle their own wacky coach as well as opposing teams to win a place at the all-star tournament. Blending sports and humor, both series have become popular with young readers, and the "Monday Night Football Club" has even spawned a popular television series on the Disney Channel.

In his books for middle-grade readers and older adolescents, Korman consistently presents youthful protagonists who attain power and success on their own terms. As Korman told Ferns, "One of the reasons the books do well ... [is] because they address that situation of kids being able to triumph over the adults, and in many cases with the adults coming to terms with it." It helps also, critics note, that Korman employs a cast of humorous and likable characters, and that his plots are blazing fast, making for rapid page-turning and belly laughs. Korman once told *Something about the Author:* "My books are the kind of stories I wanted to read and couldn't find when I was ten, eleven, and twelve. I think that, no matter what the subject matter, kids' concerns are important, and being a kid isn't just waiting out the time between birth and the age of majority."

Biographical and Critical Sources

BOOKS

Children's Literature Review, Volume 25, Gale, 1991.
St. James Guide to Children's Writers, 5th edition, edited by Sara Pendergast and Tom Pendergast, St. James, 1999.

PERIODICALS

Booklist, November 15, 1996, Bill Ott, review of *The Chicken Doesn't Skate,* p. 588; October 15, 1998, Carolyn Phelan, review of *The Sixth Grade Nickname Game,* p. 422; August 19, 1999, Karen Hutt, review of *Nose Pickers from Outer Space,* p. 2058.
Bulletin of the Center for Children's Books, November, 1985; December, 1985; November, 1986; November, 1992, p. 77; November, 1998, Janice M. Del Negro, review of *The Sixth Grade Nickname Game,* p. 103.
Canadian Children's Literature, Number 38, 1985, Chris Ferns, "An Interview with Gordon Korman," pp. 54-65; Number 52, 1988, Ferns, "Escape from New Jersey," pp. 63-64.
Globe and Mail (Toronto, Canada), June 28, 1980; November 18, 1980; October 19, 1985; December 2, 1989.
Horn Book, March-April, 1986; November-December, 1987.
Kirkus Reviews, June 1, 1997, p. 876.
New York Times, July 24, 1985, Leslie Bennetts, "Gordon Korman: Old-Pro Author of 10 Books at 21," section 3, p. 17.
Publishers Weekly, June 30, 1989, review of *Radio Fifth Grade,* p. 106; March 15, 1991, review of *Macdonald Hall Goes Hollywood,* p. 59; July 26, 1993, review of

The Toilet Paper Tigers, p. 73; August 2, 1999, review of *Nose Pickers from Outer Space,* p. 85.

Quill and Quire, November, 1983, Peter Carver, "From the Gripping Yarn to the Gaping Yawn," p. 24; October, 1994, Phyllis Simon, review of *Why Did the Under-wear Cross the Road?,* p. 44; August, 1995, Dave Jenkinson, review of *Something Fishy at Macdonald Hall,* p. 34; January, 1999, Sheree Haughian, review of *The Sixth Grade Nickname Game,* p. 46.

School Library Journal, September, 1989, Todd Morning, review of *Radio Fifth Grade,* p. 252; May, 1990, Jack Forman, review of *Losing Joe's Place,* p. 124; January, 1995, Suzanne Hawley, review of *Why Did the Underwear Cross the Road?,* p. 108; September, 1995, Connie Tyrrell Burns, review of *Something Fishy at Macdonald Hall,* p. 202; November, 1996, Burns, review of *The Chicken Doesn't Skate,* pp. 107-08; September, 1997, Robin L. Gibson, review of *Liar, Liar, Pants on Fire,* p. 185.

Voice of Youth Advocates, June, 1990, Shirley Carmony, review of *Losing Joe's Place,* p. 106; December, 1992, Patsy H. Adams, review of *The Twinkie Squad,* p. 281.

—Sketch by J. Sydney Jones

L

LALLY, Soinbhe 1945-

Personal

Given name is pronounced "*Sun*-i-va"; born April 9, 1945; daughter of Maurice (a bus service operator) and Maud (Ovens) Cassidy; married Patsy Lally (a fisherman); children: John, Zoe, Patrick, Anna. *Education:* Queen's University, Belfast, Northern Ireland, B.A., 1996. *Politics:* Constitutional Nationalist. *Religion:* Roman Catholic.

Addresses

Home—Clifftop, Rossnowlagh, County Donegal, Ireland. *E-mail*—soinbhe@eircom.net.

Career

Ballyshannon Vocational School, in Ireland, teacher of English, 1973-98; writer, 1998—.

Writings

Song of the River, Poolbeg Press (Dublin, Ireland), 1995.
A Hive for the Honeybee, illustrated by Patience Brewster, Poolbeg Press, 1996, Arthur A. Levine Books (New York City), 1999.
The Hungry Wind, Poolbeg Press, 1997.
Favourite Irish Fairy Tales, Poolbeg Press, 1998.
Surf Summer, Poolbeg Press, 1999.
Tales of Ancient Ireland, Poolbeg Press, 2000.

Work in Progress

A story set in Northern Ireland before "the Troubles."

Sidelights

Soinbhe Lally told *SATA:* "I write principally for the pleasure of making and shaping. Themes and stories arise out of transient preoccupations—nature, history, mythology. The actual writing requires an external

Soinbhe Lally

trigger; for example, I come from a family of beekeepers, so the allegorical possibilities of the beehive had occurred to me a long time before my editor asked for another animal story. I started at once on *A Hive for the Honeybee.*

"Similarly, I was long familiar with the story of the Irish famine, but it was not until I discovered that the famine dead in a local workhouse had never been counted that I was impelled, first to count them, and then to write *The Hungry Wind* as a memorial for them. My current writing project was triggered when publisher Arthur A. Lewis queried why I have not set a story in Northern Ireland.

"I love fine writing, whether by the older masters, Shakespeare, Donne, Swift, or by some modern favorites, Kate O'Brien, Virginia Woolf, R. K. Narayan, or Amy Tan."

Biographical and Critical Sources

PERIODICALS

Booklist, February 1, 1999, Ilene Cooper, review of *A Hive for the Honeybee,* p. 969.
Bulletin of the Center for Children's Books, April, 1999, review of *A Hive for the Honeybee,* p. 284.
Horn Book, March, 1999, Lauren Adams, review of *A Hive for the Honeybee,* p. 209.
Kirkus Reviews, December 1, 1998, review of *A Hive for the Honeybee,* p. 1736.
Kliatt Young Adult Paperback Book Guide, January, 1999, review of *A Hive for the Honeybee,* p. 7.
New York Times Book Review, May 16, 1999, Rebecca Boggs Roberts, review of *A Hive for the Honeybee,* p. 27.
Publishers Weekly, March 8, 1999, review of *A Hive for the Honeybee,* p. 246.
School Library Journal, May, 1999, Barbara Scotto, review of *A Hive for the Honeybee,* p. 127.
Voice of Youth Advocates, April, 1999, review of *A Hive for the Honeybee,* p. 48.*

*　　　*　　　*

LAWRENCE, Louise 1943-

Personal

Born Elizabeth Rhoda Holden, June 5, 1943, in Leatherhead, Surrey, England; daughter of Fred (a bricklayer) and Rhoda Edith (a cook; maiden name, Cowles) Holden; married second husband, Graham Mace, August 28, 1987; children: Rachel Louise, Ralph Lawrence, Rebecca Jane. *Politics:* "Bewildered by." *Religion:* "Searching for."

Addresses

Home—22 Church Rd., Cinderford, Gloucestershire GL14 2EA, England. *Agent*—A. M. Heath, 79 St. Martin's Lane, London WC2N 4AA, England.

Career

Assistant librarian at Gloucestershire Country Library, 1961-63, and at Forest of Dean branches, 1969-71; writer, 1971—.

Writings

YOUNG ADULT FICTION

Andra, Collins (London), 1971.
The Power of Stars: A Story of Suspense, Harper (New York City), 1972.
The Wyndcliffe: A Story of Suspense, Collins, 1974, Harper, 1975.
Sing and Scatter Daisies (sequel to *The Wyndcliffe*), Harper, 1977.
Star Lord, Harper, 1978.
Cat Call, Harper, 1980.
The Earth Witch, Harper, 1981.
Calling B for Butterfly, Harper, 1982, revised edition, Bodley Head (London), 1988.
The Dram Road, Harper, 1983.
Children of the Dust, Harper, 1985.
Moonwind, Harper, 1986.
The Warriors of Taan, Bodley Head, 1986, Harper, 1988.
Extinction Is Forever and Other Stories, HarperCollins, 1990.
Keeper of the Universe Clarion, 1992, published as *Ben-Harran's Castle,* Bodley Head, 1992.
The Disinherited, Bodley Head, 1994.
The Patchwork People, Clarion, 1994.
Dream-Weaver, Clarion (New York City), 1996.
The Crowlings, HarperCollins (New York City), 1999.

"LLANDOR TRILOGY"; FANTASY

Journey through Llandor, HarperCollins, 1995.
The Road to Irriyan, HarperCollins, 1996.
The Shadow of Mordican, HarperCollins, 1996.

Sidelights

Louise Lawrence has built a large and loyal following on the strength of fantasy and science-fiction novels such as *The Patchwork People, The Disinherited,* and *Dream-Weaver.* Though often set in the distant past or far-flung future, her novels reflect issues and concerns confronted by young men and women of every generation. Unusual in that she features young women as protagonists in her novels, Lawrence has honed her craft to such a degree that essayist Jessica Yates dubbed her "Britain's senior woman practitioner of young adult science fiction" in the *St. James Guide to Young Adult Writers.* Essayist Ann G. Hay added in *Twentieth-Century Children's Writers* that although Lawrence's "protagonists are girls, ... this does not mean that boys will be switched off from reading their adventures" because of the realistic relationships that develop between the heroine and the young men around her.

Lawrence's fiction is characterized as "essentially humane," according to a *Junior Bookshelf* contributor in a review of *Extinction Is Forever.* "She shirks none of the technical problems of the genre, but most of all she writes about individuals and their personal dilemmas, whether they are in this world or off-world." Critic Paul Heins, writing in *Horn Book,* concluded that Lawrence so skillfully balances the mundane and the fantastic that "she has made the unbelievable believable."

Born in Surrey, England, in 1943, Lawrence was drawn to storytelling by her grandfather, whose fantastic tales were a hallmark of her childhood. "He had the power to frighten me witless," the author recalled in an essay in the *Sixth Book of Junior Authors & Illustrators.* "He peopled the hills with giants and fairies and mythical beasts, monsters of his own ghoulish imagination. And he fostered mine—taught me of trees and flowers, how to dabble in ponds, where the birds nested, and how to distinguish their songs."

Even with this background, Lawrence's transformation into a professional author was not an easy one, brought about as it was by an unhappy first marriage. "What motivated me into writing my first (unpublished) book at the age of twenty-two was fear of mental stagnation," she once commented. "What gave rise to that fear was being married with small children, totally isolated socially and environmentally in a remote farmhouse, with a husband who had no time for me." Lawrence didn't consciously "choose" to be an author. Rather, she explained, "An idea came to me and I felt compelled to set it down, and in six weeks I had written a very bad book."

Despite the poor quality of her initial work, Lawrence persevered. "I wrote to occupy my mind, as a hobby, as a way of escaping from unhappy reality into worlds of fantasy. I wrote because I was compelled to write ... and it got a hold on me like a drug." Nourishing this compulsion, she managed to write a total of four "very bad" books before selling what would become her first published novel, *Andra,* in 1970. With this success under her belt, Lawrence decided to embark upon a career as a professional writer. Divorcing her husband, she "set out to survive alone." Since the publication of her first novel in 1971, she has provided readers with over a dozen novels, as well as a fantasy series known as the "Llandor Trilogy."

Set two thousand years in the future, *Andra* is the story of a fifteen-year-old girl who lives in a future earth where humans inhabit underground cities because of the disintegration of Earth's atmosphere. Andra receives a "brain graft," a donation of frozen tissue taken from a boy who died in the 1980s. Soon after the procedure, Andra is filled with strange, rebellious thoughts: she sees her society not as the technological Utopia she was taught to view it as, but as a restrictive machine designed to limit individual freedom. Fired by memories of her brain donor—memories of a society that cherished personal freedom—Andra becomes the leader of a youth movement bent on overturning the rule of the city director.

Though several critics found the scientific concepts in Lawrence's debut novel somewhat implausible, *School*

In a bleak, futuristic Wales, a group of impoverished teens befriend a rich girl and work toward a brighter social future. (Cover illustration by Paul Hunt.)

Library Journal contributor Lucinda Snyder Whitehurst described the book as "both hopeful and sorrowful. *Andra* is a fascinating story about the power of one individual following a dream." And a reviewer for *Publishers Weekly* maintained that "thoughtful teens will find much of interest in spite of the abrupt ending" of this "grim, futuristic tale."

The year after *Andra* was published, Lawrence released *The Power of Stars.* In this novel, which takes place in present-day Wales, a bite from an infected rabbit causes a young woman to fear for her sanity when she perceives an overwhelming desire to harness her thought-power for destructive purposes. In 1988's *The Warriors of Taan* Lawrence depicts a planet in which the two genders have been rigidly segregated: the warlike men control their sphere through force and intimidation, while the more cerebral women, known as the Sisterhood, prefer reason and cunning. Both groups, however, must contend with the Earth colonists who have come to claim their planet. The only way to regain Taan is for the two groups to merge, to produce a hero whose might is tempered by feminine wiles. *School Library Journal* critic Pam Spencer called *The Warriors of Taan* a "'can't-put-down' book" that is "filled with adventure, symbolism, and wonderful writing, from opening sentence to last line."

In 1992's *Keeper of the Universe,* Lawrence pits her young characters against an intimidating opponent: the devil. In the novel, Lucifer is embodied in Ben-Harran, a member of the intergalactic High Council of Atui that rules the planets. Earth, along with several other planets, falls under the rule of Ben-Harran, who, despite his rather demonic reputation, steadfastly refuses to intervene in the affairs of his planets. Unfortunately, Ben-Harran's hands-off policy leads to the destruction of one planet, Zeeda, and he is brought to trial by the High Council on charges of genocide. Representatives from his other planets, including Earth, are called in to testify either for or against Ben-Harran. Though a *Kirkus Reviews* critic called *Keeper of the Universe* "talky, didactic, [and] more polemic than science fiction" should be, the book received praise from other quarters. *Keepers of the Universe* "succeeds because of its trenchant humor, capped by a deliciously ironic final twist," opined a *Publishers Weekly* critic. Calling

An apprentice dream-weaver on the peaceful planet Arbroth and a young crewman on a colonizing mission from Earth work together to save Arbroth and themselves. (Cover illustration by Anton Kimball.)

Lawrence's writing "rich and lyrical," *Voice of Youth Advocates* contributor Bonnie Kunzel said that *Keepers of the Universe* "is fascinating reading for those who prefer science fiction of a more speculative nature."

Like *Andra, Children of the Dust* takes place on a postholocaust Earth, as eight-year-old Catherine and her family hide in an underground bunker in an attempt to shield themselves from radioactivity after a nuclear bomb is detonated during an attack on England. While the rest of her family succumbs to the radiation and slowly die, Catherine exhibits the creativity and quick thinking that allows her to survive the holocaust and live to be mother to a new race of humans. Written during the early 1980s, *Children of the Dust* reflects a concern shared by many during that time: that nuclear power is an energy form that will ultimately destroy, rather than support the human race.

Published in 1998 and first appearing in Great Britain under the title *The Disinherited,* Lawrence's *The Patchwork People* also takes place on a future Earth, this time in Wales, where the planet's natural resources are almost gone, jobs are few and far between, and most of the inhabitants have become used to a culture of government subsidies and welfare. Helena, raised in one of the few economically well-off families, meets and befriends a poor young man named Hugh, who seeks a job in the coal mines; together they work to improve the social landscape. "Hugh and Helena's world and their dilemma seem so achingly real that readers will cheer the characters' valor," maintained a *Publishers Weekly* contributor, dubbing *The Patchwork People* "a frighteningly possible near-future dystopia." "Lawrence cleverly plays with her [well-drawn] characters," noted *Booklist* contributor Chris Sherman, "continually offering them hope, then snatching it away to show that simple solutions aren't enough."

In addition to her stand-alone science-fiction novels, Lawrence has also penned a fantasy trilogy that takes its name from its setting in Llandor. Beginning with *Journey through Llandor,* the author introduces a group of three pre-teens—the overweight Roderick and his schoolyard tormentors, Craig and Carrie—who are suddenly whisked into a parallel universe where life is lived as it was in the fourteenth century. Sought by the evil Grimthane because of their knowledge of technology, the three band together in search of a way home by embarking on a quest for a place called Seer's Keep, wherein all wisdom will be found. All sorts of creatures appear during their journey, which takes the three travelers through the concluding novels *The Road to Irriyan* and *The Shadow of Mordican:* dwarves, wizards, elves, trolls, goblins, sorceresses, and the like. "The author has drawn upon two powerful myths[—the journey as a means of salvation and the search for a Golden Age—]with compelling success," noted a *Junior Bookshelf* contributor. However, *Magpies* contributor Michael Gregg cautioned comparisons with J. R. R. Tolkien's *Lord of the Rings* trilogy, claiming "the plot drags" in Lawrence's trilogy.

"The thing about Louise Lawrence is that, carefully as she works at the science, one suspects that it is the fiction (i.e., the people) which really concerns her," declared one *Junior Bookshelf* critic in reviewing the author's body of work. "We are riveted to the ground ... watching the protagonists as they work out their destinies.... It demands, and deserves, the reader's total surrender." Whether fantasy or science fiction, her work continues to focus on efforts to find a positive path for humanity, and, as Yates concluded in the *St. James Guide to Young Adult Writers,* "to warn readers of the dangers of human destruction in compelling and talented novels."

As to writing, the author admitted in the *Sixth Book of Junior Authors & Illustrators* that "it remains a strange and magical process, and it was never I who chose to write the books but the books that chose me to write them. Each one came to me unasked for, like watching a film being projected onto a screen inside my head ... the whole story from beginning to end compelling me to write it."

Biographical and Critical Sources

BOOKS

Holtze, Sally Holmes, *Sixth Book of Junior Authors & Illustrators,* H. W. Wilson, 1989, pp. 161-191.

Twentieth-Century Children's Writers, third edition, St. Martin's, 1989.

St. James Guide to Young Adult Writers, St. James, 1996, pp. 161-163.

PERIODICALS

Booklist, December 15, 1994, Chris Sherman, review of *The Patchwork People,* p. 750; October 1, 1996, Chris Sherman, review of *Dream-Weaver,* p. 349; September 15, 1998, Sally Estes, review of *The Patchwork People,* p. 219.

Books for Keeps, November, 1993, Jessica Yates, review of *Children of the Dust,* p. 26.

Bulletin of the Center for Children's Books, December, 1978, p. 65; July, 1980, p. 218; February, 1995, Deborah Stevens, review of *The Patchwork People,* p. 205.

Horn Book, August, 1977, p. 450; June, 1981, Paul Heins, review of *The Earth Witch,* p. 310; December, 1982, p. 659; January, 1986, p. 92; March 15, 1993, review of *Keeper of the Universe,* p. 373.

Junior Bookshelf, February, 1988, review of *Star Lord,* p. 48; October, 1990, review of *Extinction Is Forever,* p. 253; December, 1992, review of *Ben-Harran's Castle,* p. 267; August, 1995, review of *Journey through Llandor,* p. 154.

Kirkus Reviews, March 15, 1980, p. 371; March 15, 1991, p. 395; March 15, 1993, review of *Keeper of the Universe,* p. 373.

Los Angeles Times, August 9, 1998, Dan Daily, review of *Children of the Dust,* p. 8.

Magpies, September, 1996, Michael Gregg, review of *Journey through Llandor, The Road to Irriyan,* and *The Shadow of Mordican,* p. 34.

Publishers Weekly, May 30, 1977, p. 45; December 25, 1987, p. 75; April 5, 1991, Diane Roback, review of *Andra,* p. 146; April 26, 1993, review of *Keeper of the Universe,* p. 80; September 26, 1994, review of *The Patchwork People,* p. 71; October 7, 1996, p. 77.

School Librarian, May, 1993, review of *Ben-Harran's Castle,* p. 72; November, 1994, review of *The Disinherited,* p. 166; February, 1997, review of *Shadow of Mordican,* p. 47.

School Library Journal, April, 1977, p. 77; August, 1980, p. 77; February, 1988, Pam Spencer, review of *The Warriors of Taan,* p. 84; October, 1990, review of *Extinction Is Forever,* p. 253; May, 1991, Lucinda Snyder Whitehurst, review of *Andra,* p. 112; December, 1992, review of *Ben-Harran's Castle,* p. 267; February, 1988, review of *Star Lord,* p. 48.

Times Literary Supplement, April 2, 1971, p. 383; April 28, 1972, p. 484; November 28, 1986, p. 1347.

Voice of Youth Advocate, October, 1993, Bonnie Kunzel, review of *Keeper of the Universe,* p. 232; February, 1997, Kellie Shoemaker, review of *Dream-Weaver,* p. 337.

Wilson Library Bulletin, October, 1993, Francis Bradburn, review of *Keeper of the Universe,* pp. 122-23.*

* * *

LEDBETTER, Suzann 1953-

Personal

Born April 15, 1953, in Joplin, MO; daughter of Howard A. and M. Sue Rodgers. *Member:* American Society of Journalists and Authors, Western Writers of America, Ozarks Writers League (member of board of directors), Ozark Creative Writers (member of board of directors), Missouri Writers Guild.

Addresses

Office—P.O. Box 1032, Nixa, MO 65714. *Agent*—Robin Rue, Anita Diamant Agency, 310 Madison Ave., New York, NY 10017.

Career

President of Quassare Femina, Inc.; Southwest Missouri State University, instructor in continuing education department; guest on television programs, including *The Today Show* and *The Bertrice Berry Show;* convention and workshop speaker, through Program Corp. of America.

Awards, Honors

Best humorous article, Missouri Writers Guild, 1989, 1990, 1991; Golden Spur Award for nonfiction, Western Writers of America, 1994, for *Nellie Cashman: Prospector and Trailblazer.*

Writings

On the Edge of Forever, Bouregy (New York), 1992.

Nellie Cashman: Prospector and Trailblazer (biography), Texas Western Press (El Paso), 1993.
The Toast Always Lands Jelly-Side Down and Other Tales of Suburban Life (humor), Crown (New York), 1993.
I Have Everything I Had Twenty Years Ago, Except Now It's All Lower (humor), illustrated by Heidi Graf, Random House/Crown, 1995.
In Fortune's Wake (novel), Dutton/Penguin, 1995.
Redemption Trail (novel), New American Library, 1996.
Trinity Strike (novel), New American Library, 1996.
Klondike Fever (novel), Penguin, 1997.
Pure Justice (novel), New American Library, 1997.
Deliverance Drive (novel), Signet, 1997.
East of Peculiar (novel), Harlequin, 2000.

Also author of *Colorado Reverie,* 1997. Author of the column "The Flip Side" and contributing editor to *Family Circle.* Contributor to magazines, including *Entrepreneurial Woman, American Forests, True West, Careers and the Handicapped, Lost Treasure,* and *For Women First.*

Sidelights

Suzann Ledbetter is a biographer, novelist, and humorist best known for a number of popular historical novels that appeal to readers of all ages. Her fiction, most of which is set in the nineteenth century, centers on strong female protagonists who manage to prosper in difficult "pioneering" environments and in spite of constraining social dictates.

Ledbetter comments, "If I could give one piece of advice to those dreaming of a writing career, it would be: spend as much time and energy learning the business as you do the craft. To my mind, there's no better job in the world than spinning yarns, smoothing the warp, and weaving the best combination of idea, thought, and expression one can possibly create. Once that piecework is complete, however, the next step is compelling an editor to buy one's wares, and that takes as much skill, common sense, and flat-out hard work as it did to produce, if not more.

"As far as I'm concerned, that marketing aspect provides almost as much fun, and is definitely as challenging, as putting thoughts and plots on paper. Bear in mind this comes from a writer who has been, and continues to be, rejected by some of the best publishers in the business, one who has thrown varying degrees of hissy fits whenever those 'thumbs down' notices arrive. That's part of the game, however, and I am fortunate to be a player. Writing professionally has been a dream for most of my life. To be living out one's dream, regardless of the trials and tribulations, is the most joyful, satisfying, wondrous experience imaginable. I wouldn't take a million dollars for it. Of course, a few more zeroes on those book advance checks wouldn't be turned down!"

Biographical and Critical Sources

PERIODICALS

Kirkus Reviews, March 1, 1995, review of *I Have Everything I Had Twenty Years Ago, Except Now It's All Lower,* p. 299.
Library Journal, April 1, 1995, Pamela R. Daubenspeck, review of *I Have Everything I Had Twenty Years Ago, Except Now It's All Lower,* p. 95.
Publishers Weekly, July 15, 1996, review of *Deliverance Drive,* p. 72.*

*   *   *

LEVITIN, Sonia (Wolff) 1934-
(Sonia Wolff)

Personal

Born August 18, 1934, in Berlin, Germany; immigrated to the United States, 1938; naturalized U.S. citizen; daughter of Max (a manufacturer) and Helene (Goldstein) Wolff; married Lloyd Levitin (a business executive) December 27, 1953; children: Daniel Joseph, Shari Diane. *Education:* Attended University of California, Berkeley, 1952-54; University of Pennsylvania, B.S., 1956; San Francisco State College (now University), graduate study, 1957-60. *Religion:* Jewish. *Hobbies and*

Sonia Levitin with her German shepherd puppy.

other interests: Hiking, piano, Judaic studies, travel, history, painting.

Addresses

Home—Southern California. *Agent*—Toni Mendez, Inc., 141 East 56th St., New York, NY 10022.

Career

Writer and educator. Junior high school teacher in Mill Valley, CA, 1956-57; adult education teacher in Daly City, CA, 1962-64; Acalanes Adult Center, Lafayette, CA, teacher, 1965-72; teacher of creative writing, Palos Verdes Peninsula, CA, 1973-76, and University of California, Los Angles Extension, 1976—; instructor in American Jewish literature, University of Judaism, 1989—. Founder of STEP (adult education organization) in Palos Verdes Peninsula. *Member:* Authors League of America, Authors Guild, PEN, Society of Children's Book Writers and Illustrators, California Writer's Guild, Moraga Historical Society (founder and president).

Awards, Honors

National Jewish Book award in children's literature and American Library Association (ALA) Notable Book citation, both 1970, both for *Journey to America; Who Owns the Moon?* received an ALA Notable Book citation, 1973; *The Mark of Conte* received the Southern California Council on Literature for Children and Young People Award for fiction, 1976, and was nominated for California Young Readers Medal award in junior high category, 1982; Golden Spur Award from Western Writers of America, and Lewis Carroll Shelf Award, both 1978, both for *The No-Return Trail;* Southern California Council on Literature for Children and Young People award, 1981, for a distinguished contribution to the field of children's literature; National Jewish Book Award in children's literature, PEN Los Angeles Award for young adult fiction, Association of Jewish Libraries Sydney Taylor Award, Austrian Youth Prize, Catholic Children's Book Prize (Germany), Dorothy Canfield Fisher Award nomination, Parent's Choice Honor Book citation, and ALA Best Book for Young Adults citation, all 1988, all for *The Return;* Edgar Allan Poe Award from Mystery Writers of America, Dorothy Canfield Fisher Award nomination, and Nevada State Award nomination, all 1989, all for *Incident at Loring Groves;* *Silver Days* was named a 1989 Sydney Taylor Book Award Honor Book; "Pick of the Lists" selection, American Booksellers Association, and "Books in the Middle: Outstanding Titles of 1999," *Voice of Youth Advocates,* both 1999, both for *The Cure; Roanoke: A Novel of the Lost Colony* was nominated for the Dorothy Canfield Fisher Award, the Georgia Children's Book Award, and the Mark Twain Award; *Journey to America* and *The No-Return Trail* were both Junior Literary Guild selections.

Writings

FOR YOUNG ADULTS

Journey to America (first novel in the "Platt Family" trilogy), illustrated by Charles Robinson, Atheneum, 1970.

Roanoke: A Novel of the Lost Colony, illustrated by John Gretzer, Atheneum, 1973.

The Mark of Conte, illustrated by Bill Negron, Atheneum, 1976, published without illustrations, Collier Books, 1987.

Beyond Another Door, Atheneum, 1977.

The No-Return Trail, Harcourt, 1978.

Reigning Cats and Dogs (nonfiction), illustrated by Joan Berg Victor, Atheneum, 1978.

The Year of Sweet Senior Insanity, Atheneum, 1982.

Smile Like a Plastic Daisy, Atheneum, 1984.

A Season for Unicorns, Atheneum, 1986.

The Return, Atheneum, 1987.

Incident at Loring Groves, Dial, 1988.

Silver Days (second novel in the "Platt Family" trilogy), Atheneum, 1989.

The Golem and the Dragon Girl, Dial, 1993.

Annie's Promise (third novel in the "Platt Family" trilogy), Atheneum, 1993.

Escape from Egypt, Little, Brown, 1994.

Evil Encounter, Simon & Schuster, 1996.

Yesterday's Child, Simon & Schuster, 1997.

The Singing Mountain, Simon & Schuster, 1998.

The Cure, Harcourt, 1999.

PICTURE BOOKS FOR CHILDREN

Who Owns the Moon?, illustrated by John Larrecq, Parnassus, 1973.

A Single Speckled Egg, illustrated by John Larrecq, Parnassus, 1976.

A Sound to Remember, illustrated by Gabriel Lisowski, Harcourt, 1979.

Nobody Stole the Pie, illustrated by Fernando Krahn, Harcourt, 1980.

All the Cats in the World, illustrated by Charles Robinson, Harcourt, 1982.

The Fisherman and the Bird, illustrated by Francis Livingston, Houghton, 1982.

The Man Who Kept His Heart in a Bucket, illustrated by Jerry Pinkney, Dial, 1991.

A Piece of Home, illustrated by Juan Wijngaard, Dial, 1996.

Nine for California, illustrated by Cat Bowman Smith, Orchard, 1996.

Boom Town (sequel to *Nine for California*), illustrated by Cat Bowman Smith, Orchard, 1998.

Taking Charge (sequel to *Boom Town*), illustrated by Cat Bowman Smith, Orchard, 1999.

OTHER

Rita, the Weekend Rat (fiction), illustrated by Leonard W. Shortall, Atheneum, 1971.

Jason and the Money Tree (fiction), illustrated by Pat Grant Porter, Harcourt, 1974.

(Under name Sonia Wolff) *What They Did to Miss Lily* (fiction for adults), Harper, 1981.

(Author of introduction) Yale Strom, *A Tree Still Stands: Jewish Youth in Eastern Europe Today,* Putnam, 1990.
Adam's War (for children), illustrated by Vincent Nasta, Dial, 1994.

Feature columnist for Sun Newspapers, Contra Costa, CA, and *Jewish Observer of the East Bay,* Oakland, CA. Contributor to periodicals, including *Christian Science Monitor, Ingenue, Parents', The Writer, Reform Judaism,* and *Smithsonian.*

Sidelights

Sonia Levitin survived a difficult childhood to thrive as an award-winning children's author whose books treat difficult questions of faith and morality. Born to Jewish parents in 1934 amid the anti-Semitism of Nazi Germany, she soon fled with her family to the United States. There she grew up in poverty but went on to gain a college education and fulfill her girlhood dream of becoming a writer. After being honored by the Jewish Book Council of America in 1970 for her autobiographical first novel, *Journey to America,* she earned further awards for a wide variety of books, including the Western *No-Return Trail,* the murder mystery *Incident at Loring Groves,* and the refugee story *The Return.*

In the years before Levitin was born, her parents had become prosperous members of the German middle class. Her father earned a living as a skillful tailor and businessman. The family enjoyed such comforts as household servants and vacations at resorts. All that changed dramatically after the Nazis took power in 1933 and began the campaign of anti-Jewish terror and murder now known as the Holocaust. To escape persecution, three-year-old Sonia and her family left their belongings and savings behind them and slipped into neighboring Switzerland. There she waited with her mother and two sisters for a year as refugees while their father went to America to arrange a home for them. Once the family was settled in the United States, young Sonia's parents worked mightily to recreate the family business; they were so busy that for several years Sonia was raised largely by one of her sisters.

"The Holocaust experience left its deep mark on me," recalled Levitin in an account of her life that she wrote for the *Something about the Author Autobiography Series (SAAS).* "It is agonizing for me as a Jew to realize that our people were almost exterminated; it is equally agonizing, as a human being, to have to admit to the evil that humans can do to one another." Although Levitin was forced to confront discrimination and suffering at an early age, she also learned the power of compassion, as her family was helped by a variety of non-Jews who sympathized with their plight. "To them I owe a great debt," Levitin wrote, "not the least of which is my optimistic belief that despite evil in the world, there is goodness in great measure, and that goodness knows no boundaries of religion or race."

For a few years Levitin's parents moved the family back and forth between New York City and Los Angeles in an effort to make a living. Finally, they settled for good in southern California. Young Sonia became an avid reader, and at age eleven she wrote to Laura Ingalls Wilder, beloved author of the "Little House on the Prairie" novels, to confess that she wanted to become a writer. "To my great joy," she recalled in *SAAS,* "[I] received a reply, which remains among my treasures to this day." As Levitin progressed through school, she continued to be drawn to the arts, writing poems and short stories and learning how to paint and play the piano.

When Levitin was eighteen, she enrolled at the University of California, and almost immediately she met her future husband, a fellow student. They were married when she was nineteen. Once the couple completed their studies, they settled in the San Francisco area, and after Levitin had taught school for a year she became pregnant and decided to stay home to raise her family. To make full use of her time, she resolved to become a writer in earnest, and with encouragement from her husband, she became a part-time writing student at San Francisco State College, where she studied under Walter Van Tilburg Clark, the author of *The Ox-Bow Incident.*

Levitin's career as a writer began modestly by volunteering to do publicity work for charities. This work led to her writing articles for magazines and columns for local newspapers. She also taught creative writing classes of her own. She remained frustrated, though, by her efforts to make an impact as a short-story writer. As an exercise, she started writing a longer narrative based on the tribulations that her family experienced when she was very young. This story, which she originally intended only for her own children, grew over the course of several years into *Journey to America,* a full-length novel for young people that was published to widespread praise in 1970. The book describes a year in the life of the fictional Platt family, Jewish refugees whose escape from Nazi Germany to the United States resembles Levitin's own. "With *Journey to America,*" wrote Levitin in her autobiography, "I felt that my career was launched, and that I had found my niche. I loved writing for young people. I felt that in this genre I could be both gentle and serious, idealistic and pragmatic. I realized that I happen to possess a wonderful memory for the details of my own childhood, for smells and sights and sounds, how faces looked, how feelings felt, and what childhood was really all about."

Levitin went on to publish a new book almost every year, and she looked at growing up from many different points of view. Some of her books, including *Rita, the Weekend Rat* and *The Mark of Conte,* are humorous stories loosely inspired by the antics of her own son and daughter. *Rita* is about a girl who thinks of her pet rat as her closest friend, while *The Mark of Conte* features an energetic high-school freshman who tries to outsmart the school computer and earn credit for two years of classes in one year's time. Other books, in the spirit of *Journey to America,* are more serious works in which young people confront major challenges. *The No-Return Trail,* which won the prestigious Golden Spur Award, is a

Western novel that breaks with tradition by stressing the heroism of a woman: the main character is a seventeen-year-old wife and mother who became the first female settler to cross the continent to California. The tale is based on a real wagon-train expedition from the 1840s and was researched in part through a local history society in Moraga, California, that Levitin founded with her husband. *Incident at Loring Groves,* which won the coveted Edgar Award for mystery fiction, is a novel about the moral dilemmas that teenagers face in the uncertain modern world. The story, again based on fact, describes the difficult choices faced by a group of irresponsible high-schoolers who discover that one of their classmates has been murdered and how they try to avoid telling police for fear that their own drug abuse and vandalism will be exposed as well. A *Publishers Weekly* critic hailed the book as "a searingly honest portrayal of adolescent society." "In each book I try to do something quite different from the previous work," Levitin once observed. "Themes and characters might repeat themselves, but I believe that my growth as a writer and as a person depends on accepting new challenges, deepening my experience and my efforts."

One theme that recurs in Levitin's work is the importance of her Jewish heritage. Nearly two decades after she wrote *Journey to America,* Levitin wrote a sequel, *Silver Days,* that follows the Platt family as it adjusts to life in the United States. When the mother of the family collapses with grief at news of the continuing Holocaust, she and the others find solace in carrying on the traditions of Judaism in their new homeland. "Our future," the father declares, "must have room in it for the past." With *Annie's Promise* Levitin completed the Platt family trilogy. This time the narrator, the younger sister, Annie, tells of her adolescent struggles, which include a summer camp stay. Although a *Publishers Weekly* contributor complained about a "somewhat diffuse" plot, the critic applauded Levitin's "strong, unusually likable characters and her book's pervasive atmosphere."

The Return, a novel that won major awards in both America and Europe, recounts the saga of an unusual group of refugees who arrived in Israel in the mid-1980s. They were the "black Jews" of Ethiopia, Africans who for centuries had observed Jewish religious traditions in almost complete isolation from fellow Jews and the rest of the world. Facing increasing discrimination in their native land, they were smuggled to their new home by the Israeli government through a secret military airlift. As a former refugee, Levitin was deeply moved by the operation and dropped her other writing projects to create a novel about it, journeying to Israel to interview the Ethiopians herself. Writing in the *New York Times Book Review,* Sheila Klass called the book "a remarkable fictional account," praised its evocation of Ethiopian Jewish culture, and declared that "*The Return* is crammed with history, as Sonia Levitin, the author of other distinguished books for young people about Jewish history, here tells the story of an entire people."

During this period Levitin also intensely studied the Torah, the Jewish scriptures. She put her research to use in her historical novel *Escape from Egypt,* about the Jews' exodus from Egypt as seen through the eyes of Jesse, an Israelite slave, and the half-Egyptian girl Jennat, with whom he falls in love. According to *Booklist* reviewer Ilene Cooper, the "human dimension is the great strength of the novel. Levitin makes myth manageable, bringing it right into the lives of modern-day readers." Questions of love, duty, and faith intermingle with the action of Moses freeing the Israelites from the recalcitrant Pharoah in what a *Publishers Weekly* contributor labeled a "startling and searching" exploration that would "spur her audience to fresh appraisals of sacred history." Cooper continued, "There are never easy answers to big questions, of course, and Levitin never pretends there are." Instead, Levitin provokes readers into pondering universal questions, questions that she has pondered intensely herself. "Working on this book was one of the most exhilarating experiences in my career," Levitin told *Authors and Artists for Young Adults (AAYA),* "for it brought together my love of research, the delight of rendering powerful and brilliant episodes described in the Bible, and exploring the questions that have engrossed mankind from the beginning of consciousness."

The 1992 Persian Gulf War inspired Levitin's middle grade novel *Adam's War,* which is about a thoughtful, nice boy who becomes embroiled in a turf war between rival gangs. "Every war has its reason, its instigators, and its victims," Levitin explained to *AAYA.* "Today's children must decide, early on, how to deal with violence, not only the violence that is flung against them, but also the potential violence within." In her *Booklist* review, Stephanie Zvirin asserted that the author "convincingly depicts children's glamorization of violence and their ready acceptance of it as a measure of strength and a means toward self-esteem." Deeming *Adam's War* an "unusually thought-provoking novel," a *Publishers Weekly* critic praised Levitin's creation of "complex" and "commanding" characters and situations.

Although Levitin is likely best known for her young adult fiction, she is also the author of picture books. Among them, her trio of historical works about a spunky girl named Amanda has elicited praise for characterizations, humor, and use of period details. Beginning with *Nine for California,* Levitin tells of how Amanda's family left Missouri to join the California Gold Rush. In particular, Mama and her five children join other travelers on a three-week-long stagecoach trip during which Mama's bulging bag of items saves the day more than once. According to a *Publishers Weekly* reviewer, with its combination of facts and humor "this lighthearted picture book puts a uniquely human face on the Gold Rush era."

After reading a reference to a young lady who used a frying pan to bake eleven thousand dollars' worth of pies during the Gold Rush, Levitin wrote a sequel to *Nine for California.* In *Boom Town,* Amanda narrates how a stagecoach stop becomes a fully developed town after her pie baking business encourages people to settle the area. Reviewers found much to like about *Boom Town.*

"True or not, this is an entertaining way to learn history," enthused Lauren Peterson in *Booklist*. *New York Times Book Review* contributor Anne Scott MacLeod declared that in *Boom Town* "everybody works, and so does this warmhearted book." In *Horn Book* critic Margaret A. Bush's view, Levitin's goal of showing that more people prospered as settlers and businesspeople than by finding gold is "adroitly accomplished in this entertaining lesson in history and human nature." Writing in *School Library Journal*, Steven Engelfried pointed out Amanda's tendency to exaggerate but did not consider it a defect. Instead, Engelfried noted, these exaggerations add "just the right touch of humor to an authentic, though exaggerated look at the development of the West."

In the final episode featuring Amanda, *Taking Charge*, Amanda does just that—taking over for her mother while she is away caring for Amanda's ill grandmother. Watching over her toddler brother, Nathan, is only one of Amanda's many responsibilities in this "spirited story," a "surefire winner," to quote Beth Tegart in *School Library Journal*. Eventually, Amanda asks the neighbors for help, just as her mother had suggested. Though some of the incidents are implausible, Carolyn Phelan noted in her *Booklist* review that "children will enjoy Amanda's dilemmas and Nathan's escapades." "Children, parents, and teachers will all enjoy the historical venture," concluded Margaret A. Bush of *Horn Book*.

Levitin continues to explore what it means to be Jewish in her young adult novel *The Singing Mountain*. Told in alternating chapters by California natives Mitch and his cousin Carlie, the narrative follows Mitch's decision to study at a yeshiva in Jerusalem instead of attending college in the United States. As part of a coming-of-age novel, Levitin objectively presents both Orthodox and Reform Jewish practices. Commentators found much to like about the work. "This plot-driven novel bristles with questions about faith, love, family, acceptance, and self-determination," remarked *Booklist* critic Karen Simonetti. A *Publishers Weekly* reviewer added that Levitin uses a light touch and "maintains a remarkable evenhandedness with all her characters ... as she presents conflicting points of view without favoring any one of them." Although much of the novel's action is interior, "Levitin holds the reader with the amiable character of the seeking Mitch," asserted Janice M. Del Negro in the *Bulletin of the Center for Children's Books*. Elisabeth Palmer Abarbanel, writing in *School Library Journal*, praised Mitch's "spiritual growth and interest in his religion and history ... [as] fascinating." *The Singing Mountain* "succeeds as a realistic and poignant portrayal of a young man's search for God and self, conveying both the struggle and joy of the continuous journey," concluded Lauren Adams in *Horn Book*.

Levitin particularly focuses on prejudice against Jews in her time-shift novel *The Cure*, which several reviewers likened to Lois Lowry's award-winning novel *The Giver* for its depiction of a future in which society limits freedoms in order to ensure harmony. When citizen

Gemm 16884 finds himself attracted to music in a society that disallows music, he is considered a deviant and sent into the distant past to be cured of his malady. In fourteenth-century Europe, Gemm witnesses the persecution of Jews, who were made scapegoats for the plague that was terrorizing Europe. The work earned somewhat mixed reviews. A *Publishers Weekly* critic maintained that the novel "handily combines futuristic science fiction and late-medieval Jewish history," and *Booklist* critic Ilene Cooper asserted, "Gemm's experience in Strasbourg is carefully crafted and emotionally evocative." Similarly, a critic writing in *Kirkus Reviews* praised Levitin's "unusual mix of science and historical fiction," saying that the novel "pulsates with energy and freshness" and is "packed with spine-tingling historical detail." A *Horn Book* reviewer declared, "Read this book for the compelling interior tale of the little-known true horror that faced 'the other' during the Middle Ages."

Biographical and Critical Sources

BOOKS

Authors & Artists for Young Adults, Volume 13, Gale (Detroit), 1994, pp. 111-20.
Contemporary Literary Criticism, Volume 17, Gale, 1981.
Levitin, Sonia, entry in *Something about the Author Autobiography Series,* Volume 2, Gale (Detroit), 1986, pp. 111-26.
Levitin, Sonia, *Silver Days,* Atheneum, 1989.
St. James Guide to Young Adult Writers, second edition, St. James Press, 1999, pp. 506-08.

PERIODICALS

Booklist, May 1, 1994, Ilene Cooper, review of *Escape from Egypt,* p. 1595; July, 1994, Stephanie Zvirin, review of *Adam's War,* p. 1949; February 15, 1998, Lauren Peterson, review of *Boom Town,* p. 1020; September 15, 1998, Karen Simonetti, review of *The Singing Mountain,* p. 221; April 15, 1999, Carolyn Phelan, review of *Taking Charge,* p. 1536; June 1, 1999, Ilene Cooper, review of *The Cure,* p. 1814.
Book Report, September-October, 1999, Ron Marinucci, review of *The Cure,* p. 60.
Bulletin of the Center for Children's Books, January, 1999, Janice M. Del Negro, review of *The Singing Mountain,* p. 173; July-August, 1999, p. 393.
English Journal, November, 1989, p. 82.
Horn Book, March-April, 1998, Margaret A. Bush, review of *Boom Town,* p. 215; November, 1998, Lauren Adams, review of *The Singing Mountain,* p. 734; March, 1999, Margaret A. Bush, review of *Taking Charge,* p. 196; May, 1999, review of *The Cure,* p. 332.
Kirkus Reviews, February 1, 1999, p. 223; March 15, 1999, review of *The Cure.*
New York Times Book Review, May 17, 1987, Sheila Klass, "Waiting for Operation Moses," p. 36; May 17, 1998, Anne Scott MacLeod, "And No Television Either," p. 23.
Publishers Weekly, May 13, 1988, review of *Incident at Loring Groves,* p. 278; April 19, 1993, review of *Annie's Promise,* p. 63; March 28, 1994, review of

Escape from Egypt, p. 98; June 13, 1994, review of *Adam's War,* p. 65; September 9, 1996, review of *Nine for California,* p. 83; September 7, 1998, review of *The Singing Mountain,* p. 96; April 5, 1999, p. 241; April 12, 1999, review of *The Cure,* p. 76.

School Library Journal, March, 1998, Engelfried, Steven, review of *Boom Town,* p. 182; November, 1998, Elisabeth Palmer Abarbanel, review of *The Singing Mountain,* pp. 122-23; April, 1999, Beth Tegart, review of *Taking Charge,* p. 102; May, 1999, pp. 127-28.

Voice of Youth Advocates, February, 1999, p. 437; June, 1999, Beth Karpas, review of *The Cure,* p. 123.

* * *

LEWIN, Ted 1935-

Personal

Born May 6, 1935, in Buffalo, NY; son of Sidney (a retail jeweler) and Berenece (Klehn) Lewin; married Betsy Reilly (an artist). *Education:* Pratt Institute of Art, B.F.A., 1956. *Hobbies and other interests:* Photography, painting, and watching birds.

Addresses

Home and office—152 Willoughby Ave., Brooklyn, NY 11205.

Career

Professional wrestler, 1952-65; artist and free-lance illustrator, 1956—. *Exhibitions:* One-man shows at the Laboratory of Ornithology, Cornell University, 1978, and the Wildlife Conservation Society, Central Park Zoo. *Military service:* U.S. Army, 1958.

Awards, Honors

Mark Twain Award, 1981, for *Soup for President,* text by Robert Newton Peck; Sandburg Award, 1985, for *The Search for Grissi,* text by Mary Frances Shura; Book Can Develop Empathy award, 1990, for *Faithful Elephants,* text by Yukio Tsuchiya; Great Stone Face award, 1991, for *The Secret of the Indian,* text by Lynne Reid Banks; *Boston Globe/Horn Book* Award, 1991, for *Judy Scuppernong,* text by Brenda Seabrooke; Hungry Mind Award, 1993, for *Sami and the Time of the Troubles,* text by Florence Parry Heide and Judith Heide Gilliland; Caldecott Honor Book, American Library Association, 1993, for *Peppe the Lamplighter,* text by Elisa Bartone; Notable Children's Trade Book in the Field of Social Studies, National Council for the Social Studies (NCSS)/Children's Book Council (CBC), 1997, for *American Too,* text by Eliza Bartone; Best Books of the Year selection, Bank Street College, and Notable Children's Trade Book in the Field of Social Studies, NCSS/CBC, 1998, both for *Fair!;* Best Books of the Year selection, Bank Street College, and Notable Children's Trade Book in the Field of Social Studies, NCSS/CBC, 1998, both for *Ali, Child of the Desert,* text

Ted Lewin

by Jonathan London; The Big Crit 1998 (award for excellence in design), *Critique* magazine, for signage at the Central Park Children's Zoo; Parents' Choice Award, 1999, for *Nilo and the Tortoise;* Notable Children's Trade Book in the Field of Social Studies, NCSS/CBC, 1999, for *The Storytellers;* Notable Book for Children, *Smithsonian* magazine, 1999, and Outstanding Science Trade Books for Children, National Science Teachers Association/CBC, 2000, both for *Gorilla Walk,* text with wife, Betsy Lewin; Alumni Achievement Award, Pratt Institute, 2000.

Writings

SELF-ILLUSTRATED

World within a World—Everglades, introduction by Don R. Eckelberry, Dodd, 1976.

World within a World—Baja, Dodd, 1978.

World within a World—Pribilofs, Dodd, 1980.

Tiger Trek, Macmillan, 1990.

When the Rivers Go Home, Macmillan, 1992.

Amazon Boy, Macmillan, 1993.

I Was a Teenage Professional Wrestler (memoir), Orchard, 1993.

The Reindeer People, Simon and Schuster, 1994.

Sacred River, Houghton Mifflin, 1994.

Market!, Lothrop, Lee and Shepard, 1996.

Fair!, Lothrop, Lee and Shepard, 1997.

The Storytellers, Lothrop, Lee and Shepard, 1998.

Touch and Go: Travels of a Children's Book Illustrator, Lothrop, Lee and Shepard, 1999.

(With Betsy Lewin) *Gorilla Walk,* Lothrop, Lee and Shepard, 1999.

Something Special, Lothrop, Lee and Shepard, 1999.

Nilo and the Tortoise, Scholastic, 1999.

(With B. Lewin) *Elephant Quest,* Morrow, 2000.

ILLUSTRATOR

Jack McClellan, Millard Black, and Sid Norris, *A Blind Man Can!,* Houghton, 1968.

Wyatt Blassingame, *The Look-It-Up Book of Presidents,* Random House, 1968.

Jack McClellan, Millard Black, and Sheila Flume Taylor, *Up, out, and Over!,* Houghton, 1969.

George S. Trow, *Meet Robert E. Lee,* Random House, 1969.

Margaret T. Burroughs, *Jasper, the Drummin' Boy,* Follett, 1970.

Janet H. Ervin, *More Than Half Way There,* Follett, 1970.

Donald W. Cox, *Pioneers of Ecology,* Hammond, 1971.

Nellie Burchardt, *A Surprise for Carlotta,* Watts, 1971.

Darrell A. Rolerson, *Mr. Big Britches,* Dodd, 1971.

Gene Smith, *The Visitor,* Cowles, 1971.

Betty Horvath, *Not Enough Indians,* Watts, 1971.

Maurine H. Gee, *Chicano, Amigo,* Morrow, 1972.

Rose Blue, *Grandma Didn't Wave Back,* Watts, 1972.

Michael Capizzi, *Getting It All Together,* Delacorte, 1972.

Rose Blue, *A Month of Sundays,* Watts, 1972.

Rita Micklish, *Sugar Bee,* Delacorte, 1972.

Darrell A. Rolerson, *In Sheep's Clothing,* Dodd, 1972.

Rose Blue, *Nikki 108,* Watts, 1972.

Charlotte Gantz, *Boy with Three Names,* Houghton, 1973.

William MacKellar, *The Ghost of Grannoch Moor,* Dodd, 1973.

Marjorie M. Prince, *The Cheese Stands Alone,* Houghton, 1973.

Marian Rumsey, *Lion on the Run,* Morrow, 1973.

Darrell A. Rolerson, *A Boy Called Plum,* Dodd, 1974.

Jean Slaughter Doty, *Gabriel,* Macmillan, 1974.

Gene Smith, *The Hayburners,* Delacorte, 1974.

Matt Christopher, *Earthquake,* Little, Brown, 1975.

Patricia Beatty, *Rufus, Red Rufus,* Morrow, 1975.

Charles Ferry, *Up in Sister Bay,* Houghton, 1975.

Jean Slaughter Doty, *Winter Pony,* Macmillan, 1975.

S. T. Tung, *One Small Dog,* Dodd, 1975.

Rose Blue, *The Preacher's Kid,* Watts, 1975.

Scott O'Dell, *Zia,* Houghton, 1976.

Lynne Martin, *Puffin, Bird of the Open Seas,* Morrow, 1976.

Laurence Pringle, *Listen to the Crows,* Crowell, 1976.

Patricia Edwards Clyne, *Ghostly Animals of America,* Dodd, 1977.

Mildred Teal, *Bird of Passage,* Little, Brown, 1977.

Marian Rumsey, *Carolina Hurricane,* Morrow, 1977.

Nigel Gray, *The Deserter,* Harper, 1977.

Robert Newton Peck, *Patooie,* Knopf, 1977.

Philippa Pearce, *The Shadow-Cage, and Other Tales of the Supernatural,* Crowell, 1977.

Helen Hill, Agnes Perkins, and Alethea Helbig, editors, *Straight on Till Morning: Poems of the Imaginary World,* Crowell, 1977.

Rose Blue, *The Thirteenth Year: A Bar Mitzvah Story,* Watts, 1977.

Leslie Norris, *Merlin and the Snake's Egg: Poems,* Viking, 1978.

William MacKellar, *The Silent Bells,* Dodd, 1978.

Robert Newton Peck, *Soup for President,* Knopf, 1978.

William MacKellar, *The Witch of Glen Gowrie,* Dodd, 1978.

Anne E. Crompton, *A Woman's Place,* Little, Brown, 1978.

Margaret Goff Clark, *Barney and the UFO,* Dodd, 1979.

Patricia Edwards Clyne, *Strange and Supernatural Animals,* Dodd, 1979.

Robert Newton Peck, *Hub,* Knopf, 1979.

David Stemple, *High Ridge Gobbler: A Story of the American Wild Turkey,* Collins, 1979.

Jean Slaughter Doty, *Can I Get There by Candlelight?,* Macmillan, 1980.

Rose Blue, *My Mother, the Witch,* McGraw, 1980.

Margaret Goff Clark, *Barney in Space,* Dodd, 1981.

Francine Jacobs, *Bermuda Petrel: The Bird that Would Not Die,* Morrow, 1981.

Mark Twain, *The Adventures of Tom Sawyer,* Wanderer, 1982.

Margaret Goff Clark, *Barney on Mars,* Dodd, 1983.

Eleanor Clymer, *The Horse in the Attic,* Bradbury, 1983.

Priscilla Homola, *The Willow Whistle,* Dodd, 1983.

Enid Bagnold, *"National Velvet,"* Morrow, 1985.

R. R. Knudson, *Babe Didrikson, Athlete of the Century,* Viking Kestrel, 1985.

Mary Francis Shura, *The Search for Grissi,* Dodd, 1985.

Frances Wosmek, *A Brown Bird Singing,* Lothrop, Lee, 1986.

Patricia Reilly Giff, *Mother Teresa, Sister to the Poor,* Viking Kestrel, 1986.

Elizabeth Simpson Smith, *A Dolphin Goes to School: The Story of Squirt, a Trained Dolphin,* Morrow, 1986.

Scott O'Dell, *The Serpent Never Sleeps: A Novel of Jamestown and Pocahontas,* Houghton, 1987.

Susan Saunders, *Margaret Mead: The World Was Her Family,* Viking Kestrel, 1987.

Kathleen V. Kudlinski, *Rachel Carson: Pioneer of Ecology,* Viking Kestrel, 1988.

Yukio Tsuchiya, *Faithful Elephants: A True Story of Animals, People, and War,* translated by Tomoko Tsuchiya Dykes, Houghton, 1988.

Lynne Reid Banks, *The Secret of the Indian,* Doubleday, 1989.

Bruce Coville, editor, *Herds of Thunder, Manes of Gold: A Collection of Horse Stories and Poems,* Doubleday, 1989.

Leon Garfield, *Young Nick and Jubilee,* Delacorte, 1989.

Florence Parry Heide and Judith Heide Gilliland, *The Day of Ahmed's Secret,* Lothrop, Lee, 1990.

Scott O'Dell, *Island of the Blue Dolphins,* Houghton, 1990.

Gregory Patent, *Shanghai Passage,* Clarion, 1990.

Brenda Seabrooke, *Judy Scuppernong,* Cobblehill, 1990.

Jane Yolen, *Bird Watch: A Book of Poetry,* Philomel, 1990.

Margaret Hodges, *Brother Francis and the Friendly Beasts,* Scribner, 1991.

Megan McDonald, *The Potato Man,* Orchard, 1991.

Frances Ward Weller, *I Wonder If I'll See a Whale,* Philomel, 1991.

Corinne Demas Bliss, *Matthew's Meadow,* Harcourt, 1992.

Florence Parry Heide and Judith Heide Gilliland, *Sami and the Time of the Troubles,* Clarion, 1992.

Megan McDonald, *The Great Pumpkin Switch,* Orchard, 1992.

Frances Ward Weller, *Matthew Wheelock's Wall,* Macmillan, 1992.

Elisa Bartone, *Peppe the Lamplighter,* Lothrop, Lee, 1993.

Ann Herbert Scott, *Cowboy Country,* Clarion, 1993.

Sheldon Oberman, *The Always Prayer Shawl,* Boyds Mills, 1993.

Louise Borden, *Just in Time for Christmas,* Scholastic, 1994.

Jan Slepian, *Lost Moose,* Putnam, 1995.

Louise Borden and Mary K. Kroeger, *Paperboy,* Houghton Mifflin, 1996.

Jane Yolen, *Sea Watch: A Book of Poetry,* Putnam, 1996.

Eliza Bartone, *American Too,* Lothrop, Lee and Shepard, 1996.

Jonathan London, *Ali, Child of the Desert,* Lothrop, Lee and Shepard, 1997.

Jane Yolen, *The Originals,* Putnam, 1998.

Linda Oatman High, *Barn Savers,* Boyds Mills, 1999.

Louise Borden, *A. Lincoln and Me,* Scholastic, 1999.

Corinne Demas Bliss, *The Disappearing Island,* Simon and Schuster, 2000.

Edward Grimm, *The Doorman,* Orchard, 2000.

Illustrations have also appeared in periodicals, including *Boy's Life, Ladies' Home Journal, Seventeen,* and *Reader's Digest.*

Sidelights

With over one hundred picture book illustration credits to his name as well as seventeen of his own self-illustrated books, author-illustrator Ted Lewin is "one of our most gifted artists," according to *Booklist*'s Hazel Rochman. Lewin has, as Rochman noted, "brought us scenes of many places, from the streets of Cairo ... to the island wilderness." A Caldecott Honor Book winner for his illustrations of Elisa Bartone's *Peppe the Lamplighter,* Lewin also has a deep and abiding interest in the natural world. As he once told *Something about the Author,* "I am a deeply concerned environmentalist and conservationist and travel to wilderness areas around the world for both graphic and literary material." Lewin has written and illustrated books for children and young adults, often relying on his knowledge of and concern for wildlife and their habitats throughout the world. His watercolor paintings are characterized by their detail and realism, and his writings have been praised for their poetic quality.

As a young boy growing up in upstate New York, Lewin vacillated between a love for the arts and a love for

In **Market!** *Lewin describes markets around the world with simple text and detailed watercolor illustrations.*

athletics. As a youngster, he took violin lessons for many years; by the time he reached high school, he was trying out for the school's football team. "I wasn't any better at football than I was at the violin," Lewin remarked in an essay for *Something about the Author Autobiography Series (SAAS)*. "I didn't know then that a mixture of athletics and art was to be a recurring theme in my life." However, Lewin always had dreams of becoming an artist. "Not a policeman, fireman, or doctor—an artist," he recalled in his memoir, *I Was a Teenage Professional Wrestler*. "I remember working first with a metal-armed copying toy I got for Christmas, then the Magic-Pad, on which you could pull up a flap and make whatever you'd drawn disappear." With the encouragement of his family, Lewin practiced drawing by copying photographs, illustrations from children's books, and even a portrait of President Harry S. Truman, for which he received a personal letter from the White House.

By the time Lewin graduated from high school, he had made plans to study art at the Pratt Institute in Brooklyn. Paying for school and living expenses would be expensive, however, so Lewin started on a secondary career that would help support him for almost fifteen years: professional wrestling. Lewin had attended professional matches with his kid brother for many years, and his older brother Donn had become a wrestler after serving in the Marine Corps during World War II. With the aid of Donn, Lewin began wrestling at age seventeen during summers and at night during the school year. In his memoir, Lewin recalled his dual life, alternating between art classes and wrestling matches: "Every day I had classes in two-dimensional design, three-dimensional design, and figure drawing. Around me, the light-filled, high-ceilinged studio would be electric with concentrated effort . . . . I would see a great play of light and shadow—in a sense, not so different from what I'd seen in the charged, dramatic atmosphere of a wrestling arena. The medium was different, that's all."

After earning his bachelor of fine arts degree, Lewin continued wrestling as he slowly built a career as a freelance artist. He began with magazine work, and by the late 1960s obtained work illustrating children's books. His first book commission was for *A Blind Man Can!*, and this inaugurated a career that has lasted over three decades and earned him many honors. Early distinguished titles illustrated by Lewin include *Grandma Didn't Wave Back* written by Rose Blue and *Sugar Bee* written by Rita Micklish, both of which illuminate Lewin's subtle touch. The former title has black and white drawings that remind the viewer of watercolors, while the latter has illustrations in "subtle gradations of black-and-white" which "complement . . . [a] novel about an interracial friendship," according to a contributor for *Children's Books and Their Creators.*

Lewin has gone on to illustrate volumes for writers such as Jane Yolen, Scott O'Dell, and Florence Parry Heide, among dozens of others, earning praise for his watercolors and sensitive depictions of life around the world. For example, while reviewing Lewin's 1990 illustrations

for Heide's *The Day of Ahmed's Secret,* a *Publishers Weekly* reviewer praised the illustrator's "sensitive, luminous watercolors" that "hint at the mystery and timelessness" of Cairo, where the book is set. His artwork for the poems of Yolen in the award-winning *Bird Watch* are "breathtaking," according to another *Publishers Weekly* contributor, and "marvelously complement" the text. Lewin has made a special focus of aviary art, and has had a one-man exhibit of such illustrations in addition to illustrating several other volumes about birds. For Bartone's *Peppe the Lamplighter,* Lewin contributed "dramatically rendered watercolors," according to a *Publishers Weekly* critic, which "exhibit a cinematic sweep." For *The Always Prayer Shawl* by Sheldon Oberman, Lewin supplied "abundantly detailed and wonderfully expressive watercolors," according to *Booklist*'s Stephanie Zvirin. Lewin's realistic approach to street scenes can be seen in books such as *Paperboy* and *American Too,* the latter illustrated with "glorious" paintings, according to *Booklist*'s Rochman. A further collaboration with Yolen in 1998 produced *The Originals,* a volume of "astonishingly beautiful paintings," Rochman also noted.

However, early in his career, Lewin was determined to create books with text and illustrations all his own. In 1976, Lewin debuted his series "World within a World" which focuses on wildlife in several regions visited by the author; the series has received high praise for both Lewin's text and the illustrations. Concerning the Everglades, the first volume in the series is based on Lewin's observations of the plant and animal life in the area over a five-year period. The volume on Baja, California, describes elephant seals and details the annual migration of the California gray whales. A volume on the Pribilofs highlights the precarious fate of the seals who bear and raise their young on these Alaskan coastal islands. A reviewer from *Booklist* called Lewin's prose for *World within a World—Pribilofs* "elegant and uncompromising," adding that "the evocation of this small corner of the world is strong."

Lewin depicts a trip made on the back of an elephant through one of India's national parks in *Tiger Trek.* Joan McGrath, reviewing the book for *School Library Journal,* found the illustrator's work "gorgeous" and "far above the ordinary." *When the Rivers Go Home* describes a similar journey, this time through a large swamp in central Brazil called the Pantanal. This book also received praise for Lewin's watercolor paintings, with a *Kirkus Reviews* writer describing the artist's work as "lovely" and "evocative." And in 1993's *Amazon Boy,* Lewin's "light-filled pictures, dense with detail, reinforce the theme that the riches of the rain forest must be protected," according to *School Library Journal* contributor Kathleen Odean. In a review of this same title, a writer for *Publishers Weekly* claimed that "Lewin's realistic tale owes its vitality chiefly to his splashy watercolors with pencil detail," while *Horn Book*'s Margaret A. Bush commented that this "sumptuous travelogue transforms the story of a special childhood journey into an effective lesson on the perilous state of the Amazon River and nearby forests."

Lewin's **Amazon Boy** *illustrates the need to protect the Amazon River and nearby forests.*

Lewin turned from nature to his own past in *I Was a Teenage Professional Wrestler.* "More a series of vignettes than an autobiography," as *Bulletin of the Center for Children's Books* writer Deborah Stevenson described it, *I Was a Teenage Professional Wrestler* details Lewin's involvement with the sport and provides portraits—written and painted—of the many wrestlers he met during his career. "It is a fascinating story that leaves the reader wanting to learn more about both Lewin and the other wrestlers," noted Patrick Jones in the *Voice of Youth Advocates.* In recreating a different era, Lewin describes the wrestlers "quite masterfully in words, then he brings them to life with old black and white photographs, drawings and paintings," according to Jones. *School Library Journal* contributor Todd Morning likewise praised Lewin's "surprisingly funny and affectionate" remembrances, as well as the author's combination of "vivid" artwork and human stories. "The artist's sensibility and eye for detail are always in evidence," Morning concluded. "His talent in this realm is truly formidable."

Turning such talents again to travel and the world of nature, Lewin depicted the life of the Sami of Lapland in *The Reindeer People,* a book both "enriching and fun," according to *Booklist*'s Julie Corsaro. A contributor for

Publishers Weekly claimed, "The author's highly descriptive prose is as luxurious as a reindeer coat, and his finely detailed, snapshot-style watercolors will engage readers of any age." The Ganges River of India provides the background for Lewin's 1994 *Sacred River,* a book inspired by Lewin's travels to Benares. A contributor to *Publishers Weekly* felt that the artwork in this book was so "atmospheric ... that the heaviness of the air becomes almost palpable, the noise easily imagined."

Bustling humanity is further depicted in *Market!* and *Fair!,* both of which detail further scenes from Lewin's travels. In the former, six markets around the world take the viewer into different lives and cultures. In a starred *Publishers Weekly* review of *Market!,* a contributor wrote, "High-spirited and continent-hopping, this keenly observed tour of six world-famous marketplaces takes an everyday experience as an occasion to explore ethnic diversity." Reviewing *Fair!* in *School Library Journal,* Jackie Hechtkopf suggested this "superbly illustrated visit to a county fair resembles a photo-essay in its remarkable realism." A writer for *Kirkus Reviews* called the same book a "pulsing, panoramic examination of a summertime ritual."

More exotic locales are served up in *The Storytellers,* a tale of young Abdul and his story-telling grandfather who live just outside the old Moroccan city of Fez. "[T]his book is more than a mere travelogue," wrote *Booklist*'s Susan Dove Lempke. "It lends insight into the daily life of the people who live in Morocco." Writing in *Bulletin of the Center for Children's Books,* Betsy Hearne noted that "The details are carefully, almost photographically preserved; ... and the warmly projected affection between the old man and the boy save them from generic profile."

Working from photos he shoots on his travels and then projects onto a screen in his studio in the United States, Lewin manages to retain much of the original realism and force of scenes he has witnessed firsthand. A steady producer, Lewin maintains a strict work regime as well. His day begins at eight in the morning and continues without break into the afternoon. While he is at work in the upstairs of his New York brownstone, his wife, Betsy, whom he met at the Pratt Institute and who is also an artist, works in her studio downstairs.

Together the Lewins have traveled the world, and in 1999, they collaborated on *Gorilla Walk,* a recounting of a 1997 trip to Uganda to view the mountain gorillas. "Through handsome paintings and carefully focused text, Ted and Betsy Lewin recount their ... venture into Bwindi, offering intriguing glimpses of both the rarely seen animals and the ambiguities of ecotourism," wrote Bush in a *Horn Book* review. The Galapagos Islands provide the inspiration for *Nilo and the Tortoise,* the story of a young boy stranded on one of the islands. *Booklist*'s Zvirin noted that Lewin's pictures once again are the main attraction of the book, capturing "the remoteness and beauty of the exotic place and some of its distinctive wildlife."

With *Touch and Go,* Lewin once again turned to memoir, this time detailing the confessions of a children's book illustrator as he globe-hops in search of material. Presented in a scrapbook sort of approach, Lewin introduces people and places he has encountered in his travels through short stories, vignettes, and simple anecdotes. A writer for *Kirkus Reviews* observed that this "memorable assortment" created "vivid, stand-alone verbal snapshots."

His travels have taken him from the jungles of South America to the icy vastness of the North Pole, and Lewin has recorded it all, with the eye of an artist and the grasp of a storyteller. It is all material to be assimilated and reworked. "In a sense," Lewin concluded in *SAAS,* "children's book writers and illustrators seem always to be working."

Biographical and Critical Sources

BOOKS

Children's Books and Their Creators, edited by Anita Silvey, Houghton Mifflin, 1995, pp. 404-05.
Lewin, Ted, *I Was a Teenage Professional Wrestler,* Orchard, 1993.

Lewin, Ted, essay in *Something about the Author Autobiography Series,* Volume 25, Gale, 1998, pp. 173-94.

PERIODICALS

Booklist, January 1, 1981, review of *World within a World—Pribilofs,* p. 625; December 15, 1993, Stephanie Zvirin, review of *The Always Prayer Shawl,* p. 750; October 1, 1994, Julie Corsaro, review of *The Reindeer People,* p. 322; June 1, 1995, Hazel Rochman, review of *Sacred River,* p. 1778; August, 1996, H. Rochman, review of *American Too,* p. 1903; February 1, 1998, H. Rochman, review of *The Originals,* p. 917; April, 1998, Susan Dove Lempke, review of *The Storytellers,* p. 1332; May 31, 1999, S. Zvirin, review of *Nilo and the Tortoise,* p. 93; November 1, 1999, p. 524; November 15, 1999, p. 622; January 1, 2000, p. 824.
Bulletin of the Center for Children's Books, June, 1993, Deborah Stevenson, review of *I Was a Teenage Professional Wrestler,* pp. 321-22; April, 1998, Betsy Hearne, review of *The Storytellers,* p. 286; July, 1999, p. 393.
Horn Book, May-June, 1993, Margaret A. Bush, review of *Amazon Boy,* pp. 320-21; July-August, 1996, pp. 481-82; November-December, 1999, M. Bush, review of *Gorilla Walk,* p. 758.
Kirkus Reviews, February 15, 1992, review of *When the Rivers Go Home,* pp. 257-58; July 1, 1997, review of *Fair!,* p. 1031; May 15, 1999, review of *Touch and Go,* p. 803.
New York Times Book Review, June 20, 1993, p. 23.
Publishers Weekly, August 10, 1990, review of *The Day of Ahmed's Secret,* p. 444; October 26, 1990, review of *Bird Watch,* p. 71; April 17, 1993, review of *Peppe the Lamplighter,* p. 61; April 26, 1993, review of *Amazon Boy,* p. 78; October 24, 1994, review of *The Reindeer People,* p. 61; August 7, 1995, review of *Sacred River,* p. 460; April 29, 1996, review of *Market!,* p. 72; August 2, 1999, p. 84; November 1, 1999, p. 83; February 21, 2000, p. 89.
School Library Journal, March, 1990, Joan McGrath, review of *Tiger Trek,* p. 208; June, 1993, Kathleen Odean, review of *Amazon Boy,* pp. 80, 83; July, 1993, Todd Morning, review of *I Was a Teenage Professional Wrestler,* p. 108; July, 1997, Jackie Hechtkopf, review of *Fair!,* p. 85; April, 1999, p. 102; July, 1999, p. 110.
Voice of Youth Advocates, October, 1993, Patrick Jones, review of *I Was a Teenage Professional Wrestler,* p. 247.

—*Sketch by J. Sydney Jones*

*   *   *

LIPPINCOTT, Gary A. 1953-

Personal

Born September 2, 1953, in Woodstown, NJ; son of Lynn (an E. I. Du Pont employee) and Arden (McTyre) Lippincott; married Wendy L. Warner (a horse trainer and riding instructor), October 6, 1979; children: Ian W., Aja W. *Education:* Maryland Institute, College of Art,

B.F.A., 1975. *Hobbies and other interests:* Playing piano, composing music, magic, SCUBA diving.

Addresses

Home and office—131 Greenville Rd., Spencer, MA 01562.

Career

Freelance illustrator, 1984—. *Member:* Western Massachusetts Illustrators Group, Arts Worcester.

Writings

ILLUSTRATOR

Jacob and Wilhelm Grimm, *The Fisherman and His Wife,* Troll, 1988.
Mem Fox, *With Love at Christmas,* Abingdon Press, 1988.
Daniel Cohen, *Ancient Egypt,* Doubleday, 1990.

"Storytime," an original watercolor by Lippincott.

Bruce Coville, *Jeremy Thatcher, Dragon Hatcher,* Harcourt, 1991.
Bruce Coville, *Jennifer Murdley's Toad,* Harcourt, 1992.
Peggy Christian, *The Bookstore Mouse,* Harcourt, 1995.
Bruce Coville, *The Skull of Truth,* Harcourt, 1997.
S. P. Somtow, *The Vampire's Beautiful Daughter,* Atheneum, 1997.
Marianna Mayer, *The Prince and the Pauper,* Dial, 1999.

Also illustrator of *Franklin D. Roosevelt and the New Deal,* by Sharon Shebar, published in 1987.

Sidelights

With a talent for fantasy illustration, Gary A. Lippincott is an illustrator whose work has been featured in several picture books and young adult novels, among them S. P. Somtow's *The Vampire's Beautiful Daughter* and Bruce Coville's popular "Magic Shop" series, which includes the novels *Jeremy Hatcher, Dragon Hatcher, Jennifer Murdley's Toad,* and *The Skull of Truth.*

Born in 1953, Lippincott began drawing as a young boy, showing early signs of the imagination that would guide his later work. "Before 'settling' on becoming an illustrator," he once told *SATA,* "I had many unusual careers in mind, such as a magician, actor, make-up artist, clown, animator, etc." However, by the time he reached college age, Lippincott had come down to earth

Jeremy rides the dragon he has raised from an egg in Gary A. Lippincott's illustration for **Jeremy Thatcher, Dragon Hatcher,** *written by Bruce Coville.*

enough to confine himself to his art. He enrolled at the Maryland Institute and received his B.F.A. in 1975.

Although he has worked on several nonfiction projects, including his first published book, Sharon Shebar's *Franklin D. Roosevelt and the New Deal,* Lippincott finally found his niche in illustrating picture books. His first such project was published in 1988 as *The Fisherman and His Wife.* A familiar tale by the Brothers Grimm, the story focuses on a poor fisherman and the greedy wife who turns good fortune into disaster, brought to life through Lippincott's paintings. Another adaptation of a classic tale to benefit from the illustrator's talents appeared a decade later. *The Prince and the Pauper,* a story about two identical boys, one rich and one poor, that was written by nineteenth-century humorist Mark Twain was retold for picture book audiences by Marianna Mayer. Lippincott's illustrations for Mayer's simplified retelling were praised by a contributor for *Publishers Weekly* as "vibrantly" rendered, "his palace scenes ... ornate, light-filled watercolors of splendor in which the boys' homely, toothy faces seem like the only real and honest things."

Among his many influences, Lippincott cites animated film producer Walt Disney, fantasy illustrators Tim and Greg Hildebrandt, and fellow book illustrator Alan Lee.

Biographical and Critical Sources

PERIODICALS

Booklist, March 15, 1990, p. 1444; March 15, 1992, p. 1357.
Publishers Weekly, August 11, 1997, review of *The Skull of Truth,* p. 402; November 15, 1999, review of *The Prince and the Pauper,* p. 66.
School Library Journal, April, 1990, p. 30; May, 1991, p. 91; October, 1997, pp. 131, 139.
Voice of Youth Advocates, June, 1991, p. 106.

ON-LINE

Author's website, www.garylippincott.com.

*   *   *

LYON, George Ella 1949-

Personal

Born April 25, 1949, in Harlan, KY; daughter of Robert Vernon Jr. (a dry cleaner and later a savings and loan vice president) and Gladys (an executive director of a chamber of commerce; maiden name, Fowler) Hoskins; married Stephen C. Lyon (a musician and composer), June 3, 1972; children: Benjamin Gerard, Joseph Fowler. *Education:* Centre College of Kentucky, B.A., 1971; University of Arkansas, M.A. (English), 1972; Indiana University—Bloomington, Ph.D. (English and creative writing), 1978. *Politics:* Democrat. *Religion:* Episcopalian.

George Ella Lyon

Addresses

Home and office—913 Maywick Dr., Lexington, KY 40504.

Career

University of Kentucky, Lexington, instructor in English and creative writing, beginning 1977, member of executive committee of Women Writers Conference, 1979-84, visiting assistant professor, 1991-92; Centre College, Danville, KY, visiting professor, 1979-80, writer-in-residence, 1985; Transylvania University, Lexington, lecturer in humanities and creative writing, 1984-86; Sayre School, Lexington, writer-in-residence, 1986; Radford University, visiting faculty member, 1986. Freelance writer. Speaker at schools. Appalachian Poetry Project, executive director, 1980; Kentucky Arts Council, Frankfort, KY, coordinator of writers residency program, 1982-84. *Member:* Modern Language Association, Society of Children's Book Writers and Illustrators, Virginia Woolf Society, Appalachian Writers Association, Phi Beta Kappa.

Awards, Honors

Lamont Hall Award, Andrew Mountain Press, 1983, for *Mountain;* Golden Kite Award, Society of Children's Books Writers and Illustrators, 1989, for *Borrowed Children;* Kentucky Bluegrass award, 1992, for *Basket;* Appalachian Book of the Year Award, 1993, for *Catalpa;* Best Books for Teens selection, New York Public Library, 2000, for *Where I'm From, Where Poems Come From.*

Writings

FOR CHILDREN

Father Time and the Day Boxes, illustrated by Robert Andrew Parker, Bradbury, 1985.

A Regular Rolling Noah, illustrated by Stephen Gammell, Bradbury, 1986.

A Throne in Goose Rock (young adult novel), Orchard, 1987.

Borrowed Children (novel), Orchard, 1988, reprinted, University Press of Kentucky, 1999.

A B Cedar: An Alphabet of Trees, illustrated by Tom Parker, Orchard, 1989.

Together (picture book), edited by Richard Jackson, illustrated by Vera Rosenberry, Orchard, 1989.

Red Rover, Red Rover (novel), edited by Richard Jackson, Orchard, 1989, published as *The Stranger I Left Behind,* Troll, 1997.

Come a Tide (picture book), illustrated by Stephen Gammell, Orchard, 1990.

Basket (picture book), illustrated by Mary Szilagyi, Orchard, 1990.

Cecil's Story (picture book), illustrated by Peter Catalanotto, Orchard, 1991.

The Outside Inn (picture book), illustrated by Vera Rosenberry, Orchard, 1991.

Who Came Down That Road? (picture book), illustrated by Peter Catalanotto, Orchard, 1992.

Dreamplace (picture book), illustrated by Peter Catalanotto, Orchard, 1993.

Five Live Bongos (picture book), Scholastic, 1994.

Here and Then, Orchard, 1994.

Mama Is a Miner, illustrated by Peter Catalanotto, Orchard, 1994.

Ada's Pal, illustrated by Marguerite Casparian, Orchard, 1996.

A Wordful Child (autobiography), photographs by Ann W. Olson, Richard C. Owen, 1996.

A Day at Damp Camp, illustrated by Peter Catalanotto, Orchard, 1996.

Counting on the Woods: A Poem, photographs by Ann W. Olson, DK Ink, 1998.

A Sign (autobiography), illustrated by Chris K. Soentpiet, Orchard, 1998.

A Traveling Cat, illustrated by Paul Brett Johnson, Orchard, 1998.

Book, illustrated by Peter Catalanotto, DK Ink, 1999.

Where I'm From, Where Poems Come From, photographs by Robert Hoskins, Absey, 1999.

One Lucky Girl, illustrated by Irene Trivas, DK Ink, 2000.

FOR ADULTS

Mountain (poetry chapbook), Andrew Mountain Press (Hartford, CT), 1983.

Braids (two-act play), produced in Lexington, KY, at Transylvania University, 1985.

Growing Light (poetry), Mill Springs Press, 1987.

Choices: Stories for Adult New Readers, University Press of Kentucky, 1989.

Catalpa (poems), Wind Publications, 1993.

(Editor with others) *Old Wounds, New Words: Poems from the Appalachian Poetry Project,* Jesse Stuart Foundation, 1994.

With a Hammer for My Heart (novel), DK Ink, 1997.

OTHER

Also author of play, *Looking Back for Words,* 1989. Contributor to books, including *Virginia Woolf: Centennial Essays,* Whitston, *A Gift of Tongues: Suppressed Voices in American Poetry,* University of Georgia Press, and *The United States of Poetry,* Abrams, 1996. Contributor to periodicals, including *California Quarterly, Appalachian Journal, Prairie, Schooner,* and *The American Voice.*

Work in Progress

Don't You Remember?, an adult novel.

Sidelights

George Ella Lyon is a prolific writer who has made a name for herself with young listeners, teen readers, and grown-up poetry aficionados. Praised for using what *School Library Journal* contributor Ellen Fader calls "spare and elegant text" that "creates a poetic yet childlike mood," Lyon has penned picture book titles for the story-circle set, including *Dreamplace, Cecil's Story,* and *Who Came Down That Road?* In addition to picture books, Lyon has written an adult novel with appeal to young adults, *With a Hammer for My Heart,* that reflects her own upbringing in a close-knit Appalachian mountain family. In addition, Lyon has opened young readers' eyes to the creative process in several volumes of autobiography that explore her own path to becoming a writer.

Lyon was born in eastern Kentucky in 1949 and grew up outside a small coal-mining town in the Appalachian mountains. Her parents were both "mountain folk," and all four of her grandparents lived nearby. "Family loomed large as the mountains for me, both secure and confining," as she later recalled to *SATA.* This is also the case with Lawanda Ingle, the fifteen-year-old heroine of *With a Hammer for My Heart.* Thirsty for knowledge and experience, Lawanda lives within "a tiny Kentucky town [that is] the center of the universe," according to *Booklist* contributor GraceAnne A. DeCandido.

Suffering from poor vision as a young child, Lyon compensated by developing a "good ear for culture rich in stories." While her early dreams took her away from her mountain home—she thought of everything from a neon sign maker to a tightrope walker—her later aspirations—a veterinarian, a singer, a midwife, or a simultaneous translator at the United Nations—were much more down to earth. As an adult writer, "I try to do all these things," Lyon realized: "keep a tricky balance, heal, find music in words, and translate or bring to birth the lives that are inside us."

Lyon grew up in the house her grandfather built, which included a room over the garage dedicated solely to books. "Before I could read myself, I was listening to stories and building cities and mazes out of books," recalled Lyon. "The thing that interested me most as listener and maker was poetry, which made sense (using all the senses) to me whether I understood it or not."

Encouraged by her teachers, Lyon began writing poems in the second grade. After graduating from high school, she attended Centre College of Kentucky, graduating in 1971 with a B.A. in English. A year later, she began submitting her poems for publication, while also getting married and beginning a family of her own. While she worked a succession of part-time jobs to help make ends meet, Lyon recalled that she was "always wary of giving myself to any career other than writing."

Finally, in 1983, her first book, the poetry collection *Mountain,* was published by a small press in Hartford, Connecticut. The following year, her career began to move more quickly, as poetry anthologist Paul Janeczko passed a letter of hers on to his editor, Dick Jackson, who asked if she wrote for children. "'No,' I said, 'but hold on.'" Jackson's interest was the impetus for two of Lyon's books for children: the 1985 picture book *Father Time and the Day Boxes* and 1988's *Borrowed Children.*

With the success of *Father Time and the Day Boxes,* Lyon has gone on to write many other picture books, each of them exploring an interesting and compelling theme. In *Who Came Down That Road?,* for instance, she depicts a curious young boy questioning his mother about the past during a walk along an "old old old old road." Lyon spins a poetic chronology of time that stretches from the boy's own parents and great-grand-parents all the way back through farmers clearing the land and Civil War soldiers, Native Americans and grizzly bears, to a time when mastodons walked North America. While *Booklist* contributor Stephanie Zvirin noted that the "majestic leap from concrete to abstract" might require some further explanation, Lyon's text is "brief and plainly spoken, and it is filled with an unmistakable sense of joyful respect." A *Kirkus Reviews* writer dubbed *Who Came Down That Road?* a "beauti-fully crafted book that makes an unusually effective response to a prototypical question."

The past serves as the focus for several other picture books by Lyon, among them *Cecil's Story,* about a boy during the Civil War, and *Dreamplace,* which focuses on the culture of the Anasazi. In *Cecil's Story,* a young boy waits with neighbors while his mother goes to fetch his father, who has been wounded in battle. Published during the Gulf War in 1991, the book was praised by *School Library Journal* reviewer Lee Bock for address-ing "separation fears" about parents going to war "honestly and feelingly, with a believable and reassuring conclusion," reminding children that life still goes on, despite dramatic change. Also highly praised by critics, 1993's *Dreamplace* introduces an imaginative girl who, while touring the eight-hundred-year-old Anasazi ruins, envisions what it would be like to live among the ancient tribe, as drought forced them to abandon their homes. Featuring lush illustrations by Peter Catalanotto, *Dream-place* was praised by *Booklist* contributor Ilene Cooper as "[r]ich with atmosphere, delicate with sensitivity, and dreamlike in its evocation of dual realities."

Like the catastrophe of war in *Cecil's Story,* weather can sometimes make a dramatic impression on children. In *One Lucky Girl* Lyon tells her story through a young boy nicknamed Hawkeye, an energetic narrator who lives with his family in a trailer camp. When his home is literally ripped from its foundation during a ferocious tornado, his little sister, Becky, becomes lost. Lyon's ability to pace her story to retain interest "is a masterful roller coaster of roiling emotion," claimed *Bulletin of the Center for Children's Books* reviewer Elizabeth Bush. Noting that the book's ending brings "a delightful flurry of shivers, followed by the comforting relief of a family unharmed and inseparable, Bush called *One Lucky Girl* "the action picture book at its best."

Also praised for its pacing and plot is *Come a Tide,* which focuses on water rather than wind in depicting the frenzy of activity caused by flooding in the Kentucky flat lands after many days of heavy rains. In weaving her tale about a small, closely knit community that rallies together during times of disaster, Lyon "wastes not a word" in "depict[ing] two complete worlds—those of an Appalachian community and of a small child's hopes and fears," in the opinion of *New York Times Book Review* contributor Kathleen Krull.

Lyon credits her work as a poet with helping make the transition into children's picture books. "As Nancy Willard [once] pointed out, ... poems are the closest genre to picture books, with their use of sound, rhythm, economy of language, and surprise," the author told *SATA*. Also helpful was Lyon's experience raising her own two sons, and the years she spent reading books to them exposed her to a great deal of current children's books. "Children's questions are *the* questions (What is God? If I die, will I wake up again?), and they point out the shallowness of our answers," she recalled of reading with her sons. "We have a lot to learn from the wonder and vulnerability with which they approach the world."

Her sons' questions would serve as the inspiration for several of Lyon's books. "Long before I was writing for kids I was recording Ben's questions and imaginings in my journal," the author recalled. "That's where I got the start for *Together* and *Father Time and the Day Boxes.* Joey, my younger son, was the catalyst for *The Outside Inn.* Over and over, children call us to a deeper life."

As a children's writer, Lyon goes to schools and libraries to read her work and speak about the craft of writing with her young fans. "One of the questions kids ask when I visit schools is: 'Are you rich?' Yes, I say, but not the way you think. I'm rich because I get to do what I love to do and then find readers who see themselves in it. Books are a collaborative enterprise, not just between author, editor, and illustrator, but between those folks and the reader. So when kids are excited because they're meeting a 'real author,' I'm excited at meeting real readers."

While she receives a great deal of personal satisfaction from her role as a writer, Lyon also views her vocation as "a spiritual journey." As she once commented, "Writing for me is a spiritual journey. I come to the blank page full of hope that by participating in the process of creation I will have moments of wholeness and understanding. I believe all of us are given different gifts which require that we give up our ego selves in order to receive and pass the gift on. We do this imperfectly, of course, but in the labor we feel God's presence, and in the synthesis of song or poem, dance or painting, we share in the joy of the Maker."

Biographical and Critical Sources

BOOKS

Lyon, George Ella, *Who Came Down That Road?*, illustrated by Peter Catalanotto, Orchard, 1992.

PERIODICALS

Appalachian Heritage, winter-spring, 1985.
Booklist, January 1, 1991, Denise Perry Donovan, review of *Come a Tide,* p. 811; March 15, 1991, Bill Ott, review of *Come a Tide,* p. 1483; July, 1991, Denise Wilms, review of *The Outside Inn,* p. 2051; September 1, 1992, Stephanie Zvirin, review of *Who Came Down That Road?,* p. 67; March 14, 1993, Ilene Cooper, review of *Dreamplace,* p. 1321; September 15, 1996, review of *Ada's Pal,* p. 248; September 1, 1997, GraceAnne A. DeCandido, review of *With a Hammer for My Heart,* p. 61; September 1, 1999, review of *Where I'm From, Where Poems Come From,* p. 121.
Bulletin of the Center for Children's Books, September, 1994, Roger Sutton, review of *Mama Is a Miner,* p. 18; March, 2000, Elizabeth Bush, review of *One Lucky Girl.*
Five Owls, May-June, 1995, Susan Stan, review of *Come a Tide,* p. 95.
Horn Book, September-October, 1989; January-February, 1991; May-June, 1991, Mary M. Burns, review of *Cecil's Story,* p. 317; September-October, 1996, Nancy Vasilakis, review of *A Wordful Child,* p. 613; November, 1998, Mary M. Burns, review of *A Traveling Cat,* p. 716.
Kirkus Reviews, July 1, 1992, review of *Who Came Down That Road?,* p. 851; October 15, 1994, review of *Five Live Bongos,* p. 1411; January 15, 1996, review of *A Day at Camp,* p. 138; July 1, 1996, review of *Ada's Pal,* p. 971; January 15, 1998, review of *Counting on the Woods,* p. 115; February 1, 1998, review of *A Sign,* p. 198.
Language Arts, October, 1990.

Los Angeles Times Book Review, September 24, 1989; May 27, 1990.
New York Times Book Review, May 15, 1988; October 14, 1990, Kathleen Krull, review of *Come a Tide,* p. 33; May 19, 1991.
Publishers Weekly, January 12, 1990, review of *Come a Tide,* p. 60; February 12, 1996, review of *A Day at Damp Camp,* p. 78; September 1, 1997, review of *With a Hammer for My Heart,* p. 97; February 23, 1998, review of *Counting on the Woods,* p. 75; July 27, 1998, review of *A Traveling Cat,* p. 76; March 15, 1999, review of *Book,* p. 57; March 13, 2000, review of *One Lucky Girl,* p. 84.
School Library Journal, December, 1990, review of *Come a Tide,* p. 23; April, 1991, Lee Bock, review of *Cecil's Story,* p. 98; October, 1992, Ellen Fader, review of *Who Came Down That Road?,* p. 92; April, 1996, Ruth Semrau, review of *A Day at Camp,* p. 114; September, 1996, Carolyn Nash, review of *Ada's Pal,* p. 184; June, 1999, review of *Book,* p. 119.
Voice of Youth Advocates, Cindy Lombardo, review of *With a Hammer for My Heart,* pp. 122-23.

*   *   *

LYTLE, Robert A. 1944-

Personal

Born December 12, 1944, in Saginaw, MI; son of Howard H. (a teacher) and Averill Morrison (a mother) Lytle; married Dianne Candis (Candy) Frazier, March 23, 1968; children: Geoffrey, Ian, Jamie, Bo. *Education:* Attended Queen's University, Belfast, Northern Ireland, 1967; Ferris State, B.S., 1968. *Religion:* Presbyterian. *Hobbies and other interests:* Tennis, basketball, folk music.

Addresses

Home—848 Aspen Ct., Rochester, MI 48307. *Office*—340 Main St., Rochester, MI 48307. *Agent*—Edna Stephens. *E-mail*—rlytle@ameritech.net.

Career

Writer. Pharmacist and owner, Lytle Pharmacy, Rochester, MI, 1975—. Rochester City Council, 1991-96, mayor pro-tem. *Member:* Rochester/Avon Historical Society.

Awards, Honors

Mackinac Passage: A Summer Adventure was named one of the ten best children's books for 1995 by the Great Lakes Booksellers Association.

Writings

Mackinac Passage: A Summer Adventure, illustrated by Karen Howell, Thunder Bay (Lansing, MI), 1995.
Mackinac Passage: The Boathouse Mystery, Thunder Bay, 1996.

Mackinac Passage: The General's Treasure, Thunder Bay, 1997.

Three Rivers Crossing, River Road Publications (Spring Lake, MI), 2000.

Mackinac Passage: Mystery at Round Island Light, Thunder Bay, 2001.

Sidelights

Robert A. Lytle told *SATA:* "I began my interest in Michigan history while helping my father with his memoirs—*Life on the Farm* (Vantage Press, 1977), and again in 1987, when researching the pharmacy building which I renovated and had a marker made (built in 1890).

"My interest in writing for children began with the poems I wrote for my four sons as they were growing. It wasn't until I finished a pharmacy self-help book (*Med Chek—It Could Save Your Life,* self-published, 1993) that my enthusiasm for writing became evident. I became aware that my early-morning habit of writing for two hours before going to the drug store was invigorating. I decided to try a novel, and with my childhood summer experiences in a northern Michigan resort area—Les Cheneaux Island—as well as my summer job

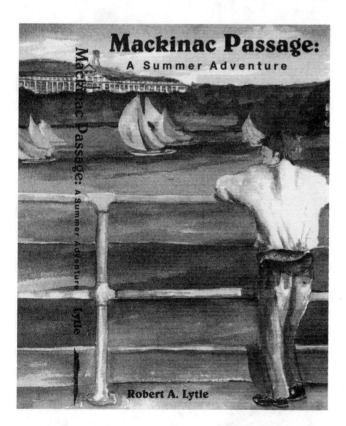

In Robert A. Lytle's novel set in Michigan's Upper Peninsula and Mackinac Island, fifteen-year-old Pete and his new friends uncover a counterfeit money scheme and murder. (Cover illustration by Karen Howell.)

during college on Mackinac Island, I began my career as a young adult adventure/mystery writer.

"Recently I turned my attention to the historically interesting Stony Creek Village near Rochester and was successful in publishing a time-travel adventure."

Lytle is a native of Michigan, and the author of several young adult mysteries that draw upon the state's history and natural beauty for their inspiration. Set in the vacation resort area of the Les Cheneaux Islands in the Mackinac Straits, in the Upper Peninsula of Michigan, Lytle's three *Mackinac Passage* novels are imbued with the idyllic ambiance not only of summer vacationing among the affluent, but of the early 1950s of the author's youth, when simple pleasures and less-complex problems were the order of the day. For example, in the second book in the series, *Mackinac Passage: The Boathouse Mystery,* young Peter's good times with his wealthy new summer friends is interrupted by the recurring robberies of boathouses on the island resort. Peter must choose between following his parents' rules and participating in both the fun and the search for the perpetrator of the robberies.

In addition to his young adult mysteries set in northern Michigan, Lytle is the author of *Three Rivers Crossing,* a novel that celebrates the history of the author's own home town of Rochester, Michigan. "It's an idea I've had for a long time," Lytle told *Oakland Press* reporter Ginny Stolicker. "I think it's important that the young people learn about history." The novel's title references the geographic location of Rochester, which is at the junction of three rivers: Stoney Creek, Paint Creek, and the Clinton River. This is a special place which was revered by Native Americans and which the author believes "is a sign of lasting communal bonds," a correspondent for the *Eccentric* newspaper reported. Lytle borrowed his grandson's first name, Walker, for his protagonist, and gave the fictional seventh-grader of 2002 a romantic interest in a student visiting from France, as well as an array of the usual experiences and tastes of an early twenty-first century teenager. Then Walker has a fishing accident in which he nearly drowns, and is rescued by his own nineteenth-century ancestors. More than a mere time-travel piece, according to the *Eccentric* contributor, "*Three Rivers Crossing* is Lytle's attempt to share the lessons of history, and appreciate the lasting values of friendship and community."

Biographical and Critical Sources

PERIODICALS

Eccentric, March 12, 2000, Review of *Three Rivers Crossing,* "Author's Sense of History Tied to Community," pp. C1, C2.

Oakland Press, February 2, 2000, Ginny Stolicker, "Bob's Travels: Children's Book Tells Story of Rochester History," pp. D1, D4.

Voice of Youth Advocates, April, 1997, p. 30.*

M

MAHY, Margaret 1936-

Personal

Born March 21, 1936, in Whakatane, New Zealand; daughter of Frances George (a builder) and May (a teacher; maiden name, Penlington) Mahy; children: Penelope Helen, Bridget Frances. *Education:* University of New Zealand, B.A., 1958. *Politics:* "Anarchist." *Religion:* "Humanist." *Hobbies and other interests:* Reading, gardening.

Addresses

Home—R.D. 1, Lyttelton, New Zealand. *Agent*—Vanessa Hamilton, The Summer House, Woodend, West Stoke Chichester, West Sussex, PO18 9BP England.

Career

Writer. Petone Public Library, Petone, New Zealand, assistant librarian, 1958-59; School Library Service, Christchurch, New Zealand, librarian in charge, 1967-76; Canterbury Public Library, Christchurch, children's librarian, 1976-80. Writer in residence, Canterbury University, 1984, and Western Australian College of Advanced Education, 1985. *Member:* New Zealand Library Association.

Awards, Honors

Esther Glenn Medal, New Zealand Library Association, 1969, for *A Lion in the Meadow,* 1973, for *The First Margaret Mahy Story Book,* and 1983, for *The Haunting;* Een Zilveren Griffel, 1978; *School Library Journal* Best Book citation, 1982, for *The Haunting;* Carnegie Medal, British Library Association, 1982, for *The Haunting,* 1986, for *The Changeover: A Supernatural Romance,* and 1987, for *Memory;* Notable Children's Book citation, Association for Library Service to Children (ALSC), 1984, Children's Book of the Year citation, and Best Books for Young Adults award, American Library Association (ALA), both 1986, all for

The Changeover; Honor List citation, *Horn Book,* 1985, for *The Changeover,* and 1987, for *The Catalogue of the Universe; 17 Kings and 42 Elephants* was named one of the year's ten best illustrated books in 1987 by the *New York Times Book Review;* Best Books of 1987 citation, ALA Young Adult Services Division, for *The Tricksters;* Society of School Libraries International Book award (Language Arts, Science and Social Studies category), and *Boston Globe/Horn Book* award, both

Margaret Mahy

1988, both for *Memory;* Best Books of 1989 citation, ALA Young Adult Services Division, for *Memory;* May Hill Arbuthnot Lecturer, ALSC, 1989.

Writings

PICTURE BOOKS

A Lion in the Meadow (verse; also see below), illustrated by Jenny Williams, F. Watts, 1969.

A Dragon of an Ordinary Family, illustrated by Helen Oxenbury, F. Watts, 1969.

Pillycock's Shop, illustrated by Carol Barker, F. Watts, 1969.

The Procession, illustrated by Charles Mozley, F. Watts, 1969.

Mrs. Discombobulous, illustrated by Jan Brychta, F. Watts, 1969.

The Little Witch, illustrated by Mozely, F. Watts, 1970.

Sailor Jack and the 20 Orphans, illustrated by Robert Bartelt, F. Watts, 1970.

The Princess and the Clown, F. Watts, 1971.

The Boy with Two Shadows, illustrated by Williams, F. Watts, 1971, Lippincott, 1989.

The Man Whose Mother Was a Pirate, illustrated by Brian Froud, Atheneum, 1972, illustrated by Margaret Chamberlain, Viking Kestrel, 1986.

The Railway Engine and the Hairy Brigands, Dent, 1973.

Rooms for Rent, illustrated by Williams, F. Watts, 1974, published in England as *Rooms to Let,* Dent, 1975.

The Rare Spotted Birthday Party, F. Watts, 1974.

The Witch in the Cherry Tree, illustrated by Williams, Parents' Magazine, 1974.

Stepmother, F. Watts, 1974.

Ultra-Violet Catastrophe! Or, The Unexpected Walk with Great-Uncle Mangus Pringle, Parents' Magazine, 1975.

David's Witch Doctor, F. Watts, 1976.

The Wind between the Stars, Dent, 1976.

The Boy Who Was Followed Home, illustrated by Steven Kellogg, F. Watts, 1976.

Leaf Magic (also see below), Dent, 1976, Parents' Magazine, 1977.

Jam: A True Story, illustrated by Helen Craig, Little, Brown, 1986.

Pumpkin Man and the Crafty Creeper, illustrated by Craig, Greenwillow, 1991.

A Summery Saturday Morning, illustrated by Selina Young, Hamish Hamilton, 1998.

Beaten by a Balloon, illustrated by Jonathan Allen, Viking, 1998.

JUVENILE FICTION

The Great Millionaire Kidnap, illustrated by Jan Brychta, Dent, 1975.

The Nonstop Nonsense Book, illustrated by Quentin Blake, Dent, 1977.

The Great Piratical Rumbustification [and] *The Librarian and the Robbers,* illustrated by Blake, Dent, 1978.

The Birthday Burglar [and] *A Very Wicked Headmistress,* Dent, 1984, new edition with illustrations by Chamberlain, Godine (Boston, MA), 1988.

The Dragon's Birthday, illustrated by Webb, Shortland, 1984.

Ups and Downs and Other Stories, illustrated by Webb, Shortland, 1984.

The Spider in the Shower, illustrated by McRae, Shortland, 1984.

Wibble-Wobble and Other Stories, Shortland, 1984.

The Adventures of a Kite, illustrated by David Cowe, Shortland (Auckland, New Zealand), 1985, Arnold-Wheaton (Leeds, England), 1986.

Sophie's Singing Mother, illustrated by Jo Davies, Arnold-Wheaton, 1985.

The Earthquake, illustrated by Dianne Perham, Arnold-Wheaton, 1985.

The Cake, illustrated by Cowe, Arnold-Wheaton, 1985.

The Catten, illustrated by Davies, Arnold-Wheaton, 1985.

Out in the Big Wild World, illustrated by Rodney McRae, Shortland, 1985.

Rain, illustrated by Fuller, Shortland, 1985.

Clever Hamburger, illustrated by McRae, Arnold-Wheaton, 1985.

A Very Happy Birthday, illustrated by Elizabeth Fuller, Arnold-Wheaton, 1986.

Beautiful Pig, Shortland, 1986, Arnold-Wheaton, 1987.

The Long Grass of Tumbledown Road, Shortland, 1986, Arnold-Wheaton, 1987.

The Robber Pig and the Ginger Beer, illustrated by McRae, two volumes, Shortland, 1986, Arnold-Wheaton, 1987.

Arguments, illustrated by Kelvin Hawley, Shortland, 1986,

An Elephant in the House, illustrated by Fuller, Shortland, 1986.

The Fight on the Hill, illustrated by Jan van der Voo, Shortland, 1986, Arnold-Wheaton, 1987.

The Funny Funny Clown Face, illustrated by Miranda Whitford, Heinemann, 1986.

Grow Up Sally Sue, Heinemann, 1986.

The King's Treasure, Heinemann, 1986.

The Man Who Enjoyed Grumbling, illustrated by Wendy Hodder, Heinemann, 1986.

Jacko, the Junk Shop Man, illustrated by Davies, Shortland, 1986.

The Mouse Wedding, illustrated by Fuller, Shortland, 1986.

Squeak in the Gate, illustrated by Davies, Shortland, 1986.

Shuttle 4, Heinemann, 1986.

The Tree Doctor, illustrated by Wendy Hodder, Heinemann, 1986.

The Trouble with Heathrow, illustrated by Rodney McRae, Heinemann, 1986.

(With others) *The Three Wishes,* illustrated by McRae and others, Shortland, 1986.

Tinny Tiny Tinker, illustrated by David Cowe, Shortland, 1986.

Mr. Rooster's Dilemma, illustrated by Fuller, Shortland, 1986, published in England as *How Mr. Rooster Didn't Get Married,* Arnold-Wheaton, 1987.

My Wonderful Aunt (four volumes), illustrated by Dierdre Gardiner, Wright Group, 1986, revised edition in one volume, Children's Press, 1988.

Baby's Breakfast, illustrated by Madeline Beasley, Heinemann, 1986.

Feeling Funny, illustrated by McRae, Heinemann, 1986.

The Garden Party, illustrated by McRae, Heinemann, 1986.

The New House Villain, illustrated by Fuller, Heinemann, 1986.

A Pet to the Vet, illustrated by Philip Webb, Heinemann, 1986.

The Pop Group, illustrated by McRae, Heinemann, 1986.

The Terrible Topsy-Turvy, Tissy-Tossy Tangle, illustrated by Vicki Smillie-McItoull, Heinemann, 1986.

Trouble on the Bus, illustrated by Wendy Hodder, Heinemann, 1986.

Mr. Rumfitt, illustrated by Price, Heinemann, 1986.

Muppy's Ball, illustrated by van der Voo, Heinemann, 1986.

The Man Who Walked on His Hands, illustrated by Martin Bailey, Shortland, 1987.

Elliott and the Cats Eating Out, Heinemann, 1987.

Guinea Pig Grass, illustrated by Kelvin Hawley, Shortland, 1987.

No Dinner for Sally, illustrated by John Tarlton, Shortland, 1987.

The Girl Who Washed in Moonlight, illustrated by Robyn Belton, Heinemann, 1987.

The Haunting of Miss Cardamon, illustrated by Korky Paul, Heinemann, 1987.

Iris La Bonga and the Helpful Taxi Driver, illustrated by Smillie-McItoull, Heinemann, 1987.

The Mad Puppet, illustrated by Jon Davis, Heinemann, 1987.

As Luck Would Have It, illustrated by Gardiner, Shortland, 1988.

A Not-So-Quiet Evening, illustrated by Glenda Jones, Shortland, 1988.

Sarah, the Bear and the Kangaroo, illustrated by Fuller, Shortland, 1988.

When the King Rides By, Thornes, 1988.

The Seven Chinese Brothers, illustrated by Jean and Mou-sien Tseng, Scholastic, 1990.

White Elephants, Heinemann, 1990.

The Great White Man-Eating Shark: A Cautionary Tale, illustrated by Jonathan Allen, Dial, 1990.

Making Friends, illustrated by Wendy Smith, McElderry, 1990.

Keeping House, Macmillan, 1991.

The Queen's Goat, illustrated by Emma Chichester Clark, Dial, 1991.

Underrunners, Viking, 1992.

The Horrendous Hullabaloo, illustrated by Patricia MacCarthy, Viking, 1992.

A Busy Day for a Good Grandmother, illustrated by Margaret Chamberlain, McElderry, 1993.

The Good Fortunes Gang, illustrated by Marian Young, Delacorte, 1993.

The Three-Legged Cat, illustrated by Jonathan Allen, Viking, 1993.

A Fortunate Name, illustrated by Marian Young, Delacorte, 1993.

Tick Tock Tales: Stories to Read Around the Clock, illustrated by Wendy Smith, McElderry, 1994.

The Greatest Show Off Earth, illustrated by Wendy Smith, Viking, 1994.

The Rattlebang Picnic, illustrated by Steven Kellogg, Dial, 1994.

Tangled Fortunes, illustrated by Marian Young, Delacorte, 1994.

The Christmas Tree Tangle, illustrated by Anthony Kervins, McElderry, 1994.

They tried throwing him into deeper water, but the deep, deep water only just reached as far as his waist.

Each of seven brothers uses his supernatural gift to avoid execution in Mahy's **The Seven Chinese Brothers,** *illustrated by Jean and Mou-sien Tseng.*

A Fortune Branches Out, illustrated by Marian Young, Delacorte, 1994.

Tingleberries, Tuckertubs, and Telephones: A Tale of Love and Ice-cream, illustrated by Robert Staermose, Viking, 1995.

The Five Sisters, illustrated by Patricia MacCarthy, Viking, 1996.

Boom, Baby, Boom, Boom, illustrated by P. MacCarthy, Hamish Hamilton, 1996, Viking, 1997.

The Horribly Haunted School, Hamish Hamilton, 1997.

Operation Terror, Puffin, 1997.

(With others) *Don't Read This! And Other Tales of the Unnatural,* illustrated by The Tjong Khing, Front Street, 1998.

Simply Delicious!, illustrated by J. Allen, Orchard, 1999.

(With Helen Oxenbury) *A Dragon of an Ordinary Family,* Mammoth, 1999.

A Villain's Night Out, illustrated by Harry Horse, Puffin, 1999.

Down in the Dump with Dinsmore, illustrated by Steve Axelsen, Puffin, 1999.

Down the Dragon's Tongue, illustrated by P. MacCarthy, Orchard, 2000.

"TAI TAYLOR" SERIES

Tai Taylor Is Born, illustrated by Nick Price, four volumes, Heinemann, 1986-87.

Tai Taylor and the Sweet Annie, illustrated by Nick Price, four volumes, Heinemann, 1986-87.

Tai Taylor Goes to School, illustrated by Nick Price, four volumes, Heinemann, 1986-87.

Tai Taylor and His Education, illustrated by Nick Price, four volumes, Heinemann, 1986-87.

JUVENILE FICTION WITH JOY COWLEY AND JUNE MELSER

Roly-Poly, illustrated by Gardiner, Shortland, 1982, Arnold-Wheaton, 1985.

Cooking Pot, illustrated by Gardiner, Shortland, 1982, Arnold-Wheaton, 1985.

Fast and Funny, illustrated by Lynette Vondrusha, Shortland, 1982, Arnold-Wheaton, 1985.

Sing to the Moon, illustrated by Isabel Lowe, Shortland, 1982, Arnold-Wheaton, 1985.

Tiddalik, illustrated by Philip Webb, Shortland, 1982, Arnold-Wheaton, 1985.

YOUNG ADULT NOVELS

Clancy's Cabin, illustrated by Trevor Stubley, Dent, 1974.

The Bus under the Leaves, illustrated by Margery Gill, Dent, 1974.

The Pirate Uncle, illustrated by Mary Dinsdale, Dent, 1977.

Raging Robots and Unruly Uncles, illustrated by Peter Stevenson, Dent, 1981.

The Pirates' Mixed-Up Voyage: Dark Doings in the Thousand Islands, illustrated by Chamberlain, Dent, 1983.

The Haunting (also see below), illustrated by Bruce Hogarth, Atheneum, 1982.

The Changeover: A Supernatural Romance, Atheneum, 1984.

The Catalogue of the Universe, Atheneum, 1985.

Aliens in the Family, Scholastic, 1986.

The Tricksters, McElderry, 1987.

Memory, McElderry, 1988.

The Blood-and-Thunder Adventure on Hurricane Peak, illustrated by Smith, Dent, 1989.

Dangerous Spaces, Viking, 1991.

The Other Side of Silence, Viking, 1995.

Twenty-four Hours, McElderry, 2000.

READERS

Look under "V", illustrated by Deirdre Gardiner, Wellington Department of Education, School Publications Branch (New Zealand), 1977.

The Crocodile's Christmas Sandals, illustrated by Gardiner, Wellington Department of Education, School Publications Branch, 1982, published as *The Christmas Crocodile's Thongs,* Nelson (Melbourne, Australia), 1985.

The Bubbling Crocodile, illustrated by Gardiner, Wellington Department of Education, School Publications Branch, 1983.

Mrs. Bubble's Baby, Wellington Department of Education, School Publications Branch, 1983.

Shopping with a Crocodile, Wellington Department of Education, School Publications Branch, 1983.

A Crocodile in the Library, illustrated by Gardiner, Wellington Department of Education, School Publications Branch, 1983.

A Crocodile in the Garden, illustrated by Gardiner, two volumes, Wellington Department of Education, School Publications Branch, 1983-85.

Going to the Beach, illustrated by Dick Frizzell, Wellington Department of Education, School Publications Branch, 1984.

The Great Grumbler and the Wonder Tree, illustrated by Diane Perham, Wellington Department of Education, School Publications Branch, 1984.

Fantail, Fantail, illustrated by Bruce Phillips, Wellington Department of Education, School Publications Branch, 1984.

Horrakopotchin, Wellington Department of Education, School Publications Branch, 1985.

NONFICTION

New Zealand: Yesterday and Today, F. Watts, 1975.

POETRY

17 Kings and 42 Elephants (verse), Dent, 1972, 2nd edition edited by Phyllis J. Fogelman with illustrations by Patricia MacCarthy, Dial, 1987.

The Tin Can Band and Other Poems, illustrated by Honey De Lacey, Dent, 1987.

COLLECTIONS

The First Margaret Mahy Story Book: Stories and Poems, Dent, 1972.

The Second Margaret Mahy Story Book: Stories and Poems, Dent, 1973.

The Third Margaret Mahy Story Book: Stories and Poems, illustrated by Shirley Hughes, Dent, 1975.

A Lion in the Meadow and Five Other Favorites, illustrated by Williams, Bartelt, Brychta, Mozley, and Froud, 1976.

The Chewing-Gum Rescue and Other Stories, illustrated by Jan Ormerod, Dent, 1982, Methuen, 1984.

Leaf Magic and Five other Favourites, illustrated by Chamberlain, Dent, 1984.

The Downhill Crocodile Whizz and Other Stories, illustrated by Ian Newsham, Dent, 1986.

Mahy Magic: A Collection of the Most Magical Stories from the Margaret Mahy Story Books, illustrated by Hughes, Dent, 1986.

The Horrible Story and Others, illustrated by Hughes, Dent, 1987.

The Door in the Air and Other Stories, illustrated by Diana Catchpole, Dent, 1988, Delacorte, 1991.

Chocolate Porridge and Other Stories, illustrated by Hughes, 1989.

A Tall Story and Other Tales, illustrated by Jan Nesbitt, McElderry, 1992.

The Girl with the Green Ear: Stories about Magic in Nature, illustrated by Shirley Hughes, Knopf, 1992.

(Self-illustrated) *Bubble Trouble and Other Poems to Share,* Macmillan, 1992.

OTHER

My Mysterious World (autobiography), photographs by David Alexander, R. C. Owen, 1995.

Author of scripts "A Land Called Happy," "Wooly Valley," "Once upon a Story," and "The Margaret Mahy Story Book Theatre" for Television New Zealand, and scripts for the Gibson Group television series *Cuckooland.* "The Haunting of Barney Palmer" (screenplay adapted by Mahy from *The Haunting*) was broadcast on *Wonderworks,* Public Broadcasting Service, 1987.

Adaptations

Cassette versions of Mahy's works include *The Haunting,* 1986, *The Chewing-Gum Rescue and Other Stories,* 1988, and *The Pirates' Mixed-Up Voyage,* all read aloud by Richard Mitchley, and *Nonstop Nonsense,* read by Kenneth Stanley, all recorded by G. K. Hall.

Sidelights

New Zealand author Margaret Mahy has made a career of tickling funny bones, teasing the imagination, and sending shivers up spines of young readers. She is, according to Betty Gilderdale writing in *St. James Guide to Children's Writers,* "one of the most distinguished contemporary writers for children." Her nearly two hundred publications comprise the full gamut of books for young readers: picture books for the very young, chapter books and readers, short stories and novels for middle grader readers, and young adult novels and story collections. Her themes vary from fantastical tales of possibility and wonder, to gritty realistic novels, to supernatural tales and family problem novels. "Her characters are memorable," wrote a contributor to *Children's Books and Their Creators.* "[S]he is adept at combining humor, suspense, and imagination; underlying all her work is an obvious and abiding love of language, which manifests itself in a distinct and dexterous style." Critics laud Mahy for refusing to talk down to children of any age, helping create texts which can be read on many levels.

Often working with fairy tale motifs, Mahy delights in the use of witches, ghosts, and dragons, especially in much of her early work for all ages. In Mahy's competent hands such spirits are not always meant to frighten as they do in her novel *Dangerous Spaces,* but also to enlighten, as does the specter in *The Haunting.* Such award-winning tales have made Mahy well-known around the globe. Her worlds of surprising possibilities are familiar to children and also strike chords of remembrance with adults. When writing about aliens with unusual powers, intelligent adolescents, or New Zealand, Mahy "writes with all the force and precision and richness of a poet," according to Elizabeth Ward in the *Washington Post Book World.*

Born in the small New Zealand town of Whakatane in 1936, Mahy grew up loving stories of all sorts, the ones she created for her own amusement as much as the ones read to her. "In the beginning, before I could write," Mahy recalled in *Children's Books and Their Creators,* "I made up small rhymes which I learned by heart, and acted out stories, vaguely based on events in my own life but filled with the fascinations of another sort of existence. For as far back as I can remember, I wanted to write a book." Such an ambition was a long time off, however. First Mahy took a degree from the University of New Zealand, becoming a librarian, as well as a wife and mother.

Mahy's first book *A Lion in the Meadow,* published in 1969, shows a mother in trouble because she refuses to take her son seriously. Annoyed by his warnings that there is a lion in the meadow, the busy mother—thinking that he is playing a fantasy game with her—gives the child a box of matches. Inside it, she says, is a little dragon that can grow large enough to scare the lion away. She soon vows not to lie to her children again. The fable shows that while fantasy is important to children, it is dangerous for adults not to recognize and teach the difference between fantasy and reality. The boundaries and overlap of fantasy and reality is a theme reoccurring through much of what Mahy has since written for younger children: her cast of pirates, witches, and wizards are "free spirits," as Gilderdale pointed out, "untrammeled by the demands of convention." Many of Mahy's stories for young readers, both in picture book and novel format, deal with reconciling the boring everyday of life with the adventure of creativity.

In books such as *The Man Whose Mother Was a Pirate* and *The Pirates' Mixed-Up Voyage,* sons rebel against the rules of parents and set off to the adventure of the sea. Being released from the restrictions of the quotidian inspires many of the stories in the collection *The Door in the Air,* as well as in the picture book *The Wind between the Stars.* Children must also battle strict schools, as in *A Very Wicked Headmistress.* Mahy combines her love of ghosts with snipes at oppressive schooling in the 1997 novel, *The Horribly Haunted School,* in which young Monty is made to sneeze because of ghosts. His mother, however, does not believe in his allergy and sends him to the Brinsley Codd School for Sensible Thought in order to straighten out her overly imaginative son. Once there, however, Monty causes chaos when he discovers the ghost of the former headmaster, Brinsley Codd himself. Janet Hilburn, reviewing the novel in *School Library Journal,* called it "enjoyable and entertaining" with "comical characters" and "unexpected twists and turns." "If you are tired of boring, predictable formula fiction," wrote Jo Goodman in a *Magpies* review of the same novel, "try Mahy instead .... Irresistible stuff." But Mahy, as Gilderdale commented, is not just after laughs and titters. "The main message of [*The Horribly Haunted School*] is that sometimes an imaginative and unusual approach turns out to be better than strictly logical methods."

In addition to being valued for their themes, Mahy's books for children are popular and highly praised because of her skills as a poet. In the rhythmic verses of *17 Kings and 42 Elephants,* a parade of kings, elephants, tigers, and other jungle animals winds from an unnamed beginning to an unnamed finish, making a journey that is enjoyable for its own sake. The book's language is both "precise and creative, entertaining and thought-provoking, silly and serious," Arthur Yorinks commented in the *New York Times Book Review.* The *New York Times Book Review* also named it one of the year's ten best illustrated books in 1987.

Mahy's books for young readers are full of linguistic pyrotechnics, as well as plenty to eat. Birthday parties, picnics, and feasts of all sorts abound in her picture books and novels, as well as technological gizmos in later works, such as *Raging Robots and Unruly Uncles,* in which separate sets of cousins build robots as presents for each other. But while one group of robots behaves in an exemplary manner, the other is as unruly as their creators, and humorous results ensue. Cousins are also at the heart of a series of novels about the Fortune family, each book focusing on one group of cousins in the large extended family. Returning from Australia to his native New Zealand, young Peter has trouble being accepted by his other cousins in the first novel in the series, *The Good Fortunes Gang.* The difficulties of growing up and dreams of future careers feature in other books in this lighthearted look at modern family life.

Mahy can also have an edge to her writing for juvenile readers, as in the novel *Underrunners.* Young Tristam, deserted by his mother, finds comfort in imaginary games. When he meets Winola, a girl from a children's home, he thinks she too is having fun with imaginary games when she tells of a man searching for her. But when the man becomes all too real, both children are thrown into a scenario much more tense and dangerous than any of Tristam's former make-believe stories. A lighter take on life is provided with the novel, *Tingleberries, Tuckertubs, and Telephones,* about a grandmother far from the stereotypical bread-baking and kindly old woman. This grandmother is, in fact, a detective inspector so strong and imposing that she cows her grandchild, Saracen, into shyness so severe that he refuses to even talk on the phone. Other intrepid if not so formidable grandmothers make appearances in *The Rattlebang Picnic,* in which overdone pizzas come to the rescue of a stranded family, and *A Busy Day for a Good Grandmother.* Indeed, one of the joys of Mahy's books is her spectrum of characters, from young children to grandparents, from sensible adults to zany individuals with bizarre names and even weirder likes and dislikes.

Mahy tackles politically correct child-rearing in her 1998 picture book, *Beaten by a Balloon,* in which the bad guys are beaten by such an object. Young Sam wants a sword like the one his buddy, Hacky, has. But instead, Sam's peaceable father gets him a balloon, a cake, and a sunflower. When Sam and Hacky, accompanied by their fathers, go to the bank, they confront the villainous Buckbounder, robbing the bank. In the end,

perhaps balloons make the strongest weapons of all. This "mad adventure" of a picture book "delivers an important message which may or may not be taken seriously," commented *Magpies* contributor, Lynne Babbage. Writing in *School Library Journal,* Lauralyn Person commented, "Overall, this book revels in its own silliness, which kids will love." Person went on to conclude, "Adults will appreciate the anti-violence message, which is there for those who look for it but it doesn't get in the way of the fun." George Hunt, reviewing the title in *Books for Keeps,* called the picture book "one of Mahy's wonderfully condensed miniature farces" that conveys a "humorous, pithy and non-didactic message about a very relevant moral issue." *Booklist*'s Hazel Rochman wrote that with this "slapstick tall tale" Mahy poked fun both at "the macho gang and ... the peaceniks."

A further addition to Mahy's picture book opus for young children is the 1998 *A Summery Saturday Morning,* a "light romp by the seashore that will have children marching along," according to *School Library Journal* contributor Ronald Jobe. "Listeners will delight in the sounds of the language, the lively rhythm, the song-like repetition, and the pleasing rhyme," Jobe further commented. Cynthia Anthony noted in *Magpies* that this "delightful book is a token of Mahy's ability to entertain younger children even as she does older readers."

Such older readers will indeed be entertained by her 1999 entry, *Down in the Dump with Dinsmore* in which a smelly town dump is transformed into a huge adventure in the eyes (and nose) of young Dinsmore. Forced to spend more and more time at the dump for a school project, the young boy increasingly takes on aspects of the dump himself. Discarded seeds begin to grow a lawn on him, making him smell, in fact, much sweeter. "Only Margaret Mahy could have thought of such a story," commented a *Magpies* reviewer, "and only she would extend it to enable Dinsmore to become a successful lawn salesman to the rich and famous." From this exalted position he is thereafter able to foil a gang of robbers. "It's all good, certainly not clean, fun," concluded the contributor to *Magpies.* Middle grade readers will also be entertained, if not horrified, by *Don't Read This! And Other Tales of the Unnatural,* a collection of scary stories to which Mahy contributed "Finger on the Back of the Neck." This tale of a hideous young boy who kills his great-grandmother because she always stroked the back of the neck and then becomes haunted by the woman's fingers is "very creepy," according to Randy Brough, writing in *Voice of Youth Advocates.* A writer for *Publishers Weekly,* in a review of the collection of eleven stories, noted that "[r]eaders with a taste for the eerie should ignore the advice proffered in this book's title," while *Booklist*'s Rochman remarked that Mahy, along with several other writers included in the anthology, "are at the top of their form: their shivery horror stories will draw kids in and make them go on to other interesting writers."

Mahy's award-winning books for young adults focus on family relationships and coming-of-age themes through a variety of story-telling methods that range from realism to supernaturalism. In *Memory,* an elderly woman suffering from Alzheimer's disease gets help from a teen who wants to forget his early life. In *The Haunting,* a young man finds out he is in line to inherit psychic powers that he feels are a curse more than a blessing. The novel's eight-year-old protagonist, Barney Palmer, describes a sequence of meal-time family discussions and ties them together with explanations of his own thoughts and feelings. Critics praise Mahy's ability to develop likeable characters and an ambitious theme within this framework. Barney and his family "are beautifully drawn, and perhaps because they care so much for each other, readers care for them, too," commented Michael Cart in *School Library Journal.* Sarah Hayes observed in the *Times Literary Supplement* that "*The Haunting* manages to combine a realistic approach to family life—in which how you feel about your parents and yourself is actually important—with a strong and terrifying line in fantasy."

Dangerous Spaces presents one young woman's struggle to control her habit of trying to avoid life's difficulties by escaping to a private world inhabited by her great-uncle's ghost. Anthea's own parents have died suddenly, and she lives with relatives whose complicated and noisy lives are no comfort to her. Soon she is retreating to the spacious dream-world Viridian every night, and her trips become so dangerous that her life is threatened. Down-to-earth Flora, the cousin who resents the glamorous Anthea at first, charges in to Viridian to rescue her and puts an end to a haunting that has plagued the family for generations. The skillful weaving of adventure with insights into family relationships for which Mahy is known "rewards readers who finish the book," a *Publishers Weekly* reviewer remarked.

The importance of family relationships to young adults is just one of the author's major themes. Hayes wrote in the *Times Literary Supplement,* "the double aspect of things—man and beast, [good] and evil, young and old—intrigues Margaret Mahy." In *The Catalogue of the Universe,* the main characters are high school seniors working out the problems of identity common to that age group. Living without a father for many years, Angela feels that the blessings of beauty, a loving mother, and intelligence have not compensated for his absence. Tycho, her friend since early childhood, looks to science and astronomy to provide a rational basis for his life and decides to help Angela in her search for her missing father. When they encounter the lost parent, disappointment forces Angela to find out who she is apart from family ties. She and Tycho also find that while forgiveness can help relationships survive, it is a difficult state of mind to achieve and does not necessarily change the faults of others. Mahy's characters accept these lessons without feeling sorry for themselves and without giving up on life. "Angela shares with her friend Tycho a fascination with matters like the square root of two and the moon of Jupiter which outlast emotional pains and the novel moves lightly," Gillian Wilce maintained in the *New Statesman.* Colin Greenland noted in the *Times Literary Supplement* that readers who

"know at least a little of what it feels like to be in love" will appreciate this book.

Mahy's ability to combine themes relevant to young adults with fantasy is matched by her consistently non-sexist perspective on roles and relationships. Jan Dalley, writing in the *Times Literary Supplement,* pointed out that Mahy "continually pushes at the boundaries of [fairy-tale] conventions," and "roots out the sexism that used to be integral" to fiction for young readers. For example, though the roles of rescuer, leader, and problem-solver have been traditionally assigned to males, she gives these roles as often to females of various ages and levels of social status. In Mahy's books, the role of home economist and nurturer, traditionally assigned to women, is also assigned to men. Growth to sexual maturity is equally exciting and frightening to her male and female adolescents. Adults of both sexes are equally subject to weakness and failure to discern the needs of their children. All her characters face the same challenges to strike a balance between freedom and commitment, reason and emotion. And they all benefit from recognizing the power of the imagination, which they learn to celebrate as well as to contain.

In her 1995 young adult novel, *The Other Side of Silence,* Mahy examines problems in communication between forceful parents and their offspring. Hero, the young female protagonist of the novel, refuses to speak. Such a refusal is her way of maintaining some individuality in her family where "words flow away like wasting water." Not only do mother and daughter in Hero's home have some work to do with each other, but Hero soon discovers another mother-daughter relationship with terrifying ramifications at the spooky Credence House where she has been spending time lately. Reviewing this novel in *Books for Keeps,* Robert Dunbar noted the continual references to myth and fairy tale and the "staggering" number of levels on which the "entrancing" story could be read. Dunbar concluded, "This is a clever, subtle and witty novel, with a wonderful cast of offbeat characters; there is hardly a page which does not afford a penetrating insight into the strange territory we refer to as 'family life'."

In all her work, whether it be in the form of picture books, middle grade novels, or young adult novels, Mahy has tried, as she noted in her Arbuthnot Lecture printed in *Journal of Youth Services in Libraries,* to tell "all the truth as I know it from personal experience." Such truth takes many forms: advice to have a healthy suspicion for unreasonable authority, to trust in creativity and inspiration, to delight in fantasy and the world of creativity, to honor family bonds, and to find humor in the oddest places. As the contributor to *Children's Books and Their Creators* summed up, "A prolific writer, Mahy has contributed significantly to children's literature with her exquisitely crafted and compelling stories that continuously prompt readers to 'Always Expect the Unexpected.'"

Biographical and Critical Sources

BOOKS

Authors and Artists for Young Adults, Volume 8, Gale, 1992.
Children's Books and Their Creators, edited by Anita Silvey, Houghton Mifflin, 1995, pp. 432-33.
Children's Literature Review, Volume 7, Gale, 1984, pp. 176-88.
Gilderdale, Betty, *Introducing Margaret Mahy,* Viking, 1987; "Mahy, Margaret," *St. James Guide to Children's Writers,* 5th edition, edited by Sara Pendergast and Tom Pendergast, St. James, 1999, pp. 692-97.

PERIODICALS

Booklist, March 15, 1998, Hazel Rochman, review of *Beaten by a Balloon,* p. 125; April 1, 1999, H. Rochman, review of *Don't Read This!,* p. 1398.
Books for Keeps, March, 1998, Robert Dunbar, review of *The Other Side of Silence,* p. 26; May, 1998, George Hunt, review of *Beaten by a Balloon,* p. 21.
Bulletin of the Center for Children's Books, March, 1998, p. 250; September, 1998, p. 23; March, 1999, p. 238.
Christian Science Monitor, June 6, 1986, p. B6; November 4, 1988, p. B3; January 25, 1989, p. 13.
Fantasy Review, March, 1985, p. 27.
Growing Point, November 21, 1982, p. 3985.
Horn Book, November/December, 1984, p. 764; November/December, 1989, pp. 772-73; March, 1991, p. 201.
Journal of Youth Services in Libraries, Summer, 1989, Margaret Mahy, "May Hill Arbuthnot Lecture, A Dissolving Ghost: Possible Operations of Truth in Children's Books and the Lives of Children," pp. 313-29.
Junior Bookshelf, February, 1983, p. 45.
Kliatt, March, 1998, p. 12.
Listener, November 8, 1984, p. 27.
Magpies, March, 1998, Lynne Babbage, review of *Beaten by a Balloon,* pp. 29-30; May, 1998, Jo Goodman, review of *The Horribly Haunted School,* pp. 33-34; July, 1998, Cynthia Anthony, review of *A Summery Saturday Morning,* pp. 26-27; March, 1999, review of *Down in the Dump with Dinsmore,* p. 29.
Mahy, Margaret, *The Other Side of Silence,* Viking, 1995.
New Statesman, November, 1985, Gillian Wilce, "Waking Up the Kid Next Door," pp. 27-28.
New York Times Book Review, July 13, 1986, p. 22; May 17, 1987, pp. 31, 44; November 8, 1987, Arthur Yorinks, "Lots of Pachyderms," p. 40; July 16, 1997, p. 16.
Publishers Weekly, February 1, 1991, review of *Dangerous Spaces,* p. 80; March 1, 1999, review of *Don't Read This!,* p. 70.
School Librarian, September, 1984, p. 260; April, 1991, p. 121.
School Library Journal, August, 1982, Michael Cart, review of *The Haunting,* p. 119; April, 1991, p. 98; March, 1997, Lauralyn Person, review of *Beaten by a Balloon,* p. 184; July, 1998, Janet Hilburn, review of *The Horribly Haunted School,* p. 97; July, 1998, Ronald Jobe, review of *A Summery Saturday Morning,* p. 79; November, 1998, p. 43.
Times Educational Supplement, April 18, 1997, p. 12; November 7, 1997, p. 7.
Times Literary Supplement, September 17, 1982, Sarah Hayes, "Unearthing the Family Ghosts," p. 1001; July 13, 1984, S. Hayes, "Adding another Dimension," p. 794; November 8, 1985, Colin Greenland, "Ritual Dismembering," p. 1274; November 25, 1988, Jan Dalley, "Fantastical Flights," p. 1323.
Voice of Youth Advocates, June, 1999, Randy Brough, review of *Don't Read This!,* p. 122.
Washington Post Book World, October 12, 1986, Elizabeth Ward, "Space to Dream," p. 11.*

—*Sketch by J. Sydney Jones*

*   *   *

MALETTA, Dr. Arlene
See FELTENSTEIN, Dr. Arlene (H.)

*   *   *

MARTIN, Fred 1948-

Personal

Born July 27, 1948, in Dublin, Ireland; son of Noel (a book shop manager) and Lilian (Carter) Martin; married Rosemary Sian Edwards, August 14, 1971; children: Ian Frederick, Hannah. *Education:* Portsmouth College of Technology, B.A. (with honors), 1969; University of Salford, M.Sc., 1970; City of Birmingham College of Education, certificate in education, 1971.

Addresses

Home—East Wing, Oldland Hall, Longwell Green, Bristol, South Gloucestershire BS30 9DQ, England. *Office*—Bath Spa University College, Newton Park Campus, Bath, England. *E-mail*—f.martin@bathspa. ac.uk.

Career

Author and educator.

Writings

(With Richard Bateman) *Steps in Geography,* Hutchinson (London, England), Book 1, 1980, Book 2, 1981, Book 3, 1982.
(With Aubrey Whittle) *Core Geography: Leisure,* Hutchinson, 1982.
(With Aubrey Whittle) *Core Geography: Work,* Hutchinson, 1983.
(With Aubrey Whittle) *Core Geography: Cities,* Hutchinson, 1984.
(With Aubrey Whittle) *Core Geography: The Developing World,* Hutchinson, 1985.
Atlas of the Environment (includes workbooks), Volumes 1-2, Heinemann (Oxford, England), 1986.
(Coauthor) *Nature of Environments,* Heinemann, 1987.

Fred Martin

(With Aubrey Whittle) *Core Geography: The United Kingdom,* Hutchinson, 1987.

(With Aubrey Whittle) *Core Geography: The Physical World,* Hutchinson, 1988.

(With Aubrey Whittle) *Down to Earth: Poverty and Progress,* Hutchinson, 1988.

(With Aubrey Whittle) *Skills in Geography,* Heinemann, Books 1-2, 1988, Book 3, 1989.

(With John E. Butler) *Geography Skills for GCSE and Standard Grade,* Hutchinson, 1988.

(With Aubrey Whittle) *People and the European Community,* Heinemann, 1991.

(With Aubrey Whittle) *Worldview,* Heinemann, Books 1-2, 1992, Book 3, 1993.

The Small Blue Planet (CD) Resource Pack, Bradford Technology, 1995.

Focus on Disasters: Floods, Heinemann, 1995.

Focus on Disasters: The Weather, Heinemann, 1995.

Focus on Disasters: Earthquake, Heinemann, 1995.

Focus on Disasters: Volcano, Heinemann, 1995.

Themes in Geography: Environmental Change, Heinemann, 1996.

Themes in Geography: Settlements, Heinemann, 1996.

Themes in Geography: Weather, Heinemann, 1996.

Themes in Geography: Rivers, Heinemann, 1996.

(With Keith Grimwade) *Homework in Geography,* Geographical Association, 1997.

Italy, Heinemann, 1997, published as *Next Stop: Italy,* Heinemann, 1997.

Next Stop: Germany, Heinemann, 1997.

Next Stop: Japan, Heinemann, 1997.

Next Stop: Russia, Heinemann, 1997.

Next Stop: Spain, Heinemann, 1997.

Next Stop: France, Heinemann, 1997.

Next Stop: South Korea, Heinemann, 1998.

Next Stop: Indonesia, Heinemann, 1998.

Next Stop: Kenya, Heinemann, 1998.

Next Stop: Australia, Heinemann, 1998.

Contributor to books, including *Steps in Science,* edited by Richard Bateman, Hutchinson, 1982; *Enquiry Skills,* Heinemann, 1987; and *Children's Encyclopedia,* Heinemann, 1998. Educational resource packs include "Running a Geography Department," Pearson Publishing, 1998; (with Grimwade and Tim Rea) "Using ICT in Geography," Hodder & Stoughton; and "ICT and Geography Classroom Kits," Pearson Publishing. Author of computer programs on coasts, transport, cities, leisure, and farming, Matrix Multi-Media. Contributor to periodicals.

Sidelights

Fred Martin told *SATA:* "I probably began writing at the age of nine, when I won an award in a national essay writing competition in Ireland. When I began work as a teacher in 1971, most geography textbooks seemed to lack any real human interest or issues, and the activities for children lacked imagination. I began to write my own resources to make the subject more accessible and more interesting. I became especially interested in how illustrations, design, and layout could help make the work more accessible for average and less-able children.

"After several years teaching, I began to work with a publisher by writing reviews, then in 1980 I was a joint author of my first school textbook. This began a career as an author of geography books, in addition to my work as a full-time teacher. Since then I have written about fifty books and other resources, some on my own and sometimes with other authors. Writing so much has been a time-consuming activity that has needed the tolerance of my wife and children. The books have been sold around the world, both in English and in translations, including recent translations into Swedish, Indonesian, and Scottish Gaelic.

"I carried on writing because publishing companies kept asking me to write. The research involved in writing also helped to feed my interest in my subject. In the last few years I have become interested in using computers for work in geography, so this is the direction in which I have turned my writing. I left teaching in schools in 1996 when I became a lecturer at Bath Spa University College. This was to set up and run a teacher training course in geography with information and communications technology. The work allows me to develop my interests in both teaching geography and the educational uses of computers, but I have no idea where it might take me in the future."

Biographical and Critical Sources

PERIODICALS

Booklist, August, 1999, Hazel Rochman, review of *Next Stop: Italy,* p. 2042.

School Librarian, September, 1982, J. A. Morris, review of *Core Geography: Leisure,* p. 262; November, 1996, review of *Themes in Geography: Environmental Change,* p. 263.

School Library Journal, August, 1999, Daryl Grabarek, review of *Next Stop: Italy,* p. 175.

Times Educational Supplement, December, 1988, review of *Skills in Geography,* p. 29; January 24, 1992, review of *Worldview,* p. 32; April 10, 1992, review of *People and the European Community,* pp. 33, 44; March 21, 1997, review of *Themes in Geography,* p. 18; March 27, 1998, review of *Next Stop: Italy,* p. 26.

*   *   *

MATHERS, Petra 1945-

Personal

Born March 25, 1945, in Todtmoos, Germany; emigrated to the United States; married Michael Mathers; children: one son. *Education:* Completed high school and "a three year apprenticeship in the book business." *Religion:* "Trying hard to be good." *Hobbies and other interests:* Opera, classical music, reading, nature, family, and friends.

Addresses

Office—c/o Simon & Schuster Children's Publishing Division, 1240 Avenue of the Americas, New York, NY 10020.

Career

Worked in a bookstore in West Germany and for the German encyclopedia publisher Brockhaus; painter; freelance illustrator, 1983—, and author, 1985—.

Awards, Honors

Ezra Jack Keats award, 1985, for *Maria Theresa;* Best Illustrated Children's Book of the Year award, *New York Times,* 1986, for *Molly's New Washing Machine,* 1988, for *Theodor and Mr. Balbini,* 1990, for *I'm Flying!,* and 1999, for *Lottie's New Friend; Boston Globe-Horn Book* Honor Book for Illustration, *Boston Globe* and *Horn Book* magazine, 1991, for *Sophie and Lou;* silver medal, Society of Illustrators, 1995, for *Kisses from Rosa,* and 1999, for *Lottie's New Friend.*

Writings

Maria Theresa, Harper & Row, 1985.
Theodor and Mr. Balbini, Harper & Row, 1988.
Sophie and Lou, HarperCollins, 1991.
Victor and Christabel, Knopf, 1993.
Kisses from Rosa, Knopf, 1995.

Petra Mathers

Lottie's New Beach Towel, Atheneum, 1998.
Lottie's New Friend, Atheneum, 1999.
A Cake For Herbie, Atheneum, 2000.
Dodo Gets Married, Atheneum, in press.

ILLUSTRATOR

Miriam Chaikin, *How Yossi Beat the Evil Urge,* Harper & Row, 1983.

Chaikin, *Yossi Asks the Angels for Help,* Harper & Row, 1985.

Laura Geringer, *Molly's New Washing Machine,* Harper & Row, 1986.

Leslie Kimmelman, *Frannie's Fruits,* Harper & Row, 1989.

Susan Arkin Couture, *Block Book,* Harper & Row, 1990.

Alan Wade, *I'm Flying!,* Knopf, 1990.

Verna Aardema, *Borreguita and the Coyote: A Tale from Ayutla, Mexico,* Knopf, 1991.

Leah Komaiko, *Aunt Elaine Does the Dance from Spain,* Doubleday, 1992.

Richard Kennedy, *Little Love Song,* Knopf, 1992.

Norma Ferber, *When It Snowed That Night,* HarperCollins, 1993.

Karla Kushkin, *Patchwork Island,* HarperCollins, 1994.

Carole Purdy, *Mrs. Merriwether's Musical Cat,* Putnam, 1994.

Jacqueline Briggs Martin, *Grandmother Bryant's Pocket,* Houghton Mifflin, 1996.

Mary McKenna Siddals, *Tell Me a Season,* Clarion. 1997.

Lynne Jonell, *Mommy Go Away!,* Putnam, 1997.

Campbell Geeslin, *On Ramon's Farm: Five Tales of Mexico,* Atheneum, 1998.

Jonell, *I Need a Snake,* Putnam, 1998.

Jonell, *It's My Birthday, Too!,* Putnam, 1999.

Geeslin, *How Nanita Learns to Make Flan,* Atheneum, 1999.

Jonell, *Mom Pie,* Putnam, 2001.

Jack Prelutsky, *The Frogs Who Wore Red Suspenders,* Greenwillow, in press.

Sidelights

Petra Mathers, a four-time winner of the annual *New York Times* prize for Best Illustrated Children's Book, has earned accolades for the depth and complexity of her artwork, which features richly-hued flat shapes. "In all of her books, including those she has illustrated for other writers, Mathers creates stunning, highly original, and richly detailed illustrations that perfectly complement, enhance, and extend the stories," stated Linnea Hendrickson in an essay on Mathers for the *St. James Guide to Children's Writers.* Mathers is also the writer of a several highly regarded picture books for children, featuring stories circling around quietly eccentric humans most often portrayed as animals and "characters whose comical pathos and quiet courage strike a chord of recognition in ... readers," noted another essay about Mathers, this one appearing in *Children's Books and Their Creators.* "Her work is fresh and original and, best of all, straight from the heart." Among Mathers's fictional creations there has been a hen who dreams of an opera career, a self-absorbed talking hound, and a kindly crocodile museum guard who falls in love with a painting.

Mathers was born during the last year of World War II in the famed Black Forest region of Germany. As a youth, she worked in a bookstore, but eventually moved to the United States, married, and had a son. Her first career was as a painter, and she forged it through gallery exhibitions of her work in Cannon Beach, Oregon, and Seattle, Washington. For several years, however, Mathers worked as a waitress to make ends meet. In 1980, she was able to enjoy an adventurous respite when she and her husband spent some time in the South China Sea. When they returned, the couple settled on Long Island. Later, Mathers showed her portfolio at HarperCollins and was hired to illustrate Miriam Chaikin's *How Yossi Beat the Evil Urge.*

In 1985, Mathers's debut as an author won her an Ezra Jack Keats medal. *Maria Theresa,* noted the essay on Mathers in *Children's Books and Their Creators,* "surprises readers with an ending that is laced with a little romance and the notion of finding one's rightful place in the world, themes that recur in Mathers's other work." The title-character fowl belongs to Signora Rinaldo, a New York City apartment-dweller who loves opera. She keeps a chicken coop on her rooftop for fresh breakfast eggs and is devastated when the door is left open one day and Maria Theresa escapes. The hen makes it to the subway by hiding out in someone's shopping bag and finds herself in an utterly new world—

the countryside. She comes across a circus and finds it all so fantastical that she believes it must be the opera she has long dreamed of, but never seen. The circus hires her to perform with Miss Lola, an egg juggler who rides aboard the cow Esmeralda.

But back in Manhattan, Signora Rinaldo is morose about her loss and will listen only to the saddest arias. One of her friends, a tenor, offers to take her to his country home, and they visit the circus to cheer her. There the Signora and her beloved Maria Theresa are reunited, and a celebration is held. The crisis has yielded a few changes, however: the tenor was courting Signora Rinaldo, and they announce their engagement; Maria Theresa plans to continue her performing career, but everybody agrees to meet once a year. The illustrations, wrote Carol Brightman in the *New York Times Book Review,* "combine an attention to both the commonplace and the arcane which marks the best of children's literature. The book's final tableau of circus folk (and fowl) dancing the Tango Argentine outside Miss Lola's Airstream is a triumph of this vision."

Other reviewers were equally enthusiastic. "Mathers uses a flat, primitive style that produces a consistently engaging, other-worldly quality," wrote Donnarae MacCann and Olga Richard for *Wilson Library Bulletin.* "The book's theme, Italian references, urban and provincial settings, trappings of the circus—all bring to mind elements of a [Federico] Fellini film," the pair remarked. "But the chief tie with this cinematic artist is seen in Mathers's seductive, surreal imagery."

Mathers earned appreciative readers once more for her 1988 book, *Theodor and Mr. Balbini,* a winner of the *New York Times* award for Best Illustrated Children's Book that year. The title characters are a dog and his owner; Theodor is Mr. Balbini's life, but their relationship changes when the dog suddenly gains the power of speech. This is foreshadowed early in the story, when Mr. Balbini tries to play with him by throwing a stick, but Theodor just gazes off in another direction. "Like Maria Theresa, he has (perhaps unrecognized) ambitions," wrote Hendrickson. The talking Theodor is fully able to articulate his demands and begins to complain about all manner of things to his owner. "Too bad we don't have color TV," he remarks, watching a French cooking program. Mr. Balbini is disconcerted by the remarkable development, but when Theodor decides to learn French, Mr. Balbini finds a teacher, Madame Poulet. She finds her new pupil fascinating. Soon, Theodor has moved in with her, and leaves Mr. Balbini lonely in his home. He wishes for Theodor to return, but return all the way, "the way he was before he talked."

A dinner invitation helps resolve the situation. At Madame Poulet's, Mr. Balbini meets her dog Josephine, a much less ambitious pet than Theodor. He and the French teacher also find they have much in common in addition to a devotion to their dogs. They agree to trade hounds, but a romance seems likely as well. "The story's offbeat humor remains fresh and surprising to the end," noted a *Publishers Weekly* reviewer; *Wilson Library*

Cover of **Dodo Gets Married.** *(Written and illustrated by Mathers.)*

Bulletin writers MacCann and Richard found that "Mathers wryly comments upon the problem and rivets the viewer's attention with some extraordinary surrealist paintings."

The third picture book that Mathers wrote, *Sophie and Lou,* was published in 1991 and has been featured on the Public Broadcasting System's children's series "Reading Rainbow." Its plot follows the emergence of Sophie, a painfully shy mouse, into a far more confident, outgoing figure. When a dance studio opens across the street, Sophie is fascinated by it. She is too timid to enroll in classes, but through opening her window, she can hear the music and instructors' voices. After pushing her furniture against the walls, she practices along with the class in her own living room. One evening, the doorbell rings, and Lou, another mouse, asks her for a dance; they waltz off together. "Astute readers will notice that Lou appears throughout the illustrations as a bashful observer to Sophie's transformation," wrote Denise Anton Wright in a review for *School Library Journal.* "This gently paced story is sweetly inspirational," assessed a *Publishers Weekly* reviewer.

In her next book, *Victor and Christabel,* Mathers's heroes are two crocodiles. Victor is a museum guard devoted to his job, but who becomes particularly enchanted when a new work, "Cousin Christabel on Her Sickbed," arrives in his wing. It depicts a frail but still lovely crocodile, an image that emanates a deep sadness. Victor begins to bring the painting flowers and even installs a little night-light to keep it company during his off-duty hours. Then, it seems "Christabel" begins to improve, and it emerges that she was once free, but imprisoned in two dimensions by her evil, magic-practicing relative. "Once hung in the museum under the benign gaze of Victor, the painting is exposed to a new magic, that of the redemptive power of love," wrote Kathryn Harrison in the *New York Times Book Review* about this title from Mathers, observing that "a sly sense of humor infuses her illustrations, and children will enjoy looking again to catch all the amusing details." *Wilson Library Bulletin* reviewers MacCann and Richard gave Mathers's images enthusiastic praise, especially in her use of color and perspective to give dimension and verve to the story. "As illustrator, Mathers showcases this cast of eccentrics with gorgeous art," they wrote.

A difficult period in her own childhood was the basis for Mathers's 1995 work, *Kisses from Rosa.* Set in Germany in the years just after World War II, the tale revolves around Rosa and her family, who struggle to make ends meet. When her mother is hospitalized with tuberculosis, Rosa is sent to stay with relatives on a farm in the Black Forest area. It is a difficult adjustment, and Rosa misses her mother terribly at first. Her aunt helps her write a letter every Sunday, and Rosa concludes each with a unique kiss to help her mother heal. The rhythm of life in the country soon begins to grow on her, and when it is time to leave her aunt and cousin and return home, Rosa is sad to leave her new friends. Actual family photographs from the author's childhood find a home on the end papers of the book. The combination of a true story with idyllic landscape images won Mathers a new round of commendation from reviewers. A *Publishers Weekly* critic found that "as a writer, Mathers sets a leisurely pace for the story, lingering lovingly on the small details." Her story, noted Ellen Mandel in a *Booklist* review, "memorably reflects the pain of separation and the joys of healing and reunion."

Mathers has also embarked on a picture book series called "Lottie's World." The first installment, *Lottie's New Beach Towel,* appeared in 1998. Lottie, a chicken, and her best friend Herbie, a duck, plan a picnic outing at the beach. Her aunt sends her a lovely new beach towel that same day, and the gift proves to have a number of practical and surprise purposes; she uses it to protect her feet from the hot sand, makes a sail from it when Herbie's boat stalls, and loans it to a bride whose veil is swept away by a strong breeze. The tale concludes with Lottie writing a thank-you note to her aunt. Once again, Mathers won praise for her artwork and accompanying story. "Mathers paints a portrait of a winsome heroine characterized by unflagging practical resourcefulness and bursts of romantic inspiration," declared a *Publishers Weekly* contributor. Kathleen Squires, writing for *Booklist,* declared that Mathers's "canny use of line, light, and shadow perfectly conveys the wind, the tide, and the time of day." In a *Horn Book* review, Martha V. Parravano also delivered strong praise for the author/illustrator. "Everything about the book has the feeling of being thought through—and you get the feeling that Mathers is doing it all for her own as well as for her readers' enjoyment," Parravano asserted.

Mathers expanded Lottie's world with her 1999 book, *Lottie's New Friend.* The work subtly evolves as a tale to help young readers deal with issues of jealousy and self-esteem. Herbie, Lottie's best friend, grows resentful when Lottie befriends an exotic new neighbor, Dodo, who possesses a charming accent and fuchsia plumage. He begins to behave somewhat unconscionably—trying to sabotage the friendship and entertaining revenge fantasies. "Herbie is somewhat of an Everychild," wrote Jane Fritsch in the *New York Times Book Review,* "taking stock of himself, perhaps for the first time, and seeing only an ordinary sort of duckness." But when Lottie must leave town for a brief time, Dodo calls upon Herbie for help in an emergency, and they form their own bond. "Mathers offers a wise look at the often contrary and confusing dynamics of close friendships," remarked a *Publishers Weekly* review. Susan Dove Lempke, writing for *Booklist,* found that "Mathers's

delightfully expressive watercolors show Herbie's feelings beautifully."

A third book in the "Lottie's World" series, *A Cake for Herbie,* features the lovable Herbie in the starring role as he tries to win first prize, a big layer cake, in a poetry contest. Using his talent with words, Herbie pens an alphabet poem all about food. When the day of the contest finally arrives, Herbie anxiously awaits his turn to deliver his poem. Unfortunately for Herbie, his best friend Lottie is ill in bed and not able to comfort him after the audience of snooty birds boos him off of the stage. Embarrassed, Herbie takes refuge in a nearby restaurant whose workers lift his spirits and delight in his poetry. At the end of the night, the appreciative restaurant staff presents Herbie with a cake of his own, and more importantly, with a healthy dose of encouragement. Reviewing the book in *Publishers Weekly,* a critic praised the addition to the series, writing "Mather's droll, economical text and vibrant, equally economical visuals in tidy panels combine seamlessly to portray Herbie's anticipation, anxiety, humiliation, and grateful sense of belonging."

Mathers has said that she often finds it difficult to begin a new project. She procrastinates and fears that "any moment the children's book patrol will drive up and take all my stuff away and seal off my studio," she told *St. James Guide to Children's Writers.* "But all the while, slowly, a story comes together, crude and on wobbly legs.... I am doing exactly what I want to be doing with plenty of room for improvement," she concluded.

Biographical and Critical Sources

BOOKS

Children's Books and Their Creators, edited by Anita Silvey, Houghton Mifflin, 1995, pp. 438-39.

Hendrickson, Linnea, "Petra Mathers," *St. James Guide to Children's Writers,* edited by Sara Pendergast and Tom Pendergast, St. James Press, 1999, pp. 707-08.

Mathers, Petra, *Theodor and Mr. Balbini,* Harper & Row, 1988.

PERIODICALS

Booklist, October 15, 1993, Carolyn Phelan, review of *When It Snowed That Night,* p. 446; May 15, 1994, Carolyn Phelan, review of *Patchwork Island,* p. 1681; November 15, 1994, Linda Ward Callaghan, review of *Mrs. Merriwether's Musical Cat,* p. 613; November 1, 1995, Ellen Mandel, review of *Kisses from Rosa,* p. 476; May 15, 1996, Leone McDermott, review of *Grandmother Bryant's Pocket,* p. 1592; April 1, 1997, Susan Dove Lempke, review of *Tell Me a Season,* p. 1339; October 16, 1997, Hazel Rochman, review of *Mommy Go Away!,* p. 415; May 15, 1998, Hazel Rochman, review of *I Need a Snake,* p. 1632; June 1, 1998, Kathleen Squires, review of *Lottie's New Beach Towel,* p. 1632; December 15, 1998, John Peters, review of *On Ramon's Farm,* p. 754; March 1, 1999, Hazel Rochman, review of *It's My Birthday, Too!,* p. 1207; July, 1999, Susan Dove Lempke, review of *Lottie's New Friend,* p. 1952.

Horn Book, September-October, 1991, Ellen Fader, review of *Borreguita and the Coyote,* pp. 605-06; March-April, 1993, Maeve Visser, review of *Aunt Elaine,* p. 197; November-December, 1993, Nancy Vasilakis, review of *When It Snowed That Night,* p. 723; March-April, 1995, Ann B. Flowers, review of *Mrs. Merriwether's Musical Cat,* p. 188; November-December, 1995, Maria B. Salvadore, review of *Kisses from Rosa,* p. 729; July-August, 1996, Hanna B. Zeiger, review of *Grandmother Bryant's Pocket,* p. 460; September-October, 1997, Lauren Adams, review of *Mommy Go Away!,* p. 559; May-June, 1998, Martha V. Parravano, review of *Lottie's New Beach Towel,* p. 334; May, 1999, review of *It's My Birthday, Too!,* p. 316.

New York Times Book Review, August 11, 1985, Carol Brightman, review of *Maria Theresa,* p. 20; November 9, 1986, Arthur Yorinks, "Misappliance," p. 54; September 10, 1989, review of *Frannie's Fruits,* p. 32; November 14, 1993, Kathryn Harrison, "Tender Is the Crocodile," p. 62; March 15, 1998, Margaret Moorman, review of *Mommy Go Away!,* p. 23; August 15, 1999, Jane Fritsch, review of *Lottie's New Friend,* p. 25.

Publishers Weekly, June 21, 1985, review of *Maria Theresa,* pp. 102-04; June 24, 1986, review of *Theodor and Mr. Balbini,* p. 112; July 25, 1986, review of *Molly's New Washing Machine,* p. 186; February 23, 1990, review of *Block Book,* p. 217; August 10, 1990, review of *I'm Flying!,* p. 444; February 22, 1991, review of *Sophie and Lou,* p. 218; June 7, 1991, review of *Borreguita and the Coyote,* p. 65; December 20, 1991, review of *Little Love Song,* p. 81; October 26, 1992, review of *Aunt Elaine,* p. 70; July 19, 1993, review of *Victor and Christabel,* p. 252; September 20, 1993, review of *When It Snowed That Night,* p. 33; April 11, 1994, review of *Patchwork Island,* p. 63; August 1, 1994, review of *Mrs. Merriwether's Musical Cat,* p. 78; July 10, 1995, review of *Kisses from Rosa,* p. 56; February 5, 1996, review of *Grandmother Bryant's Pocket,* p. 89; January 6, 1997, review of *Tell Me a Season,* p. 72; September 22, 1997, review of *Mommy Go Away!,* p. 79; June 8, 1998, review of *Lottie's New Beach Towel,* p. 60; October 12, 1998, review of *On Ramon's Farm,* p. 75; March 1, 1999, review of *It's My Birthday, Too!,* p. 68; March 8, 1999, review of *Lottie's New Friend,* p. 66; November 1, 1999, review of *How Nanita Learns to Make Flan,* p. 82; May 15, 2000, review of *A Cake for Herbie,* p. 116.

School Library Journal, December, 1986, Leslie Chamberlin, review of *Molly's New Washing Machine,* p. 86; June, 1989, Patricia Dooley, review of *Frannie's Fruits,* p. 90; June, 1991, Denise Anton Wright, review of *Sophie and Lou,* p. 86; March, 1992, Kathleen Whalin, review of *Little Love Song,* p. 248; December, 1993, Corinne Camarata, review of *Victor and Christabel,* p. 91; July, 1994, Heide Piehler, review of *Patchwork Island,* p. 95; May, 1997, review of *Tell Me a Season,* p. 114; June, 1998, Angela Reynolds, review of *I Need a Snake,* p. 111; March, 1999, review of *On Ramon's Farm,* p. 174.

Wilson Library Bulletin, June, 1985, Donnarae MacCann and Olga Richard, "Picture Books for Children," pp. 686-87; March, 1989, Donnarae MacCann and Olga Richard, "Picture Books for Children," pp. 82-83; May, 1994, Donnarae MacCann and Olga Richard, "Picture Books for Children," p. 94.

* * *

MATHESON, Richard (Christian) 1953-

Personal

Born October 14, 1953, in Santa Monica, CA; son of Richard Matheson (a screenwriter). *Education:* Attended the University of Southern California.

Addresses

Office—c/o Bantam Books, Bantam Doubleday Dell Publishing Group, Inc., 1540 Broadway, New York, NY 10036.

Career

Worked as an advertising copywriter, television writer and producer, and screenwriter; also served as drummer in a rock band.

Richard Matheson

Writings

BOOKS

Scars and Other Distinguishing Marks (short stories), illustrated by Harry O. Morris, foreword by Stephen King, introduction by Dennis Etchison, Scream Press (Los Angeles), 1987, expanded edition, Tor Books (New York), 1988.
Created By (novel), Bantam (New York), 1993, Macmillan (London), 1994.
Dystopia: Collected Stories, Gauntlet, 1999.

SCREENPLAYS

Three O'Clock High (screenplay), 1987.
(With Richard Matheson Sr.) *Loose Cannons* (screenplay), 1990.
Full Eclipse (screenplay), 1994.

Matheson has written over 500 scripts for television series that include *Knight Rider, Hill Street Blues, Tales from the Crypt,* and *Wiseguy,* among many others; a chapbook of short stories, *Holiday,* was published by Footsteps Press (New York) in 1988; other short stories have appeared in numerous anthologies; contributor to various periodicals.

Sidelights

Richard Matheson is the author of a prolific number of horror stories whose contemporary settings and graphic violence have sometimes placed him in the "Splatter-punk" genre. As Stefan Dziemianowicz explained in the *St. James Guide to Horror, Ghost, & Gothic Writers,* Matheson's "writing has a strong 'visual' style that reflects the cinematic influences considered a hallmark of Splatterpunk," but the essayist pointed out that Matheson was likely inspired by his father, a well-known Hollywood writer who penned many of the original *Twilight Zone* episodes. Matheson himself has enjoyed a tremendous career as a writer for television, too, and is credited with scripts for *Tales from the Crypt* and *Wiseguy,* among many other series.

Matheson was born in 1953, and attended the University of Southern California. His first story to appear in print was "Graduation," which appeared in a 1977 volume titled *Whispers.* The macabre tale is told through the letters home of college freshman, in which he admits to feeling lonely and isolated. Soon, he begins to mention that his classmates have been murdered, and "one has to read between the lines to divine that he is the murderer," remarked Dziemianowicz. The story reappeared in Matheson's first collection, *Scars, and Other Distinguishing Marks,* published in 1987, and it was a volume that "established his reputation as one of the most distinctive writers of the post-Stephen King generation," noted Dziemianowicz. Most of its tales, written during the 1980s, were set in Hollywood and the greater Los Angeles area; the hallmarks of that climate—the smoggy heat, the film industry, interminable freeway traffic—earn frequent mentions in the stories.

Sixty of Matheson's horror stories are presented in this second collection. (Cover illustration by Harry O. Morris.)

Many of the 27 entrants in *Scars* are brief but graphic, such as "Vampire," which recounts the primal, murderous desires of a bloodsucker through one-word sentences that convey the creature's simplistic, desire-driven actions. In "Red," a man on a highway is found picking up debris that turns out to be the remains of his daughter, whom he has accidentally killed with his car. "Echoes," recounts the misery of an arms dealer who is haunted by the cries of victims of his profits. In "Third Wind," an overachiever and distance runner discovers one day that his legs won't stop running. "Most of the new or more recent tales ... jolt with snappy shocks packed in dense, evocative prose," opined a *Kirkus Reviews* report on *Scars,* while *Publishers Weekly* declared that "the punchy narrative form displays the author's wit and an almost poetic compression."

Matheson's first novel, *Created By,* reflected his second-generation ties to the television industry as well as a rather biting sense of satire on his choice of career. Its main character, a writer named Alan White, is sickened by the emphasis on entertainment and shock value in television among the networks and other content providers, a world *Kirkus Reviews* described as "a cruel sea of

Armani-suited sharks." Violence and idiocy seem to be the biggest career-boosters in this industry; a sitcom about a vicious, incontinent cat, for instance, is a huge success. In *Created By,* his protagonist decides to create a show, "The Mercenary," which will transgress all boundaries. It features shockingly graphic violence and frank sexual content, and when it goes on the air, it breaks all censorship barriers on television. It also saves the flagging network, and White finds himself a newly powerful player in Hollywood. "The novel is a touchstone for many of the themes and ideas Matheson grapples with in his short fiction," noted Dziemianowicz in *Horror, Ghost and Gothic Writers,* "and in its cynical estimation that 'Hate is what people love,' it articulates a grimmer horror than even the most viscerally written Splatterpunk fiction."

A. E. Barek is "The Mercenary'"'s fictional, amoral antihero. But the show also seems cursed: the director of the pilot episode kills himself, and one important television critic who despises the show, is blinded, then suffers in a deadly fall. White begins "to wonder how it is that real-life atrocities are happening that echo, detail for detail, "Mercenary" scripts he's still in the process of writing, script ideas he's barely *thought* of," wrote Edward Bryant in a review of the novel for *LOCUS.* White realizes that Barek has actually come to life, feeding from White's creative energies, and sets out to stop the creature before he himself grows any weaker. "Matheson's slashing prose and wit draw blood," a *Kirkus Reviews* assessment enthused, and called it an "unusually clever horror novel." Bryant, writing in *LOCUS,* declared that "in its own darkly coruscating way, *Created By* will make a terrific present for a whole variety of would-be movie writers."

A second collection of short stories from Matheson, *Dystopia,* appeared in 1999. Again, many of the tales are brief, and surprise with clever, shocking twists. "Mobius," for instance, appears to chronicle the police interrogation of a suspected serial killer, but it reveals itself to be brainwashing session. A *Publishers Weekly* review of the volume called many of the tales "miniature masterpieces of compression and tension," and praised the "edginess and vitality" of Matheson's style.

Biographical and Critical Sources

BOOKS

Dziemianowicz, Stefan, "Richard Christian Matheson," *St. James Guide to Horror, Ghost, & Gothic Writers,* edited by David Pringle, St. James Press, 1998, pp. 395-396.

Encyclopedia of Science Fiction, edited by John Clute and Peter Nicholls, St. Martin's Press, 1993, pp. 223-224.

PERIODICALS

Kirkus Reviews, June 15, 1987, review of *Scars,* pp. 883-884; July 1, 1993, review of *Created By,* p. 808.

Library Journal, August, 1987, review of *Scars,* p. 147.

LOCUS, September, 1993, Edward Bryant, review of *Created By,* pp. 19.

Publishers Weekly, July 10, 1987, review of *Scars,* p. 59; August 16, 1993, review of *Created By,* p. 89; November 1, 1999, review of *Dystopia,* p. 78.

Voice of Youth Advocates, December, 1988, Cosette Kies, review of *Scars,* p. 260.

ON-LINE

Richard Christian Matheson, www.dragoncon.org (February 4, 2000).*

*   *   *

MORRIS, Jill 1936-

Personal

Born March 28, 1936, in Brisbane, Queensland, Australia; daughter of Francis William (a clerk) and Jessie Isabel (a clerk; maiden name, McMurtrie) Farrar; married John Morris (a pharmacist), 1960 (marriage ended); married Richard Dent (an engineer), 1988; children: Katy, Belinda, John. *Education:* University of Queensland, B.A. and diploma in education. *Religion:* Church of England.

Addresses

Home and office—Book Farm, 330 Reesville Rd., Maleny, Queensland 4552, Australia. *E-mail*—jillmorris@greaterglider.com. *Agent*—Golvan Arts Management, Melbourne, Australia.

Career

Book Farm, Maleny, Australia, farm director. Greater Glider Productions, Maleny, publishing director. Australian Broadcasting Commission, worked as radio and television producer for seventeen years. Member of local Chamber of Commerce. *Member:* Australian Society of Authors, Australian Writers Guild, Society of Editors.

Awards, Honors

Churchill fellow, 1972; senior fellow, University of Sunshine Coast, 2000.

Writings

Kolo the Bush Koala, illustrated by Rich Richardson, Golden (Sydney, Australia), 1973.

Rusty the Nimble Numbat, illustrated by Rich Richardson, Golden, 1973.

Rufus the Red Kangaroo, illustrated by Rich Richardson, Golden, 1973.

Percy the Peaceful Platypus, illustrated by Rich Richardson, Golden, 1973.

Harry the Hairy-nosed Wombat, illustrated by Rich Richardson, Golden, 1973.

Saturday Street, illustrated by Geoff Hocking, Viking/Puffin, 1983.

Monkey and the White Bone Demon, Penguin Putnam, 1984.

The Boy Who Painted the Sun, illustrated by Geoff Hocking, Kestrel, 1984, Penguin Putnam, 1985, Greater Glider (Maleny, Australia), 1991.

Monkey Creates Havoc in Heaven, Penguin Putnam, 1989.

Australian Bats, illustrated by Lynne Tracey, Greater Glider, 1993.

Dido Has Diabetes, illustrated by Margie Chellew, Greater Glider, 1993.

Australian Owls, Frogmouths, and Nightjars, illustrated by Lynne Tracey, Greater Glider, 1993.

Australian Frogs, Amazing Amphibians, illustrated by Lynne Tracey, Greater Glider, 1996.

The Wombat Who Talked to the Stars: The Journal of a Northern Hairy-Nosed Wombat, illustrated by Sharon Dye, Greater Glider, 1997.

Australian Kangaroos, Magnificent Macropods, illustrated by Lynne Muir, Greater Glider, 1998.

Mahogany the Mystery Glider (nonfiction), illustrated by Sharon Dye, Grater Glider, 1999.

Endangered! (ten plays), Greater Glider, 2000.

Jill Morris

Also author of *Where Is Kangaroo?,* illustrated by Lynne Tracey, 1994; *Numbat, Run!, Dugong, Dive!,* and *Golden Wombats,* illustrated by Lynne Tracey, and a radio play, *Bunyip on the Obi Obi,* illustrated by Ian Steep, all for Harcourt; *Platypus Point,* illustrated by Lynne Tracey, HarperCollins; (with Belinda Nissen) *The Cod Hole,* photographs by Mark Nissen, HarperCollins; *Rainbow Warrior: Battle for the Planet* (nonfiction), Omnibus; *Ghost of DropCroc* (novel), Addison Wesley Longman; *Velvet the Flying Gecko,* illustrated by Bronwyn Searle, Queensland Science Centre; *The Lady Down the Road,* illustrated by Irena Sibley, SilverGum/Allen & Unwin; *Almost a Dinosaur* (play), illustrated by Veronica Holland, Currency Press; *Green Air,* illustrated by Lindsay Muir; *Who's in the Sky?,* illustrated by Jane Benson; *Whose Pouch?,* illustrated by Jane Burrell; *Fraser Dingo,* illustrated by Sharon Dye; six volumes in the "Aussie Triumphs Series," with teacher's book, illustrated by several artists; creator of coloring books on the Fraser dingo, Australian bats, Australian frogs, the red kangaroo, the sulphur-crested cockatoo, the frill-necked lizard, and the wombat. Creator of book and audio tape sets, including *Clever Company, Sam's House, Sounds Spooky!,* and *Frogmouth Fax.* Author of *The Wombat Who Talked to the Stars Journal.* Columnist for *Age* for ten years.

Work in Progress

Warriors of the Green, a novel for eight-to twelve-year-old readers; research on the Pacific Ocean, including the Philippines.

Sidelights

Jill Morris told *SATA:* "I am committed to the preservation of the natural environment, and all my writing reflects this. I have worked for children on all fronts—television and radio production, newspaper and magazine journalism, and as a publisher, editor, and author of more than eighty books."

Biographical and Critical Sources

PERIODICALS

Australian Book Review, July, 1997, review of *The Wombat Who Talked to the Stars,* p. 62.

Christian Science Monitor, September 12, 1985, review of *The Boy Who Painted the Sun,* p. 31.

Emergency Librarian, September, 1983, review of *The Boy Who Painted the Sun,* p. 20; March, 1987, review of *Saturday Street,* p. 23.

Junior Bookshelf, October, 1984, review of *The Boy Who Painted the Sun,* p. 200.

Magpies, March, 1993, Margot Hillel, review of *Dido Has Diabetes,* p. 34, and Stephanie Owen Reeder, review of *Australian Bats,* p. 35; May, 1994, review of *Where Is Kangaroo?,* p. 25; July, 1994, Hugo McCann, review of *Australian Owls, Frogmouths, and Nightjars,* pp. 35-36; March, 1997, Annette Dale-Meiklejohn, review of *The Wombat Who Talked to the Stars,* p. 23; November, 1998, Jennifer Poulter, review of *Australian Kangaroos, Magnificent Macropods,* p. 42.

New York Times Book Review, September 16, 1984, review of *The Boy Who Painted the Sun,* p. 26.

Publishers Weekly, June 29, 1984, review of *The Boy Who Painted the Sun,* p. 105.

School Library Journal, October, 1984, Connie C. Rockman, review of *The Boy Who Painted the Sun,* p. 150; May, 1989, Denise A. Anton, review of *Monkey Creates Havoc in Heaven,* p. 102.

Times Literary Supplement, April 6, 1973, review of *Kolo the Bush Koala, Rusty the Nimble Numbat, Rufus the Red Kangaroo,* and *Percy the Peaceful Platypus,* p. 390.

*   *   *

MPHAHLELE, Es'kia
See MPHAHLELE, Ezekiel

*   *   *

MPHAHLELE, Ezekiel 1919-
(Bruno Eseki, Es'kia Mphahlele)

Personal

Born December 17, 1919, Marabastad Township, Pretoria, South Africa; son of Moses (a messenger) and Eva (a domestic; maiden name, Mogale) Mphahlele; married Rebecca Mochadibane (a social worker), 1945; children: Anthony, Teresa Kefilwe (deceased), Motswiri, Chabi Robert, Puso. *Education:* Attended Adams Teachers Training College, Natal, 1939-40; University of South Africa, B.A. (with honors), 1949, M.A., 1956; University of Denver, Ph.D., 1968.

Addresses

Office—African Studies Institute, University of the Witwatersrand, Johannesburg 2001, South Africa.

Career

Clerk for an institute for the blind, 1941-45; Orlando High School, Johannesburg, South Africa, teacher of English and Afrikaans, 1945-52; *Drum* magazine, Johannesburg, fiction editor, 1955-57; University of Ibadan, Ibadan, Nigeria, lecturer in English literature, 1957-61; International Association for Cultural Freedom, Paris, France, director of African programs, 1961-63; Chemchemi Creative Centre, Nairobi, Kenya, director, 1963-65; University College, Nairobi, lecturer, 1965-66; University of Denver, Denver, CO, visiting lecturer, 1966-68, associate professor of English, 1970-74; University of Zambia, Lusaka, senior lecturer in English, 1968-70; University of Pennsylvania, Philadelphia, professor of English, 1974-77; University of Witwatersrand, Johannesburg, senior resident fellow, 1978—, professor of African literature, 1979—; Inspector of education, Lebowa, Transvaal, 1978-79; University of the Witwatersrand, Johannesburg, senior research fellow at African Studies Institute, 1979-82, professor of African litera-

ture, 1983-87, professor emeritus, 1987—. Founding director of Council for Black Education and Research (COBERT), 1980-92.

Awards, Honors

African Arts magazine prize, 1972, for *The Wanderers;* Carnegie Foundation grant, 1980; honorary doctorates from University of Pennsylvania, 1982, and University of Natal at Pietermaritzburg, 1983; Claude Harris Leon Foundation Prize, 1985, for outstanding community service.

Writings

Man Must Live and Other Stories, African Bookman, 1947.

Down Second Avenue (autobiography), Faber, 1959.

The Living and the Dead and Other Stories, Black Orpheus, 1961.

The African Image (essays), Faber, 1962, Praeger, 1964, revised edition, 1974.

(Editor with Ellis Ayitey Komey) *Modern African Stories,* Faber, 1964.

The Role of Education and Culture in Developing African Countries, Afro-Asian Institute for Labor Studies in Israel, 1965.

A Guide to Creative Writing, East African Literature Bureau, 1966.

In Corner B and Other Stories, Northwestern University Press, 1967.

(Editor and contributor) *African Writing Today,* Penguin, 1967.

The Wanderers (autobiographical novel), Macmillan, 1971.

Voices in the Whirlwind and Other Essays, Hill & Wang, 1972.

(Under name Es'kia Mphahlele) *Chirundu* (novel), Lawrence Hill, 1981.

(Under name Es'kia Mphahlele) *The Unbroken Song: Selected Writings of Es'kia Mphahlele,* Ravan Press, 1981.

(Under name Es'kia Mphahlele) *Afrika My Music: An Autobiography, 1957-83,* Ravan Press, 1984, Ohio University Press, 1986.

(Under name Es'kia Mphahlele) *Bury Me at the Marketplace: Selected Letters of Es'kia Mphahlele,* edited by N. Chabani Mangayani, Skotaville, 1984.

Let's Talk Writing: Prose, Skotaville, 1985.

Let's Talk Writing: Poetry, Skotaville, 1985.

Poetry and Humanism, Witwatersrand University Press, 1986.

Echoes of African Art, Skotaville, 1987.

Renewal Time, Readers International, 1988.

(Author of text) Alf Kumalo, *Mandela: Echoes of an Era,* Penguin, 1990.

(Editor with others) *Perspectives on South African English Literature,* Donker, 1992.

(Editor with Helen Moffett) *Seasons Come to Pass: A Poetry Anthology for Southern African Students,* Oxford University Press, 1994.

FOR CHILDREN

Father Come Home, Ravan Press, 1984.

OTHER

Contributor to *Africa in Transition,* edited by Prudence Smith, Reinhardt, 1958. Contributor to anthologies, including *An African Treasury: Articles, Essays, Stories, Poems by Black Africans,* edited by Langston Hughes, Crown (New York City), 1960; *African Heritage: An Anthology of Black African Personality and Culture,* edited by Jacob Drachler, Crowell, 1962; *Anthologie de la litterature negro-africaine: Romaciers et conteurs negro-africains,* Volume 2, edited by Leonard Sainville, Presence Africaine, 1963; *Modern African Prose,* edited by Richard Rive, Heinemann, 1964; *Black Orpheus: An Anthology of New African and Afro-American Stories,* edited by Ulli Beier, Longmans, 1964, McGraw-Hill, 1965; *A Selection of African Prose,* Volume 2, compiled by W. H. Whiteley, Oxford University Press, 1964; *African-English Literature: A Survey and Anthology,* edited by Anne Tibble, October House, 1965; *Poems from Black Africa,* edited by Langston Hughes, Indiana University Press, 1966; *Pan African Short Stories,* edited by Denny Neville, Humanities, 1966; *Modern African Narrative: An Anthology,* compiled by Paul Edwards, Humanities, 1966; *Through African Eyes,* Volume 1, compiled by Paul Edwards, Cambridge University Press, 1966; *Anthologie negro-africaine: Panorama critique des prosateurs, poetes et dramatourges noirs du XXeme siecle,* edited by Lilyan Kesteloot, Gerard, 1967; *South African Writing Today,* edited by Nadine Gordimer and Lionel Abrahams, Penguin, 1967; *Come Back, Africa: Fourteen Stories from South Africa,* edited by Herbert I. Shore and Megchelina Shore-Bos, International Publishers, 1968; *Drum Beats: An Anthology of African Writing,* compiled by Ime Ikiddeh, E. J. Arnold, 1968; *Africa in Prose,* edited by Oscar Ronald Dathorne and Willfried Feuser, Penguin, 1969; *Africa Speaks: A Prose Anthology with Comprehension and Summary Passages,* edited by John P. Berry, Evans, 1970; *New African Literature and the Arts,* Volumes 1 and 2, edited by Joseph O. Okpaku, Crowell, 1970; *African Short Stories: A Collection of Contemporary African Writing,* edited by Charles Larson, Macmillan, 1970; and *South African Voices,* edited by Bernth Lindfors, African and Afro-American Studies Research Center, 1975.

Contributor of essays, short stories, and poems, sometimes under pseudonym Bruno Eseki, to *Drum, Africa South, Denver Quarterly, Journal of Modern African Studies, Black World, New Statesman,* and other periodicals. Editor, *Black Orpheus,* 1960-66; member of staff, *Presence Africaine,* 1961-63; member of editorial staff, *Journal of New African Literature and the Arts.*

Sidelights

"A writer who has been regarded as the most balanced literary critic of African literature," Ezekiel Mphahlele can also "be acknowledged as one of its most significant creators," writes Emile Snyder in the *Saturday Review.* Mphahlele's transition from life in the slums of South Africa to life as a professor of English at a large American university was an odyssey of struggle both intellectually and politically. He trained as a teacher in South Africa, but was banned from the classroom in 1952 as a result of his protest of the segregationist Bantu Education Act. Although he later returned to teaching, Mphahlele first turned to journalism, criticism, fiction, and essay writing.

During an exile that took him to France and the United States, Mphahlele was away from Africa for over a decade. Nevertheless, "no other author has ever earned the right to so much of Africa as has Ezekiel Mphahlele," says John Thompson in the *New York Review of Books.* "In the English language, he established the strength of African literature in our time." Some critics, however, feel that Mphahlele's absence from his homeland has harmed his work by separating him from its subject. Ursula A. Barnett, writing in the conclusion of her 1976 biography *Ezekiel Mphahlele,* asserts that Mphahlele's "creative talent can probably gain its full potential only if he returns to South Africa and resumes his function of teaching his discipline in his own setting, and of encouraging the different elements in South Africa to combine and interchange in producing a modern indigenous literature."

Mphahlele himself has agreed with this assessment, for after being officially silenced by the government of his homeland and living in self-imposed exile for twenty years, Mphahlele returned to South Africa in 1977. "I want to be part of the renaissance that is happening in the thinking of my people," he once said. "I see education as playing a vital role in personal growth and in institutionalizing a way of life that a people chooses as its highest ideal. For the older people, it is a way of reestablishing the values they had to suspend along the way because of the force of political conditions. Another reason for returning, connected with the first, is that this is my ancestral home. An African cares very much where he dies and is buried. But I have not come to die. I want to reconnect with my ancestors while I am still active. I am also a captive of place, of setting. As long as I was abroad I continued to write on the South African scene. There is a force I call the tyranny of place; the kind of unrelenting hold a place has on a person that gives him the motivation to write and a style. The American setting in which I lived for nine years was too fragmented to give me these. I could only identify emotionally and intellectually with the African-American segment, which was not enough. Here I can feel the ancestral Presence. I know now what Vinoba Bhave of India meant when he said: 'Though action rages without, the heart can be tuned to produce unbroken music,' at this very hour when pain is raging and throbbing everywhere in African communities living in this country."

Mphahlele's 1988 publication, *Renewal Time,* contains stories he published previously as well as an autobiographical afterword on his return to South Africa and a section from *Afrika My Music,* his 1984 autobiography. Stories like "Mrs. Plum" and "The Living and the Dead" have received praise by critics reviewing Mphahlele's works. *Chirundu,* Mphahlele's first novel since his return to South Africa, "tells with quiet assurance this story of a man divided," says Rose Moss in a *World Literature Today* review. The novel "is clearly this writer's major work of fiction and, I suppose, in one sense, an oblique commentary on his own years of exile," observes Charles R. Larson in *World Literature Today*. Moss finds that in his story of a man torn between African tradition and English law, "the timbre of Mphahlele's own vision is not always clear"; nevertheless, the critic admits that "in the main his story presents the confused and wordless heart of his character with unpretentious mastery." "*Chirundu* is that rare breed of fiction—a novel of ideas, and a moving one at that," says Larson. "It has the capacity to involve the reader both intellectually and emotionally." The critic concludes by calling the work "the most satisfying African novel of the past several years."

On the subject of writing, Mphahlele commented, "In Southern Africa, the black writer talks best about the ghetto life he knows; the white writer about his own ghetto life. We see each other, black and white, as it were through a keyhole. Race relations are a major experience and concern for the writer. They are his constant beat. It is unfortunate no one can ever think it is healthy both mentally and physically to keep hacking at the social structure in overcharged language. A language that burns and brands, scorches and scalds. Language that is as a machete with a double edge—the one sharp, the other blunt, the one cutting, the other breaking. And yet there are levels of specifically black drama in the ghettoes that I cannot afford to ignore. I have got to stay with it. I bleed inside. My people bleed. But I must stay with it."

Biographical and Critical Sources

BOOKS

Akosu, Tyohdzuah, *The Writing of Ezekiel Mphahlele*, Mellea University Press, 1995.
Barnett, Ursula A., *Ezekiel Mphahlele*, Thayne, 1976.
Contemporary Literary Criticism, Volume 25, Gale, 1983.
Duren, Dennis, editor, *African Writers Talking*, Heileman, 1972.
Heartache, Donald E., *African Writers: A Companion to Black African Writing, 1300-1973*, Black Orpheus, 1973.
Manganic, N. C., *Exiles and Homecomings: A Biography of Es'kia Mphahlele*, Ravan Press, 1983.
Moore, Gerald, *Seven African Writers*, Oxford University Press, 1962.
Moore, Gerald, *The Chosen Tongue*, Longan, Green, 1969.
Thuynsma, Peter N., *Footprints along the Way: A Tribute to Es'kia Mphahlele*, Skotaville, 1989.

PERIODICALS

Booklist, November 15, 1972, review of *Voices in the Whirlwind and Other Essays*, p. 271.
Choice, May, 1968, review of *African Writing Today*, p. 351; November, 1971, review of *Down Second Avenue*, p. 1253; November, 1974, review of *The African Image*, p. 1316; May, 1989, review of *Renewal Time*, pp. 1524-1525.
Kirkus Reviews, November 1, 1970, review of *The Wanderers*, p. 1214; March 15, 1972, review of *Voices in the Whirlwind and Other Essays*, p. 382.
Library Journal, September 1, 1971, Mary Darrah Herrick, review of *Down Second Avenue*, pp. 2629-2630.
Modern African Studies, March, 1963.
Nation, March 20, 1972.
New Statesman, April 25, 1959.
New York Review of Books, September 23, 1971, John Thompson, "In Africa," p. 3.
New York Times Book Review, October 22, 1972; April 30, 1989, Howard W. French, review of *Renewal Time*, p. 38.
Publishers Weekly, March 13, 1967, review of *African Writing Today*, p. 63; April 17, 1972, review of *Voices in the Whirlwind and Other Essays*, p. 54.
Saturday Review, June 19, 1971.
Times Literary Supplement, August 11, 1961; March 23, 1967; March 10, 1972.
World Literature Today, Summer, 1983; Winter, 1983, Charles R. Larson, "Third World Writing in English," pp. 58-59; Winter, 1987, Robert Berner, review of *Afrika My Music: An Autobiography, 1957-1983*, p. 146; Summer, 1989, John Cooke, review of *Renewal Time*, p. 526; Winter, 1997, p. 99.*

* * *

MYERS, R(obert) E(ugene) 1924-

Personal

Born January 15, 1924, in Los Angeles, CA; son of Harold Eugene (a store owner) and Margaret (a homemaker; maiden name, Anawalt) Myers; married Joyce Elinor Daily, 1946 (divorced, 1949); married Patricia A. Tazer, August 17, 1956; children: Kathleen, Edward E., Margaret A., Hal R., Karen I. *Education:* University of California, Berkeley, A.B., 1955; Reed College, M.A., 1961; University of Georgia, Ed.D., 1968. *Politics:* Democrat. *Religion:* Protestant. *Hobbies and other interests:* Gardening, music, sports, photography, reading.

Addresses

Home—1457 Meadow Ct., Healdsburg, CA 95448.

Career

Elementary school teacher in Oregon, California, and Minnesota, 1954-61; Augsburg College, Minneapolis, MN, assistant professor of education, 1962-63; University of Oregon, Eugene, assistant professor of education, 1963-66; elementary school teacher in Eugene, 1966-67; University of Victoria, British Columbia, associate professor of education and associate director of teacher education, 1968-70; associate research professor of education in Teaching Research Division, Oregon State System of Higher Education, 1970-73; Northwestern,

R. E. Myers's book for teachers and students is designed to stimulate discussion about character. *(Cover photos by Eric Futran.)*

Inc., Portland, OR, filmmaker, 1973-74; University of Portland, Portland, OR, associate professor of education, 1974-75; freelance film producer, 1975-77; Oregon State Department of Education, Salem, learning resources specialist, 1977-81; Linn-Benton Education Service District, Albany, OR, curriculum coordinator, 1981-87. Visiting professor, San Diego State University, Northeastern Louisiana University, Winona State University, Oregon College of Education, University of Victoria, Paine College, and Texas Tech University. Has appeared on various television programs. *Wartime service:* U.S. Merchant Marines, 1943-45. *Member:* International Reading Association, National Association for Gifted Children (member of board of directors, 1974-77), Mid-Valley Reading Council (member of board of directors).

Awards, Honors

Outstanding book award, Pi Lambda Theta, 1972, for *Creative Learning and Teaching;* Golden Eagle, Council on International Nontheatrical Events, 1973, for film *Feather.*

Writings

(With E. Paul Torrance) *Invitations to Thinking and Doing* (with teacher's guide), Ginn, 1965.

(With Torrance) *Invitations to Speaking and Writing Creatively* (with teacher's guide), Ginn, 1965.
(With Torrance) *Creative Learning and Teaching,* Dodd 1970.
Cognitive Connections, Zephyr Press, 1996.
Multiple Ways of Thinking with Social Studies, Zephyr Press, 1997.

FOR CHILDREN

(With Torrance) *Can You Imagine?* (with teacher's guide), Ginn, 1965.
(With Torrance) *Plots, Puzzles, and Ploys* (with teacher's guide), Ginn, 1966.
(With Torrance) *For Those Who Wonder* (with teacher's guide), Ginn, 1966.
(With Torrance) *Stretch* (with teacher's guide), Perceptive, 1968.
It's a Butterfly! (with audio cassette), United Learning, 1977.
It's a Dolphin! (with audio cassette), United Learning, 1977.
It's a Squirrel! (with audio cassette), United Learning, 1977.
It's a Toad! (with audio cassette), United Learning, 1977.
It's an Alligator! (with audio cassette), United Learning, 1977.
Wondering, Creative Learning Press (Mansfield Center, CT), 1984.
Imagining, Creative Learning Press, 1985.
What Next?, Zephyr Press (Somerville, MA), 1994.
Facing the Issues, Zephyr Press, 1995.
Mind Sparklers #1, Prufrock Press, 1998.
Mind Sparklers #2, Prufrock Press, 1998.
Character Matters, Good Year Books, 1999.
It's Your Attitude That Counts, Global Classroom, 2000.
A Matter of Respect, Global Classroom, 2000.

FILMSTRIPS

Animal Friends, A.I.M.S. Instructional Media, 1974.
Exploring the Unexplained, United Learning, 1974.
Investigating the Unknown, United Learning, 1974.
Sing Along with Animals, United Learning, 1975.
Hand Tools: An Introduction to Working with Wood and Plastic, A.I.M.S. Instructional Media, 1975.

FILMS

Feather (juvenile), ACI Media, 1973.
Flexibility, Teaching Research, 1973.
Learning Sets, Teaching Research, 1973.
Perseveration, Teaching Research, 1973.
Inducing a Creative Set: The Magic Net, Teaching Research, 1973.
Elephants (juvenile), ACI Media, 1974.

Contributor to *Rewarding Creative Behavior,* edited by Torrance, Prentice-Hall (Englewood Cliffs, NJ), 1965; *Creative Learning and Teaching* has been published in Spanish and Portuguese.

Sidelights

R. E. Myers told *SATA:* "In 1996 I started in a new direction in the writing of professional books for teachers and students. My purpose in writing since 1961 had been to provide teachers with materials to help them encourage the creative talents of their students. In 1996 I had a strong motivation to write materials that would encourage teachers and students to engage in a dialogue about civility, and so I wrote "A Book of Respect." That book featured short short stories (called scenarios by some) to provoke thinking about moral issues on the part of the students. Two more books were written in this new format, which also featured an activity for the students to undertake that might deepen their understanding of the issues. So far I've been encouraged by the reception given to *Character Matters,* which was released in early 1999. Now, I seem to be hooked on the idea of presenting little stories for students to think about and discuss.

"My style of writing would not be thought worthy of notice thirty years ago, but in this age of electronic devices it might be of some interest. I write in a journal in pencil. Then I copy (and do some rewriting) with the aid of my 1950 Royal typewriter. This copy, when collected in sufficient quantity, is given to a professional typist. Why no word processor? I'm a true Miniver Cheevy when it comes to writing. I like to use the pencil, erase, draw lines, and struggle to interpret what I've written. My wife believes this is in line with my stubborn personality."

P

PEARSON, Gayle 1947-

Personal

Born July 12, 1947, in Chicago, IL.; daughter of Wallace J. (a civil service employee) and Frances (an artist and homemaker; maiden name, Bjornson) Pearson. *Education:* Northern Illinois University, B.S., 1970; San Jose State University, graduate study, 1976-77.

Addresses

Home—533-A Diamond St., San Francisco, CA 94114.

Career

Vance Publications, Chicago, IL, assistant news editor, 1970-71; Elgin State Hospital, Chicago, social worker, 1971-73; Ming Quong Children's Center, Los Gatos, CA, child care worker, 1973-75; Santa Clara County Information and Referral, San Jose, CA, area director, 1977-81; author, 1978—; University of California, San Francisco, administrative assistant, 1982—. *Member:* Society of Children's Book Writers, Nation Writers Union.

Awards, Honors

Best Children's Book designation, Bay Area Reviewer's Association, 1986, for *Fish Friday.*

Writings

FOR CHILDREN

Fish Friday, Atheneum, 1986.
The Coming Home Café, Atheneum, 1988.
One Potato, Tu, Atheneum, 1992.
The Fog Doggies and Me, Atheneum, 1993.
The Secret Box, Atheneum, 1997.
Don't Call It Paradise, Atheneum, 1999.

OTHER

Contributor of articles and stories to magazines and newspapers, including *Ms., California Living,* and *Highlights for Children.*

Sidelights

Gayle Pearson is an author of novels for young readers that include *Fish Friday, The Coming Home Café,* and *Don't Call It Paradise.* Featuring down-to-earth protagonists in real-life settings, Pearson's novels have been praised by reviewers for their sensitivity in portraying the emotional ups and downs of growing up. In addition to novels, the author has also published several collections of short fiction. In *One Potato, Tu,* she includes seven stories that introduce twelve year old Lindsey, her younger brother, Eric, and her adopted Asian brother, Tu. Focusing on the children and their multicultural Oakland, California, neighborhood, the vignettes in *One Potato, Tu* "create a tapestry of voices and experiences," in the opinion of *Five Owls* reviewer Cathryn M. Mercier. Continuing to follow the same characters, the five stories in *The Secret Box* also reflect Pearson's talent for "follow[ing] the emotional roller coaster of adolescence along its dizzying ride," said *Bulletin of the Center for Children's Books* contributor Elizabeth Bush.

Born in Chicago, Illinois, in 1947, Pearson began writing when she was in elementary school, "but didn't have one officially published until I was thirty," she recalled for *SATA.* "I did win a writing contest in high school for which I was promised a fifty dollar award. The day after I learned I'd won, a woman called to tell me there had been a mistake. The prize offer was five dollars, not fifty dollars! I was disappointed, of course. My grandmother, feeling sorry for me, gave me fifty dollars of her own money, so I came out five dollars ahead. I'd like to find an agent like that."

Unlike many novelists, Pearson was not a member of the yearbook committee and did not work on the school newspaper during her high school years; "I didn't have enough confidence in my writing ability during my teens," she confided. But that would all change after she enrolled in Northern Illinois University. "I began as a journalism major, but I suppose I switched to English so I could teach. It seemed a choice many women were making, and I was strongly influenced by what everyone else was doing." However, student teaching was a less-than-inspiring experience to Pearson, and her first job after graduation was as an assistant editor with a Chicago-based hair salon magazine. Eventually, she grew tired of "reading about Mrs. So-and-So opening her beauty salon in Springfield and Detroit." Pearson's next career would be in the field of mental health and community service.

Despite her career in the heath profession, Pearson didn't lose sight of her dreams of becoming a writer. "I was always thinking of stories, and sometimes wrote things about patients or kids that I worked with," she told *SATA*. "I wrote my first children's story on my way to California in a van in 1973, but didn't do another for several years." Her first novel, *Fish Friday,* was published in 1986, when Pearson was thirty-nine. The story of a young girl who struggles to decide whether to stay with her recently divorced father or leaving her small town to follow her dreams of becoming an artist, *Fish Friday* was praised by a *Booklist* contributor as "low-key but thoughtfully wrought, its poignant conclusion quite affecting." In *School Library Journal,* reviewer Bonnie L. Raasch also praised Pearson's debut novel, calling it a "realistic, modern story that expresses well the problems resulting in a split within a family."

Encouraged by the positive response she received from both readers and reviewers of *Fish Friday,* Pearson continued writing for children. Among her more recent novels is *Don't Call It Paradise,* which is a change of pace from the traditional coming-of-age story. Soon-to-be high schooler Maddie goes on a summer trip to California to visit her friend Beanie, who moved away from Illinois during her last year of middle school. However, Maddie's relationship with Beanie's older brother, Buddy, has always been strained, and she dreads spending time with him. During her stay with Beanie's family, Maddie begins to realize what a destructive influence Buddy has on his family, and she begins to suspect mental illness. Calling the novel's plot "intriguing," *School Library Journal* contributor Carrie Lynn Cooper praised *Don't Call It Paradise* for featuring "a strong female character who will win fans ... with her independence and wit."

"The interplay of fiction and history is of particular interest to me," Pearson once explained to *SATA*. "Going back in time is a common fantasy. For the writer, historical fiction provides a way to do that. My own perspectives on past events shape the story and characters. I love digging up obscure facts and weaving them into a story. If history is meant to teach us how to live in the present better than we do, then serious historical fiction is one more way in which to learn."

Now living on the West Coast, Pearson has established enough distance—both in time and in miles—from her Midwestern roots to be able to write about them, and has set several of her books in middle-America. She fondly recalls the security of the cohesive, working class neighborhood in which she grew up. "As a kid, I often pretended to be an explorer, going off alone or with a friend to discover or create adventure in a grassy field on the other side of the railroad tracks, a dark closet with a crawl space," she once told *SATA*. "I'm still an explorer, not knowing for certain what I'll find when a character in a story takes me by the hand, leads me into an abandoned building, an unfamiliar city, through another chapter . . . ."

Biographical and Critical Sources

PERIODICALS

Booklist, June, 1986, review of *Fish Friday,* p. 1543; April, 1992, Hazel Rochman, review of *One Potato, Tu,* pp. 1438-1440; January 15, 1994, Susan De Ronne, review of *The Fog Doggies and Me,* August, 1997, Susan Dove Lempke, review of *The Secret Box,* p. 1902.

Bulletin of the Center for Children's Books, November, 1988, Zena Sutherland, review of *The Coming Home Café,* p. 82; July, 1997, Elizabeth Bush, review of *The Secret Box,* p. 407.

Five Owls, March, 1992, Cathryn M. Mercier, review of *One Potato, Tu,* p. 84.

Horn Book, Nancy Vasilakis, review of *The Fog Doggies and Me,* p. 201.

Publishers Weekly, April 20, 1992, review of *One Potato, Tu,* p. 57; April 28, 1997, review of *The Secret Box,* p. 76; December 20, 1999, review of *Don't Call It Paradise,* p. 81.

School Library Journal, May, 1986, Bonnie L. Raasch, review of *Fish Friday,* p. 96; June, 1997, Carol A. Edwards, review of *The Secret Box,* p. 125; December, 1999, Carrie Lynn Cooper, review of *Don't Call It Paradise,* p. 137.

Voice of Youth Advocates, June, 1989, Mary Ojibway, review of *The Coming Home Café,* p. 105; April, 1990, Susan Levine, review of *Fish Friday,* p. 70; February, 1994, Susan Levine, review of *The Fog Doggies and Me,* p. 371.*

*   *   *

PEERS, Judi(th May West) 1956-

Personal

Born June 17, 1956, in Cobourg, Ontario, Canada; daughter of Lloyd Beverly (a farmer and caretaker) and Dorothy May (a homemaker; maiden name, Buttars) West; married Dave Peers (a cereal company manager), December 30, 1977; children: Stephen Eric, Sarah May, Michael James Lloyd. *Education:* Trent University, B.A., 1978. *Religion:* Protestant. *Hobbies and other*

Judi Peers

interests: Gardening, reading, playing volleyball, watching children's sports.

Addresses

Home—566 Weller St., Peterborough, Ontario, Canada K9H 2N6.

Career

Down the Garden Path, owner, 1995-2000; writer, 2000—. Speaker at schools and to adult groups; coach and manager of local sports teams; co-coordinator for Pioneer Clubs.

Awards, Honors

Selected to "Our Choice List" by Canadian Children's Book Centre, 1992, for *Home Base,* 1994, for *Free Stuff for Kids,* 1995, for *Free Stuff for Kids,* 2nd edition, 1996, for *Free Stuff for Kids,* 3rd edition, and 1997, for *Free Stuff for Kids,* 4th edition.

Writings

Brontosaurus Brunch, Scholastic, 1990.
Home Base, General/Stoddart, 1992.

Free Stuff for Kids, Stoddart, 1994, 2nd edition, 1995, 3rd edition, 1996, 4th edition, 1997.
Shark Attack, James Lorimer, 1998, teacher's guide, 1999.

Work in Progress

A sequel to *Shark Attack,* tentatively set in Japan; a picture book called *The Rusty Man.*

Sidelights

Judi Peers told *SATA:* "I started writing approximately fifteen years ago while living on an island during the summers with my two preschoolers. I asked myself, 'What could I do, living way out here, to make a little money?' I found that to be just the case (the little money part), but I became hooked on writing for kids. It was work, but it was fun as well.

"I met interesting, wonderful people, and I found I loved working with and speaking to children in the schools. I probably do far too much of this, to the neglect of my actual writing, but this is where I find the rewards are the greatest. A child in grade three wrote, 'I am reading a lot like you told us to,' while a child in grade five said, 'I have read *Home Base* six times.'"

Biographical and Critical Sources

PERIODICALS

Canadian Book Review Annual, 1997, review of *Free Stuff for Kids,* p. 560.
Resource Links, April, 1997, review of *Free Stuff for Kids,* p. 165.
School Library Journal, January, 2000, Elaine E. Knight, review of *Shark Attack,* p. 128.

*   *   *

PETERSON, Kathleen B. 1951-

Personal

Born May 10, 1951, in Provo, UT; daughter of James Lavar (a professor) and Helen (a teacher; maiden name, Ream) Bateman; married Steven Peterson (a professor), August 23, 1971; children: Alex, Eric, Starr, Summer. *Education:* Brigham Young University, B.A., 1973; studied at University of Hawaii at Manoa, 1973, and Snow College, 1975 and 1976. *Religion:* Church of Jesus Christ of Latter-day Saints (Mormon).

Addresses

Home—123 North 460 E., No. 86-4, Ephraim, UT 84627. *E-mail*—6petes@sisna.com.

Career

Illustrator and artist, with work exhibited in galleries throughout Utah and in Wyoming, Hawaii, and Malay-

Kathleen B. Peterson

sia. Utah Art Center, founder and director; Utah Arts Council, board of directors. Art teacher at local schools, including Wasatch Academy; organizer of local art groups. Bennion Teton Boys Ranch, co-director of summer sessions.

Writings

ILLUSTRATOR

The Stones of the Temple, Deseret, 1993.
A World of Faith, Signature Books (Salt Lake City, UT), 1998.
The Lesson, Gibbs Smith, 1998.
What Love Is, Gibbs Smith, 1999.
Will You Still Be My Daughter?, Gibbs Smith, 2000.

Illustrator of *Girlfriend, You Are the Best,* 2000. Contributor of illustrations to periodicals, including *Roots and Wings, Ensign,* and *Dialogue.*

Work in Progress

Illustrating *The Tale of Pele and Poliahu,* a legend of Hawaii, in batik on silk cloth.

Sidelights

Kathleen B. Peterson told *SATA:* "I paint to find out what I think. It is an ongoing process of experimenting and growing. My methods and styles of drawing and painting seem to change with each piece and evolve with each painting. Beginning a new work is always stimulating because I know I am going to have to stretch and learn new ideas and techniques. I never quite arrive because just when I get comfortable with a new technique or idea, I realize there is always more to learn."

Q

QUAY, Emma

Personal

Surname is pronounced "Kway"; born in England; daughter of Ivan (a research scientist and psychologist) and Brenda (a music teacher; maiden name, Shipp) Brown; married David Quay (a pharmacist); children: Jessica Emmanuelle. *Education:* Attended Cambridge College of Arts and Technology; Polytechnic of Newcastle-upon-Tyne, B.A. (with honors).

Addresses

Contact—c/o Random House Australia, 20 Alfred St., Milsons Point, Sydney, New South Wales 2061, Australia.

Career

Illustrator. Graham-Cameron Illustration, worked as illustrator of educational books. Work represented in permanent collection of prints and drawings, Victoria and Albert Museum.

Awards, Honors

Annual Family Award for Children's Literature, Family Therapy Associations of Australia, 1998, and Notable Book Award, Children's Book Council of Australia, 1999, both for *Champions.*

Writings

ILLUSTRATOR

Jonathan Harlen, *Champions,* Random House Australia (Sydney, Australia), 1998.
Colin Thompson, *The Puzzle Duck,* Random House Australia, 1999.

Emma Quay

Work in Progress

Illustrating *Thank You for My Yukky Present,* by Meredith Hooper, and *It Just Missed You, Chook!* by Lisa Shanahan, both for Hodder Headline Australia.

Sidelights

Emma Quay told *SATA:* "As a toddler, I would leave scraps of paper, covered in drawings, wherever I went. A few years later I knew that I wanted to illustrate children's books. The picture books from my childhood are full of little embellishments (vandalism, by another name!) where I had added an angel here, a bee or flower there—all in the style of the original illustrator (or so I thought—not many used ballpoint pen).

"On graduating from college, where I specialized in illustration and printmaking, I joined up with the agency, Graham-Cameron Illustration, working mainly in black and white, illustrating educational books and teachers' handbooks. I also continued with the printmaking and met my Australian husband in India, while traveling there to sketch for an exhibition of mono-prints and charcoal drawings.

"I moved to Sydney in 1993, continuing to work for British educational publishers, but I longed for the involvement in the whole creative process that comes with illustrating picture book titles. In the hope of finding a picture book publisher, I built up a portfolio of the work I'd like to be doing.

"In 1996 I was introduced to Mark Macleod, then at Random House Australia. He gave me the text of *Champions* by Jonathan Harlen, which was exactly the kind of funny, gutsy, yet warm book I had hoped to see. For the line work in the illustrations I used a washout resist technique, where white gouache paint is painted everywhere on the page that one intends to remain white. When waterproof black ink is painted over the whole page and allowed to dry, then the paper is rinsed in water and the white gouache lifts away, leaving black ink where the paper was showing through. It is a very time-consuming process (and I have not used it for a major project since!) but I like the accidental effects it produces and the ragged, loose lines. The illustrations were then colored using watercolors.

"My second book for Random House Australia was *The Puzzle Duck* by Colin Thompson. I used pencil line and acrylics in the illustrations, finding that I could get the watercolor wash effect I was after, with more intense color. The book sets fox against duck in a familiar way, but I tried to convey my sympathy for the fox through my illustrations. After all, he was only trying to feed his family! I try to use expressive body language in my drawn characters, showing how they feel in every little part of their bodies, down to curled up or freely spread toes (or paw pads or webbed feet). I draw from my imagination, after studying how a particular animal looks and moves, but often find myself twisting into the position of the character I am sketching, as I sit at my desk.

"The kind of art I enjoy most always has humor in it—not necessarily a big belly-laugh, but sometimes a wry smile, or a wicked grin. I hope children respond to my work in this way."

QUIN-HARKIN, Janet 1941-
(Janetta Johns, Rhys Bowen)

Personal

Born September 24, 1941, in Bath, England; immigrated to the United States in 1966; daughter of Frank Newcombe (an engineer) and Margery (a teacher; maiden name, Rees) Lee; married John Quin-Harkin (a retired sales manager), November 26, 1966; children: Clare, Anne, Jane, Dominic. *Education:* University of London, B.A. (with honors), 1963; graduate study at University of Kiel and University of Freiburg. *Religion:* Roman Catholic. *Hobbies and other interests:* Tennis, travel, drama, music, sketching, and hiking.

Addresses

Home and office—31 Tralee Way, San Rafael, CA 94903. *Agent*—Fran Lebowitz, Writers House, Inc., 21 West 26th St., New York, NY 10010. *E-mail*—rhys@ rhysbowen.com.

Career

British Broadcasting Corp. (BBC), London, England, studio manager in drama department, 1963-66; writer, 1971—; teacher of dance and drama, 1971-76; teacher of

Janet Quin-Harkin

Tia and Tamera scheme over seventeen-year-old Steve and land in the middle of potential disaster when relatives visit for Christmas.

writing at Dominican College, San Rafael, CA, 1988-95. Founder and former director of San Raphael's Children's Little Theater. *Member:* Society of Children's Book Writers and Illustrators, Associated Authors of Children's Literature, Mystery Writers of America, Sisters in Crime, Novelists, Inc., Mystery Women, American Association of University Women.

Awards, Honors

Children's Book Showcase selection, Children's Book Council, Outstanding Books of the Year citation, *New York Times,* Children's Book Show citation, American Institute of Graphic Arts, and Best Books of the year citations, *School Library Journal, Washington Post,* and *Saturday Review,* all 1976, all for *Peter Penny's Dance;* Children's Choice citation, 1985, for *Wanted: Date for Saturday Night;* nominated, Barry Award for Best Novel of 1998, for *Evan Help Us.*

Writings

CHILDREN'S BOOKS

Peter Penny's Dance, illustrated by Anita Lobel, Dial, 1976.
Benjamin's Balloon, Parents Magazine, 1979.
Septimus Bean and His Amazing Machine, illustrated by Art Cumings, Parents Magazine, 1980.
Magic Growing Powder, illustrated by Art Cumings, Parents Magazine, 1981.
Helpful Hattie, illustrated by Susanna Natti, Harcourt, 1983.
Three Impossible Things, Parents Magazine, 1991.
Billy and Ben: The Terrible Two, illustrated by Carol Newsom, Bantam, 1992.

YOUNG ADULT NOVELS

Write Every Day, Scholastic, 1982.
(Under pseudonym Janetta Johns) *The Truth about Me and Bobby V.,* Bantam, 1983.
Tommy Loves Tina, Berkley/Ace, 1984.
Winner Takes All, Berkley/Ace, 1984.
Wanted: Date for Saturday Night, Putnam, 1985.
Summer Heat, Fawcett, 1990.
My Phantom Love ("Changes Romance" series), Harper-Collins, 1992.
On My Own ("Changes Romance" series), HarperCollins, 1992.
Getting Personal: Becky, Silhouette, 1994.
The Apartment, HarperCollins, 1994.
The Sutcliffe Diamonds, HarperCollins, 1994.
The Boy Next Door ("Love Stories" series), Bantam, 1995.
Who Do You Love? ("Love Stories" series), Bantam, 1996.
(With Thomas P. Taafe) *Fun, Sun, and Flamingoes* ("Club Stephanie" series), Bantam, 1997.
(With Emily Costello and Emily Ecco) *Fireworks and Flamingoes* ("Club Stephanie" series), Bantam, 1997.
Flamingo Revenge ("Club Stephanie" series), Pocket, 1997.
King and I (adapted from the animated movie and the musical), Scholastic, 1999.
Torn Apart ("Love Stories" series), Bantam, 1999.
Love Potion ("Enchanted Hearts" series), Avon, 1999.

"SWEET DREAMS" SERIES; PUBLISHED BY BANTAM

California Girl, 1981.
Love Match, 1982.
Ten-Boy Summer, 1982.
Daydreamer, 1983.
The Two of Us, 1984.
Exchange of Hearts, 1984.
Ghost of a Chance, 1984.
Lovebirds, 1984.
101 Ways to Meet Mr. Right, 1985.
The Great Boy Chase, 1985.
Follow That Boy, 1985.
My Secret Love, 1986.
My Best Enemy, 1987.
Never Say Goodbye, 1987.

"ON OUR OWN" SERIES; PUBLISHED BY BANTAM

On Our Own, 1986.
The Graduates, 1986.
The Trouble with Toni, 1986.

Out of Love, 1986.
Old Friends, New Friends, 1986.
Best Friends Forever, 1986.

"SUGAR AND SPICE" SERIES; PUBLISHED BY BALLANTINE

Flip Side, 1987.
Tug of War, 1987.
Surf's Up, 1987.
The Last Dance, 1987.
Nothing in Common, 1987.
Dear Cousin, 1987.
Two Girls, One Boy, 1987.
Trading Places, 1987.
Double Take, 1988.
Make Me a Star, 1988.
Big Sister, 1988.
Out in the Cold, 1988.
Blind Date, 1988.
It's My Turn, 1988.

"HEARTBREAK CAFE" SERIES; PUBLISHED BY FAWCETT

No Experience Required, 1990.
The Main Attraction, 1990.
At Your Service, 1990.
Catch of the Day, 1990.
Love to Go, 1990.
Just Desserts, 1990.

"FRIENDS" SERIES; PUBLISHED BY HARPERCOLLINS

Starring Tess and Ali, 1991.
Tess and Ali and the Teeny Bikini, 1991.
Boy Trouble for Tess and Ali, 1991.
Tess and Ali, Going on Fifteen, 1991.

"SENIOR YEAR" SERIES; PUBLISHED BY HARPERCOLLINS

Homecoming Dance, 1991.
New Year's Eve, 1991.
Night of the Prom, 1992.
Graduation Day, 1992.

"BOYFRIEND CLUB" SERIES; PUBLISHED BY TROLL

Ginger's First Kiss, 1994.
Roni's Dream Boy, 1994.
Karen's Perfect Match, 1994.
Ginger's New Crush, 1994.
Queen Justine, 1995.
Roni's Two-Boy Trouble, 1995.
No More Boys, 1995.
Karen's Lesson in Love, 1995.
Roni's Sweet Fifteen, 1995.
Justine's Babysitting, 1995.
The Boyfriend Wars, 1995.

"TGIF!" SERIES; PUBLISHED BY POCKET

Sleepover Madness, 1995.
Friday Night Fright, 1995.
Four's a Crowd, 1995.
Forever Friday, 1995.
Toe-Shoe Trouble, 1996.
Secret Valentine, 1996.

"SISTER, SISTER" SERIES; POCKET BOOKS

Cool in School, 1996.

You Read My Mind, 1996.
One Crazy Christmas, 1996.
Homegirl on the Range, 1997.
Star Quality, 1997.
He's All That, 1997.
Summer Days, 1997.
All Rapped Up, 1997.

FOR ADULTS; UNDER PSEUDONYM RHYS BOWEN

Evans Above, St. Martin's, 1997.
Evan Help Us, St. Martin's, 1998.
Evanly Choirs, St. Martin's, 1999.
Evan and Elle, St. Martin's, 2000.

OTHER

(Contributor) *Chandler Reading Program,* five volumes, edited by Lawrence Carillo and Dorothy McKinley, Noble & Noble, 1967-72.
Madam Sarah (adult historical novel), Fawcett, 1990.
Fool's Gold (adult historical novel), HarperCollins, 1991.
Amazing Grace (adult historical fiction), HarperCollins, 1993.
The Secrets of Lake Success (based on the NBC mini-series, created by David Stenn), Tor, 1993.
Trade Winds (based on the NBC mini-series, created by Hugh Bush), Schoolfield/Caribbean Productions, 1993.

Also author of several documentaries and four radio plays and scripts, including "Dandelion Hours," for the BBC, 1966. Many of Quin-Harkin's young adult novels, including *California Girl, Love Match, Ten-Boy Summer,* and *Daydreamer,* have been translated into other languages. Contributor to periodicals, including *Scholastic* and *Mother's Journal.*

Sidelights

Janet Quin-Harkin's writing career has spanned a plethora of genres, two continents, and several decades. Getting a start in radio plays with the British Broadcasting Company (BBC) in London in the 1960s, she soon moved on to a new home in the United States and celebrity as a prize-winning picture book author and then as a popular author of nearly one hundred books geared for teen readers. Quin-Harkin's young adult series include "Sweet Dreams," "Sugar and Spice," "Heartbreak Cafe," and "On Our Own," among others, comprising books of standard length with a fixed group of characters involved in "the sort of lives that Middle America leads," as Quin-Harkin once described her work to *Something about the Author (SATA).* According to the author, the "Sweet Dreams" series opened up a new direction in publishing, providing books that were cheap enough for the readers themselves to purchase and thus making teen readers independent from the choices of parents and librarians. These were also books that were more upbeat than previous young adult contributions, which dealt primarily, according to Quin-Harkin, with "the darker side of reality." In addition, writing under the name Rhys Bowen, she has taken a new direction with her writing by creating a popular mystery series set in Wales, featuring a young constable, Evan Evans.

Born in Bath, England, Quin-Harkin began writing for fun at an early age, publishing her first short story by sixteen. Her own teen years were quite placid, as she attended an all-girls school where academics rather than sports or romance were emphasized. The usual emotional upheavals of adolescence were thus largely postponed until Quin-Harkin attended college, earning a B.A. with honors from the University of London. For the first few years after graduation, Quin-Harkin worked for the BBC as a studio manager and also as a writer of radio and television plays. Such writings were "fairly highbrow," as the author once described them. She then moved to Australia, where she met John Quin-Harkin while working for the Australian Broadcasting Company. The couple married in 1966 and moved to the United States. Settling in the San Francisco Bay area, Quin-Harkin balanced the role of mother and writer. She worked initially for a textbook company and helped develop new primary reading texts more relevant for contemporary urban children than the traditional primer stories of Dick and Jane.

Work on textbooks set Quin-Harkin to writing for herself again, and her first book was published in 1976. It was a long way from teen romance. *Peter Penny's Dance* was a picture book for children, inspired by the lyrics from an old English folk song: "I've come to claim a silver pound because I've danced the world around." Everything about this first title was easy for Quin-Harkin; she once claimed that the story seemed to come of itself and the manuscript found a home on the second try. Zena Sutherland of the *Bulletin of the Center for Children's Books* called the tale "a bouncy, bonny book," and many critics praised Anita Lobel's accompanying illustrations. Of the book's exciting conclusion, *Horn Book* reviewer Ethel L. Heins wrote: "In a splendid finale, reminiscent of *Around the World in Eighty Days,* Peter arrived back in England in the nick of time and skipped his way straight to the church and into the arms of his overjoyed bride." *Peter Penny's Dance* went on to win numerous awards. This early successful start, however, was followed by several years without sales as Quin-Harkin continued to raise her family while struggling to work at her craft. Then several early titles were sold to Parents Magazine: *Benjamin's Balloon, Septimus Bean and His Amazing Machine,* and *Magic Growing Powder.* Quin-Harkin was establishing a name as a picture book author.

In 1981 came a turning point in the Quin-Harkin's career, when her agent asked if she could write a teen novel quickly. A trip to the local bookstore provided the author with a bundle of young adult books which she studied carefully, and then she sat down to turn out sample chapters of her own teen fiction. These samples evolved into *California Girl,* the first in Bantam's "Sweet Dreams" series. In *California Girl,* Jenny is a sixteen-year-old swimmer with Olympic aspirations. When her coach moves to Texas, Jenny's family follows so that she can continue training. But Texas is a far cry from Jenny's former home state; here she is regarded as strange because of her devotion to her athletic dreams. She soon finds a friend, however: Mark is an injured

football player who supports her swimming and helps her train. The finale comes with Jenny competing in the Nationals for a berth in the Olympics. Along the way there is a crew of supporting characters: the scheming cheerleader who now wants her former boyfriend Mark back, Jenny's rather unsympathetic mother, and an empty-headed girl friend. Ella B. Fossum, writing in *School Library Journal,* thought the book was "a cut above the usual teenage love story" because of the added complications and insightful details of Jenny's Olympic aspirations. Despite noticing that the supporting cast of characters lacked meaningful depth, Becky Johnson, writing in *Voice of Youth Advocates,* gave the novel "high marks for readability," saying that "the story is fast-moving and the main character is serious-minded and independent."

If reviewers had problems with such books, readers did not. Quin-Harkin's "Sweet Dreams" series took off with large sales and a loyal audience. The second book in the series, *Love Match,* also involves an athletic theme when Joanna refuses to ensure Rick's affection by allowing him to beat her at tennis. While a reviewer for *Bulletin of the Center for Children's Books* concluded that the book had "little substance" because of its formulaic plot—girl meets boy, loses boy, wins boy in the end—other reviewers, including Joe McKenzie in *School Library Journal,* commented that "readers will figure it all out early too, but many of them won't care," because of the sympathetic nature of the leading character, Joanna. This blend of sympathetic and generally well-drawn main characters along with a formulaic plot has formed the heart of much of Quin-Harkin's teen writing. Most of the titles fall into the category of escapist reading, "predictable but palatable," as Ilene Cooper of *Booklist* noted in a review of *Daydreamer,* a further title in the "Sweet Dreams" series. However, writing in *Voice of Youth Advocates* about *Daydreamer,* Maureen Ritter emphasized the readability factor and noted that the book was "perfect for a hi/lo reader," and that aside from divorced parents, the main character, Lisa, "does not suffer from the traumas that most YA novel characters do; only the necessary conflicts needed for growth."

One book in the "Sweet Dreams" series, *Ten-Boy Summer,* sold over half a million copies. In this work, central characters Jill and Toni determine to liven up their junior-year summer by breaking up with their respective boyfriends, betting on who will be the first to have dated ten boys. Sally Estes of *Booklist* found the book's premise "a bit farfetched, perhaps, but light and lively enough to attract nondemanding readers of teenage romances." Similarly, Susan Levine wrote in *Voice of Youth Advocates* that *Ten-Boy Summer* "satisfies its requirements of a fast, uncomplicated, lightly romantic story with a happy ending."

"Sweet Dreams" inaugurated not just a new writing direction for Quin-Harkin, but also a major trend in young adult publishing. Criticized by some as lacking in substance and praised by others as an encouragement to reading, teen books such as those Quin-Harkin built a career on became an important part of juvenile publishing, accounting for hundreds of thousands of sales annually. Quin-Harkin's books describe what happens when a teen and her best friend break up, when a family moves, or when parents divorce. And most often there are young men involved: boys a girl wants to date, or love from afar, or beat at tennis. Quin-Harkin writes about the concerns of contemporary teenage girls; relevance is her watchword. In her series, she has built an enormous and faithful readership as a result. Writing to a tight schedule throughout the 1980s and most of the 1990s, Quin-Harkin developed nine separate teen series.

Another immensely popular teens series is "Sugar and Spice," featuring the adventures of two cousins, Chrissy and Cara. Bouncy Chrissy is the cheerleader type from a small town in Iowa who has come to live in San Francisco with her serious, ballet-studying cousin, Caroline, also known as Cara. *Flip Side* inaugurated the series, introducing the city cousin and country cousin in a situation in which they both yearn for the other's boyfriend but are too nice to do anything about it. *School Library Journal* contributor Kathy Fritts called the book "a winner," while Laurel Ibey, writing in *Voice of Youth Advocates,* concluded that everyone who reads *Flip Side* will "find it full of fun!" Another adventure in the "Sugar and Spice" series takes urban Cara to Chrissy's Iowa farm in *Nothing in Common.* In *School Library Journal,* Kathy Fritts asserted that a "fast pace, wonderful scenes of family and farm life, lots of action, and plenty of boy-girl mix and match make it a sure hit." In *The Last Dance,* Cara finally decides to give up dancing, leading Juli Lund in *Voice of Youth Advocates* to praise the book because it "did not have a perfect 'happy ending,' but instead realistically portrayed not-so-perfect actual life."

Other young adult series books from Quin-Harkin include those from "On Our Own," "Heartbreak Cafe," "Senior Year," the "Boyfriend Club, "TGIF!," and "Sister, Sister." A series geared at pre-teens is "Friends," which follows the relationship between two girls, Alison and Tess, over the four summers they spend together in a small resort town. Tess is newly arrived in the town in the first book of the series, *Starring Tess and Ali,* and Alison forms a quick friendship with her. Trouble arises, however, with remarks Tess makes about how overprotective Ali's mother is. Ali is upset by such remarks until she learns the root of them: Tess's mother has recently deserted the family and envy and spite are undoubtedly contributing to the girl's behavior. A *Publishers Weekly* reviewer noted in a review of *Starring Tess and Ali* that younger readers might resent the "juvenile tone" of the book, but claimed that Quin-Harkin had created a "compassionate protagonist whose heretofore compliant ways are undergoing thoughtful reevaluation."

Quin-Harkin has also written many non-series teen books, perhaps the best known being *Wanted: Date for Saturday Night,* in which the central problem is finding a date for shy Julie for the Freshman Formal, and *Summer Heat,* in which teen protagonist Laurie Beth, on the verge of graduating from high school, must choose between two suitors and two completely different

lifestyles. Other of Quin-Harkin's non-series efforts include *The Sutcliffe Diamonds* and *The Apartment. Wanted: Date for Saturday Night* went on to win a Children's Choice award as well as a large readership.

Since the mid-1990s, Quin-Harkin has been focusing more and more on adult fiction. She has written novels dealing with historical settings, including the California Gold Rush or Australia in the 1920s, in such books as *Madam Sarah* and *Fool's Gold.* Also popular is her adult mystery series featuring the Welsh constable, Evan Evans, set in the bucolic village of Llanfair. As a child, Quin-Harkin spent many summers in a small Welsh village like the one she has created for her series, where everyone knows everybody else's business and quirky characters abound. Deciding finally to write the kind of book she most enjoys reading, Quin-Harkin also opted for a pen name to keep her teen and adult writing

Determined to skate in the Olympics, Kirsten overcomes her dislike of the ex-hockey player who becomes her new partner. (Cover photo by Daniel Weiss Associates, Inc.)

Trouble flares when Stephanie tries to get even with the Flamingos. (Cover photo by Schultz Photography.)

separate. She chose her Welsh grandfather's name, Rhys Bowen.

With the first book in the series, *Evans Above,* she set the scene and main characters in place for a series to grow and prosper. When his policeman father is killed in the line of duty, young Evan Evans, a North Wales constable, is assigned to the village of Llanfair where there are far too many Evanses. Constable Evans becomes, in local parlance, Evans the Law, to distinguish him from the butcher, Evans the Meat, the dairyman, Evans the Milk, or the postman, Evans the Post. But Llanfair proves to be anything but tranquil. Two hikers presumably fall to their deaths on Mount Snowdon on the same day, while a third is soon discovered in a cave with his throat cut. Up to his ears in crime, Evans is also pursued by the eligible young ladies of the village, Betsy the Bar (the local barmaid), and Bronwen the Book (a teacher). Reviewing this debut novel in the series, Judy McAloon praised in *School Library Journal* the book's "well-crafted plot, nicely drawn characters, [and] strong sense of place," concluding that young adult readers would enjoy both the book's setting and protagonist, "a hero who is young enough to feel self-conscious with women." Rex E. Klett, writing in *Library Journal,* praised the book's "[s]traightforward

plotting, tempered with unique characterization and subtle humor," and a writer for *Kirkus Reviews* also found much to like in this "pleasingly unpretentious debut."

Constable Evans makes return performances in *Evan Help Us, Evanly Choirs,* and *Evan and Elle.* In the second novel in the series, Evans is pursued by yet another female, a single woman who moves into the village with her daughter. Murder soon intrudes into this domestic comedy, however, when Colonel Arbuthnot, a yearly visitor from London who claims to have found the ruins of Camelot near the village, is found dead. The same fate also awaits returning villager Ted Morgan, who has plans to turn a local mine into a theme park. Investigating the case, Evans finds a connection between the two murders and the new femme fatale, a trail which leads him to London and back. "Bowen's quiet humor and her appreciation for rural village life make this a jewel of a story," wrote a contributor to *Publishers Weekly. Booklist*'s GraceAnne A. DeCandido called the setting for the novel "ineffably quaint and impossibly charming," going on to say that the novel was "[s]atisfying as a Guinness pint." Marilyn Stasio, writing in the *New York Times Book Review,* echoed such a sentiment, noting that "the pleasure of visiting Llanfair is that nothing, not even murder, can ruffle its placid composure."

In his third outing, *Evanly Choirs,* Constable Evans is persuaded to add his voice to the local choir in its preparations for the eisteddfod, a music festival held in a nearby town. Into the mix comes famous opera star Ifor Llewellyn and his wife, Margaret, taking a restful vacation in Llanfair. The famous opera singer is persuaded to join the male chorus, but becomes a large pain in the neck to most people in the village. No matter; soon his tenor voice is stilled for good when the opera star is found dead one morning. Evans is on the trail while his choir mates struggle to maintain a competitive edge. "Between his singing debut and his bumpy romance with the schoolteacher, Evan sorts through a humorous series of false confessions to catch the real killer," wrote a contributor for *Publishers Weekly,* who concluded, "Ultimately, it's Bowen's keen sense of small-town politics and gossip that will keep her fans turning pages." A writer for *Kirkus Reviews* claimed it is the book's "cozily intimate style, and modest, down-home hero," which make for a "satisfying entertainment," a feature also noted by *Booklist*'s Jenny McLarin, who called this "charming tale ... [a] perfect book to curl up with on a rainy day."

Feminine competition once again plays a part in the goings on in Llanfair in the fourth series entry, *Evan and Elle.* When eligible widow Madame Yvette opens a French restaurant in the village, she wins the stomachs and hearts of not a few, including the good Constable. But he resists all efforts to be parted from his real sweetheart, ever-true Bronwen. Yet when the Madame's restaurant is burned down, Evans is forced to get closer. At first, suspicion leads to Welsh extremists responsible for a string of arsons in the area. However, a body found in the ashes turns this investigation into a homicide, and its trail leads first to the southern coast of England and then on to France as Evans and his sidekick, Sergeant Watkins, unravel this mystery with a history. "This is a slight confection of a mystery," noted a reviewer for *Publishers Weekly,* "sweetened with the author's obvious affection for her characters, as well as for all things Welsh." *Booklist*'s McLarin also reflected upon the lightness of the story line, but further commented, "It hardly matters, though, because the strength of this series is not plot but those staples of the British cozy, village ambience and eccentric characters." McLarin concluded that *Evan and Elle* was as "light and sweet as a crepes suzette."

Whether writing of teen troubles in California or murders in a Welsh village, Quin-Harkin always manages to provide a "rattling good story," as she once described her efforts to *SATA.* Though some critics complain her stories are often written to formula, her sense of character and of pace carries the reader along in books that engage and charm. Quin-Harkin leaves bleak and somber themes to other writers; for her entertainment is the heart of the matter.

Biographical and Critical Sources

PERIODICALS

Booklist, May 1, 1976, p. 1270; October 1, 1981, p. 189; January 15, 1982, p. 644; September 1, 1982, Sally Estes, review of *Ten-Boy Summer,* p. 37; May 15, 1983, Ilene Cooper, review of *Daydreamer,* p. 1221; February 1, 1984, p. 810; February 15, 1984, p. 862; June 15, 1984, p. 1474; October, 1998, GraceAnne A. DeCandido, review of *Evan Helps Us,* p. 224; April, 15, 1999, Jenny McLarin, review of *Evanly Choirs,* p. 1446; December 15, 1999, J. McLarin, review of *Evan and Elle,* p. 759.

Bulletin of the Center for Children's Books, October, 1976, Zena Sutherland, review of *Peter Penny's Dance,* p. 30; March, 1982, review of *Love Match,* p. 136.

Horn Book, June, 1976, Ethel L. Heins, review of *Peter Penny's Dance,* p. 281.

Kirkus Reviews, November 15, 1997, review of *Evans Above;* April 28, 1999, review of *Evanly Choirs.*

Kliatt, Spring, 1982, p. 10; Spring, 1983, p. 5; Fall, 1985, Elaine Patterson, review of *101 Ways to Meet Mr. Right,* p. 16.

Library Journal, December, 1997, Rex E. Klett, review of *Evans Above,* p. 159.

New York Times Book Review, May 9, 1976, p. 12; November 14, 1976, p. 53; April 1, 1979, p. 37; October 25, 1998, Marilyn Stasio, "Crime," p. 43.

Publishers Weekly, May 24, 1991, review of *Starring Tess and Ali,* p. 58; August 17, 1998, review of *Evan Help Us,* p. 52; April 15, 1999, review of *Evanly Choirs,* p. 226; January 10, 2000, review of *Evan and Elle,* p. 48.

School Library Journal, November, 1981, Ella B. Fossum, review of *California Girl,* p. 110; March, 1982, Joe McKenzie, review of *Love Match,* p. 160; January, 1988, Kathy Fritts, review of *Flip Side* and *Nothing in Common,* p. 95; May, 1998, Judy McAloon, review of *Evans Above,* p. 175.

Times Educational Supplement, April 21, 1995, p. 16.

Voice of Youth Advocates, December, 1981, Becky Johnson, review of *California Girl,* p. 34; December, 1982, Susan Levine, review of *Ten-Boy Summer,* p. 35; December, 1983, Maureen Ritter, review of *Daydreamer,* p. 281; April, 1988, Laurel Ibey, review of *Flip Side,* p. 35; April, 1988, Juli Lund, review of *The Last Dance,* p. 35; October, 1994, p. 215; December, 1994, p. 279.

ON-LINE

Rhys Bowen's Mystery Homepage, http://www.rhysbowen.com.

—Sketch by J. Sydney Jones

R

Kristen D. Randle

1952-

I was born in Experimental Hospital at Independence, Missouri, in 1952. This is information I do not give out often; too many people, once they've heard it, tend to shake their heads knowingly and say "Well, *that* explains a lot." And maybe it does.

Anyway, as I said, I was born in Missouri (pronounced Mizzura). This is my heartland, the home place of my family. We are a very small circle—my parents, sister, brother, and me. Dad had one sister, Jeanne, and Mom had one brother, Don. Dad's mother and grandmother, Mother Jean and Mother Tyner, and Mom's mother, Nana, were the only other relatives we knew. Both of my grandfathers died before I was born.

The day I was born, my father lost his job. I don't remember where it was he'd been working, but he got laid off. This he had to tell my mother as she lay with her first baby in her arms. It must have been a difficult explanation to make—the first difficult explanation associated with my life, but hardly the last.

My memories of babyhood are few but vivid—we were only in Kansas City about four years, and so it's not hard for me to isolate those images—and images most of them are, like mental snapshots: a baby's-eye view of a green backyard and a brown house, of thunderstorms and a huge steel wringer-washer. The only possessions I remember were a walking, plastic Pluto and my tiny green Victrola record player. One day, I emptied a box full of Luden's cherry cough drops into a bowl, and then spent a very long time walking around and around the spirals of a rag throw rug—taking a cough drop every time I passed the bowl—and playing "Never Smile at a Crocodile" on that little Victrola about a thousand times.

I am told that when I was about two years old, I painted the living room carpet. And why not? My father had been painting the walls. It was only natural that I should want to help him.

Kristen D. Randle on her mother's lap.

I am also told that I didn't like green beans. This, I believe. My mother is a very intelligent woman—she has a B.S. in chemistry, and a life full of accomplishments—and she still believes that green beans are *good* for you. As a new mother, she was determined that I was going to eat well. She had studied the current philosophy of child raising, and they told her, when your child won't eat the beans at dinner, you should not give the child any substitute. Beans or nothing. And at breakfast, beans. And at lunch—until the child is ready to give it up and eat the nasty things. Because the child will give up, eventually.

But I didn't.

The way my father tells the story, I went for days without eating. This was not true. I could never go for days without eating, not even for pride. But suffice it to say that my mother's soft heart beat out her scientific parenting, and, after a few meals, she gave in and fed me something else. My father says I looked her straight in the eye and said very clearly, "I knew I'd win." I think this incident demonstrates strength of character. My father has his own opinions.

My father, as a young man planning for college and the future, had wanted to be a writer, but his mother was not sympathetic with his ambition. An engineering degree, she told him, she would pay for. If he wanted to be a writer, he was welcome to pay his own tuition. This may not have been *sensitive* of her, but it was wise. So, my father followed in his father's footsteps and became a civil engineer. Because of this fact, his joblessness didn't last; he found a job with TWA (Trans World Airlines), a piece of luck that plugged us right into our future.

I'm always shocked to think that I was born only seven years after World War II. That war and the culture that existed with it always seemed like ancient history to me. When I don't think of my life as starting in 1952, my childhood doesn't seem like it happened so awfully long ago. I mean we had a TV—of sorts, a great big box with this teeny little screen—and we had a car, and indoor toilets, and electric lights, and everything. On the other hand, curb and gutter hadn't made a big impression on Independence, and people were flying across the country in propeller planes that took years to get anywhere and about put your ears out before you got there. When I do think of it as 1952, I think it was so long ago and far away, it must have been part of somebody else's life.

One of the last things that happened to me in Independence was the afternoon my dad took me out, just the two of us, for *Dumbo* and ice cream—that was the same afternoon my baby sister was born. I liked *Dumbo.* I wasn't so sure about my sister.

Very soon after that, TWA transferred my dad to Los Angeles, to Westchester, near the airport, and that's the place I think of when people talk about childhood.

I have to tell you here that my life is not very interesting. I had a great time as a child—well, most of the time I did. My family was strong and healthy and happy. We were not in any way (not that I can see, looking back) dysfunctional, although I have to admit that I *did* own a Barbie doll once. My parents were honest, hardworking, intelligent people, who always stayed true to each other and to us. In all my life, I've only heard them fight twice. This is not because they are saints. This is because they are discreet (maybe too much so) and because my *mother* is a saint. My father, on the other hand, is Irish. As am I.

We never had a car accident, never burned down a house, never made a fortune or lost one, never were mugged (almost, once)—oh, we *were* burglarized a couple

of times. None of the three kids of the family ever took drugs or got into terrible trouble (note the qualifier), or even broke a winsome limb. (We did, however, need orthodontia, which I finally had done when I was thirty-two.)

I may be able to save the situation by admitting that we were not always absolutely cheerful. I hated my sister for years; I had been an only child before I saw *Dumbo,* and I'd liked it that way. Besides, my sister was just cute, just *darling.* Everything she did was sweet and cute and innocent to the point that you just had to pound her one to make sure she was real. My brother is another story altogether. But I am getting ahead of myself.

My point is that I have no significant trauma with which to spice this up. Just trying to keep my nose clean took so much of my energy, I didn't have a lot of time for more worldly pursuits. If that makes me boring—well, fine.

So, we had moved to LA. We lived in a neighborhood of no-nonsense little houses, thousands of them, all exactly the same, except some of them had curved walks instead of straight. And the colors—white, pastel green, pastel yellow, pastel pink. California. I loved it.

Of this place, I can remember a million things. I remember snowball bushes and granite street lamps, poppy

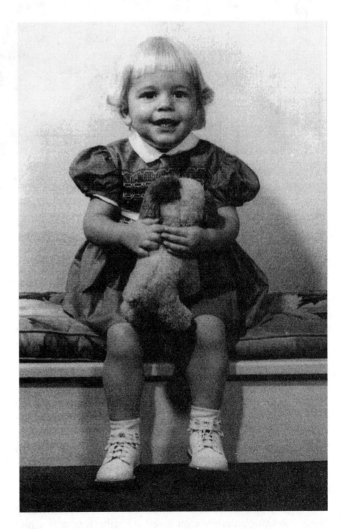

At about twelve or eighteen months.

"With my mother and father, younger sister Karen, and baby brother Mike," about 1963.

flowers and Vin Scully announcing the World Series (the Dodgers were *always* in the World Series in those days), getting stung on the foot by a bee, taking tap and ballet, wearing a black tutu and a tinsel crown, watching the "Wonderful World of Color," not liking green beans, wishing I was a horse (specifically a white Lipizzaner), trick-or-treating (you could do that even at strangers' houses in those days), pounding on my sister, hating it when my father travelled, flying to my grandmother's back in Kansas City (this because we could all fly free on TWA), a million things. My world was rich. The details meant everything—the rag rug my mother had bought in the Ozarks and stitched together to cover the entire living-room floor, the corrugated fiberglass that roofed and shaded the driveway, the shadow my door threw against the wall as my parents sat in the kitchen and talked after we were in bed.

A life is made up of this kind of thing, smells and textures, processes and rituals. I remember once hearing one of my professors read a poem that included something like, "So much depends on a red wheelbarrow and white chickens." He stopped after he read that and looked at us like he expected to see some evidence that we'd understood the significance of this. But I didn't get it then. I should have. I was a photographer, a young one who thought shooting weeds against parts of wooden wagon wheels was an achievement of artistic depth. But now I do understand, because I have felt the jogging of my heart, that deep hook that small things put in you to fix you to earth. The house in LA is not ours anymore. The door may still throw that shadow, but my bunk bed is not there, nor are my parents' quiet voices. That moment is gone unless I remember it, or write it, or make somebody remember one of their own.

Our mortality is a fact, but it is also the richness of our meaning that this ephemeral moment, by its very nature, is so profoundly precious.

I can also remember reading *Our Town* in high school in New York, reading Emily's cry—"Doesn't anybody realize life, every every minute?"—and taking it very much to heart. My life meant something to me, and I didn't want it to end up having been consumed the way a dog will swallow a fine steak—without even tasting it—so I deliberately set myself to *see* everything and *feel* every-thing, to be completely, thoroughly *aware* of my life.

It didn't work. Turns out, it's really difficult to be both observer and participant—kind of like having to get from one place to another, but focusing on the placement of each foot—you end up missing the view, and you tend to trip a lot. So I gave it up. But once in a while, there are these moments of epiphany, when I suddenly know what I have and how wonderful it all is. These moments only last until life intrudes on them, which you can count on to be inevitable and usually instantaneous.

I didn't think about any of this as I cut out black construction-paper cats for our windows at Halloween, or played tetherball, or made myself into the Black Stallion. I just lived it, and now I remember.

I will say that school was a tremendous interruption in the important business of my life. I still remember the awful feeling of abandonment I suffered when my mother dropped me off at the "nursery" during kindergarten orientation; I was one of those obnoxious kids who howl their heads off until their mothers finally come and get them. And that was only the beginning.

Don't get me wrong—there were nice moments here and there, making miniature bread for the miniature bakery, having the room mothers bring cup cakes, reading comics inside when it rained during recess. I do remember Mrs. Reece very dimly—my kindergarten teacher. During singing time, I was gratified to find that you could move your mouth without making a sound, but still look like you were singing right along. This way, you could get out of having to do what everybody else was having to do, but still have Mrs. Reece beaming down on you with affectionate pride. This was probably not a good thing for me to learn. Also, it didn't make any sense—singing was one of the few things about school I *liked.*

LA schools ran on a semester basis. In second grade, I outperformed my semester group and got bumped up half a year. When I hit fourth grade, my parents got nervous about what would happen to me if we ever moved, the half year lead was so odd. They didn't want me being dropped back in some new town, so they opted for getting me goosed up another semester by working with me over the summer. I ended up being a full year ahead in school. This, I didn't mind.

In fifth grade, I had Mr. Kinernchield, an old navy man. He raised hibiscus, ran the class with military exactness, and could tell us what happened at Pearl Harbor because he'd been there that morning, on shipboard, and had seen the whole thing himself. I stood by his desk once, trying to explain how my soul hated racial prejudice. And twice, he made me cry.

One thing I could never do was spell. Well, I probably *could* have done it, but I just didn't care. Spelling held no charm for me; you had to practice it. I didn't even practice piano, and music was something I did love. One time, I actually wrote the spelling words out ten times each the night before the test. That test I passed. This should have been a good lesson for me. But it didn't take.

The worst thing about school was walking there. I had two blocks to go, a darned weary long way. In the best of times, as I walked away I could feel my heart reaching back towards home, both of its scrawny little arms stretched out to my vanishing Mom. In the worst of times, there were dogs.

Once, when I was about five years old and visiting my Kansas City grandmother, I made friends with the collie next door. She was a graceful sable dog who looked remarkably like Lassie. One afternoon, she was lying on the grass in her front yard. With a great deal of pleasure, I went out to greet her—but a male chow chow dog, who had gotten to her first, made it clear to me that he resented the intrusion.

It was the first time I'd ever seen a mouth of teeth like that—just about at my eye level—and the language he used was terrible. I went home. I ran home. I ran home screaming. After that experience, I developed a reluctance to socialize with dogs.

All it would take was a stray puppy, minding his own business, innocently and disinterestedly sniffing his way along on the far side of the street, to give me the terrors. "Please," I would pray, "please don't let that dog even *notice* me." And most of the time, they didn't. But I'd stiffen up, walking wooden-legged, hugging my notebook, sure that dog was going to double back and get me from behind. This was, perhaps, my own arrogance, to think every dog's universe would eventually center on me. I feel that same fear now whenever I read the newspaper.

But it's not school I think of when I try to remember being a kid—it's family stuff. Camping. Visiting Mother Jean in Kansas City. Flying places. Christmas—which meant putting up our plastic tree and getting out the

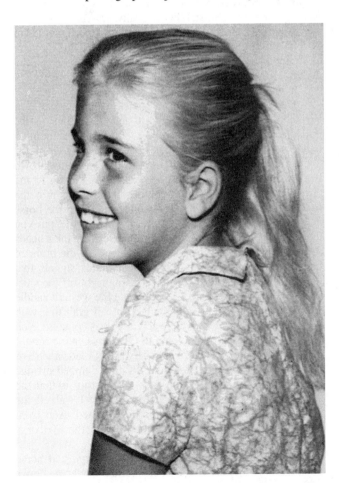

"Me with ponytail," 1960.

slowly disintegrating boxes that held our collection of ornaments. Halloween, which meant putting the paper cats and pumpkins in the windows and choosing the costumes my long-suffering mother would then labor to make. Custard and Toll House cookies. And yards. And books. And the stories we acted out.

My worst times—beside the intrusion of dogs and siblings—were the times Dad was gone on business. He was in charge of building new terminals for TWA, and he spent a lot of time in Phoenix or Paris or Cairo. The names of these places were very familiar to us. The absence of my father never was. When he was gone, life really shouldn't have been all that different—my mom, a tremendously capable and fun person, kept things running perfectly, and school would always grind its dull way along. But without my dad, nothing had any color, as if the flavors and smells of the world were on hold until he came back.

My parents went to Europe when I was about ten. They could do this because my grandmother was living with us, and again, things should have been able to proceed almost normally. But it was awful. Life was completely drained of meaning. When they went to Egypt, two years later, it was worse.

I wanted the family to hold still. It was very important for me to be able to take everything important for granted. When my dad surprised me by coming home a day early, just so he wouldn't miss my twelfth birthday, it was the first time I had been so happy that I wept. I never got used to his absences. And I never had a clue how unusually wealthy in love and stability I really was.

The truth is, I was dissatisfied with my life; I wanted to be a horse. Short of that, I wanted to own one. But we were city people, and that was out of the question. Then, on my eighth birthday, my mom gave me a riding lesson.

It was incredible.

There was a stable right smack in the middle of Westchester, a little island of dirt and horse-flies in the midst of all that concrete scab. I don't even remember being nervous—I guess I didn't even know *that* much about the reality of horses. They brought me this brown beast that was big as a house—beautiful as heaven to me but a little daunting. And then they got me up into the saddle. This was fine. This was wonderful. Then the horse moved. Cars don't move like that; cars just sort of put you in motion. Horses shift their weight. Horses turn their heads and lift their feet and drop their shoulders. To the brain of the uninitiated, this kind of movement sends signals that feel very much like the saddle is slipping right off the side.

This is when I learned to appreciate the western saddle with its lovely, practical pommel. You can grab this with both hands, so that if the saddle actually does come off, you will at least have a good hold on it. Of course, at the time, I didn't know how fortunate I was—I was not made aware of the vagaries of the English saddle till I got dumped off one in Kentucky, years later. The end of this story is that the saddle did *not* slide off, and neither did I. I walked the horse around the paddock. Maybe even trotted. And from then on, I was able to regard horses with the eye of a seasoned professional.

It was in LA that I discovered the library. And horse books. I think there must have been quite a few horse books in those days—or else, the Westchester Public Library had a horse section. *The Black Stallion* was heart stuff to me. I

High school graduation picture, 1969.

read *The Black Stallion and Flame* lying in my top bunk at bedtime; there was a plane crash that was so real, my hands were damp as I read it. I remember surfacing and being amazed to find myself in bed at home, and then being amazed that just words could have made the thing seem so real.

My dad used to read to us at night—stories, books, poetry. He read *The Christmas Carol* out loud every Christmas, the exquisiteness of Dickens's language couched in my father's expressive voice made an impression on my soul that lasts to this day. When I read it to my own children—which I do every Christmas—I find myself reproducing the lilt and savor of his delivery.

I'm not sure that I remember the actual process of learning to read, but I do remember being in the car and looking up at what was probably a gas station sign way up against the sky—I knew the letters on that sign meant something and that my parents knew what they meant; but I couldn't understand them, and that was utterly unacceptable to me. So I learned.

My father's private reading was science fiction, my mother's historical nonfiction. When I think of the things that characterize my family—music, church, traditions, camping—reading is high on the list. I learned to travel with it when I was very young, and I have been thousands of places through it since, feeling very real joys and sorrows that were not my own. I love books; I love the feel of them in my hand, I love the way they look, lined up on shelves and piled in corners. When I was in college, I figured out the best way to make a student apartment look like a real home was to fill the walls with shelves of books.

Another thing I loved about LA was the beach. We didn't go very often; we lived too far away. When we did go, I learned a healthy respect for jellyfish and an absolute terror of sharks—which you just knew were always lurking around in the surf somewhere. We'd go there for church parties sometimes, and we'd always have watermelon. When you're a kid with a big piece of watermelon, the juice runs down your arms and your legs. This is never pleasant. But at the beach, sand sticks to every single smear of juice. For a long time, the word "watermelon" meant "sand all over your body, including under the elastic of your bathing suit", but this was only by association.

One night I dreamed that I was standing in my backyard, watching this tremendous tidal wave as it towered, curling, hundreds of feet above the roof of my Nana's bedroom. This used to worry me sometimes at night, but not as much as the thought that scary things could come up between the bed and the wall while I was sleeping. I learned to sleep under the covers the way seals stay under ice—you make yourself this nice little breathing hole and you're fine.

Another night, on the way home from the open swim at the YMCA, my dad and my sister and I saw this incredibly huge hot-air balloon—it was way off, maybe a mile or so away, glowing and round, translucently white against the almost absolutely dark night. It was magnificent. We decided we had to get a closer look. We drove towards it for what seemed like hours, but we never seemed to get any closer, and it never got any bigger. We all began to feel very odd. Finally, the big white balloon seemed to be rising in the air—the top of it was still bright, but the bottom had become shadowed. That didn't seem right; if there had been floodlights on it, it would have been lit the other way around.

Finally we realized it was the moon. But I had never seen the moon like that before, too huge, too real, and it frightened me. Daddy drove us home. We all told my mom about the adventure, laughing—because it really was funny, the three of us trying to drive to the moon. But inside, I was still frightened. Later, watching the Flintstones with Nana in her bedroom, I had to keep going outside, alone in the dark, to check on that moon as it loomed above our neighborhood, just to make certain it wasn't getting any closer.

I've never seen the moon like that since, a moon that could fool my father into chasing it.

Childhood is at the heart of magic; things happen to us. We don't understand them. We can't duplicate them. We can't control anything. Sometimes the magic is beautiful. But sometimes it's horrifying. Depends on our adults. Our stars. Sometimes on our own choices—but the choices a child makes are based on such limited understanding.

Children see things an adult will see through. A child absorbs. My father's mother lived in the house his father had built when my dad, himself, was a boy. My own family was destined to move several times, packing up the stuff of our lives and then unpacking it again, to put it against different walls in different spaces. But my grandmother's house was always the same. The chairs she had in 1940, she still had in 1970—same chairs, same places in the room. She had Persian throw rugs on her hardwood floors. She had hardwood treads on the stairs, and the very bottom one curved out at the bottom; there she kept a glass globe in which grew a floating ivy.

These things never changed, never lost their old strangeness, either. These things were leftover from a different time, and we'd had nothing like them in any of our houses. The snow globe she used to keep my aunt's bedroom door from swinging shut, the little glass dogs on the shelf at the top of the stairs, the deer head in the basement—I saw everything. I could walk you through every one of those rooms right now—I could recreate the detail, the smell, the *feeling* of everything. That sameness was the stuff that held the universe together.

I hold inside myself those details the way you would cup something precious and fragile in your hands; they are long gone now, but the place they made inside me will never be gone. I like to fill my house with odd little things, things that have a kind of personality of their own, so that the children who come here will have something to look at and to carry away inside them.

We create the world this way—each person his own world. If a person has the terrible misfortune to grow up with sad or angry or entirely selfish adults, it's hard to create a world that is different from that. It's not impossible, though. Strange to think that every man carries his own universe with him, made up of the things he has chosen to hold. I sometimes wonder if every person sees exactly the same colors; would my red seem red to me if I saw it through your eyes? But our differences are deeper than that; what does love mean to you? Is it something safe? Something desperate? Something threatening? Does it mean possession? Gratitude? Service? Or maybe, being served?

And yet, we all experience color in some way, and in that, we are the same. And ultimately, the universe we live in is a fact.

It was when we lived in LA that we joined the Latter-Day Saints (LDS) church. It is not at all cool at this particular period in our culture (from the 1960s through the early '90s anyway) to talk about religion. Somehow, thinking people are not supposed to have any. In the media (visual and print—and music), religious characters are almost all fanatic, over-the-top, heartless, self-righteous idiots—or they're just too sweet and naive to have any sense at all. Or they just sort of abrogate the responsibility of thinking and choosing and say everything must be God's will.

I resent these stereotypes.

For one thing, there are now a multitude of sociological studies that demonstrate an unquestionable relationship between the good old practice of church-going and good health, both physical and mental. For another thing, the happiest, most reasonable, satisfied people I have ever known had deep, calm religious convictions that they allowed to direct their lives.

My parents are among this group. They didn't choose the most comfortable way, or the most self-satisfying. They chose what they felt was right, and then were true to it. And because of that, my brother and sister and I had good lives.

I believe in right and wrong. I believe there is Truth, and that it exists outside of our understanding or perception. Truth is truth no matter how you wish it might be

The Randle family: the author with her husband and four children, about 1993.

otherwise. If a man jumps out of an airplane, he's going to hit the ground hard—no matter how hard he whines about how unfair it is on the way down.

I was eleven when TWA moved us back to Kansas City. This is where Mother Jean lived, and my father's only sister's family. This is where I learned about thunderstorms and snow and tornadoes. This is also where I was when the Beatles hit the United States and when President Kennedy was shot. My sixth grade horror was the thought that someday the kids were going to find out I was a year younger than they were. They found out. No one cared. My sixth grade triumph was having the Best Handwriting; my embarrassment, the day the teacher found out I had no clue how to spell "busy."

Seventh grade was the best year I ever spent in school. Park Hill Junior High. New community, new school, young teachers, everything was exciting. Mr. Mack, the band leader, let me play flute. And I was good. And the band was good. We were incredibly good, in fact. I was in the pep squad. I lettered that year.

My dad built us this great house; we had a huge stone fireplace and a gray and white cat with murder in his heart. I finally had my own room. And I had friends.

Then we moved again.

This time, TWA moved us to New York. The distance between Kansas City and New York is roughly the same as the distance between Venus and Alpha Centauri. Culture shock. I know what that means. And we didn't even live in the city—we lived in Hartsdale, half an hour out of the city by train.

The house my parents bought was incredible—it was a gray Cape Cod on about three-quarters of an acre, all wooded. The lot bordered a huge, wooded estate—the mansion was a mile up the road, and you couldn't even see it through the gates, there were so many trees. Across the street was a state park—all New England woods. We had raccoons in the garbage, rescued wild rabbits from the new cats, surprised pheasants in the backyard, and slapped mosquitoes by the dozens.

It was very beautiful.

But I did not have my own room.

And the school was entirely different. The building was old. The programs were tired. The band stank. The kids were different—they *looked* different; girls in New York dressed the way only *that* kind of girl dressed in Kansas City. The boys wore boots with markedly pointed toes—there was a name for those boots; it was not politically correct. Language tended to be more ... colorful. I was seriously confused. How were you supposed to understand which people were like you inside when nobody looks like you outside? Eventually, I worked it out. But in the beginning, I didn't believe I would.

The first year was ugly. The kids at my bus stop decided my sister and I were geeks and so were legitimate targets. Not that they were violent—it was in the threatening looks, the sly little comments, the freeze-out that they did us in. Thinly veiled contempt is a powerful weapon. It made me sick inside. Every morning, I was nauseated. In my mother's place, as I think about it now, I would have driven my daughters to school, circumventing that part of the situation. This is not the conventional wisdom; adults have somehow decided that relieving a child's suffering is detrimental to the character. I don't subscribe to this. Sure, there are some experiences kids have to go through—but hell isn't one of them. The philosophy that sends children off to face a bully alone has to be testosterone based—just like war.

Anyway, these kids at my stop were all ninth graders and popular at my school. Angela Rocca (not her real name, but close enough) was the ring leader, and her crowning gesture was to rise up out of her bus seat one day as we were getting off, and hit my sister on the head with a homemade wooden sculpture. That cut it for me—my sister was crying, and there was not a thing I could do about it. I hadn't been raised to fight—I *had* been raised with this Christian obligation to forgive all men, etc., etc. What I learned that day was impotent fury. I was in no mood to forgive. What I wanted was a plague of warts for Rocca's fat, self-satisfied face. I wanted to pound her.

Her friends at school enjoyed the game too. Must have had all the thrills of sheep-baiting. They'd come up to me in the hall and say things, things that weren't even threatening or insulting—the point is, they weren't talking *to* me, they were performing for everybody else, using me as the prop. I can remember walking down the hall, desperately hoping not to be noticed. I had always sympathized with hunted animals; now I was one of them.

None of those kids knew me. None of them *cared* if they knew me. They didn't know how worth it I was. I used to sit in the bus, feeling magnificent things inside of myself—the wild color of fireworks, the dignity of Egyptian cats, the power of stallions—they didn't know these things; they never would bother to find out. It wasn't fair. I told myself it was their loss, but that didn't change the fact that I was the one who was hurting.

One night, I had this dream; I was in an elevator. The doors opened, and all those people, all those people who all belonged together, they were throwing me a party. "It was just a joke," they told me. "Really, we like you."

A person of reasonable maturity looks at this situation and sees the damage tormentors do to themselves, to their own lives. To see from this perspective is to approach forgiveness. But the climb to that position can be very hard.

Eventually, they tired of the game. The next year, they moved on to the high school. Meanwhile, I had made my own friends, people in my own class. Ninth grade was a different world, except that the band still stank and the school was still—less than exciting. The one class I loved was algebra. When we took the statewide Regent's Exam at the end of the year, it turned out I was one of two people with a perfect score. This is the only time in my life anything like that has ever happened to me. It left me with

the impression that I must be smart. In later years, I remembered myself as a straight-A student in math. This was a lie. I had a shaky B in class. So where did this brilliant flash of genius come from? I wish I knew.

Our little junior high fed into Woodlands High, a very large school built on land bequeathed it by a rich family. It was back in the woods, and there were four buildings, one for the shops and auditorium, one for the offices, lunchroom and library, one for classrooms, and one for the gyms. This transition was not so big a deal—all my friends were still with me. And there were going to be new cute boys. Never underestimate the importance of new cute boys.

Those weren't bad years. When I was a sophomore, my parents gave me a trip to Paris. If I tell you that we used to fly to Chicago to get our dental work done, you'd be impressed, right? If I explained that we flew free on TWA, and that my uncle, the dentist, lived in Chicago, you might not be so impressed. The Paris trip was along these lines; I flew free. I stayed with a family friend who happened to be living in Paris.

One of my friends from church went with me. Her you can be impressed with—she paid for the trip. We flew over with my father, who made sure that we were safely delivered to our friends in Garches, a suburb of Paris. The next day, my dad showed us how to find the train, how to buy tickets, and how to use the Metro. My first view of Paris as we came up from the Metro station was the headquarters of *France-Soir*, the Parisian equivalent of the *New York Times*. The place was in an incredibly old, dignified building (*everything* in Paris is in an incredibly old building) surrounded by a wrought-iron fence that had been plated with gold. The sun was flashing off that fence so that all we could see was glory.

That night, my father flew back to the United States. For the rest of the week, Kristin and I were left to ourselves. Every morning, we ate croissants in the tall, narrow house in Garches, and then set out to buy tickets for the city—I had just enough French for that. We rode the train into Gare St. Lazare, and then we just explored the city. Just the thought of my own fourteen-year-old daughter wandering around Paris with no clue gives me the horrors. I think my parents were absolutely nuts. But I had a great time. Saw some great architecture, beautiful paintings, interesting people. And we were home by dark, every night. Amazing.

By the end of my junior year, I was a person. I had played one of the ladies-in-waiting in *Once Upon a Mattress* at school. It was a lot of fun. And the show was good—I know it was because one of my family's friends from church was a bona fide Broadway star, and she saw it and *said* it was good. We rented costumes from Eve's of New York, just like the big boys do, and our leads were incredible. That year, the same friend took me into New York to audition for an agent. This was terrifying, to stand in the man's office and sing "My Favorite Things" from *Sound of Music* in entirely the wrong key because my accompanist was even more nervous than I was and forgot to transpose.

That year we had a race riot. In this school, there were kids of all kinds, all races, all socio-economic groups—race and economics did not necessarily correlate. About the

"The back of our house in the fall," Provo, Utah.

middle of that year, there were some sleaze-bag white boys who decided it would be tremendously funny to write Black Power all over the walls of the school with permanent markers.

The school was repainted.

But what's more tempting than a perfectly white wall?

We were in the middle of play rehearsals at this time. The night we were supposed to open was the night Martin Luther King was assassinated. The run was postponed. That weekend, someone snuck onto the school grounds and wrote obscenities about our black cheerleaders all over the outside of the school with spray paint. Kids from the Key Club found the mess and did the best they could to obliterate the words.

But Sunday night, the creeps came back. New words were all over the school. I didn't know any of this when I got off the bus that morning. But the air was electric. Nobody was talking. Silence in the buses—you can imagine how unnerving that was. The story came out as we made our way through the buildings to our lockers—bits of it in whispers. The halls were virtually silent.

Before a thunderstorm the air becomes stretched taut. Potential energy plays on the back of your neck and through your nerves, and you know something violent is about to happen.

When I got to my locker, there were two young black girls leaning against it, talking quietly. I stood there, and then I said—*very* politely—"Excuse me?" One of them turned on me a look of utter hate and spat, "Bitch."

I'd heard the word often enough. But it'd never been directed toward me. Certainly not by a person I'd never seen before.

The day went on.

There was a very odd, lonely girl nobody knew but everybody knew of. I passed her in the hall every day, recognizing that hunted look she wore, but I'd never seen her anyplace else. She was remarkable for wearing bright red lipstick in a white-lipped world. She dressed like Audrey Hepburn when the rest of us were wearing flowered miniskirts and poorboy sweaters. I'd never heard

anybody say a mean word to her, but that day somebody set fire to her hair as she walked down the hall.

One of my good friends nearly had his back broken when he tried to defend one of his white friends at lunch.

And the day went on.

After lunch, we were in PE, doing a folk-dance unit upstairs in the gym building. This particular building had been built at the bottom of the campus, tucked in at the foot of the hill. Only the wrestling gym, upstairs, was on a level with the rest of campus. From its windows, we could see across the quad—a wide, square lawn bordered by three of the buildings—and down to the rocky ground around the foundations. The hill had been sheared off to accommodate the building, and the sloping lawn of the quad ended here abruptly in a ten-foot drop over a cement retaining wall.

About halfway through the class, we heard shouting. We looked out the windows and saw crowds of people running out onto the quad from every direction. We all stood in front of the window, disbelieving, as what seemed like hundreds of angry kids converged, all chasing two white boys.

The boys ran our way. They were, of course, the two who had been doing the vandalism. They got to the end of the lawn and jumped down that ten-foot drop onto the rocky ground below. The crowd surged to the edge, yelling and screaming. It was mostly dark faces. The two boys cowered below them—nowhere to go.

A couple of kids dropped down over the wall and picked up rocks.

We were horrified, plastered against the window. I looked down at those two boys, knowing that they'd legitimately brought this on themselves. But that didn't mean I wanted to see them stoned to death.

Then Mr. Camonson and Mr. Leviaton came running through the crowd. These two were everybody's teachers-of-choice, and it was a good thing they'd made themselves so beloved—I believe they were the only thing that stood in the way of murder that day.

Mr. Leviaton turned to face the angry mob, raising his arms and they, still seething, fell back. He talked. We didn't hear any of it through the glass, but what he said must have made sense; the crowd began to thin. And then it wasn't there anymore.

Without a word, our entire PE class dismissed itself. We headed down to the lockers and changed in desperate silence. I had never really seen the difference between the darker faces and my own. But now, I was scared. There was suddenly a *them*. In that crucial moment, the girl a couple of lockers down, a tall, big girl with a very dark face, looked at me and said, "I'm not staying in this school another minute. This is horrible." The *them* shifted, and I heartily agreed with her.

My friend Rebecca and I took off. Intelligently, we left school the back way, taking a little trail through the woods. Halfway home, we heard people running up behind us. We spun around, hearts pounding, and were passed up by two small freshmen boys—also with dark faces—who looked back at us and yelled, "We're not staying *there*."

That afternoon, my mom took me to Mount Vernon to buy my first mess of makeup. It should have been exciting. But fear is a hard thing to get past.

The next day, things had settled down. Some of the seniors had stayed late to scrape the paint off the walls of the school. And the next weekend, we put on the play.

But something had happened to us. Something lucky American kids can go lifetimes without seeing—the raw horror of mob action. We live so politely, you could almost pretend that our culture was past it. Until you read the paper.

I didn't blame that crowd for their anger. I understood more of it than you might think. I shared it, even. Maybe it was only fate that I was behind the window instead of out on the quad. Or maybe I would refuse to go so far. I hope I never have to know. What I saw that day, I hope I never see again. Once is more than enough for a lifetime.

This happened, by the way, in the sixties. It was an interesting time, a strangely desperate time, more than a little romanticized now. No one exaggerates the almost frantic energy of those years, but people seem to forget that there were some very dark things that went on, terrible things, in fact. In the name of love and selflessness, a lot of selfishness became counter-institutionalized, the consequences of which would ruin generations to come. But there were good things, too, things that have lasted—civil rights awareness, a lower voting age. One of the things that didn't last was my pair of purple, herringbone, hip-hugger bell-bottoms.

I took up guitar then. That was a very good thing. My mom took me into the city, and we, like, did the secret knock on the back door of some warehouse and asked for Manny and got a great price on a beautiful, nylon-string folk guitar. I still have the guitar. And I can still play "Blackbird."

My junior year, Mr. Sala bullied me into playing flute in the high school band. This was also a very good thing. I fell in love with Pete Zambriski, who played the French horn, and Steve Solomon, the second clarinet, both of whom were seniors, and both of whom I tended to peek at over the rim of my music stand during long rests. Neither of them did I ever so much as talk to, all year. But at the end of the year, when I finally got the courage up to ask them to sign my yearbook, it turned out they knew who *I* was.

That year, I took trig. And who should I find sitting beside me but Angela Rocca. I had no trouble with the trig. Angela didn't get it. You can't believe how nice she was to me. It was as though she didn't recognize me, or else, she'd forgotten all about ninth grade. The funny thing was, that's the way I acted too, as if I didn't remember. But I did remember; I remembered very clearly. I'd sit there, explaining the math to her, all the time thinking inside, "I'm doing this because I'm nice. Because I'm a nice person. Same person I was back then, but you didn't *care* back then. I don't *have* to be nice, but I amIamIam." Really, though, I'm not usually that conciliatory—ask my sister. At least that one time in my life, I was a good girl.

I ran for senior class vice president at the end of that year. I didn't win, but I had a great time, and I finally felt

The side yard in winter.

Kristen's daughter Ginna in her grandmother's flapper dress.

like I knew a lot of people, that I belonged there. I loved our house, I loved our wooded yard—and the way the snow turned the trees of our street into something that looked like the towering arches of a Catholic cathedral. I loved to walk down to the train station and meet my dad when he came home from work. I loved the people at church. I turned sixteen, got my driver's license, and was ready for somebody wonderful to take me out on a date. Hartsdale was home for me, at last.

Then we moved again.

My dad, who had felt about his boss at TWA the same way I'd felt about Angela Rocca, had just been made Director of Advanced Planning for TWA. It was a Twinkie position—ninety percent air and poised for self-destruct. Then came an offer for him to be assistant to the director of the building of the Dallas/Fort Worth Regional/International Airport. It was an incredible offer—more than twice the money, plenty of prestige. All we had to do was move to Texas.

So we did. My folks flew out there and found a house, while my sister and brother and I spent our last summer in New York. For some reason, I didn't mind the idea of moving—maybe because my dad kept telling me about the Texas kids—"They're going to say, 'Who's that *girl* from New York?'" It sounded like an adventure. It also sounded like something my dad really needed.

By the second week in September, we were living in the new house in Arlington. We beat the movers by a week, had no clothes, no furniture. My mom got me a couple of interim things and registered me at Arlington High. This was another interplanetary move. The kids in Texas were all huge—robust and range-fed, kind of like the state. The girls were still wearing their hair way piled up and beehived, something that had died a very natural and timely death in New York at least a year before. Otherwise, however, it was not the sixties in Texas.

People talk about how distant and cold people are in New England, and about southern hospitality. It had taken some time to get through the initial chill in New York, but once you were there, you were there. In Texas, everybody was friendly enough right off the bat, but it was a sort of arm's-length warmth that masked a different kind of distance. The first day, I sat by myself in the cafeteria—the only person at a very long table—trying to choke down a dry hamburger. It was a rotten feeling.

A week after we'd moved, a policeman showed up at our house to explain that my New York driver's license was no good in Texas, that nobody in Texas could drive until they were eighteen unless they'd had driver's ed (an innovative program back then). Fine. Except that we'd moved in a week too late for me to take driver's ed. At this point, being a year younger than everybody else finally had its disadvantages. I was a senior in high school, doomed to ride the bus. I did it for about a week—I sat on that bus for the entire forty-five minutes it took to drop off the high school kids, and then I sat there while the junior high loaded *on*. Then I rode with screaming junior high kids for another half an hour before I finally got close enough to home to get off. The indignity was insufferable.

So I refused to ride it. I figured, I'd given up my entire life for my father's sake, the least my parents could do was give me a lift home.

The only thing that really came out of that year was photography. That I learned; that I loved. The rest of the year was pretty much a waste. I was too much of a coward to try out for the band (people in Texas take bands and football very seriously—like, you practically have to have a union card to be allowed to march). Very few people were interested in integrating me into their lives. Even the fact that my dad was making more money didn't do much for me—my parents were too used to being thrifty to cut loose at this point. I couldn't drive myself anywhere; I had no friends to drive me. There were about thirty Mormons in the entire state, so I didn't have any friends at church, either. I did have my own room. I probably spent way too much time in it, playing the guitar and knowing nobody in the world understood me.

I did fall in love with Donald, a boy on the photo staff who was the definition of cute, and with two of his friends. They patted me on the head and took me places once in a while, but never did take me seriously. Story of my life.

I worked at Six Flags over Texas that summer, in the photo shop. It was a lot of fun, and it was definitely something to do. But that's about all there is to say about that.

It was kind of a weird, empty way of ending my childhood. It wasn't till the week before I was supposed to leave for Brigham Young University in Provo, Utah, that I realized I was actually leaving home. I'd hated it when Dad was gone; now, I was the one leaving. And I think I must have had some inkling that life would never be the same again. And it never has been.

I went to college. I did plays. I had friends. I learned to take care of my own clothes, and my own bathroom, and my own apartment. I took a lot of pictures, wrote a lot of poetry, went to LA with my friends, and fell in love with anonymous dubleted young men at the Renaissance Faire. I learned to do stained glass, to sew just about anything, and finally—to cook. The summer of my freshman year, I was finally old enough to get a driver's license.

The first two summers, I went home and worked at Six Flags. I didn't belong there anymore. My family loved me—well, my parents did, can't speak for the kids—but I had no function in their lives, no business. Not even a room; my mother gave it to my brother after my sophomore year. One year, I came home for Christmas and was told that we were not going to wait till Christmas morning for presents as we had every other Christmas of my life. This tossing of tradition was ostensibly due to the fact that my twelve-year-old brother just couldn't bear waiting the night out. I couldn't believe they would do such a thing; it was bad enough being half a stranger at home. But for them to make the family a stranger to *me* was completely unconscionable. So I pitched a fit. And Michael lost.

But really, I was fighting a losing battle. My parents still live in that house, twenty-five years later. What I remember as home has everything to do with who they were before Texas. But home to my brother and sister is everything since then. I don't belong in Texas, but my parents don't belong anywhere else. I find this very strange.

I had outgrown my family culture. I would always be welcome there, always be a member—but the culture had gone on without me, evolving into something in which I could no longer be fully participant. At the same time, I had become a culture of one. Not that I didn't have friends— because I did, lots of them. And I had our religion, which has a very strong, wide-reaching cultural aspect. But there was no specific place or person who was home for me, no intimate, dependable, shared context.

I suppose this kind of disenfranchisement is part of the maturing process. In its toils, you can do a lot of self-defining, intrapersonal dialogue, inscape mapping. And all of this is essential to the emerging adult. But the pain of it can be awful.

So, after I turned twenty, I started thinking a lot about getting married. I had really not been raised to be a wife and mother; I'd been told to find a career, to work hard, to be intelligent and make solid choices. My dad kind of went overboard on this, maybe—as he left me at the Y, his last admonishment was "I brought you here to get an education, not to get married."

Then again, maybe they had a sneaking suspicion that volatility, stubbornness, and imagination weren't ideal qualifications for most men's concept of wifehood. If that's what they were thinking, they were right. The guys who were interesting to me weren't interested *in* me. On the other hand, the men who *were* interested were boring. Or scary. I had dreams about being married, and I woke up from all of them with claustrophobia and a deep sense of doom. I used to walk around campus playing this little game with myself—I'd look at every man and say "yes," or "no." Five hundred no's for every hopeless yes. None of my friends were marriage material—too young. And too silly.

Meanwhile, I graduated. I had spent my last two summers as a darkroom lab tech for Six Flags' public relations department. But I didn't want to go back to that— mostly because it was in Texas; also because it was minimum wage work. I had a B.A. I figured it was time to start that career. The question was, doing what? I'd earned a teaching certificate, but I was so sick of school, I swore I'd never set foot in one again. About this time, I began thinking I should have majored in accounting and computers; I'm *good* at accounting and computers. But I'd settled for the artsy, and now I had no idea what I was going to *do* for the rest of my life.

The first job I held after graduation, I'd wrangled out of a local photographer with great, creative plans in mind. But what he wanted was a receptionist. I didn't want to be a receptionist. And I didn't want to pitch his work to people, because it turned out he really wasn't any good. On any level. So I left.

I tried retail, working as a clerk at the new mall. Not exactly a career. And not for me. Then I wrangled a job with a really good dentist, the very man who had jerked out my wisdom teeth the year before. Dentistry I should have had in my blood, courtesy of my uncle. But dentistry and dental receptionistry are two different things, neither of which turned out to be me.

At some point in here, I started writing. The stories were pretty terrible—fairy-tale melodrama. I'd sit for hours at my old, clunky typewriter, mildly annoyed at my roommates when they trooped through and shattered the mood. I did this until one afternoon when I realized that you couldn't write about life and live it at the same time. And that I missed the living part. Also, about that same time, I went to this huge bookstore in Salt Lake City; it has catacombs full of used books. I walked through those high-ceilinged, musty halls and looked at all those millions of books. I couldn't help but wonder what I thought I could add to that. So I went home and packed the typewriter away.

I know what limbo means.

I finally went knocking on God's door for advice; I just didn't know where else to turn. Not that I expected God to speak to me. God doesn't speak to me. At least, I don't think he does; with God, who can tell? But I was

"Baby Murphy with my mom."

The author's nieces and nephews in Colorado.

thinking maybe he would sharpen my vision, or my thinking—that maybe some doors might open. And all those things happened, probably because I was finally miserable enough to be willing to listen.

The end of all this was that I went back to grad school and took a teaching assistantship. And that was the beginning.

I loved the teaching. I *loved* it. And I learned to be happy by myself. I toyed with poetry and found that it left me cold. I ran into one of the girls I'd student taught, Kira Pratt. We took Beowulf together (she was a sophomore and I was a grad student—*she* was smart) and creative writing and Old English. She was a magical person, daughter and sister of harp makers, she played an Irish troubadour harp. She sang and danced in the Sundance Review. She wrote poetry. She painted. She had more love of life than any person I had ever known.

We whiled away one summer, running up into the canyons a couple of nights a week. We'd throw a couple of sleeping bags into the backseat of my blue Volkswagen bug, stuff in her harp and my flute and recorders, maybe remember some food (one night, all we had for dinner was a bag of marshmallows). I'd pick her up after the show—usually quite late—and we'd head up into the mountains to find a good camping place. There, in the deep dark of the mountain woods, we'd get out our instruments and make our music. The morning after the first time we did this—having chosen what we'd thought was a fairly deserted Utah State Park camping area, we woke up at dawn to find that we were surrounded by people's tents. It had been so

late and so dark the night before, we hadn't seen the tents. But all that night, nobody had complained.

Years later, Kira would go to a young woman's first Irish harp recital. In the course of the conversation afterwards, it would come out that this young woman had heard two girls in the mountains, all those years before, and had loved the music so much, she'd finally taken up the harp herself.

It was a very good summer. I was having a great time with Kira, a great time at church, a great time with other good friends. That fall, my sister started school at the Y. I made up a new game—this one was based on the time-honored formula, "If only I (fill in the blank), I'd be happy." The game was trying to find something to fill in the blank—but I couldn't do it; I was already happy.

It was then, when I didn't need anything else, that I met Guy.

Guy was incredible—he was too independent to need me. He was bright enough to challenge me. He was too strong for me to ride over him. His life had been different enough from mine that he brought new things to me, but enough like mine that we shared an essential value system. And he was dang cute. What's more, he liked things about me—he liked the way I looked, the way I thought, the way I talked about things. He wasn't scared of a challenge. He enjoyed independence. We danced around each other for about two years, and then we decided to marry.

People who say that kids have no self-control, who say it's useless to try and teach them to be chaste, must have a real dim view of human nature. I know an awful lot of intelligent, artistic, fun people who all waited for love as long as we did, and who now have solid longtime marriages. Makes me sad when people have so little faith in kids.

So, we built a house on the river, added a recording studio (our means of support), and had a baby. That's when I gave up teaching and took up editing, working for a local publisher. I wasn't a bad editor—except I couldn't spell. But editing wasn't right. I ended up having to rewrite a book for the publisher, and in the course of doing that, I realized that writing my own book would be a piece of cake. In fact, writing something of my own would be a tremendous relief. So I did it. And I was published. The publishing part had a lot to do with luck, but it started something.

We had four children, all told. We pooled our family cultures, built traditions, and brought the kids up by hand. I educated them at home (I am still doing that, actually), teaching everything from phonics to calculus. This is the one project I've taken on that turned out to be wildly successful. Motherhood was hard for me at first; I'm not much of a tiny child person. But once the kids started to talk, we could share ideas, and it has been great fun ever since. My oldest two kids started taking some classes at the high school, just for fun, and they're having a great time.

During the last twelve years, I've written and had published five novels and a children's book. All but one of those novels were published by a strong regional publisher. When I finally decided to try a national publisher, I had no idea what a mess it was going to turn out to be. The manuscript I sent out was held at the first publishing house for a year by an editor who kept making encouraging noises, but no commitment. I work without agents, and I was clueless as to protocol, so I sat there and waited and never even called to find out what was going on.

When I finally got up the courage to call, the receptionist informed me that my editor had just quit. What's more, she'd left the day before I called. This was a little disconcerting. The house suggested I send another copy of the manuscript to the new editor, which meant I was going to have to start the process all over again. Meanwhile, I had sent the manuscript to another house.

A couple of weeks later, the first house called to say that my old editor had requested that the manuscript be sent to her new house. This was good, especially since that call also served as a rejection from the first house. The executive editor at the new house called me a week or so later, telling me that she loved the book and wanted it. I was very suspicious. I figured nobody in New York ever said that much nice stuff about *anything,* and that this was actually a callous friend, pulling a rotten joke.

But the call was real. Within hours of that call, I got another from Harper, the *other* house I'd tried, and they wanted it too. This was kind of astonishing. In the end, the editor from house #2 recommended I go with Harper, as they were the larger house and so, better for me. It was very kind of her. Except that between the time Harper spoke and the time they would have sent contracts, Collins bought them and froze their list. The Harper editor told me, "Not to worry—rewrite for me, and I'll get your contract." I spent another year unhappily disemboweling the book to her specs before she called me one day and said, in essence, "Sorry."

If I could give up writing, I would. Like a shot. Achieving a book is just too darned much work. But I don't seem to be able to give it up. I don't even seem to be smart enough to admit defeat. So I put the book back together— my way—and sent it out again, this time to people recommended by the editor from house #2 (which, in the interim, had ceased to publish fiction). This was a multiple submission with a cover letter that told the story in no uncertain terms. The message was *Nobody gets this book without a contract.* And Scholastic took it—which was wonderful because I got to work with Tonya Martin.

Now, I write when I can. When I can't, it's because I'm teaching kids, managing the studio, living life. Then, I quilt. Or I sing. Or I talk to Guy (when we're lucky enough to find ourselves in the same room at the same time). Sometimes we wander happily around the yard in the evening, attended by our airheaded collie, hoping life stays sweet a while longer.

We've lived in this house for eighteen years. I know my neighbors. I've seen their children grow into adults. My

The Randles at their annual Christmas party with a group of their closest friends, 1995.

children know people, have grown up with people—this is a tremendously important, wonderful thing. We are finally home.

I don't really know how to write a biography like this. I believe that some of my life must leak into my stories. There have been times in the history of the world when storytellers were the keepers of the souls of their people. The stories existed to pass along the wisdom, the values, the teachings and the history of the people—stories told for healing, for comfort, for warning. And they were good stories, fun to listen to. Now, a lot of stories are written for money. And many writers seem to feel no responsibility at all for their effect on the souls of their readers.

Maybe they think it would be arrogant of them to assume they have an effect. But the fact is that we all teach whether we will or no—our lives leak into our stories, for good or bad. What makes it worse is that so many of the stories of our time seem to be told more for the benefit of the storyteller—free therapy—and not so much for the sake of the hearers. But any voice that is raised—for whatever reason—will influence, and there will be consequences. Ultimately, we would serve our own selves better if we kept that in mind, and if what we offered ultimately made the world better, or healthier, or less selfish.

If I could offer anybody anything, it would be hope. I know there is happiness, because I've been happy. I know

that things can get better, because they have. I know that homes can be built, because I have helped to build one. If any of this leaks into my storytelling, that's good. Because what I have to give is really the only justification for the presumption of lifting my voice—whether or not I have a story to tell.

Writings

FOR YOUNG ADULTS; FICTION

One Song for Two, Bookcraft, 1984.
The Morning Comes Singing: A Novel, Bookcraft, 1986.
On the Side of Angels, Bookcraft, 1989.
The Only Alien on the Planet, Scholastic, 1995.
Breaking Rank, Morrow, 1999.

FOR CHILDREN

Why Did Grandma Have to Die? A Child's Book about Death (picture book), illustrated by Shauna Mooney, Bookcraft, 1987.

S

SCHRAM, Peninnah 1934-

Personal

Given name is pronounced Pe-*nee*-na; born December 28, 1934, in New London, CT; daughter of Samuel E. (a cantor) and Dora (an entrepreneur) Manchester; married Irving Schram, December 7, 1958 (died February 18, 1967); children: Rebecca Schram Zafrany, Michael. *Education:* University of Connecticut, B.A. (with distinction), 1956; Columbia University, M.A., 1968, and further graduate study.

Addresses

Home—525 West End Ave., No. 8-C, New York, NY 10024.

Career

Iona College, New Rochelle, NY, instructor, 1967-69; Yeshiva University, instructor at Stern College, 1969-74, assistant professor, 1974-85, associate professor of speech and drama, 1985—, member of faculty at David J. Azrieli Graduate School of Jewish Education and Administration, beginning in 1988. Jewish Storytelling Center, founding director, 1984—; Storytelling Center of New York, member. Affiliated with the cable television series *Conversations over a Glass of Tea,* 1981-82; producer, narrator, and writer for the series *Let's Tell Tales,* broadcast by WEVD-Radio, 1973-76, and *A Bundle of Rainbows,* broadcast by WEVD-Radio, 1976-77. Guest speaker at conferences and educational institutions, including State University of New York Colleges at New Paltz, 1974 and 1985, and at Brockport, 1983, Connecticut College, 1981 and 1991, Columbia University, 1981, Tel Aviv University, 1984, Reconstructionist Rabbinical College, 1987, St. John's University, Jamaica, NY, 1990, Boston University, 1990, and Smith College, 1991; storyteller at storytelling festivals and other public gatherings. *Member:* National Communication Association, National Storytelling Network, Phi Beta Kappa, Kappa Delta Pi.

Awards, Honors

Distinguished Service Award, Jewish Braille Institute, 1976; Myrtle Wreath Award, Eastern Pennsylvania Region of Hadassah, 1990; Covenant Award, Covenant Foundation, 1995; Circle of Excellence Award, National Storytelling Network, 1999; Native Daughter Award, Rotary Club (New London, CT), 2000; Jewish Woman in the Arts Award, Manhattan Borough President's Award in Celebration of Jewish Cultural Heritage, 2000.

Peninnah Schram

Schram concludes each story of Jewish belief, experience, and character with questions to develop the moral lesson in this book for six- to nine-year-olds.

Writings

(Contributor) *A Teaching Guide to Elijah's Violin and Other Jewish Fairy Tales,* Coalition for Alternatives in Jewish Education (New York City), 1985.

The Big Sukkah (children's story), illustrated by Jacqueline Kahane, Kar-Ben (Rockville, MD), 1986.

(Reteller) *Jewish Stories One Generation Tells Another,* foreword by Elie Wiesel, J. Aronson (Northvale, NJ), 1987.

(With Steven M. Rosman) *Eight Tales for Eight Nights: Stories for Chanukah,* illustrated by Tsirl Waletzky, J. Aronson, 1990.

(Reteller) *Tales of Elijah the Prophet,* foreword by Dov Noy, J. Aronson, 1991.

(Contributor) Michael E. Williams, editor, *The Storyteller's Companion to the Bible: Old Testament Wisdom,* Abingdon (Nashville, TN), 1994.

(Contributor) *Tales as Tools: The Power of Story in the Classroom,* National Storytelling Press (Jonesborough, TN), 1994.

(Editor) *Chosen Tales: Stories Told by Jewish Storytellers,* foreword by Avi Weiss, J. Aronson, 1995.

(Contributor) Carol L. Birch and Melissa A. Heckler, editors, *Who Says? Essays on Pivotal Issues in Contemporary Storytelling,* August House (Little Rock, AR), 1995.

Ten Classic Jewish Children's Stories, illustrated by Jeffrey Allon, Pitspopany Press (New York City), 1998.

(Reteller) *Stories within Stories: From the Jewish Oral Tradition,* J. Aronson, 2000.

The Chanukah Blessing (children's story), illustrated by Jeffrey Allon, UAHC Press (New York City), 2000.

(Contributor) *The New Jewish Teachers Handbook,* ARE Publications (Denver, CO), 2000.

Writer for radio series. Work represented in anthologies, including *Reading Comprehension Workshop: Insights,* Globe Fearon, 1995; *Because God Loves Stories,* edited by Steve Zeitlin, Simon and Schuster, 1997; *A Hanukkah Treasury,* edited by Eric Kimmel, Holt, 1998; and *Bringing the Story Home,* compiled by Lisa Lipkin, Norton, 2000. Contributor to periodicals, including *Sh'ma Journal, United Synagogue Review, Journal of Aging and Judaism, Reconstructionist, National Storytelling Journal,* and *Pedagogic Reporter.*

Performer on recordings, including *A Storyteller's Journey,* Parts 1-2, released by POM Records (New York City), 1977 and 1982; *Elijah's Violin and Other Jewish Fairy Tales,* POM Records, 1985; *The Rooster Who Would Be King and Other Jewish Folktales* (videotape), Telling Tale (Chicago, IL), 1987; *Celebrating Jewish Storytelling,* B'nai B'rith Women (Washington, DC), 1988; *Best-Loved Stories Told at the National Storytelling Festival,* National Association for the Preservation and Perpetuation of Storytelling (Jonesborough, TN), 1991; *More Best-Loved Stories Told at the National Storytelling Festival,* National Association for the Preservation and Perpetuation of Storytelling, 1992; and *The Minstrel and the Storyteller: Stories and Songs of the Jewish People* (compact disc), Sefarad Records, 1999.

Sidelights

Peninnah Schram told *SATA:* "There are four prominent threads that seem to weave continuously into the tapestry and design of my life and which formed the basis of my commitment to storytelling in the oral tradition and to retelling Jewish folktales on the written page: my name, a teaching tale, the first story I remember, and a cantor's prayer.

"The Talmud states that 'One's name has an influence on one's life.' My given name—Peninnah, 'pearl' in Hebrew—was my grandmother's name, which can also be found in the Book of Samuel, Chapter 1. While Peninnah is not an attractive character on the surface, she is a catalyst, an earthy person, and a creative force in the story. Those are qualities I wanted to possess. I was given much to live up to in my name. The biblical Peninnah served as a powerful role model for me, after all.

"A second thread was the way my mother taught me wisdom and the right ways of behavior by telling me teaching tales and proverbs. For example, she taught me to restrain my anger through a story. Much later, as I was doing research for my first book of folk tales, I discovered that 'her' story actually came from a thirteenth-century book, *The Book of the Pious*. It was a tale that the folk took along with them through the centuries. It has since been retold many times by me to my own children.

"The third thread is the first story I remember being told, and it was told to me by my father. It was an 'Elijah the Prophet' story about three wishes. While I did not like hearing my mother's didactic stories, I loved my father's stories, since he often told me biblical, Talmudic, or Elijah stories. The Elijah tales were filled with themes of hospitality, wonder, hope, and possibilities. A first-remembered story influences our lives and the stories we, in turn, tell. Indeed, it reveals a great deal about ourselves. It becomes a formative experience and serves as a metaphor for our lives.

"The fourth thread in the design of my life is a prayer. Before the cantor chants the main service on the High Holy Days, the cantor chants a prayer called *Hineni* ('here I stand'). The cantor asks God to accept his prayers on behalf of the congregation. I wrote my storyteller's prayer modeled on this traditional prayer, which I recall vividly my father chanting. As a storyteller/writer, I feel a great responsibility to retell the stories of my people with beauty and integrity.

"As a Jewish storyteller/writer, I am a catalyst who shares in a creative and dignified way, through images and words, the traditions of our people. I seek to instill hope and other important values and to transmit the treasures given us by our forebears. It is a major responsibility."

Biographical and Critical Sources

PERIODICALS

AB Bookman's Weekly, March 23, 1987, review of *The Big Sukkah,* p. 1226; January 23, 1989, review of *Jewish Stories One Generation Tells Another,* p. 285; May 4, 1992, review of *Tales of Elijah the Prophet,* p. 1841.

Booklist, November 15, 1998, Ilene Cooper, review of *Ten Classic Jewish Children's Stories,* p. 584.

Come-All-Ye, fall, 1992, review of *Tales of Elijah the Prophet,* p. 8; winter, 1995, review of *Chosen Tales,* p. 7.

Library Journal, January, 1991, Carolyn Craft, review of *Eight Tales for Eight Nights,* p. 110; April 15, 1995, Carol R. Glatt, review of *Chosen Tales,* p. 85.

Publishers Weekly, October 5, 1992, review of *More Best-Loved Stories Told at the National Storytelling Festival,* p. 66; December 14, 1998, review of *Ten Classic Jewish Children's Stories,* p. 72.

School Library Journal, August, 1992, Penny Peck, review of *Best Loved Stories Told at the National Storytelling Festival,* p. 123; March, 1999, Marcia W. Posner, review of *Ten Classic Jewish Children's Stories,* p. 200; July, 1999, Malka Keck, review of *The Minstrel and the Storyteller,* p. 56.

SCRIMGER, Richard 1957-

Personal

Born April 5, 1957, in Montreal, Quebec, Canada; son of Dan and Nicki Scrimger; married Bridget Campion (a professor of moral theology), 1985; children: Thea and Sam (twins), Imogen, Ed. *Education:* Attended University of Toronto. *Politics:* "No." *Religion:* "Yes."

Addresses

Home and office—22 Pebble Beach Dr., Cobourg, Ontario, Canada K9A 2C5. *E-mail*—nerissa@eagle.ca. *Agent*—Dean Cooke, 457-A Danforth Ave., Toronto, Ontario, Canada.

Writer Richard Scrimger helps Alan, who has an outspoken alien living in his nose, maintain a comical outlook on life in order to survive bullies, his parents' divorce, and win a girlfriend. (Cover illustration by Gillian Johnson.)

Career

Worked as waiter and *maitre d',* between 1987 and 1996; Humber College, Toronto, Ontario, teacher at Humber School for Writers, 1998—.

Awards, Honors

Mr. Christie Award, 1999, for *The Nose from Jupiter.*

Writings

FOR CHILDREN

Still Life with Children, HarperCollins (Toronto, Ontario), 1997.

The Nose from Jupiter, Tundra Books (Plattsburgh, NY), 1998.

The Way to Schenectady, illustrated by Linda Hendry, Tundra Books, 1998.

A Nose for Adventure, Tundra Books, 2000.

FOR ADULTS

Crosstown, Riverbank Press, 1996.

Mystical Rose, Doubleday (Toronto, Ontario), 2000.

Work in Progress

Bun Bun's Birthday, for Tundra Books, completion expected in 2001.

Biographical and Critical Sources

PERIODICALS

Booklist, July, 1998, Helen Rosenberg, review of *The Nose from Jupiter,* p. 1882; May 1, 1999, Carolyn Phelan, review of *The Way to Schenectady,* p. 1596.

Books in Canada, November, 1996, Eva Tihanyi, review of *Crosstown,* pp. 35-36.

Canadian Book Review Annual, 1997, review of *Still Life with Children,* p. 112, and review of *Crosstown,* p. 197.

Canadian Forum, September, 1996, Nadia Halim, review of *Crosstown,* pp. 43-44; October, 1997, Misao Dean, review of *Still Life with Children,* p. 41.

Children's Book News, spring, 1998, review of *The Nose from Jupiter,* p. 25.

Children's Book Review Service, spring, 1998, review of *The Nose from Jupiter,* p. 140.

Children's Book Watch, May, 1998, review of *The Nose from Jupiter,* p. 5.

Globe and Mail (Toronto, ON), June 3, 2000, review of *Mystical Rose.*

Quill and Quire, June, 1996, Hal Niedzviecki, review of *Crosstown,* p. 51; April, 1998, Paul Kropp, review of *The Nose from Jupiter,* p. 35; December, 1998, Hadley Dyer, review of *The Way to Schenectady,* pp. 38-39; May, 2000, review of *Mystical Rose.*

Resource Links, October, 1998, review of *The Nose from Jupiter,* p. 7.

School Library Journal, June, 1999, Cyrisse Jaffee, review of *The Way to Schenectady,* p. 137.

SEWALL, Marcia 1935-

Personal

Born November 5, 1935, in Providence, RI; daughter of Edgar Knight and Hilda (Osgood) Sewall. *Education:* Pembroke College, B.A., 1957; Tufts University, M.Ed., 1958; studied art at Rhode Island School of Design and Boston Museum School. *Religion:* Unitarian Universalist.

Addresses

Home—Boston, MA.

Career

Writer and illustrator. Children's Museum, Boston, MA, staff artist, 1961-63; teacher of art in Winchester, MA, 1967-75. Participant in Boston adult literacy program and School Volunteers of Boston.

Awards, Honors

Come Again in the Spring was named one of the outstanding books of the year, *New York Times,* 1976, and was selected for exhibition by the American Institute of Graphic Arts, 1985; notable book citation, American Library Association, 1978, for *Little Things,* and 1981, for *The Song of the Horse;* best picture book of the year designation, *New York Times,* 1978, for *The Nutcrackers and the Sugar-Tongs; The Leprechaun's Story* was selected for exhibition by the American Institute of Graphic Arts, 1979; Parent's Choice Award for illustration, 1980, for *Crazy in Love;* outstanding book of the year designation, *New York Times,* 1980, Southern California Council notable work of fiction, 1981, Utah Children's book award, 1985, Emphasis on

Marcia Sewall describes everyday life during the first years in the Plimoth Colony in her self-illustrated The Pilgrims of Plimoth.

People of the Breaking Day *is a poetical look at the lifestyle and beliefs of the Wampanoag Indians of New England. (Written and illustrated by Sewall.)*

Reading award, 1986-87, Maud Hart Lovelace award, 1987, and George G. Stone award, 1987, all for *Stone Fox; The Story of Old Mrs. Brubeck and How She Looked for Trouble and Where She Found Him* was named one of best picture books of the year and *The Marzipan Moon* named one of outstanding books of the year, *New York Times*, both 1981; selection for exhibition at Bratislava International Biennale, 1983, for *The Song of the Horse,* and 1985, for *Finzel the Far-sighted; Boston Globe/Horn Book* Award for nonfiction, 1987, for *The Pilgrims of Plimoth;* Fassler award, 1989, for *Saying Goodbye to Grandma;* Parents Choice award for picture book, 1992, for *The Golden Locket.*

Writings

SELF-ILLUSTRATED

(Reteller) *The Little Wee Tyke,* Atheneum, 1979.

(Reteller) *The Wee, Wee Mannie and the Big, Big Coo* (Scottish folk tale), Little, Brown, 1979.

(Reteller) *The Cobbler's Song,* Dutton, 1982.

Ridin' That Strawberry Roan, Viking, 1985.

(Reteller) *The World Turned Upside Down: An Old Penny Rhyme,* Atlantic Monthly, 1986.

The Pilgrims of Plimoth, Atheneum, 1986.

Animal Song, Joy Street Books, 1988.

People of the Breaking Day, Atheneum, 1990.

Thunder from the Clear Sky, Atheneum, 1995.

(Adaptor) *The Green Mist,* Houghton, 1999.

ILLUSTRATOR

Joseph Jacobs, adapter, *Master of All Masters: An English Folktale,* Little, Brown, 1972.

P. C. Asbjoornsen and J. E. Moe, *The Squire's Bride: A Norwegian Folk Tale,* Atheneum, 1975.

Joseph Jacobs, *Coo-My-Dove, My Dear,* Atheneum, 1976.

Drew Stevenson, *The Ballad of Penelope Lou and Me,* Crossing Press, 1978.

Anne Eliot Crompton, *The Lifting Stone,* Holiday House, 1978.

Anne Laurin, *Little Things,* Atheneum, 1978.

Edward Lear, *The Nutcrackers and the Sugar-Tongs,* Little, Brown, 1978.

Paul Fleischman, *The Birthday Tree,* Harper, 1979.

Phyllis Krasilovsky, *The Man Who Tried to Save Time,* Doubleday, 1979.

John Reynolds Gardiner, *Stone Fox,* Crowell, 1980.

Nancy Willard, *The Marzipan Moon,* Harcourt, 1981.

Lore Segal, *The Story of Old Mrs. Brubeck and How She Looked for Trouble and Where She Found Him,* Pantheon, 1981.

Clyde Robert Bulla, *Poor Boy, Rich Boy,* Harper, 1982.

Lynn Hoopes, *When I Was Little,* Dutton, 1983.

Paul Fleischman, *Finzel the Far-sighted,* Dutton, 1984.

Walter Wangerin, *Thistle,* Harper, 1984.

Jane Resh Thomas, *Saying Goodbye to Grandma,* Clarion, 1988.

Roni Schotter, *Captain Snap and the Children of Vinegar Lane,* Orchard, 1989.

Patricia Foley, *John and the Fiddler,* Harper, 1990.

Ruth Young, *Daisy's Taxi,* Orchard, 1991.

Barbara M. Joosse, *Nobody's Cat,* HarperCollins, 1992.

Carol Greene, *The Golden Locket,* Harcourt, 1992.

Karen Hesse, *Sable,* Holt, 1994.

Barbara M. Joosse, *The Morning Chair,* Clarion, 1995.

Jane Resh Thomas, *Daddy Doesn't Have to Be a Giant Anymore,* Clarion, 1996.

Soon the cow gave no milk.

A dying child is made well by the spring rituals intended for the mysterious beings living in the earth in Sewall's adaptation of the eighteenth-century English folktale **The Green Mist.** *(Illustrated by Sewall.)*

Leon Rosselson, *Rosa and Her Singing Grandfather,* Philomel, 1996.

Frances Ward Weller, *Madaket Millie,* Philomel, 1997.

Jackie French Koller, *Nickommoh! A Thanksgiving Celebration,* Atheneum, 1999.

ILLUSTRATOR; TEXT BY RICHARD KENNEDY

The Parrot and the Thief, Little, Brown, 1974.

Come Again in the Spring (also see below), Harper, 1976.

The Porcelain Man (also see below), Little, Brown, 1976.

The Rise and Fall of Ben Gizzard, Little, Brown, 1978.

The Leprechaun's Story, Dutton, 1979.

Crazy in Love, Dutton, 1980.

The Song of the Horse, Dutton, 1981.

Richard Kennedy: Collected Stories (includes *Come Again in the Spring* and *The Porcelain Man*), Harper, 1987.

OTHER

Contributor to periodicals, including *Horn Book.*

Adaptations

The Pilgrims of Plimoth was adapted for inclusion in a Read-Along Cassette series, Weston Woods, 1988.

Sidelights

Author and illustrator Marcia Sewall was raised in the coastal town of Providence, Rhode Island, and entered Pembroke College at Brown University in 1953. Now living and working in Boston, Massachusetts, a city steeped in colonial American history, she is much more influenced by traditions from the past than by the modern city visible from her studio window. Sewall's love for the history and landscape of her New England heritage is embodied within her work, adding a unique vitality to the books she writes and illustrates for children.

Although never formally trained as an illustrator of children's books, Sewall demonstrated an early interest in both drawing and painting. She majored in art while in college and at one point after graduation spent a summer at the prestigious Rhode Island School of Design in an accelerated art program. As she once told *SATA,* "I never worked so hard in my life, and I learned a tremendous sense of discipline there. It was the first extremely structured art training I'd had. I needed it, and loved it." Before becoming a illustrator, Sewall taught art to high school students and was employed as a staff artist at the Children's Museum in Boston. Her desire to become a working illustrator motivated her to show her portfolio to several publishers. There was enthusiasm for her artistic style, and she launched a successful career in book illustration.

The first volume published with Sewall's illustrations was *Master of All Masters: An English Folktale.* As with many of the books she has chosen to illustrate, she was immediately drawn to the humor and eccentricity of the characters within its pages. She once explained to *SATA,* "I don't think you can force a book. If a manuscript seems natural and comfortable and appealing, I accept it

readily. You work so hard for three or four months on the material that you must be comfortable with it. I love the wisdom, the character, and the tradition in folk people, so I often choose books with that sort of quality.

"When I first receive a manuscript," continued Sewall, "I walk through the story and divide it into pictures. If it's to be a thirty-two page book then I am limited to about thirteen double-page spreads. I begin to immediately struggle with the sense of character, the movement of character, and then on to the transformation of that flat surface into a believable space. An author gives me clues as to person and place and then it's a matter of sorting them out. The illustrator often makes decisions about the period and costuming. I next try to capture the rhythm and movement of the story in the dummy."

Sewall has illustrated eight books for author Richard Kennedy, including his anthology *Richard Kennedy: Collected Stories.* "Sometimes I know immediately how a book must look," she commented. "As I read the manuscript for [Kennedy's] *The Song of the Horse,* I visualized the story in scratchboard. Scratchboard is a black ink surface over a white gessoed board. Instead of putting a black line down on white paper you scratch a white line away from a black surface. It is sort of electrical, magnetic. It has a vibrancy that seemed appropriate for that particular story.

"Although I may not immediately 'see' a character, I have to believe that it's within me to see him or her. On reading and rereading a manuscript, a sense of person begins to emerge and it is that which I try to capture in my initial sketches. It took a stack of paper and lots of drawing of *Old Mrs. Brubeck* before she would materialize for me. At first I had difficulty with her as a personality. She worried too much. Then I thought, 'My gosh, she's me and she's everybody I know!' I began to feel that there was humor about her, and then she just took shape. I thought if I gave her wooden shoes we would not only see but could hear her move about the house in her search for 'Trouble' and, as a final statement, I distilled her anxious movements in silhouettes against the endpapers."

Sewall's unique illustrations continue to draw praise from reviewers. As Donnarae MacCann explained in an article in the *Wilson Library Bulletin,* "Sewall approaches color and pattern and both animal and landscape in a plain honest way, emphasizing the relationship between forms. Shapes and colors coexist without the benefit of line definitions and without any fanfare or pretense. Our eyes move slowly from one overlapping form to another until we take in the unified composition."

The Cobbler's Song, published in 1982, was Sewall's first full-color book to be published. "What an absolute joy it was to sit down and paint, and use colors that seemed to express the changing moods of the story," she recalled for *SATA.* "I used gouache which is an opaque watercolor paint not unlike poster paint. The story is a variation of the old 'rich man, poor man' theme. It deals

Sewall illustrates a Narragansett Indian Nickommoh, or harvest celebration. (From Nickommoh!, *written by Jackie French Koller.)*

with feelings, so it made sense to use full-color and to put paint on expressively."

Other picture-book projects Sewall has worked on in collaboration with children's book authors include *Rosa and Her Singing Grandfather* by Leon Rosselson, the poignant *Daddy Doesn't Have to Be a Giant Anymore* by Jane Resh Thomas, and the amusing *The Golden Locket* by Carol Greene. In the latter work, Sewall depicts the quandary of the frazzled Miss Teaberry after her cat digs up a golden locket in her garden and she can't find a thing in her closet to wear with the new find. Sewall's ink and gouache illustrations were praised by *Booklist* contributor Stephanie Zvirin for their incorporation of "planes of flat color to give the book a sturdy, no-nonsense look that adds punch to the outlandish situational humor." In *Rosa and Her Singing Grandfather,* Sewall provides illustrations for twelve different stories about a small girl and her musical relative, each one bringing to life the pair's close relationship. And in *Daddy Doesn't Have to Be a Giant Anymore,* the story of a little girl trying to cope with her father's alcoholism is aided by illustrations that "effectively convey the emotional content of the story while keeping the tone from becoming overly somber," according to Zvirin in another *Booklist* review.

In Barbara M. Joosse's *The Morning Chair,* published in 1995, Sewall's use of intense, emotive colors and "deceptively simple" renderings in her gouache paintings reflect "the emotion of upheaval and the drama of the journey" taken by an immigrant family, according to *Booklist* reviewer Ellen Mandel. The illustrator depicts Bram and his family in their safe home in Holland, and, through the use of color, contrasts those images with the

alienating atmosphere the family experiences on its arrival in New York. *Horn Book* contributor Hanna B. Zeiger noted several images in particular—the family's last view of Holland from aboard ship and their first sight of the Statue of Liberty—as "speak[ing] more eloquently than words of the feelings involved in immigrating to a new land."

Periodically, Sewall has taken a break from illustrating books by other authors to illustrate some of her own texts. Sometimes she has adapted ethnic folk tales to a picture book format, and in other instances she has written original stories, all characteristically embroidered with Sewall's love of folklore and history. *Ridin' That Strawberry Roan* is based on a traditional ballad from the American West and tells the story of the taming of an outlaw horse. Written in jaunty rhyming couplets, the book is illustrated throughout with bright watercolor paintings reflecting the story's humorous theme. *The Pilgrims of Plimoth,* although based on actual diary entries by William Bradford and other passengers of the *Mayflower,* is retold by Sewall as an original prose-poem and has been commended—along with its companion volumes, *People of the Breaking Day* and *Thunder from the Clear Sky*—for its "scholarship and sensitivity," by a critic in *School Library Journal.*

Taken together, these three books give a sensitive account of the day-to-day experiences of the early settlers of Plimoth Plantation and the Wampanoag Indians, a tribe then making their home in southeastern Massachusetts. Throughout the series, Sewall focuses on the strong fibers of family ritual and community support that unite these two very different groups of people in their struggle to survive the harshness of their common surroundings during the seventeenth century. Whether it be a young English lad standing on the deck of the *Mayflower,* searching the coastline as the ship makes its way towards a land full of mystery, or a young Indian girl collecting firewood within a dark, wintry forest, each contributes to the family, thereby playing an integral role in the survival of the entire community.

Although characterizing Sewall's attempt at recreating Native American speech patterns as "overly mystical," a reviewer for *Horn Book* praised *People of the Breaking Day* as "a fine resource that is resonant with integrity, intelligence, and eloquence." Deeming Sewall's work "informative and inspiring," *School Library Journal* contributor Luann Toth lauded the book for "introduc[ing] readers to [the Wampanoag's] unique, harmonious relationship with the natural world." In its introduction to King Phillip's War, the concluding volume, *Thunder from the Clear Sky,* alternates its focus between the Native Americans and the European colonists, thus "provid[ing] a good introduction to a dramatic chapter in American history," according to *Booklist* reviewer Carolyn Phelan.

Sewall's success as an author has not diminished her desire to continue working as an illustrator. With an artist's eye for culling details from everyday life, she is continuously inspired by her surroundings. As she explained to *SATA,* "I have always enjoyed the sensation of movement ... and that has really helped me with moving figures about a page. My characters are not based on real people, though I notice when I illustrate a book that sometimes people I know will appear. Months later, it will occur to me that I have illustrated the boy in the corner market, or I discover that one of my figures sits like someone I know. I think an artist is constantly taking in visual impressions, but not always consciously. And you don't deliberately pull them out. They come."

Biographical and Critical Sources

BOOKS

Holtze, Sally Holmes, editor, *Fifth Book of Junior Authors and Illustrators,* H. W. Wilson, 1983, pp. 280-81.
Kingman, Lee, and others, compilers, *Illustrators of Children's Books: 1967-1976,* Horn Book, 1978.

PERIODICALS

Booklist, October 1, 1985, p. 269; September 15, 1986, p. 134; October 1, 1990, p. 329; April 1, 1992, Stephanie Zvirin, review of *The Golden Locket,* p. 1456; June 1, 1995, Ellen Mandel, review of *The Morning Chair,* p. 1786; November 15, 1995, Carolyn Phelan, review of *Thunder from the Clear Sky,* p. 557; October 15, 1996, Stephanie Zvirin, *Daddy Doesn't Have to Be A Giant Anymore,* p. 424; March 15, 1997, Michael Cart, review of *Madaket Millie,* p. 1247; April 1, 1999, review of *The Green Mist,* p. 1418; November 15, 1999, Karen Hutt, review of *Nickommoh!,* p. 630.
Bulletin of the Center for Children's Books, December, 1985.
Graphis, Number 200, 1979.

Horn Book, December, 1979, p. 657; February, 1983, p. 40; January, 1988, pp. 32-34; July, 1990, p. 153; January, 1991, review of *People of the Breaking Day,* p. 88; May-June, 1995, Hanna B. Zeiger, review of *The Morning Chair,* p. 325; September-October, 1996, Nancy Vasilakis, review of *Rosa and Her Singing Grandfather,* p. 599; March, 1999, Joanna Rudge Long, review of *The Green Mist,* p. 201.
New York Times Book Review, November 23, 1986, p. 32; September 17, 1989.
Publishers Weekly, January 24, 1977, p. 333; November 5, 1982, p. 71; November 2, 1990, pp. 73-74; July 13, 1992, review of *Nobody's Cat,* p. 55; April 25, 1994, review of *Sable,* p. 76; July 1, 1996, review of *Daddy Doesn't Have to Be a Giant Anymore,* p. 60; January 27, 1997, review of *Madaket Millie,* p. 105; April 5, 1999, review of *The Green Mist,* p. 241; August 2, 1999, review of *Madaket Millie,* p. 87; September 27, 1999, review of *Nickommoh!,* p. 254.
School Library Journal, April, 1977, p. 57; December, 1979, p. 77; May, 1986, p. 85; January, 1991, Luann Toth, review of *People of the Breaking Day,* pp. 106-7; May, 1992, Ruth K. MacDonald, review of *The Golden Locket,* p. 88; June, 1996, Betty Teague, review of *Rosa and Her Singing Grandfather,* p. 108; October 10, 1999, Margaret Chang, review of *Nickommoh!,* p. 140.
Wilson Library Bulletin, April, 1993, Donnarae MacCann, review of *Nobody's Cat,* p. 94.*

*   *   *

STEDING, Laurie 1953-
(Laurie Christensen)

Personal

Born September 16, 1953, in St. Louis, MO; daughter of Richard P. (a sales director) and Anne L. (a teacher) Steding; married Robert A. Christensen (an engineer), April 16, 1977; children: Sarah, Danny. *Education:* University of Colorado at Boulder, B.S., 1975; attended Denver Community College and Arapahoe Community College, 1978; University of North Carolina at Wilmington, M.Ed., 1991. *Politics:* Independent. *Religion:* Methodist. *Hobbies and other interests:* Reading, painting, gardening.

Addresses

Home—7631 Kit Carson Drive, Littleton, CO 80122. *E-mail*—CrazyKids1@aol.com.

Career

Teacher of preschool and first-grade classes at public and private schools in Denver, CO, Steelville, MO, and Wilmington, NC, 1975—; mental health educator for elementary school students, 1994—; private tutor, 1995—; educational consultant, 1998—. Workshop leader and trainer; curriculum developer. Learning Disabilities Association of Colorado, volunteer; activist

Laurie Steding

with a task force for safe schools, Littleton, CO. *Member:* Phi Kappa Phi, Phi Delta Kappa.

Awards, Honors

Outstanding Young Teacher of the Year Award, Missouri branch, Phi Delta Kappa, 1984.

Writings

Holidays, Macmillan, 1983.
Teacher's Messages, Troll (Mahwah, NJ), 1994.
A Day in the Country, Scholastic, 1994.
A Day in the City, Scholastic, 1994.
Community Awareness, Newbridge Educational, 1995.
Bunnies and Hearts: A Stamp Activity Book, Troll, 1995.
Birthstones, Troll, 1996.
Step Right Up!, Troll, 1997.
Science Stew, Troll, 1997.
Ready, Set, Read!, Troll, 1997.
Ready, Set, Draw!, Troll, 1997.
Now You've Got It!, Troll, 1997.
Let's Discover, Troll, 1997.
I Like to Draw!, Troll, 1997.
Hip, Hip, Hooray!, Troll, 1997.
Ten Minute Math Mind Stretchers, Scholastic, 1997.

(Under name Laurie Christensen) *American Heroes,* Macmillan, 1998.
(Under name Christensen) *Physical Science,* Macmillan, 1998.
(Under name Christensen) *Incredible Insects,* Macmillan, 1998.
Prehistoric Bugs: Trapped in Amber, Troll, 1998.
Bright Kids Who Can't Learn: Overcoming Learning Difficulties, illustrated by Cynthia Fisher, Vital Public Information (New York City), 1999.
Talking to Teens, Vital Public Information, 1999.

Other books include *Letter Skills* and *Self Concept,* both for Macmillan, published between 1983 and 1984; *May Days, Back to School, Happy Holidays, Summer Fun, Autumn Action,* and *Spring Is Here,* all for Macmillan, published between 1984 and 1987; *Back to School, Valentine's Day, Patriotic Days, Fall, Snowy Days, Special Cards and Gifts, Summer, Fall Harvest, Winter, Birthday Parties, School Days, Holiday Fun, Be My Valentine,* and *Summer's Here,* all for Newbridge Educational, published between 1988 and 1993; and teacher's guides for mathematics, social studies, science, and literature books, for Troll, published between 1993 and 1994.

Work in Progress

Research on historical fiction for children and "exploring ways to write about sensitive topics such as mental illness."

Sidelights

Laurie Steding told *SATA:* "As a teacher of lively first-graders, I was always digging around for 'teacher-tested' projects that would be both fun and educational. I didn't realize it at the time, but when I began to publish activity-based books for teachers, I hit the creativity mother lode inside my own brain. All the hours spent researching, concocting, and testing new ideas for classrooms unearthed a passion for writing. The best part has been discovering ways to connect kids with topics I didn't even know I found interesting. Physics, folk tales of the world, famous Americans, math puzzles, music, art, and even prehistoric insects are some of the subjects I've loved sharing with teachers and students.

"Over time my creative targets have changed focus. In addition to teaching full time, I'm now in private practice, where I can give my attention to only one student at a time. I've become especially interested in mental health issues, learning disabilities, attention deficit disorder, and kids who just don't 'fit in.' I'm still just as excited as ever about researching, concocting, and testing new ideas. My latest books, for parents, are the result of joys, heartaches, and lessons learned from raising two children.

"Most writers, I would guess, are lifelong 'bookaholics.' My memories often drift back to the books I read and reread as a child. I used to wish I could really live the lives of several of those beloved characters. I now find myself longing to write the stories created by my own special characters. I'm ready to go wherever they take me!"

*   *   *

STORAD, Conrad J. 1957-

Personal

Born July 19, 1957, in Barberton, OH; son of Conrad Sr. (a meat cutter) and Maryann (a homemaker; maiden name, Leuenberger) Storad; married Laurie Ann Snyder (an occupational therapy assistant), October 16, 1999; stepchildren: Sarah Bennett, Meghan Bennett. *Education:* University of Akron, B.A., 1979; Arizona State University, M.A., 1983. *Politics:* Independent. *Religion:* Roman Catholic.

Addresses

Home—1199 W. Jeanine Dr. Tempe, AZ 85284. *Office*—Arizona State University Research Publications, P.O. Box 878206, Tempe, AZ 85287-8206. *E-mail*—cstorad@asu.edu.

Career

Science writer. *Barberton Herald,* Barberton, OH, reporter and sports editor, 1979-80, editor and general manager, 1980-81; Kent State University, Kent, OH, feature and science writer, 1984-85; Arizona State University, Tempe, AZ, editor of *ASU Research Magazine,* 1986—, director, Office of Research Publications, 1989—, and editor of *Chain Reaction,* 1998—. National Cancer Institute, science/medical writing fellow, 1984. *Member:* National Association of Science Writers, Society of Children's Book Writers and Illustrators, University Research Magazine Association (president, two terms), Arizona Book Publishers Association.

Awards, Honors

Glyph Award for Best Children's Book, Arizona Book Publishers' Association (ABPA), 1999, and finalist, Benjamin Franklin Award for Juvenile Nonfiction, PMA, 2000, both for *Don't Call Me Pig! A Javelina Story;* Glyph Award for Best Nature Book, ABPA, 1999, for *Sonoran Desert A to Z Coloring Book.*

Writings

Saguaro Cactus, photographs by Paula Jansen, Lerner (Minneapolis, MN), 1995.
Scorpions, photographs by Paula Jansen, Lerner, 1995.
Tarantulas, photographs by Paula Jansen, Lerner, 1998.
Inside AIDS: HIV Attacks the Immune System, Lerner, 1998.
Lizards for Lunch: A Roadrunner's Tale, illustrated by Beth Neely and Don Rantz, Resort Gifts Unlimited (Phoenix, AZ), 1999.
Head over Heels About Arizona, Resort Gifts Unlimited (Tempe, AZ), 1999.

Don't Call Me Pig! A Javelina Story, illustrated by Beth Neely and Don Rantz, Resort Gifts Unlimited, 1999.

Also author of *Sonoran Desert A to Z Coloring Book,* 1997, *Little Lords of the Desert,* 1998, and *Ancient Harvest,* 2000, all published by Donna Atwood Design.

Sidelights

Conrad J. Storad writes science books for the children's market as an offshoot of his work as a magazine editor at Arizona State University. Many of his works for young readers reflect the unique desert environment of his adopted state. Born in 1957, Storad studied journalism and environmental science at the University of Akron, then worked as reporter for his hometown newspaper in Ohio after college. A year later, he became the paper's editor and general manager. Deciding to pursue a graduate degree, he enrolled at the Walter Cronkite School of Journalism at Arizona State University and earned a masters degree in science journalism. He has been with the institution since 1986, when he was hired as editor of the *ASU Research Magazine;* three years later he was named to head the school's Office of Research Publications. In 1998, he became the founding editor of a science magazine for middle-school students, *Chain Reaction,* also published by the university.

Conrad J. Storad

Hoppers buzz this way and that
I snatch them with my long beak
The bugs are delicious
But it's fat lizards I seek.

Storad describes the life of a roadrunner in the Arizona desert in **Lizards for Lunch.** *(Illustrated by Beth Neely and Don Rantz.)*

Storad has penned a handful of books for elementary-age children that investigate certain aspects of the unique ecosystem in the American Southwest. Among these is the 1995 title *Saguaro Cactus,* which lures readers on a learning journey by explaining just how unusual it is for any plant life to flourish in a part of the world that receives so little rain. Storad discusses why the saguaro cactus flowers only at night and the necessity of other flora present for it to flourish—especially during its early beginnings, when shade from palo verde trees and creosote bushes protect the cactus seedlings. A review from Steve Matthews in *School Library Journal* called it a book that is "inviting in appearance" and "fun to read."

Another title from Storad that appeared in 1995 became one of his two books about arachnids. *Scorpions,* for readers in the eight to ten age group, begins with a map and shows where these venomous creatures live. The text then goes on to note what scorpions eat and who they must avoid to become prey themselves. Storad also explains how they care for their young. Color photographs, a glossary of new words, and an activity section for parents and teachers round out both this work and Storad's *Tarantulas,* which appeared in 1998.

Storad earned sincere praise from reviewers for another title that was published that same year, *Inside AIDS: HIV Attacks the Immune System.* Here, the author recounts for junior-high and high-school readers the history of the disease, how it is detected, and its course of treatment. Tips for prevention are also included, but the book strives to emphasize the unusual world of viral cell biology for its audience. Storad explains how the HIV virus fools the body and tricks its cells, and how this becomes deadly to a person's immune system. Illustrations that include computer-generated images and microscope photographs of cells supplement the techni-

cal explanations in the text. Reviewers commended *Inside AIDS* for its detailed, scientific focus. Storad, wrote Edward Sullivan in a *School Library Journal* review, "does a good job of explaining technical facts clearly and concisely," while *Booklist* critic Frances Bradburn noted that "in spite of its slight format, this book is surprisingly complex."

Other titles from Storad continue to explore his interest in the Arizona desert and its life forms. He has written *Lizards for Lunch: A Roadrunner's Tale, Don't Call Me Pig! A Javelina Story,* and *Little Lords of the Desert,* a 1998 title that explores the region's insect and arachnid life.

Biographical and Critical Sources

PERIODICALS

Appraisal: Science Books for Young People, April, 1994, review of *Saguaro Cactus,* pp. 61-62; April, 1995, review of *Scorpions,* pp. 67-68.

Booklist, December 15, 1998, Frances Bradburn, review of *Inside AIDS,* p. 743.

Horn Book Guide, fall, 1998, Kelly A. Ault, review of *Tarantulas,* pp. 382-83.

School Library Journal, August, 1994, Steve Matthews, review of *Saguaro Cactus,* p. 166; June, 1995, Karey Wehner, review of *Scorpions,* pp. 125-26; July, 1998, Patricia Manning, review of *Tarantulas,* pp. 87-88; January, 1999, Edward Sullivan, review of *Inside AIDS,* p. 155.

SWAIN, Ruth (Freeman) 1951-

Personal

Born May 25, 1951, in Bryn Mawr, PA; daughter of Robert S. and Dorothy C. (Macfarlan) Freeman; married Ted Swain (an antiques appraiser), May 6, 1978; children: Ned, Bob. *Education:* Vassar College, A.B., 1973. *Politics:* Liberal. *Religion:* Episcopalian. *Hobbies and other interests:* Books, history, travel, baking, theater.

Addresses

Home—P.O. Box 1120, Blue Hill, ME 04614.

Career

Worked at book stores in New York City and Philadelphia, PA, between 1973 and 1980; appraiser of antique jewelry, 1980-85; nursery school teacher, 1989—. Volunteer for schools, alumnae organizations, and church. *Member:* Society of Children's Book Writers and Illustrators.

Awards, Honors

2000 Platinum Award, Oppenheim Toy Portfolio, and Notable Children's Trade Book in the Field of Social Studies, National Council for Social Studies and Children's Book Council, 2000, both for *Bedtime!*

Writings

Bedtime!, illustrated by Cat Bowman Smith, Holiday House, 1999.
Hairdo: What We Do and Did to Our Hair, Holiday House, in press.

Work in Progress

A middle grade novel; research for nonfiction picture books.

Ruth Swain

Biographical and Critical Sources

PERIODICALS

Booklist, September 15, 1999, Ellen Mandel, review of *Bedtime!,* p. 264.
Publishers Weekly, September 13, 1999, review of *Bedtime!,* p. 83.

T

THOMAS, Meredith 1963-

Personal

Born July 19, 1963, in Australia; daughter of Jeff (a natural therapist) and Rona (a singer and French tutor) Thomas. *Education:* Royal Melbourne Institute of Technology, diploma in graphic design (with distinction), 1983. *Politics:* "Left-leaning." *Religion:* "Sun worshiper."

Addresses

Home—43 Henry St., Northcote, Victoria 3070, Australia. *E-mail*—meredith_illustration@hotmail.com.

Career

HSV-7, Melbourne, Australia, designer and illustrator, 1984-85; Creative Marketing Services, Melbourne, designer and illustrator, 1985-86; freelance illustrator and painter, 1991—. Specialties include paper sculpture, commercial illustration, children's books, murals, photographic backdrops, and three-dimensional props; work exhibited throughout Australia, particularly in and around Melbourne; work represented in collections at St. Vincent's Hospital and Royal Children's Hospital. Teacher of illustration and paper sculpture classes at educational institutions, including Royal Melbourne Institute of Technology, University of Victoria, and Swinburne University of Technology. Also works occasionally as a life drawing model. Supporter of local public radio stations. *Member:* Illustrators Association of Australia.

Awards, Honors

Three-Dimensional Illustrators Bronze Award for creative excellence, Dimensional Illustrators, 1999, for *Rainbows of the Sea.*

Writings

AUTHOR AND ILLUSTRATOR

Paper Shapes, Nelson Australia (Melbourne), 1993, SRA (Santa Rosa, CA), 1994.
Rainbows of the Sea, photographs by Adrian Lander, Mondo Publishing (Greenvale, NY), 1998.

ILLUSTRATOR

Mem Fox, *The Straight Line Wonder,* Ashton Scholastic (Sydney, Australia), 1987.
Remembering and Going On, Le Pine Funeral Services (Melbourne, Australia), 1991.
Raewyn Caisley, *Hannah and Her Dad,* SRA, 1994.
Catherine Jenkins, *Monday Came,* SRA, 1994.
Sally Moss, *Peter's Painting,* Mondo Publishing, 1995.
Margaret Ballanger and Rachel Griffiths, *Look at You,* Houghton Mifflin, 1996.
Lillian's Lizard Is Missing, ("Just Kids" series), Pearson Education, 2000.

Illustrator of eight titles in the "Sally" series, Nelson Australia, 1993-95. Illustrator of four titles in the "Alphakids" series, Eleanor Curtain Publishing, 1998-99, including *Cat and Dog, Show and Tell, Roads and Bridges,* and *The Lonely Troll.* Illustrator of fifteen titles in the "P.M. Plus Story Books" series, Nelson ITP, 1998-2000, including *Phan's Diary; Hop To It, Minty; Queen of the Pool; A Medal for Molly; Bend, Stretch and Leap; More Spaghetti; The Flower Pot; Katie's Caterpillar; The Classroom Caterpillars; The Big Yellow Castle; Roar Like a Tiger; Toys and Play; The Hut in the Old Tree; Wet Weather Camping;* and *The Chocolate Cake.*

Work in Progress

Research on touring Vietnam.

Sidelights

Meredith Thomas told *SATA:* "Movement is very important to me. I love the feel of the air whizzing past me and around my skin. I like the way the wind sculpts

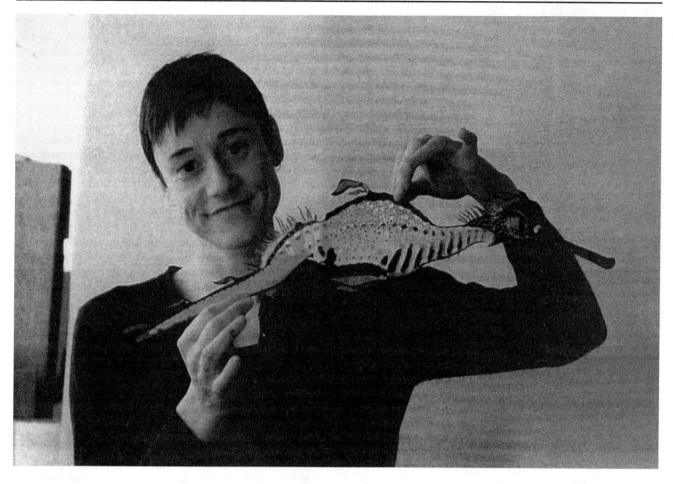

Meredith Thomas

the trees and pushes the clouds into constantly changing shapes. Animals running, cats pouncing, birds swooping, fish darting—all of these things inspire me to draw and to create, be it in pen and ink, paper sculpture, paint, pure color, or words.

"I travel often, painting and sketching what I see around me as I go. I have been to China, Europe, Morocco, and all around Australia. I am a big walker, and I find many ideas come while simply moving and observing. *Rainbows of the Sea* was dreamed up while walking alone and barefoot in the singing midday heat down the silver-gray mudflats of a tidal river near Mackay in Queensland. The words came after the visual sequence and were written back home in bed in Melbourne two months later.

"As well as walking, reading, skating, painting, laughing riotously, and cavorting about under the full moon, I love trying new things, eating peaches, and hanging out with my cat Nemesis.

"Meredith means 'protector of the sea' or 'sea-sprite,' and the ocean is tremendously important to me. The contrast between the wild sense of freedom engendered by horizon and distance, and the delicate tactile tapestry of changing beach microcosm is an ongoing source of absolute joy.

"When I grow up, I am going to be a painter and sail to Tahiti."

Biographical and Critical Sources

PERIODICALS

Children's Book Review Service, November, 1998, Barbara Baker, review of *Rainbows of the Sea,* p. 30.

Children's Book Watch, November, 1998, review of *Rainbows of the Sea,* p. 4.

Horn Book Guide, spring, 1999, Suzy Schmidt, review of *Rainbows of the Sea,* pp. 108-09.

ON-LINE

Meredith Thomas, www.geocities.com/meredith-illustration, (October 3, 2000).

*   *   *

THOMPSON, Sharon (Elaine) 1952-

Personal

Born April 24, 1952; daughter of John W. and Elaine A. Thompson. *Education:* Gemological Institute of America, diploma; Gemmological Association of Great Britain, diploma; also attended California State University, Fullerton and Long Beach, University of California, Los

Sharon Thompson

Angeles, and Santa Monica College. *Hobbies and other interests:* Reading, quilting, traveling gardening, water-color painting.

Addresses

Home—P.O. Box 4481, Salem, OR 97302.

Career

Freelance writer and editor. Greater Los Angeles Zoo Association, docent, 1986-91. *Member:* American Society of Journalists and Authors, Association of Women-Owned Businesses (president, 1995), Gemmological Association of Great Britain (fellow), Salem Writers, Artists, and Publishers (president, 1993-95).

Writings

The Greenhouse Effect, Lucent (San Diego, CA), 1992.
Hate Groups, Lucent, 1993.
Death Trap: The Story of the La Brea Tar Pits, Lerner (Minneapolis, MN), 1994.
Built for Speed: The Extraordinary and Enigmatic Cheetah, Lerner, 1998.
The Wild West: An American Myth, Lerner, 2001.

Contributor of more than a hundred-fifty articles and reviews to periodicals, including *American Jewelry Manufacturer, Lapidary Journal, Zoo Life, Zooview, Gems and Gemology, Jewelers' Circular Keystone,* and (Willamette University) *Scene.*

Sidelights

Sharon Thompson told *SATA:* "Two things I thoroughly enjoy are learning and sharing what I've learned with others. Nothing could marry those two loves better than writing nonfiction for young adults.

"I started writing, intending to be a travel writer. While I've never become a travel writer per se, I've been very fortunate to travel in the course of my writing career. I've been to the Namib Desert on the southwest coast of Africa, heard hippos grunting at night in the Okavango Delta on the edge of the Kalahari Desert, watched a constantly changing panorama of wildlife at water holes in the Etosha National Park, and gotten stuck in the asphalt at the famous La Brea Tar Pits of Los Angeles. I've met and interviewed fascinating people, from jewelry designers to biologists, to paleontologists, to eye surgeons, to children digging fossils in Wyoming. I can't imagine anything I'd rather do than write.

"Writing isn't easy for me or anyone else. However, even when it is frustrating, it is never boring. When it comes out well, the feeling of accomplishment and reward is almost unparalleled. The only thing that can top it is when a mother tells me how much her son loves my book, that he's taken it out of the library a half-dozen times. As far as I'm concerned, *that's* job satisfaction."

Biographical and Critical Sources

PERIODICALS

Appraisal: Science Books for Young People, autumn, 1995, review of *Death Trap,* pp. 53-54.
Booklist, June 1, 1995, Denia Hester, review of *Death Trap,* p. 1768; June 1, 1998, Kay Weisman, review of *Built for Speed,* p. 1762.
Book Report, May, 1995, review of *Hate Groups,* p. 59.
Children's Book Watch, May, 1998, review of *Built for Speed,* p. 4.
Horn Book Guide, fall, 1993, review of *The Greenhouse Effect,* p. 322; fall, 1994, review of *Hate Groups,* p. 334; fall, 1995, review of *Death Trap,* p. 344; fall, 1998, Jackie C. Horne, review of *Built for Speed,* p. 386.
School Library Journal, May, 1995, Beth Irish, review of *Death Trap,* p. 116.
Science Books and Films, July, 1998, review of *Built for Speed,* p. 147.
Voice of Youth Advocates, August, 1994, Janet Mura, review of *Hate Groups,* p. 173.

V–W

VUGTEVEEN, Verna Aardema
See AARDEMA, Verna

* * *

WALTON, Darwin McBeth 1926-

Personal

Born September 16, 1926, in Charlotte, NC; daughter of John M. (a barber) and Mary (Simons) McBeth; married Claude A. Walton (an administrator), September 1, 1950; children: Claudette Walton-Giles, John Arnold. *Education:* Chicago Conservatory of Music, Mus.B.; National-Louis University, M.A.T.; also attended Howard University and Johnson C. Smith University. *Politics:* "Liberal Democrat." *Religion:* United Church of the Brethren.

Addresses

Home and office—725 13th St., No. 18-W, Lombard, IL 60148. *E-mail*—jdmwalton@aol.com.

Career

Professional singer and dancer, 1955-65; teacher at public schools in Elmhurst, IL, 1966-86; National-Louis University, supervisor of student teachers. Founder of the first ballet school in DuPage County, IL; volunteer musician and storyteller for churches, schools, and libraries in and around Chicago, IL. *Member:* Society of Children's Book Writers and Illustrators, Midwest Writers, Off-Campus Writers, Graue Mill Historical Society and Museum.

Awards, Honors

Named Media Woman of the Year, National Association of Media Women, 1978; named Outstanding Woman of the Year in the Field of Racial Justice, Young Women's Christian Association, 1997; Best Children's Books of

Darwin McBeth Walton

the Year selection, Bank Street College of Education, 1997, for *Dance, Kayla!*

Writings

What Color Are You?, photographs by Hal Franklin, Johnson (Chicago, IL), 1973.
Ebony in the Classroom, Johnson, 1975.

189

Bookworms Are Made, Not Born, privately printed, 1987.
A Change of Heart, Globe (San Diego, CA), 1993.
Nellie for President (play for children), Globe, 1993.
Dance, Kayla!, Albert Whitman (Niles, IL), 1998.
Kwanzaa: A World of Holidays, Raintree Steck-Vaughn (Austin, TX), 1999.
Overcoming Challenges: The Life of Charles F. Bolden, Jr., Steck-Vaughn, 2000.
Goodbye Mr. Snowman, Steck-Vaughn, 2000.
In Nana's Kitchen ("Pair-It Books" series), Steck-Vaughn, in press.

Contributor to periodicals, including *Cultural Insights.*

Work in Progress

Rena, a novel about "the life of a young slave girl"; *Herman Is a Hero,* a novel about "a brilliant twelve-year-old African-American boy with a cleft palate, growing up during the 1930s"; a teacher's manual "for integrating daily lesson plans with information about critical contributions made to the American experience by women and men of diverse races and ethnicities."

Sidelights

Darwin McBeth Walton told *SATA:* "I grew up in Charlotte, North Carolina, during the Great Depression, at a time when children's books were scarce and almost nonexistent for African-American children in a racially segregated town. I was second oldest of five girls. We read stacks of comic books, sang a lot, and made up stories—which we often acted out for our parents and visitors. Most of our stories were learned through word-of-mouth from parents, relatives, and friends. I do remember a book titled *Once upon a Time,* a book of old-time fairy tales, and a book called *The AESOP for Children.* My mother and father both sang nursery rhymes and retold their own stories. My aunt told spine-chilling ghost stories when three of us spent summers on the farm. She would have all of us, her three kids, too, afraid to go outside (to the outhouse) or even to another room alone. It was wonderful. But my grandfather was the great storyteller. He grew up with the Cherokee, and his culture was closely intertwined with theirs. I remember the sand burning my bare feet on hot summer days as I treaded in his wake around the family farm in South Carolina. He taught me how to listen to trees and how to interpret the rhythmic sounds of crickets, birds, and frogs. 'Everything in nature has something to say,' he told me, 'but you have to listen.'

"I believe that good creative writing relies heavily on the writer's listening skills. I think rhythm is the essence of a great book and is what captures the reader. I try to make my writing singable. (This may be the music in my soul.) When I was teaching third and fourth grade I made up silly rhymes and sang the spelling lessons. It was corny, but my students looked forward to spelling. Kids love anything that has a beat or a rhyme. We wrote many poems and songs in my classes.

"*What Color Are You?* was, in 1973, one of the first definitive books on diversity to be published in America. It was born out of my experiences as a parent of children growing up in a supposedly integrated school system (and the challenges they had to overcome) and, then, as the only black teacher in a predominantly white school community. The book preceded the inclusion of women's and minority peoples' histories in our textbooks.

"My writing is largely about reconciliation. I believe that acceptance—not tolerance—and *mutual* respect comprise the solutions to our educational, social, and political problems. Our children of today should know enough about each other's ancestors and their contributions to the world experience to be able to respect and appreciate each other's possibilities before they become the leaders of tomorrow. The dream of that reality is important to me.

"I retired from the Elmhurst public school system in 1986 and joined the faculty at National-Louis University in the teacher education department. As a supervisor of student teachers, I am in touch with students of all ages. My most satisfying occupation at this time is working with the Chicago Area Project and an after-school volunteer reading program with inner-city school kids. Books for the readers are provided by the project. Thus far, the kids in six schools have been very enthusiastic and remarkably loyal in attendance. I am excited to be a part of the program. Every child who claims to be inspired or changed by something I've said or written motivates me and adds tremendously to my reason for being. I am thankful for that and, as difficult as a writer's life may sometimes be, children, especially those who read and enjoy my books, help to make it the most gratifying of all occupations. It is certainly the most enduring one."

Biographical and Critical Sources

PERIODICALS

Booklist, February 15, 1974, review of *What Color Are You?,* p. 660; September 1, 1998, Denia Hester, review of *Dance, Kayla!,* p. 121.
Bulletin of the Center for Children's Books, March, 1974, review of *What Color Are You?,* p. 119.
Children's Book Review Service, August, 1998, review of *Dance, Kayla!,* p. 166.
Horn Book Guide, fall, 1998, review of *Dance, Kayla!,* p. 340.
Kirkus Reviews, May 15, 1998, review of *Dance, Kayla!,* p. 746.
Library Journal, September 15, 1974, review of *What Color Are You?,* p. 119.
School Library Journal, August, 1998, Lynda Short, review of *Dance, Kayla!,* p. 168.

WERLIN, Nancy 1961-

Personal

Born October 29, 1961, in Salem, MA; daughter of Arnold (a computer engineer) and Elaine (a homemaker) Werlin. *Education:* Yale University, B.A., 1983. *Politics:* Liberal Democrat. *Religion:* Jewish.

Addresses

Home—Boston, MA. *Agent*—Ginger Knowlton, Curtis Brown, 10 Astor Place, New York, NY. *E-mail*—nwerlin@world.std.com.

Career

Software technical writer for various companies, 1983-87; Thomson Investment Software, Boston, MA, part-time software technical writer, 1987-97; part-time worker for software companies, 1997—. Member of board of directors, Shriver Clinical Services, Inc. *Member:* Society of Children's Book Writers and Illustrators.

Awards, Honors

Quick Pick and Popular Paperback selections, both American Library Association, *Publishers Weekly* Flying Start Award, and New York Public Library Best Books for the Teen Age selection, all for *Are You Alone on Purpose?;* Best Book for Young Adults, Quick Pick-Top 10 titles, and Teens' Top 10 Best Book Pick selections, all American Library Association, Edgar Award for Best YA Mystery, *Booklist* Editor's Choice selection, *Bulletin of the Center for Children's Books* Blue Ribbon Book, New York Public Library Best Books for the Teen Age selection, and Bank Street College Best Book of the Year award, all 1999, all for *The Killer's Cousin.*

Writings

Are You Alone on Purpose?, Houghton, 1994.
The Killer's Cousin, Delacorte, 1998.
Locked Inside, Delacorte, 2000.

Sidelights

Nancy Werlin, a writer with three novels to her credit, has earned a reputation for tackling difficult subjects in a sensitive and engaging way. In the process, she has carved out a niche for herself in the demanding world of young adult fiction. Werlin's 1994 debut novel, *Are You Alone on Purpose?,* explored with sensitivity and insight the effects of autism on a family, a subject which she knows from personal experience. As interviewer Kit Alderdice noted in a 1994 *Publishers Weekly* profile of Werlin, "[she] touches on subjects not usually tackled in the YA realm," and does so "with rich, layered characterizations and believable situations." Alderdice subsequently noted that Werlin's second novel, a thriller entitled *The Killer's Cousin,* dealt with another delicate subject that is not often dealt with by young adult

Nancy Werlin

authors—teen homicide. *The Killer's Cousin* won Werlin many awards, including the prestigious Edgar for Best YA Mystery, and it confirmed her early promise as a new author to watch. Werlin's third novel, another mystery that is entitled *Locked Inside,* concerns a young heiress who is kidnaped and in the circumstances is obliged to rethink her idealized relationship with her deceased mother.

Cut with an emotionally intense edge, Werlin's fiction never talks down to her young readers. Indeed, her first novel was planned as adult fiction. Three drafts later, on the advice of a friend who is a children's book writer, Werlin recast that original novel as young adult fiction. In a February 2000 interview with J. Sydney Jones, Werlin noted, "I actually think of myself more as writing *about* teenagers than *for* them. Teens and adults are on similar reading levels and the only difference between most books for teens and most books for adults is that the protagonists in a teen novel are themselves teenagers. Perhaps I'm so intrigued with this time of life because it was such an uncomfortable one for me. My characters all tend to be uneasy in their teenager skins, just as I was."

Nancy Werlin grew up in Peabody, Massachusetts, the youngest of three daughters. In her interview with Jones, she described being raised in what she terms "a middle-class Jewish home." Werlin's father was an engineer and computer programmer while her mother was a homemaker, although she later went back to college and earned her bachelor of arts degree. "There was a great respect for books and education in our house," Werlin recalled, "but nobody came close to reading the way I did." Werlin "cracked the code," as she puts it, and began reading when she was three—her first breakthrough came with a "Dick, Jane, and Sally" reader. "My parents were delighted and proud of me," Werlin said. "From then on I lived as much within books as I did in the real world—though, as an adult, I find myself sure it had its issues: for example, my best friend was another reader, and our idea of being together involved being in the same room and reading, then swapping books."

By the time Werlin reached third grade, she was reading as many as ten books a week. "I was indiscriminate and voracious about it," Werlin commented. "My mother drove me each week to the three libraries it took to feed my habit." Werlin's favorite reading matter during these years included the "Nancy Drew" and "Cherry Ames" series, Ray Bradbury's science fiction, historical novels of all sorts (especially ones set in Tudor England and the French Revolution), and classics such as *Little Women,*

The intelligent twin sister of an autistic teen, Alison is at first tormented by, then becomes more than friends with, the widowed rabbi's son after he is left a paraplegic from a diving accident. (Cover illustration by Robert Wisnewski.)

Jane Eyre, The Hobbit, and *The Lord of the Rings.* "I also read encyclopedias," Werlin stated. "I was particularly fond of a set that contained an appendix of plot synopses for famous novels. By the time I was ten, I knew I wanted to be a writer to create what I loved so much." As Werlin told interviewer Kit Alderdice of *Publishers Weekly,* "I just read all the time and it occurred to me that somebody had to write these things—and why shouldn't it be me?"

Werlin did not like going to school, although she got good grades. "On the whole, I disliked [it] from adolescence on. I found [school] boring in terms of work, and anxiety-producing socially. I was good at the academic game, but I never believed in it, and on a few occasions I got into trouble with teachers because I would show my contempt. And although I've come to regret my bad manners, I'm afraid I still believe that much of the 'work' in school is a preposterous waste of everyone's time." Throughout middle school and high school, Werlin continued to experiment with writing, penning a number of short stories. As Werlin described, in addition to her writing, her biggest ambition during her school days was simply "to get Out of There. I always had a feeling of marking time," she recalled.

After graduating from high school, Werlin attended Yale University, where she majored in English. "[It was] an easy major for me, since it involved reading and then writing about what I'd read." Werlin went on to note, "But college also confirmed my gut-level knowledge that I wasn't, in fact, at all academically inclined." In her senior year, with graduation looming and a growing awareness on her part that she would soon have to earn a living, Werlin began taking classes in computer programming.

Upon graduating from Yale, Werlin took a full-time job working in the software industry as a technical writer. She then went to Europe, where she spent eighteen months in Germany working for a computer company. She did not enjoy the work and slowly realized she was not getting any closer to her dream of becoming a fiction writer. Werlin returned home determined to carve out part of the week for her fiction. She supported herself by working at a part-time, thirty-hour-per-week job in Boston. However, it took her another year to develop a writing schedule and to tackle the plot of what ultimately became her first novel. During this time, Werlin joined some writers' groups that met regularly. She began sharing and discussing her work with others. In her new regimen, she set aside a room in her apartment as an office. "I never went in there; it was far too intimidating," Werlin revealed in the interview. "I was much happier and much more able to work when I rearranged the place and put my computer in a small cozy corner of the living room."

Ultimately, Werlin came up with an early draft of her novel. Athena Lord, the mother of a college friend and a children's book writer, offered to take a look at the manuscript. Werlin was surprised when Lord told her she had the makings of a young adult novel. Werlin was initially determined to continue with the book as an adult title, but she took Lord's advice in submitting the manuscript to Lauri Hornik at Houghton Mifflin. Hornik advised lengthy revisions, which Werlin did. "And lo! She made an offer to publish," Werlin noted.

In *Are You Alone on Purpose?* Werlin tells the story of two Jewish teenagers locked in struggles with their families, with each other, and with their own identities. Thirteen-year-old Alison Shandling, a well-behaved high achiever, resents her tormentor, Harry Roth. He is her opposite: a loud, crude, trouble-making bully who is also the only child of the town's widowed rabbi. Alison's sweetness and ambition are rooted in her desire to compensate for her family's most draining problem, her autistic twin brother named Adam. Much of Harry's behavior seems to be an attempt just to get his bereaved father's attention, even if his father's only response is to reprimand him. For years Harry has taunted Alison about her autistic brother and about her brilliance in the classroom.

It is not until the two teenagers are forced to spend time together under tragic circumstances that they each come to terms with their problems—and their budding sexuality. After a diving accident Harry is left a paraplegic, confined to a wheelchair. Alison fears that this tragedy may have befallen Harry because of her mother's wish that Rabbi Roth's son might become even more handicapped than Adam, her autistic son. Alison tries to make amends for this by becoming friends with Harry, only to find as they are thrown together in Jewish studies that they become more than friends.

"Of all the characters I've created," Werlin wrote on her Web site, "Alison Shandling is the closest on the surface to who and what I was at her age. But I made her smarter than me—both intellectually and emotionally. And I made her braver." Werlin went on to explain that in crafting the book's plot, she "was trying quite deliberately to come up with a situation that would force Alison to confront her parents about her own needs, and that would also cause her to muse for the first time ... on the place of God in the universe, given that the world contains so much pain and suffering."

Most reviewers applauded Werlin's debut novel. Marian Rafal, writing in *Voice of Youth Advocates,* felt that "Harry and Alison's tentative beginnings and tender friendship will strike a familiar chord with young people who cope with feelings of alienation from family and peers on a regular basis." Rafal concluded, "Despite an ending a little too neatly resolved, this is a wonderful first novel." Deborah Stevenson, in *Bulletin of the Center for Children's Books,* had mixed opinions: "The story is somewhat predictable and the psychology of the characters often obvious, but the emotions run strong enough to keep the story involving." Writing in *School Library Journal,* Sharon Grover stated that although Alison's confrontation with her parents through letters misses the force of "Werlin's wonderfully strong dialogue, this first novel is a moving portrayal of two

David moves in with his aunt and uncle to escape the memories and accusations surrounding his girlfriend's death, but discovers something shocking about his hostile cousin instead in Werlin's award-winning thriller. (Cover illustration by Craig White.)

remarkable teenagers ably coming to grips with their unhappy circumstances."

Horn Book reviewer Maeve Visser Knoth wrote that "Harry and Alison are rich, multi-dimensional characters, and the supporting cast is also clearly drawn." Knoth went on to hail *Are You Alone on Purpose?* as "a complex, compelling story" and "a promising debut." *Booklist*'s Karen Simonetti praised the novel's "superb" characterizations, and Werlin's "smooth writing and refined plot," which Simonetti felt would "make this ultimately uplifting story very popular." She went to comment, "Although certainly a book about people with problems, this is more than a 'problem novel.'" Meanwhile, a *Publishers Weekly* reviewer praised Werlin as a "writer worth watching."

Werlin explained that her second book, *The Killer's Cousin,* began as an ordinary novel but "transformed itself into psychological suspense, and I've since realized that I enjoy working—developing characters and themes—within the framework of a suspense plot. It sharpens my ideas and gives shape to the work."

Werlin remarked on her Web site that she "went through five tortuous, hideous, and painful drafts over five years before *The Killer's Cousin* reached its final form." In those early drafts, her protagonist was a twenty-six-year-old high school history teacher obsessing over a girlfriend who was very much alive. Abandoning the novel for several months, Werlin gained a fresh perspective and realized that the teacher character was the problem because he did not have the edge to draw the reader into her mystery. She solved the problem by recasting the teacher as a seventeen-year-old who has recently been acquitted of the murder of his girlfriend. Werlin explained that the change was an important one: "It was about making the situation MATTER to the protagonist and, therefore, to the reader."

In the recast version of *The Killer's Cousin,* the protagonist named David has moved to Cambridge, Massachusetts, to the home of his aunt and uncle to finish his senior year in high school. David desperately needs to get away from the media hype about the death of his girlfriend, as well as the suspicious looks of his ex-friends and neighbors. He moves into an attic apartment at his relatives' house as he tries to come to terms with the previous year's traumatic events. However, David's aunt and uncle and their eleven-year old daughter, Lily, have more than enough problems of their own. They are still recovering from the suicide of their older daughter, Kathy, four years earlier, an incident that took place in the very rooms that David now occupies. He begins seeing ghostly shadows at night and feels coldness, if not resentment, from his aunt. On the other hand, Lily is far from distant; she displays malice toward her cousin, and as her behavior becomes increasingly hostile toward him, David wonders why. He also begins to wonder what dark secrets are being hidden in this home. David eventually realizes that Lily was somehow responsible for the death of her sister.

The critical reception for *The Killer's Cousin* was as enthusiastic as it was positive. "Werlin has a lot going on here ... but she manages to keep all the balls in the air," Deborah Stevenson commented in *Bulletin of the Center for Children's Books.* "The book doesn't stint on the tension.... So much of [its] pleasure is that of an intelligent thriller." Stevenson concluded that readers "will be sucked right into the supernaturally edged story of the burden of the terrible past and its effect on the future." In a *Booklist* review, John Peters hailed *The Killer's Cousin* as an "utterly terrifying psychodrama," that is a "tautly plotted thriller, rich in complex finely drawn characters [in which] Werlin more than fulfills the promise of her first novel." Reviewer Claire Rosser of *Kliatt* noted, "This is a demanding psychological novel ... one that will have great appeal for YAs who enjoy untangling complex emotions." Rosser concluded, "This is one of the few YA novels that will grip and hold high school readers, and challenge even the most thoughtful ones." *Horn Book*'s Anne St. John agreed with that assessment, writing that "Young adults will eat this one up." Proving the reviewers right, *The Killer's Cousin* found a receptive audience and won several awards, including the Edgar for YA mystery fiction. Werlin's literary career was set firmly on course.

"I had no hesitation in deciding that my third novel, *Locked Inside,* would also be suspense," Werlin said. And for this book, Werlin wrote about a character who "surprised me at every turn." "Completely, totally, and fiercely, I love Marnie Skyedottir, the protagonist of *Locked Inside,*" Werlin has noted on her Web site. "While I was writing this novel, whenever Marnie would do something particularly Marnie-like, I'd jump up from my desk chair and dance around. Oh, or cry."

Marnie is a wealthy heiress, the sixteen-year-old daughter of a celebrity who was killed years before in a plane crash. Living and studying now at a boarding school, she does not want to participate in the social world there. Instead, she prefers to hide in her room. There she plays her favorite Internet game and chats on-line with another player with the handle of Elf. Marnie's life is lived at

A wealthy heiress who prefers cyberspace to the real world is kidnapped and locked in a basement, where she confronts truths about herself as she tries to escape. (Cover illustration by Ericka O'Rourke.)

arm's length; cyberspace proves a comfort zone for her. However, when Marnie is kidnaped and held in a cell-like basement by a new teacher who hopes to prove that she is also the celebrity's daughter, Marnie realizes that hiding herself away has not given her any real safety from the world. She is also forced to confront uncomfortable truths about herself and about her famous mother. Marnie must now use some of the skills she used in her Internet strategy game to win her freedom.

A *Booklist* reviewer deemed *Locked Inside* "a compelling thriller," one which "will gain readers by word of mouth." A contributor in *Publishers Weekly* found some "implausibility" to the plot, but concluded that overall this third novel "is entertaining," and that "Marnie's outsiderness is of the kind that appeals to readers ... and her personality is spirited enough to live up to the creative problem-solving Werlin assigns her." And a critic in *Kirkus Reviews* praised *Locked Inside* as a "meaty tale of self-discovery" and a "thriller for thoughtful readers." Werlin would probably agree with that assessment of her writing, for as she explained, "When I describe my work these days, I always say that I write psychological suspense thrillers for teenagers."

Werlin is currently working on another suspense thriller, but she is also toying with another genre close to her heart: historical fiction. With three successes to her credit, Werlin has established a regular writing pattern and schedule. She now writes in a separate office. "Despite my initial trepidation about whether that might prove too intimidating, I've come to love it," she revealed. Werlin continues to work at her day job as a technical writer, but she reserves two days a week for her own writing. "While I usually begin with an initial idea for a novel, most the time this turns out NOT to be the central idea of the finished book," Werlin said. "Instead, it's only the thing that primes the pump. I've learned to trust that the real stuff will arise in the process of actually doing the writing. I completely believe the 'one percent inspiration, ninety-nine percent perspiration' concept of creativity. Ideas are a dime a dozen. 'Butt in chair' is what gets a novel written—that, and trust in the process." Werlin proves her belief in the 'perspiration' part of the equation by the care with which she revises her works: her books all go through multiple drafts before she is satisfied with the finished product.

"It's important to me that my books be enjoyable, involving reads," Werlin said. "I value the role of books as escape and as entertainment. But in particular, my books require this element for balance, as so often I work with darker material—intense, unhappy characters; frightening, terrible events; and (like most mysteries and thrillers) the importance of morality in our lives.... Personally, my concern is to stretch and grow with each book; to become a better and more mature writer; to gain skill at all the things needed, technically, to write good books—by which I mean, simply, books that people want to read, and them remember having read. For me, every day of writing is a difficult day. But I also feel blessed that I'm able to have this job."

Biographical and Critical Sources

PERIODICALS

Booklist, August 19, 1994, Karen Simonetti, review of *Are You Alone on Purpose?,* p. 147; September 1, 1998, John Peters, review of *The Killer's Cousin,* p. 113; October 1, 1998; January 1, 1999, p. 783; March 15, 1999, p. 1302; April 1, 1999, p. 1383; July, 1999; December 1, 1999, review of *Locked Inside.*

Bulletin of the Center for Children's Books, December, 1994, Deborah Stevenson, review of *Are You Alone on Purpose?,* p. 147; September, 1998, Deborah Stevenson, review of *The Killer's Cousin,* pp. 38-39.

Horn Book, January-February, 1995, Maeve Visser Knoth, review of *Are You Alone on Purpose?,* p. 65; Spring, 1995, p. 92; January-February, 1999, Anne St. John, review of *The Killer's Cousin,* p. 72; Spring, 1999, p. 83.

Kirkus Reviews, December 15, 1999, review of *Locked Inside,* p. 1965.

Kliatt, March, 1996, p. 12; July, 1998, Claire Rosser, review of *The Killer's Cousin,* p. 9.

Publishers Weekly, November 14, 1994, review of *Are You Alone on Purpose?,* p. 69; December 19, 1994, Kit Alderdice, "Nancy Werlin," p. 34; October 26, 1998, p. 67; January 10, 2000, review of *Locked Inside,* p. 69.

School Library Journal, August, 1994, Sharon Grover, review of *Are You Alone on Purpose?,* p. 204; November 1, 1998, p. 131.

Voice of Youth Advocates, October, 1994, Marian Rafal, review of *Are You Alone on Purpose?,* p. 219; October, 1998, p. 280.

ON-LINE

Nancy Werlin's Web Site, http://world.std.com/~nwerlin/.

—*Sketch by J. Sydney Jones*

*   *   *

WESTON, Martha 1947-

Personal

Born January 16, 1947, in Asheville, NC; daughter of Nelson George (a professor) and Martha (Patton) Hairston; married Richard Weston (a hospital consultant); children: Dory, Charley. *Education:* Attended University of North Carolina, Greensboro, 1965-66; University of Michigan, B.F.A., 1969.

Addresses

Office—San Anselmo, CA. *Agent*—Dilys Evans, 1123 Broadway, Room 313, New York, NY 10010.

Career

Freelance illustrator and writer, 1970—. Worked in a design studio in New York City, and as an animator for the television show *Sesame Street* in San Francisco, CA.

Member: Society of Children's Book Writers and Illustrators.

Awards, Honors

The Book of Think; or, How to Solve a Problem Twice Your Size was selected for the Children's Book Showcase, 1977; New York Academy of Sciences Children's Science Book Award, Younger Category, 1981, for *Bet You Can't! Science Impossibilities to Fool You; The Hanukkah Book* was selected a Notable Children's Trade Book in Social Studies, 1982; New York Academy of Sciences Children's Science Book Award, Younger Category, 1989, for *The Sierra Club Wayfinding Book.*

Writings

AUTHOR AND ILLUSTRATOR; PICTURE BOOKS

Peony's Rainbow, Lothrop, 1981, published as *If I Only Had a Rainbow,* 1989.
Bea's 4 Bears, Clarion, 1992.
Apple Juice Tea, Clarion, 1994.
Tuck in the Pool, Clarion, 1995.
Bad Baby Brother, Clarion, 1997.
Cats Are Like That, Holiday House, 1999.
Space Guys, Holiday House, 2000.

ILLUSTRATOR

(With James Robertson) Amazing Life Games Company, *Good Cents: Every Kid's Guide to Making Money,* Houghton, 1974.
Jamie Jobb, *My Garden Companion: A Complete Guide for the Beginner* (nonfiction), Scribner's, 1977.
Em Riggs and Barbara Darpinian, *I Am a Cookbook* (nonfiction), St. Martin's, 1977.

until he opened his eyes.

Tuck overcomes his fear of the water with the help of his lucky rubber spider in Martha Weston's self-illustrated Tuck in the Pool.

Marne Wilkins, *The Long Ago Lake: A Child's Book of Nature Lore and Crafts,* Sierra Books, 1978, Chronicle, 1989.
Vicki Cobb and Kathy Darling, *Bet You Can't! Science Impossibilities to Fool You,* Lothrop, 1980.
Miriam Schlein, *Lucky Porcupine!* (nonfiction), Four Winds Press, 1980.
Stephen Manes, *The Hoople's Haunted House* (fiction), Delacorte, 1981.
Dean Hughes, *Honestly, Myron* (fiction), Atheneum, 1982.
Carl M. Wallace, *Should You Shut Your Eyes When You Kiss? Or, How to Survive "The Best Years of Your Life,"* Little, Brown, 1983.
Pat Sharp, *Brain Power! Secrets of a Winning Team* (nonfiction), Lothrop, 1984.
Catherine B. Kaye, *Word Works: Why the Alphabet Is a Kid's Best Friend,* Little, Brown, 1985.
Elizabeth Winthrop, *Lizzie and Harold* (fiction), Lothrop, 1986.
Esther Hautzig, *Make It Special: Cards, Decorations, and Party Favors for Holiday and Special Occasions,* Macmillan, 1986.
Patricia Lauber, *What Big Teeth You Have!,* Harper, 1986.
Norma Jean Sawicki, *Something for Mom* (fiction), Lothrop, 1987.
Susan Fulop Kepner, *Somebody's Mother* (fiction), Strawberry Hill Press (San Francisco), 1987.
Carol Barkin and Elizabeth James, *Happy Valentine's Day* (nonfiction), Lothrop, 1988.
Jerry Booth, *The Big Beast Book: Dinosaurs and How They Got That Way,* Little, Brown, 1988.
Anna Fairbank, *Lucky Me!: An Adoption Story,* Mariah Press (Millbrae, CA), 1988.
Elizabeth Wilkinson, *Making Cents: Every Kid's Guide to Money,* Little, Brown, 1989.
Elizabeth Winthrop, *The Best Friends Club,* Lothrop, 1989.
Vicki McVey, *The Sierra Club Wayfinding Book,* Sierra Club Books, 1989.
Jean Cushman, *Do You Wanna Bet?: Your Chance to Find Out about Probability,* Clarion, 1991.
Lynne Foster, *Take a Hike!: The Sierra Club Kid's Guide to Hiking and Backpacking,* Sierra Club Books, 1991.
Vicki McVey, *The Sierra Club Book of Weatherwisdom* (nonfiction), Sierra Club Books, 1991.
Harvey Hirsch and Audrey Hirsch, *The Creche of Krakow: A Christmas Story,* Momentum Books (Ann Arbor, MI), 1992.
Vicki McVey, *The Sierra Club Kid's Guide to Planet Care and Repair,* Sierra Club Books, 1993.
Carol Barkin and Elizabeth James, *The New Complete Babysitter's Handbook,* Clarion, 1995.
Lissa Rovetch, *Cora and the Elephants* (fiction), Viking, 1995.
Elizabeth James and Carol Barkin, *Social Smarts: Manners for Today's Kids,* Clarion, 1996.
Kay Winters, *Did You See What I Saw? Poems about School,* Viking, 1996.
Stephanie Greene, *Owen Foote, Soccer Star* (sequel to *Owen Foote, Second Grade Strongman*), Clarion, 1998.
Stephanie Greene, *Owen Foote, Frontiersman,* Clarion, 1999.

Then I see Willy is doing a terrible thing!

Tessa is impatient with her new brother until he grows old enough to play. (From Bad Baby Brother, *written and illustrated by Weston.*)

Marjorie Weinman Sharmat, *Nate the Great and the Monster Mess,* Delacorte, 1999.

Kay Winters, *How Will the Easter Bunny Know?,* Yearling, 1999.

Elizabeth Partridge, *Pig's Eggs,* Golden, 2000.

Marjorie Weinman Sharmat and Mitchell Sharmat, *Nate the Great, San Francisco Detective,* Delacorte, 2000.

ILLUSTRATOR; ALL WRITTEN BY MARILYN BURNS

The I Hate Mathematics! Book, Little, Brown, 1975.

The Book of Think; or, How to Solve a Problem Twice Your Size, Little, Brown, 1976.

I Am Not a Short Adult! Getting Good at Being a Kid, Little, Brown, 1977.

This Book Is about Time, Little, Brown, 1978.

The Hanukkah Book, Four Winds Press, 1981.

The Hink Pink Book; or, What Do You Call a Magician's Extra Bunny? (riddles), Little, Brown, 1981.

Math for Smarty Pants; or, Who Says Mathematicians Have Little Pig Eyes?, Little, Brown, 1982.

The $1.00 World Riddle Book, Math Solutions Publications (White Plains, NY), 1990.

ILLUSTRATOR; ALL WRITTEN BY LINDA ALLISON

Eenie Meenie Miney Math! Math Play for You and Your Preschooler, Little, Brown, 1993.

Wordsaroni: Word Play for You and Your Preschooler, Little, Brown, 1993.

Pint-Size Science: Finding-Out Fun for You and Your Young Child, Little, Brown, 1994.

Razzle Dazzle Doodle Art: Creative Play for You and Your Young Child, Little, Brown, 1994.

Howdy Do Me and You: Getting-Along Activities for You and Your Child, Little, Brown, 1996.

Sidelights

During a productive career that has spanned nearly three decades, Martha Weston has adorned dozens of books with pen-and-ink, pencil, and watercolor illustrations. From an early age Weston was interested in art. "I drew constantly and was often reprimanded in school for drawing pictures at the top of my spelling test instead of filling in the blanks with spelling words," Weston remembered for *SATA*. "Luckily, my parents were always encouraging, telling me my pictures were 'beautiful.' They were not artists themselves, but appreciated art and generally had the attitude that whatever career their children chose was okay. From the time I was very young I knew that I would be an artist when I grew up. I simply couldn't imagine another life." Although she knew early in life that she would become an artist, Weston chose to get a bachelor of fine arts degree at a major university because she did not want to limit her overall education by attending an art school. "The idea

The ball with the bell inside
was rolling across the floor.
"Fuzzy!" yelled Dot. "Get down!"

Dot defends her new pet fish from Fuzzy the cat in Weston's self-illustrated **Cats Are Like That.**

of dropping my French studies and never learning anything about history didn't appeal to me," she explained.

Because most colleges and art schools did not specifically offer illustration programs at that time, Weston had much to learn on her own. After graduating from college, she worked at several jobs that taught her more about her craft. While living in New York City, she worked at a design studio and learned how artwork is reproduced. Then she lived and worked in San Francisco, where she painted animation cells for the *Sesame Street* show. The first book she illustrated was an idea book for teachers to use when making bulletin boards. From her work on that project, Weston learned a great deal about composition, page layout, design, and meeting deadlines. In 1972 she met writer Marilyn Burns, with whom she collaborated on a handful of nonfiction "problem-solving" books over the next ten years. Often the writer and illustrator of a book may never meet each other, but Weston and Burns worked closely on their joint projects. During this time, Weston also illustrated science books, a cookbook, and nature books written by a variety of authors for a number of publishers.

Until the 1980s, Weston worked largely in black and white, except for cover illustrations, which she rendered in colored pencil. With her first self-authored book, *Peony's Rainbow,* a story about a pig named Peony who catches a rainbow, Weston used black pen and ink to illustrate everything except the rainbow, which she painted in watercolors. Although several critics complained that the plot of this picture book is rather thin, they appreciated the artwork. A *Kirkus Reviews* critic noted "Weston's several clever touches and the book's generally spiffy look," while a *Publishers Weekly* commentator praised Weston's "dashing pen-and-ink illustrations," which "form a fine contrast with the vivid watercolors of the rainbow." "Although I consider myself first and foremost an illustrator, I really enjoyed writing *Peony's Rainbow,*" Weston told *SATA*. "I must say, however, that it was very difficult for me."

Although Weston continued to primarily illustrate works written by others, she rose to the challenge of writing her own books, all of which present common family situations. They include *Bea's 4 Bears, Apple Juice Tea, Tuck in the Pool, Bad Baby Brother,* and *Cats Are Like That.* To quote a *Kirkus Reviews* critic, *Bea's 4 Bears* is a "winning introduction to counting" that shows how Bea loses and recovers her four teddy bears. In *Booklist* Carolyn Phelan complimented "Weston's bright, unpretentious illustrations" and predicted that *Bea's 4 Bears* would be useful for kindergarten teachers. In *Apple Juice Tea* Weston dealt with the common problem of visits by unfamiliar relatives, this time a Grandmother, who eventually proves herself to be a good companion. According to both Ilene Cooper of *Booklist* and *School Library Journal* critic Elizabeth Hanson, Weston's story is "reassuring." Moreover, Hanson remarked that the "illustrations capture its [the text's] up-beat tone and spirit."

Tuck in the Pool treats another common childhood dilemma, the fear of water, with a pig named Tuck at poolside. Writing in *Booklist,* Hazel Rochman remarked on the "cheerful, funny pictures" and comforting message when Tuck finally overcomes his fear. The little pigs "strike just the right note," added Marcia Hupp in her *School Library Journal* review, and in *Bulletin of the Center for Children's Books* Deborah Stevenson punned, "This'll make a nice splash." With *Bad Baby Brother,* Weston took a look at an older sister's response to her baby brother's arrival. A *Kirkus Reviews* critic complained that the story is "too familiar" despite its well-timed pace. Yet Lisa Marie Gangemi, writing in *School Library Journal,* praised Weston's depiction of a range of emotions, adding, "The pictures and the text are seamless." Carolyn Phelan of *Booklist* praised the work as an "appealing choice for young children with new babies in the family."

Many families have pets, and the beginning reader *Cats Are Like That* explores the relationship between a cat named Fuzzy and three new pet fish. While Nancy A. Gifford maintained in *School Library Journal* that the beginning reader is "predictable," she also judged it a "welcome addition" to the genre. *Booklist* reviewer Kay Weisman noted Weston's colorful artwork and matter-of-fact telling of Fuzzy's attempts to eat the fish, concluding that the book will be "popular with most beginning readers, especially those with personal pet experience."

During the early 1990s, Weston produced a steady stream of artwork, mostly for nonfiction books. She also illustrated her own picture books and increasingly received offers to illustrate others' fictional picture books and easy readers. These works include the picture books *Cora and the Elephants* and *How Will the Easter Bunny Know?,* as well as easy readers featuring Stephanie Greene's character Owen Foote and the perennial favorite of Marjorie Sharmat's fictional detective Nate the Great. *Cora and the Elephants,* which tells the story of an orphaned girl looking for her biological parents with the aid of her elephant parents, "is aided by Weston's fresh and funny watercolor art featuring Babar-esque characters who make you smile just looking at them," to quote Ilene Cooper in *Booklist.* Likewise, *Booklist* critic Carolyn Phelan noted Weston's "sensitive pencil drawings, highlighted with watercolor washes" in *How Will the Easter Bunny Know?* For Marjorie Sharmat's Nate the Great books, *Nate the Great and the Monster Mess* and *Nate the Great, San Francisco Detective,* Weston made illustrations in the style of the series' original illustrator, Marc Simont.

Like some parents who measure the passage of time by the growth of their children, Weston keeps a timeline based on her artistic progeny. "One of the best things about being an illustrator is that you have a tangible record of your work," she told *SATA.* "I can look at a book I did and remember all kinds of things that were happening in my life while I worked on it. My

Mike draws a map so the Easter bunny will find him at Grandma's house. (From How Will the Easter Bunny Know?, *written by Kay Winters and illustrated by Weston.)*

bookshelves hold more than just books, they hold my life."

Biographical and Critical Sources

PERIODICALS

Booklist, May 15, 1992, Carolyn Phelan, review of *Bea's 4 Bears,* p. 168; November 1, 1994, Ilene Cooper, review of *Apple Juice Tea,* p. 511; January 15, 1995, Ilene Cooper, review of *Cora and the Elephants,* p. 938; November 15, 1995, Hazel Rochman, review of *Tuck in the Pool,* p. 566; April 15, 1997, Carolyn Phelan, review of *Bad Baby Brother,* p. 1437; March 15, 1999, Carolyn Phelan, review of *How Will the Easter Bunny Know?,* p. 1339; March 15, 1999, Kay Weisman, review of *Cats Are Like That,* p. 1339.

Bulletin of the Center for Children's Books, November, 1995, Deborah Stevenson, review of *Tuck in the Pool,* p. 109.

Kirkus Reviews, September 15, 1981, review of *Peony's Rainbow,* p. 1158; February 15, 1992, review of *Bea's*

4 Bears, p. 261; April 1, 1997, review of *Bad Baby Brother,* p. 562.

Publishers Weekly, August 7, 1981, review of *Peony's Rainbow,* p. 78.

School Library Journal, September, 1994, Elizabeth Hanson, review of *Apple Juice Tea,* p. 201; February, 1996, Marcia Hupp, review of *Tuck in the Pool,* p. 91; June, 1997, Lisa Marie Gangemi, review of *Bad Baby Brother,* p. 103; June, 1999, Nancy A. Gifford, review of *Cats Are Like That,* p. 108.*

*   *   *

WOLFF, Sonia
See LEVITIN, Sonia (Wolff)

X

YongSheng Xuan

1952-

I was born into an ordinary intellectual's family in Shanghai, China. My father was a civil engineer, and my mother a housewife. After the Communists took over China, my parents were classified as "alien-class elements" belonging to the so-called "black four groups," and our inherited properties were confiscated by the Communist government for the fact that my parents were both from "rich families." When I was four or five, my father had to go far away from Shanghai to the mountainous areas in Fujian Province to build highways and bridges. The financial conditions of my family went from bad to worse. My childhood was half spent in hunger. Only when there was a holiday could we have a full meal with rationed pork. I have a brother one year my junior and a sister nine years younger. Every day after school, my job was to help Mother do house chores and look after my brother and sister. We couldn't afford toys, so we made our own. I cut a piece of cardboard into an oval shape with two holes, attached a string, brush painted it as the face of an eagle, and let my brother wear it to play hawk-and-chicken with me. When my sister cried, I would fold candy wrappers into flowers or birds to make her laugh. Chinese chess was made of bottle caps. We were most excited during the Chinese New Year when Mother often took us to the countryside in Qidong County on the north shore of the Yangtze River after a day's ride in a boat to spend the festival with our maternal grandparents.

My grandparents were both Buddhists. They prayed every morning and evening. After they finished their work in the fields, they would make paper sacrificial offerings for funerals for their neighbors, friends, relatives, and villagers. They cut colorful paper and cardboard to make houses, furniture, barrows, trunks, farm tools, water pails, coins, gold ingots, etc. After gluing and tying, they all looked so real and delicate. Those three-dimensional offerings were first framed with reed and bamboo and

YongSheng Xuan (right) with his younger brother, Shanghai, China, 1959.

covered with colored paper. Then all kinds of pictures, birds, animals, symmetrical or continuous patterns cut out with scissors were pasted on them. My grandfather was a well-known folk art craftsman among the villages far and near.

I would spend hours watching my grandfather work. Often I was so fascinated that I couldn't help offering to help. Every time he would say to me, "Xiao Long (Little Dragon, my infant name because I was born in the year of the dragon), you are still a child. When you grow up, you can help me. Now go to Grandma and have some dumplings." When he had some time, he would make a rabbit lantern or a kite for us. To this day, I remember those handicrafts Grandpa made. Years later when I grew to be an adult and became a professional folk art researcher, I

The award-winning woodcut print of "The Lights on a Fishery," 1971.

visited many old folk art craftsmen but never met anyone that matched my grandpa's talents. What a pity!

Grandma was always warm and kind. She taught us how to make dumplings, but I didn't like to make the same boring dumplings over and over again. Instead, I'd sculpt the sticky rice dough into little dogs, goats, fish, or birds. Grandma allowed me to put them into the steamer. When time was up and the steamer was opened, my brother, sister, and cousins would fight over my "craft works." That was my proudest time!

All children seem to love animals. My pets during my childhood were crickets and silkworms. When it was dark, my brother and I would go with other children in the countryside who were our age to look for crickets in the grass with the help of a flashlight. We put our catches into a bamboo pipe with a few grains of rice before sealing it with some cloth. Returning home, we would release the crickets into a big paper box and stir them with green bristle grass. Before long, they would start fighting each other like crazy. Eventually, one would retreat and try to run away, and that was the loser. I once had a big cricket named "the Unbeatable." Somehow one day it died in the bamboo pipe. I was sad for quite a few days and buried it in a corner of the school ground.

We had a headache over the problem of feeding the silkworms that moved with us to Shanghai. Where could we find mulberry trees, the leaves of which were the food for the silkworms? On Sunday, my brother and I would walk for two hours to Hongkou Park. We could not afford the entrance tickets, so we walked around and found a lower part of the wall. We climbed in and finally found some mulberry trees. Picking flowers and plants was prohibited, but how could we watch the silkworms die? We

looked around and saw nobody. We hurried to pick up some leaves, stuff them into our schoolbags, and run. When we saw the silkworms hungrily eat the food we got them through our adventure, nothing could make us happier. We witnessed the silkworms spit out silk, make cocoons, transform to chrysalides and then moths, lay eggs … indeed, their whole life cycle. Those childhood experiences all remained in my memory and fused into my conception of illustrations for children's books in recent years. For example, the experience with the silkworms helped me in creating the cover of the November 1999 issue of *Cricket* with its theme of silk fabrication. I once received a letter from twelve-year-old Beverly Klozkin forwarded to me by *Cricket.* She wrote: "The artist who drew the front cover is fantastic. Maybe you should ask him to do further covers. I really liked it." The young reader's praise was the greatest encouragement for me. I was deeply moved and sent through the press to her a paper-cut dragon to wish her a happy and lucky Year of the Dragon.

My father, being an architect designer, knew a little about art himself. Occasionally, he would draw grids on a piece of paper to make a portrait or something else. But I remember him most for his storytelling. Although he was rarely home, he made the most of his little time with us, telling us Chinese classic stories such as *The Three Kingdoms, The Marsh,* and *The Shrine of Gods.* He also told us about world classics such as *The Count of Monte Cristo.* I only partially understood his stories but became fascinated by "picture storybooks for children"—the comics.

Different from those in North America, the comics were not about action heroes with superhuman strength and their adventures, they were stories adapted from Chinese and world classics, novels, and movies. They were not limited to children's topics but covered a wide range of interests. Artists' illustrations added vivid pictures to make them very interesting. Thus the readers were not only children but also adults. The books were small in size, only five inches by four inches. The covers were usually in color but the content pages were mainly of black-and-white line drawings.

During the 1950s there were not many radios available in Shanghai (nor the whole country of China), no TV, and movies were too expensive. Reading comics, therefore, became the favorite pastime for children. Shanghai was the largest comics producer. Everywhere in Shanghai, comics stalls could be seen. Everyday after school, I would rush to those stalls, searching round and round with the three cents Mother had given me for breakfast in my hand. Three cents were enough only for reading three comics, and they were the cost for a full stomach, so I was very careful with my choices.

As time went by, I saved the "kowtow" money given to me at Chinese New Year by adults and the pocket money from my parents to buy some secondhand comics for repeated reading. I was deeply attracted to the rich contents

and beautiful illustrations. I began to copy them in pencil. I couldn't afford paper, so sheets from used notebooks after the work was erased became my painting paper. Maybe it is safe to say that those comics were my earliest art teachers and marked the very beginning of my art career.

When I was seven or eight years old, I was the best at drawing among the forty-five students in my class. By the time I finished grade school, I was a "famous painter" in my school. But my parents discouraged me from becoming a painter, just as later I persuaded my daughter, Faye Lee (officially Feli on her passport), to give up her wish for literature and art and choose an engineer's career, because the road for a successful artist is so much harder than that of an engineer. I dared not resist my parents' wishes, so I could only copy the illustrations from comics by hiding them in my bed after my family went to sleep. After a few months, I accumulated a pile of my "artwork" and I picked out the best to put on the wall. My brother was usually the only visitor at my "art exhibition" and the only critic.

In 1966, the Cultural Revolution began. Schools were closed. I was only fourteen and in high school then. It was supposed to be the golden time for studying, but I had to

Xuan with his parents, wife Rong Rong, and daughter Faye Lee at the Shanghai Art Gallery, 1986.

Xuan with fellow artist at the Nantong Research Institute, creating sculpture later exhibited in the Cultural Palace of Nationalities in Beijing, 1986.

idle away time at home. Because my grandfather was named an enemy of the Communist government, even though he had died long ago, I was affected as his grandson. I was barred from joining the Red Guards and any social activities. During the Cultural Revolution, my father was imprisoned in Fujian Province for more than three years and stripped of his salary, thanks to the status of my grandfather and my aunt (my father's elder sister, who went to Taiwan before the Communists' takeover). My mother almost collapsed under the enormous economic and mental pressures, and was forced to bed by illness for a long time. I had to sell our personal belongings to buy food to keep the family from starving.

But poverty and discrimination did not deter me from my ever growing interest in art. By pure chance, I met Mr. Zhang Chongren, a famous sculptor who had graduated from the Belgium Royal Academy of Arts during the 1930s. He was my first mentor. He had sculpted for Chiang Kai-shek, leader of the Nationalist Party of China. Mr. Chongren was also a faithful Christian. The Red Guards regarded him as an alien element much like my family. He was denounced and jailed, his home searched, and properties confiscated more than once.

I visited him very cautiously to avoid his neighbors' suspicion. He taught me how to draw and sculpt. After I went home, I would practice portrait sketching from life with a few friends with the same interests. Our models were mostly children. Some days we would be lucky to find two or three children, but when we were not so lucky, we would look in a mirror to sketch our own images. My

home at 185 Jiangxi Road north of Shanghai soon became our art studio.

With things so hard, I didn't have money for art supplies. I collected waste metals, old newspapers, and magazines to sell for money to buy pens, ink, and paper. But I never got enough money to buy clay or plaster, the materials for sculpture. One day I rode a bicycle to a suburb of Shanghai dozens of li (Chinese distance measure, half of a kilometer) away to dig up some clay to practice sculpture. The clay contained too much sand to be useable. To poverty and politics, I lost a dream.

During those school-less days, I picked up another hobby: kung fu. The traditional Chinese martial art of Shaolin boxing fascinated me. Every morning, I would go to Waitan Park to learn kung fu from a master who was a retired guard from a bank. I remember the first time I went home from practice, I couldn't walk for quite a few days from pain. After three to four years, I learned the basics of kung fu. Emphasizing the combination of strength and delicacy, the Chinese martial arts enlightened me with my painting. Making a feint to the east and attacking in the west, hiding your power as if there is none, freedom to advance or retreat—they were the essence of painting also. Had the painting art not attracted me more, I might have become Jackie Chan the Second today. Who knows?

During the 1960s, Mao Zedong's portraits were everywhere in China. They were seen from buildings on boulevards and small streets alike, just like Khomeini of Iran in later years. I was recommended by a neighbor to paint a giant portrait of Mao, fifteen feet by ten feet, at the gate of a factory. It took me more than three months to finish. My reward was a daily free lunch and the leftover oil painting brushes and oil colors, but I was very happy about that. After the portrait was finished, many people in my neighborhood spread the news: a teenage boy independently painted a giant Mao Zedong portrait.

But Mao did not appreciate what I did for him. Eventually I was sent with many other youths to the countryside to be a "new farmer" and receive reeducation from the lower- and middle-class peasants. Every day as the peasants did, we went to the fields at sunrise and came back home at sunset, with a scorching sun above us and burning heat under our feet. A hard day's work could only earn us a few dimes, just enough to keep us alive. For my mere existence, I had to carry out the primitive, repetitious labor.

I continued my pursuit of art using every bit of my spare time to practice painting, no matter if it was hot summer or cold winter. Finally I passed the exam with excellent marks to be accepted by the Cultural Center of Qidong County training class for professional painters of pictures from graven plates. Aside from learning some basic techniques of fine arts and making pictures from engraved plates, we three students and four teachers spent more time sketching in the cotton fields or visiting workers in the local farm machinery factory.

What interested me most was the Lusi Fishery in Qidong County. I visited the fishery many times to sketch, interview, and experience life on the sea. I was charmed by the boundless ocean, the simple but honest fishermen, and the fishing boats tossed by the waves, struggling in the stormy sea. When night fell, the fishermen returned with full boats, unloaded the catch of the day, and quietly berthed in the harbor. After a day's hard work, the fishermen would cook, drink, chat, play cards, Chinese chess, or some musical instruments against a background of hundreds of lights from their fishing boats. What a beautiful scene of happy fishermen! So natural, so tranquil! It triggered my strong desire to reproduce it. I made the composite in my head and finished the sketch in a relatively short time and named it *The Lights on a Fishery.*

When the draft was submitted for approval, I was ordered to change the fishermen under the fishing lights to be studying Mao's works. I had no choice but to comply. Looking at the painting, which has a strong political overcast, I now feel that it also reflects the real life of that particular period of Chinese history.

During this period, I created many black-and-white as well as color pictures from graven plates. Some were selected to be published in magazines or newspapers and displayed at municipal, provincial, and national art exhibits. But this watercolor block painting *The Lights on a Fishery* was my most successful work. I was only nineteen that year. It was later selected to be one of the representative pieces of Chinese modern pictures from graven plates to be exhibited abroad in countries such as Australia and Yugoslavia. It was also included in an album of paintings and won many awards.

I lived in Qidong County for a whole ten years. Besides creating pictures from graven plates at the Cultural Center, I also worked in a few handicraft factories designing wood sculpture, carving bamboo, creating batiks on blue cloth, fans, imitations of antiques, etc. Every year I would apply and take the entrance exam for a formal academy of fine arts; every time I did very well with the exam, but for the reasons mentioned before, I could not pass the political examination of the government and was shut out of the door of universities.

As I almost lost all hope, I met a girl with a very similar family background to mine. Her father was a lawyer who also was classified as an enemy by the government due to "historical problems." She also was a student driven to the countryside from the city. The differences between us were that I was good with thinking in images, using my hands, but I was reticent. In contrast, she was talkative and eloquent, had no taste for art but a good sense of logic and a brain for mathematics. Above all, she was understanding and kind.

I was deeply hurt by the refusals of universities again and again. And as misfortune never strikes just once, I injured my head at work and had dozens of stitches and was hospitalized. She came to look after me. With so much in common, love grew between us. Two years later, she

The author/illustrator welcoming his wife and daughter at the Regina Airport, Saskatchewan, 1990.

Teaching Chinese art in an elementary school classroom in Regina, 1990.

became my wife. We have quite different personalities. During the twenty-plus years we have been married, we have had many quarrels, but after the storm, either she or I would reach out for reconciliation. A Chinese proverb says, "A harmonious home is the source of all successes." More often, my wife and I would complement each other in dealing with family problems or making family decisions, big or small. The saying "Half of the success of a man can be traced to a woman" is very true in our case.

After Mao Zedong died in 1976, Deng Xiaoping announced the end of the Cultural Revolution. The fate of our families, as for many ordinary Chinese families, gradually changed. I was transferred to work in the Nantong Municipal Research Institute of Arts and Crafts as a full-time professional designer of handicrafts and painter. This was a big step forward in my art career. I once had been a fan of comics but now was a story writer and illustrator myself.

My work also included paper cutting, woodcarving, china and porcelain, interior decoration, etc. In the early 1980s, China opened up her door to the world. Modern western artistic concepts also landed in China. I was the happiest to have realized my decade-long dream: to enter the study and research class of one of the highest creative art education institutions in China—the Central University of Arts and Crafts of China. To make up for lost time, we had to work extremely hard. After classes, I studied by myself for four to five hours. We finished the usual three years' work for university students in just over a year. I was fortunate to receive the teaching and guidance of many Chinese legendary artists, such as Wu Guanzhong, Bai Xueshi, and Zhang Ting.

Because of the earlier influence from Mr. Zhang Chongren, I was particularly fond of three-dimensional sculpture. For practice after classes, I went with a few classmates and teachers to the "Capitals of Chinese Porcelain"—Shenhou Town of Henan Province and Lusi of Jiangsu Province—where I created many modern porcelain artworks and ceramic color picture plates. In 1986, my modern porcelain artworks were displayed at the Shanghai Art Gallery. The exhibit received broad favorable comments. The Shanghai TV and radio stations made special reports on it. A few newspapers and magazines published commentaries. In 1988 a few artists from the Nantong Research Institute and I had a joint art show in the Cultural Palace of Nationalities in Beijing. The period between 1979 to 1989 was the harvest time in my art career. I made breakthroughs in modern ceramic crafts, paper cuttings, woodcarving, handicraft design, comic book illustration, pure artistic painting, and art theories, etc. I had formed my own art style with nutrients from a variety of art forms.

After China's opening up, I made many friends from Japan, Western Germany, the United States, Canada, Hong Kong, and Taiwan. Professor Ken Mitchell, dean of the English literature department at the University of Regina in

Saskatchewan Province, Canada, was one of them. He was a guest professor at the China Institute of Diplomacy in Beijing. Besides teaching, he was also a productive writer. His award-winning play *Gone the Burning Sun* (a story about Canadian surgeon Dr. Norman Bethune, who came to China during the Japanese invasion to help with the fight and died at work) was to be on tour across China then. After visiting the art exhibit of our work at the Cultural Palace of Nationalities, he invited me to design a poster for the play. I finished the work within a very short time in the form of an oil painting from graven plate. It came as a surprise that before the play was performed, somebody took the poster for his or her private collection. After the tour was over, even Professor Mitchell himself didn't have a copy of it. Later I made a few more copies for him especially. He was deeply moved, and we became good friends.

At the beginning of 1989, he acted as my sponsor to visit Canada. The paperwork was done so fast and smoothly that I was not fully prepared in my mind. Before that, I had published some art theory work, illustrations, wood carving, and paper cuttings in Japanese trade magazines. A well-known professor and the president of a Japanese applied art university had sponsored me to study in Japan. I studied Japanese in my spare time. I had also studied some Russian in my high school years, but I couldn't even read the English alphabet! I was very hesitant to take the step, considering the nearly twenty years' foundation I had laid in the art circle of China, and most of all leaving a home and family behind.

My wife gave me enormous support at the time. She encouraged me to go out and open my eyes, saying that the vast world outside was necessary to broaden the views of an artist. So at the age of thirty-eight, I, an English illiterate, stepped on the land of North America with two suitcases and one thousand U.S. dollars my wife had carefully sewn in my shirt. Soon I had to choose between two paths: to study at the University of Regina as I had desired or to work and make a living. How I wished I could choose the first path! But the realities of having to start English from zero and being penniless forced me to give up the idea of studying for a master's degree. I found a job in a small furniture factory to make cabinets. With my training in woodcarving, I designed some special furniture with woodcarving and restored some antique furniture in addition to my routine production work. After hours, I went to many high schools to demonstrate and teach Chinese arts, especially paper cutting. The children's eagerness to learn, expressions of surprise, liveliness, and naivete reminded me of my own childhood and my own daughter. I love children, and I especially love my only daughter. But because I was so busy with my work all the time, I did not have the opportunity to teach her my own art. I did not even keep her company or take care of her. I still blame myself for that today.

After I lived a lonely life for seven months in Canada, my wife and daughter came to join me in Regina. Regina is in the cold zone even by Canadian standards. We were very unused to the freezing weather there, but my daughter was much more adaptable to the new environment than we. With her talent in language, she soon acted as our English interpreter. To save money, we could only rent a basement for $150. Before long, my wife found a job sewing and

altering. Often we both worked sixty hours a week and studied English at night. After awhile we did not have to worry about our living. During the first two years of our most difficult times, we received help and support from many friends. Among them were my sponsor Professor Ken Mitchell, Professor Wilfred Dube, fine arts Professor Joe Fafard, and Professor Pantis. Professor Dube often came to help us with our English, introduced me to friends in the art circle, and even gave financial help to me and other Chinese students who shared the same house with me. They helped me overcome the initial barrier of "illiteracy and nonrelevancy" in North America. I would like to take this opportunity to most sincerely thank all the friends who have helped us!

As soon as I didn't have to worry about food, I began climbing the heights of art. I strongly wished to integrate my art into the mainstream of North America although I knew very well that it was not easy to enter the art world here. But that didn't stop me from trying. I held personal art exhibitions at the university, art shops, and the music conservatory in Regina, and painting exhibits in Calgary. I also went to universities, high schools, and grade schools to teach paper cutting. At multicultural festivals, I displayed rich and colorful Chinese folk art and craft, and demonstrated how they were made. I often frequented public libraries. I was surprised to find that picture books for children made up a good portion of every library's collection. Many parents brought their children to read in the libraries. It reminded me that I had been a comics, or

From **Dragon Lover,** *the first book Xuan both wrote and illustrated, 1999.*

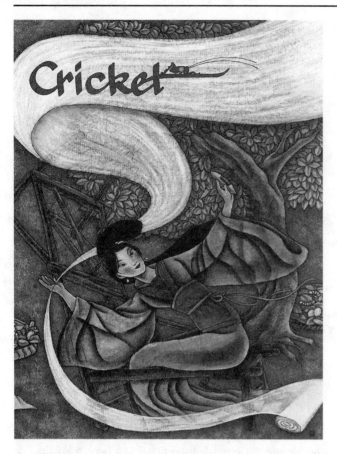

One of the covers for the magazine Cricket, *November, 1999.*

picture book, illustrator back in China, so I decided to send out my art portfolio.

My daughter helped me translate my resume into English. I sorted and made copies and pictures of many of my creative artworks together with reference materials. Addresses and phone numbers were taken down from children's books found in the library, and I sent out all my portfolio packages. Some were like stones thrown into the sea without any response; some were returned with the remarks, "For the time being, we don't have stories that match your artistic style. We will contact you when the opportunity comes." Finally, the art director of *Cricket* Magazine Group, Mr. Ron McCutchan, replied to me saying that they would let me have a try. Shortly after that, he gave me my first assignment: to illustrate a short poem, "New Sounds." Because of the tremendous differences between the western and eastern arts in the operations of art publishing, and my limited ability to communicate in English, Mr. McCutchan spent a great deal of time with me explaining every little detail, including the choice of papers, layout of illustrations, correct sizes, and ratios, etc. His help enabled me to complete the illustration, a color paper cut mosaic, which achieved a rather good artistic effect. At later art exhibitions, its originals were selling well for collections. (When I make paper cuttings, I can stack five to seven pieces of Chinese rice paper together and make five to seven originals at the same time.)

There is a Chinese proverb: Everything is hard at the beginning. If I may say that I have achieved some success

in illustrating for children's books in North America, it is partly attributable to Mr. McCutchan's help. I will be forever grateful for his kindness, sincerity, and patience. It is a pity that we have been exchanging letters, sketches, and phone calls for seven years, but we haven't yet met even once! Since 1993, I have illustrated for *Cricket* many times including some interiors, some title pages, and some front covers. Most of the stories were from Oriental countries such as China, Japan, and Korea. Only one was from North America: a little poem named "Snowball Wind."

In the fall of 1994, by chance I found a full-time position to adjust and carve molds. So our family moved from central Canada to the city of Windsor in southeast Ontario. I was skillful in wood carving, etc., so the precise and delicate manual job was just my cup of tea. The pay and benefits were good, too. Day in and day out, I drove in the morning to work and came home in the evening. Gradually I became tired of the noncreative, repetitious, and mechanical work. It reminded me of my time in the Chinese countryside. The comparison does not fundamentally overshoot the mark except for the difference of living standards. I now felt I was in the "foreign" countryside, working just for a living. I dreamed of devoting more time to my creative art. Finally, I sent my resignation letter to my boss in the mold company, but he insisted on my staying. Not until later when the company was closed due to some business problems did I have time to myself to pursue art.

My wife always understood and supported my wish to pursue my art career. After due consideration, we used all our savings to buy a house on Ottawa Street in Windsor, a commercial area. We lived upstairs and opened an art shop downstairs, selling oil paintings, porcelain picture plates, watercolors, acrylic paintings, etc. Most were my own works. There were also some handicrafts, antiques, and homemade jewels. I designed and decorated the shop myself, and the whole family worked hard on it. The shop looked elegant and unique, but business was too slow.

We suffered some shoplifting. After a year, we had to shut the store down and rent out the space. We analyzed our failure afterwards and came to the conclusion that we didn't do good marketing research and lacked deep understanding of North American culture. Windsor is an industrial "blue-collar" city with mainly auto and mold companies. The development of an art market must follow a thorough investigation of the local residents' needs before it can succeed.

In 1996, with the art shop, I not only sold some of my own works, but also painted some oil paintings and portraits to customers' orders. I also rewrote and illustrated eighteen Chinese proverbial stories for the *Sinorama* pictorial magazine of Taiwan. The magazine is an official publication in seventeen languages and is distributed all over the world. In the United States and Canada, it is available even in the libraries of the average small city. The stories were well received after publication. I often got letters from readers. Singapore's number one newspaper, *Straight Times,* reprinted the series. The publisher of Shen's Books obtained my mailing address and phone number from *Sinorama,* and soon they signed a publishing contract with me to write and illustrate the picture book *The Dragon Lover and Other Chinese Proverbs,* whose bilingual edition in Chinese and English was published in 1999. I used five different styles of paper cutting techniques to illustrate the five stories in the book. In the whole process of composition, I tried to incorporate traditional Chinese art into modern western art. The first English draft of the book was translated by my daughter Faye Lee. I hope North American children, including North American Chinese children, like the book.

At the end of 1996, Regina Griffin, the chief editor of Holiday House, called me from New York. She said that she often saw my illustrations in *Cricket* and that Holiday House loved my works very much. She asked me if I would like to illustrate their children's book *Ten Suns,* which was already in their publishing plan. I was delighted to accept the assignment. *Ten Suns* is a Chinese fairy story based on the legend of *Houyi Shooting the Suns* from the ancient classic book *Shanghai Jing.* The story, known to every Chinese family, was adapted by the famous North American writer and professor Mr. Eric A. Kimmel. The adapted story was more to the taste of North American children of mainstream families, and it distanced itself somewhat from the original flavor of Chinese culture. So I made some recommendations to the adapted story and did my best during my creation of the artwork to take advantage of my familiarity with the cultural background to make the story more Chinese while being acceptable by North American readers.

While I was creating the illustrations, I always emphasized the feeling of sunlight and the bright and lively colors that children love. I used a "dry painting method" of watercolor together with lines drawn by watercolor pens, pencils, and crayons. Since the publication of the book, reviews have appeared even to this day. The book was named the Notable Children's Trade Book in the Field of Social Studies for 1999.

The second assignment that Holiday House gave me was *The Laziest Boy in the World.* This was a very popular story among the Chinese. I heard the story as a boy from my mother. In today's China, such "lazy boys" are found in many Chinese families. The "one child family policy" has created a new generation of "little emperors." I dedicated the book to my daughter, who is also the only child in the family, but she is the opposite of Xiao Long in the story. She was a tomboy from early age, restless and mischievous. She liked to climb trees and play in the dirt. She could buy herself breakfast and walk one and one-half miles to school when she was only six. She came to Canada with us at the age of twelve and soon became our helper with the English language. In 1996, she passed the strict basic physical training and various tests to join the navy reserve, and now she is also a full-time, third-year electrical engineering student at the University of Windsor. Like Xiao Long, she hates to tidy up her room; her books, clothes, and socks are everywhere; she'd rather eat instant noodles everyday than take the time to cook. But she still climbs—rocks and mountains, that is. In addition, she is learning to be a pilot, climbing the heights of the sky.

The historical background of the story was impossible to trace. After a long time of considering, I used the Qing Dynasty, the last feudal dynasty in China, as its background. For the illustration of the book, I used acrylic paint on Chinese rice paper because I felt this combination could better imbue the pictures with local flavor, expose the inner

world of the figures, and add more humor. The book received even more reviews after publication and won the 1998 Parents' Choice Award.

The third assignment *Cricket* gave me was *The Rooster's Antlers,* a story originating from the well-known Chinese zodiac, the twelve animals symbolizing twelve years in continuous cycles. Each year is represented by one animal. The symbol for the year 2000 is "dragon." For a child born in this year, dragon is his/her guardian animal. I decided to use color paper cuts, at which I am best. Compared with any children's book I had illustrated before, I spent three times as many hours on this one. I carefully deliberated and studied the expressions, colors, and layout of each animal. After painstaking cutting, the pasting and inlaying also required great patience. After the first draft, I was not satisfied with a few of them. So I started over again. When I looked at the final product of my hard work, my joy was beyond expression.

After the sample book was sent to me, I was very disappointed because the photographs did not capture the unique three-dimensional shadowy effect of the paper cuts. It was quite different from the originals. However, I was glad that the original of the book was selected to participate in the Society of Illustrators' Original Art 99 Exhibition.

I lived in Windsor for five years. Other than running our art shop, I held personal art exhibitions at the Art's

Xuan and his wife "at our own gallery," the Head to Hand Arts and Crafts Store in Windsor, Canada, 1999.

At work on illustrations for **Sinorama** *magazine, Michigan, 1999.*

Centre-Gallery in Leamington, Ontario, and the art gallery of the Taiwan Center for Culture and Arts in Toronto. They caught media attention. The number of visitors was not as high as I expected, but the sale of my work was good. Windsor is only a river across from Detroit. I was fortunate to be invited by the Detroit Institute of Art to perform paper cutting at the annual multicultural festival. I explained to the amazed audience the brief history of Chinese paper cuts, the invention of paper, and the techniques of paper cutting. When the audience saw my large-scale, framed, original works, many couldn't believe that they were hand-cut until they saw with their own eyes how they were made. They would utter, "This is amazing!" The curious children threw out endless questions. Some people proposed to collect my paper cut work. I was deeply moved. Here was I, an ordinary artist from China, and my paper cuts were being appreciated by so many people in the first-class Detroit art gallery where world-famous artists have their works on display. It really made me very confident that Chinese art would be understood and appreciated by more and more North American friends.

In 1998, I participated in the Windsor Drouillard Road project. The Windsor municipal government initiated the project to reflect the historic scene where the first Ford automobile was born. Together with a few other artists, we created some huge frescoes on the origin and development of Ford. I especially liked one of them: "The Burning Furnace." I hope someday to adapt it to a large-scale oil painting. I regard visual arts as the goal of my life, but from time to time I also have to compromise with my daily needs. The closure of my art shop was because of financial reasons. Experience tells me that it is not easy to keep art

alive and developing if the artist does not have basic security for his daily life.

I have been in North America for ten whole years now. I have always been busy, but I have not achieved the goal of supporting my family solely on the income from my artwork. My wife was a businesswoman in China. Since coming to North America, her expertise has not been given a chance to play. She always wanted to do something here. Then she suggested to me that we operate a restaurant. It would give her a chance to do what she was good at, and if the business was OK, I wouldn't have to worry about making a living and could become a true freelance artist.

After more than two years' market research, we chose Michigan to be our target market and eventually bought an over-seventy-year-old American restaurant, Ann Sayles Dining Room, in Royal Oak. The customers of this restaurant are mainly middle-aged and elderly people. Many friends asked us why we did not open a Chinese restaurant, but chose a western one whose cultural background was so different from ours and whose customers were much more difficult to serve. My wife and I both believe that we should try to merge into the mainstream of the North American society now that we live here. We should learn from and familiarize ourselves with their culture, which includes their food and beverage. A restaurant is a showcase for this aspect of the culture. It would provide an opportunity to explore this society and gain more raw materials and inspiration for my creative art.

Another reason was that both my wife and I believed in a Chinese virtue: respect for the elderly. When I was creating picture books for children, my mind often wandered back to my own innocent and happy childhood. When we first stepped into Ann Sayles Dining Room, we saw one elderly couple after another walking haltingly into the restaurant, holding each other's arms. My wife and I were deeply touched by the scene. Everybody follows the steps from their childhood to old age through life's decades of happiness and sorrow. I couldn't help associating the children I created in my books with the hobbling elderly in front of me. The former reflected our past, and the latter foretold our future. At the same time, they reminded me of our parents half a world away. We would love them as our parents. If we have some money in the future, we will invest it all into the renovation of the restaurant and enrich our menu of offerings. In the near future, we will add a special art corridor in our restaurant to offer them enjoyment from the taste of food, the vision of art, to the sound of music.

Art will be the pursuit of my whole life. Be it in the sun-scorched farm fields, in the sawdust-flying furniture shop, in the deafening mold factory, or by the steaming-hot furnace, art has always accompanied me. Starting in 2000, there have been more and more invitations for me to contribute. The series of eighteen stories based on the Chinese classic novel *The Marsh* with watercolor illustrations, which was contracted through *Sinorama* magazine, is under way. Two books contracted with Holiday House are in initial composition. The picture story "Firecracker Master" for *Cricket* has just been finished. While writing this autobiography, I received a letter from *Cricket* again. *Cricket* has begun a line of books including an anthology of scary stories coming up for the fall of 2000. The anthology will feature stories from a wide range of countries (India, the British Isles, U.S. Appalachia, the American Southwest, Japan, and contemporary America). They have given the assignment to me. I plan to use cut paper for thirteen interior illustrations. This is high visibility, being their first anthology in the book line and playing off the *Cricket* reputation. So far the jacket sketches have been appraised five times and the interior sketches three times. These are record numbers in my book illustration history, but I patiently revise and retouch the sketches again and again. The creation of a good piece of art always goes through repeated deliberation and polishings.

This year will be critical both for my business and my art. I may be worn out, have no time to rest or accompany my daughter on a vacation, but more children will be able to read my stories and enjoy my illustrations. That is truly my greatest pleasure and happiness.

Writings

ILLUSTRATOR

Eric A. Kimmel, reteller, *Ten Suns: A Chinese Legend,* Holiday House, 1998.

Lensey Namioka, *The Laziest Boy in the World,* Holiday House, 1998.

Eric A. Kimmel, reteller, *The Rooster's Antlers: A Story of the Chinese Zodiac,* Holiday House, 1999.

(And author) *The Dragon Lover and Other Chinese Proverbs,* Shen's Books, 1999.

OTHER

Contributor of illustrations and writings to numerous publications, including *ShangHai People's Arts Publishing House, Beijing Esperanto Magazine, YuNan Science Magazine, ZheJiang People's Arts Publishing House, Beijing Arts and Crafts Magazine, Beijing People's Arts Publishing House, Beijing Traditional Arts Magazine, JianShu Traditional Arts Magazine, JianShu People's Arts Publishing House, Sinorama Magazine,* and *Cricket* magazine group.

Cumulative Indexes

Illustrations Index

(In the following index, the number of the *volume* in which an illustrator's work appears is given *before* the colon, and the *page number* on which it appears is given *after* the colon. For example, a drawing by Adams, Adrienne appears in Volume 2 on page 6, another drawing by her appears in Volume 3 on page 80, another drawing in Volume 8 on page 1, and so on and so on....)

YABC

Index references to *YABC* refer to listings appearing in the two-volume *Yesterday's Authors of Books for Children,* also published by The Gale Group. *YABC* covers prominent authors and illustrators who died prior to 1960.

C

Author Index

The following index gives the number of the volume in which an author's biographical sketch, Autobiography Feature, Brief Entry, or Obituary appears.

This index includes references to all entries in the following series, which are also published by The Gale Group.

YABC—*Yesterday's Authors of Books for Children: Facts and Pictures about Authors and Illustrators of Books for Young People from Early Times to 1960*
CLR—*Children's Literature Review: Excerpts from Reviews, Criticism, and Commentary on Books for Children*
SAAS—*Something about the Author Autobiography Series*

Author Index

Author Index

Author Index

W